Social Psychology
of the Criminal Justice System

Social Psychology of the Criminal Justice System

Martin S. Greenberg
UNIVERSITY OF PITTSBURGH

R. Barry Ruback
GEORGIA STATE UNIVERSITY

Brooks/Cole Publishing Company
Monterey, California

Dedicated to Our Parents and Grandparents

Consulting Editor: Lawrence S. Wrightsman, University of Kansas

Brooks/Cole Publishing Company
A Division of Wadsworth, Inc.

Printed in the United States of America

10 9 8 7 6 5 4 3 2 1

Library of Congress Cataloging in Publication Data

Greenberg, Martin S.
  Social psychology of the criminal justice
system.

  Includes bibliographical references and
index.
  1. Criminal justice, Administration of—
United States—Decision-making. 2. Attribution
(Psychology) 3. Social exchange. I. Ruback,
R. Barry, 1950–   II. Title.
HV8138.G73   364′.068   81-18084
ISBN 0-8185-0508-7   AACR2

Subject Editor: *Claire Verduin*
Manuscript Editor: *Rephah Berg*
Production Editor: *John Bergez*
Production Assistant: *Patricia Sobchak*
Interior Design: *Angela Lee*
Cover Photo and Design: *Debbie Wunsch*
Illustrations: *Brenda Booth*
Typesetting: *Boyer & Brass, Inc., San Diego, California*

Preface

This book examines decision making in the criminal justice system. The focus of our attention is on those who administer the system—the police, judges, prosecutors, jurors, prison guards, parole-board members, and parole officers. Our purpose is to examine not how decisions *ought* to be made but how they *are* made in practice.

In recent years there has been an explosion of knowledge concerning decision making in the criminal justice system. A variety of disciplines have contributed, including psychology, law, sociology, political science, and social work. To integrate this diverse literature we use a conceptual framework borrowed from social psychology—the attribution/exchange model. As we describe in Chapter 1, this framework views decision making as a two-step process. First, the decision maker forms certain impressions of the other person (the attribution stage); second, the decision maker evaluates the various response options with regard to their potential benefits and costs (the social-exchange stage). In subsequent chapters we use this interpretive framework to analyze decisions made at various stages of the criminal justice process, starting with the citizen's decision to notify the police and concluding with the decision to revoke parole.

This book is intended for a wide audience. It can be used as a text in both undergraduate and graduate courses in psychology, sociology, and administration of justice. In addition, it can serve as a text or as an adjunct to other texts in law school courses relating law and the behavioral sciences. Researchers and practitioners can use the text as a resource to help them integrate what is known about decision making in the criminal justice system into their professional activities.

We would like to express our appreciation to a number of people who have facilitated this endeavor. First, we want to thank Chauncey E. Wilson for his many insightful comments on Chapter 2. John Monahan of the University of Virginia and Steven Penrod of the University of Wisconsin carefully read the entire manuscript and supplied many constructive criticisms. Lawrence S. Wrightsman, Consulting Editor for Brooks/Cole, meticulously read every line (and between the lines) and provided us with incalculable assistance. We owe a special debt of thanks to Janelle Greenberg of the University of Pittsburgh, without whom the book would not have been completed. As an English legal historian, she gave us helpful guidance and suggestions concerning the discussions of the historical antecedents of the criminal justice system in the United States. We deeply appreciate her keen editorial eye and constant encouragement.

We would also like to acknowledge the competent and cheerful assistance of Deborah Sagar, Estella Saurer, and Alison Weber, who typed portions of the manuscript. Deserving of special recognition are the three Greenberg children, Joshua, Rebecca, and Steven, for their heroic patience, understanding, and consideration. We also owe a debt of gratitude to the students in our psychology and law classes, who helped us sharpen and clarify many of the ideas presented in this book.

We would be remiss if we did not acknowledge the professionalism of the staff at Brooks/Cole, particularly Claire Verduin, who gently prodded us as we labored over the final chapters; Rephah Berg, who edited the manuscript; and John Bergez and Patricia Sobchak, who helped turn the manuscript into a book.

Finally, we would like to express our indebtedness to each other. This was truly a collaborative effort, as neither of us could have written this book without the other.

Martin S. Greenberg
R. Barry Ruback

Contents

10 Summary and Conclusions   274

Table of Cases

Social Psychology
of the Criminal Justice System

CHAPTER ONE

Introduction

Being the object of a stranger's aggressive attack can be as frightening an experience as one will ever encounter. Consider the following two incidents as recounted by their victims:

> These two boys came around the corner and my purse was hanging from my arm. I had my daughter by one hand and my purse hanging on the other. He came down, grabbed my purse and yanked at it. My daughter was screaming, "Please help. Mommy, mommy." There was no one there that helped us. There were people there that had watched but nobody had come to our rescue. He yanked at it. I held on as much as possible, shaking like a leaf, very terrified. I pulled the purse away from him because I had quite a bit of money in it. . . . In fact, I held on so hard and he dragged me until the strap broke and that was the only way they got the purse. . . . Him and this other little boy took the purse and ran. My daughter and I very hysterically ran right after them.

> I was coming down the road late at night. He must have seen I was alone. He followed me to the parking lot and the car looked the same as our neighbors'. So I didn't think nothing of it. I just got right out of the car . . . which was stupid. . . . I got to the steps and I turned around 'cause I didn't hear no car doors and I always got a fear over my shoulder. So I turned around and looked and he was at my feet. . . . he come and got me from my ankles. . . . it was wintertime and I had a big fur coat on and I guess he couldn't—and I just collapsed out of fear. My legs went, I guess I was dead weight or something and he dropped me. There's a railing out front, and I hung onto that and I just screamed and I kept my legs up and together . . . he just kept trying to pull me away. I don't know what he was doing. Going up my legs or something. . . . You could see his car parked with the door open. He never closed the door. And there was another guy in the car. . . . So I just kept screaming and screaming and screaming, and I got a very big mouth, and my girlfriend heard me in one apartment downstairs and she opened her window. I didn't hear her open her window or nothing, or even say my name, but just 'cause I was screaming so loud, but he heard her and got scared. He

1

finally let me go ... she just screamed "Doris, what's the matter?" She thought I was having a fight with my husband or something. . . . All I know is when he ran, he jumped down the steps. He didn't even bother walking down. He just jumped down and took off and I just went upstairs. And then my husband called the police. . . . I fear men now. Before, I would sit and talk to anybody and think nothing of it, but now I always kinda wonder, I wonder if he's one of them. . . . I was very sick after it. I'd get up in the middle of the night crying and screaming and one time I was beating my poor husband up because I just started thinking about it. I kept thinking about it every night I went to bed [Fischer, 1977].[1]

These are but two of the millions of crimes committed each year against persons and property in the United States. Statistics collected by the Federal Bureau of Investigation (FBI) reveal that more than 12,000,000 FBI Crime Index offenses were reported in the United States in 1979 (Webster, 1980).[2] This figure is even more alarming when one considers that it includes only *reported* crimes. Recent data collected by the Law Enforcement Assistance Administration (LEAA), in collaboration with the Bureau of the Census, indicate that most crimes go unreported to the police. Considering reported and unreported crimes together, it is estimated that more than 40,000,000 criminal victimizations are committed each year (Law Enforcement Assistance Administration, 1976b). It is not surprising, therefore, to find recent public-opinion polls showing crime as one of the most serious domestic problems in the United States (Flanagan, Hindelang, & Gottfredson, 1980).

The institution created by society to deal with crime is the criminal justice system. It is entrusted with preventing and punishing criminal behavior by apprehending, prosecuting, convicting, and sentencing those members of society who violate its legal codes. The focus of this book is on the social-psychological mechanisms that underlie decision making in the criminal justice system. That is, the center of our attention is not on the causes of crime, the offender, or the victim, but the agents of the system who are responsible for deciding the fate of those who are processed by the system. These agents include police officers, prosecutors, judges, jurors, probation officers, prison administrators and guards, parole officers, and members of parole boards. Also to be examined is the role played by victims and bystanders in bringing criminal incidents to the attention of authorities. Our analysis centers on the workings of the criminal justice system as it typically functions in the urban United States. Although the system undoubtedly does not operate the same way in all urban communities, we believe that common social-psychological processes underlie its operation in these diverse communities. Finally, it should be noted that we are concerned

---

[1]Excerpts from unpublished research interviews by Constance E. Fischer, 1977. This and all other quotations from this source are reprinted by permission of the author.

[2]The seven crimes that make up the FBI Crime Index are murder, forcible rape, aggravated assault, robbery, burglary, larceny/theft, and auto theft.

with understanding the system, not with evaluating its morality. Our purpose is to analyze how the system *typically* functions, not to make judgments about how it *ought* to function. In the remaining sections of this chapter we will first describe some features of the criminal justice system and then acquaint you with the social-psychological perspective that we will use to examine decision making in the system.

THE CRIMINAL JUSTICE SYSTEM

The criminal justice system operates at the federal, state, and local levels, and at each level it consists of three interrelated components— the police, the courts, and corrections. In 1977 alone, almost $22 billion was spent to maintain this vast system (Law Enforcement Assistance Administration, 1980). Some have found it helpful to conceive of the system as a network of interconnected decision makers whose actions influence one another (Ebbesen & Konečni, 1976). For example, the length of time a person spends in prison depends on the sentence meted out by a particular judge, which is dependent on the jury's decision to convict or acquit the accused. The jury's decision is, in turn, affected by the persuasiveness of the prosecutor, whose decision to prosecute depends in part on the nature of the evidence gathered by the police. Not only are decisions made later in the system influenced by those made earlier, but very frequently earlier decisions are influenced by expected outcomes of decisions made later. Thus, a police officer's decision to make an arrest is determined in part by his or her beliefs about the prosecutor's willingness to prosecute the case. The prosecutor's decisions are, in turn, affected by his or her beliefs concerning the decision-making process of the jury. If the prosecutor believes that a persuasive case can be made to the jury, he or she is more likely to decide to prosecute. However, if the prosecutor is less sure how convinced the jury will be, he or she may decide to reduce the charges in exchange for the defendant's guilty plea. Similarly, the jury's decision of guilt or innocence may be affected by how severe a sentence a particular judge is likely to impose should the jury find the defendant guilty.

The interdependence of decision makers in the criminal justice system is illustrated by the flow chart in Figure 1-1. The chart depicts the various decision points in the system and the consequences for the defendant. Reid (1976) notes that the system

> resembles an assembly line. The accused, like a product, goes from station to station in the system; at each station something is done to him. If he "passes" inspection, he moves on to the next [part of] the system. Theoretically, if he goes through the entire system and "passes" he is ready to return to society. But if he commits another offense, and thereby becomes a recidivist, he may be "recalled to the factory" for further adjustment. But, unlike a car, he may move in and out of the system at different points [p. 260].

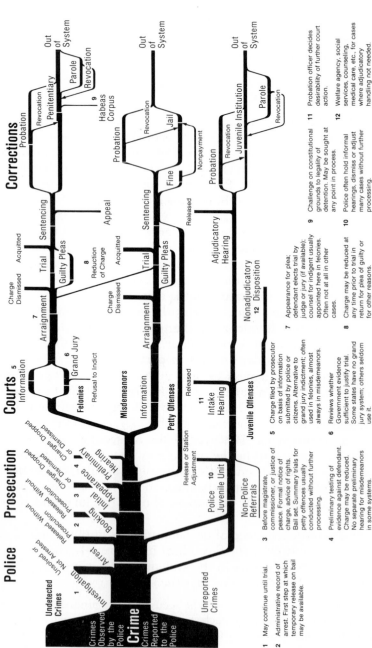

Figure 1-1. Flow chart of the criminal justice system (President's Commission on Law Enforcement and Administration of Justice, 1967a)

Attempts to analyze the working of the criminal justice system have been undertaken by legal scholars (for example, LaFave & Scott, 1972) and sociologists (Chambliss & Seidman, 1971; Quinney, 1970; Reid, 1976). Much that has been written has been highly critical, the system being variously described as "unjust," "inefficient," "overcrowded," "overworked," "underfinanced," "understaffed," and a "nonsystem." The tendency has been to criticize the system on the basis of the discrepancy between how it operates in theory and in practice. It has been pointed out that although all citizens are supposed to be treated equally before the law, in actual practice persons from certain groups are more likely to be arrested, to be prosecuted, to be convicted, and to receive stiffer sentences and are less likely to be paroled (Chambliss & Seidman, 1971). To understand why people are not treated equally by the criminal justice system, we must look closely at the everyday circumstances in which the system typically operates.

Inconsistency between Theory and Practice: The Role of Discretion

Although in theory individuals and groups should be treated equally before the law, in practice the circumstances under which agents of the system operate make this ideal very difficult to realize. What are these circumstances, and how do they affect the system? First, it must be recognized that no rule or law can be written in such a way as to remove all ambiguities. Consequently, many decisions, such as the decisions to arrest and subsequently prosecute a suspect, are left to the discretion of the particular criminal justice agents—in this case, the officer who first encounters the suspect and the prosecuting attorney in charge of the case. *Black's Law Dictionary*, (Black, 1957) defines *discretion* as the "power or right . . . conferred [by law on public officials to act] in certain circumstances, according to the dictates of their own judgment and conscience, uncontrolled by the judgment or conscience of others." Consider the following incident: A group of youths is observed congregating in front of a local drugstore on a hot summer night. The store owner calls the police because some of the youths have been intimidating her customers and she fears this will affect her business. How should the officers who arrive on the scene handle the situation? Should they disband the group with a stern warning not to congregate there in the future? Should they interrogate members of the group and take down their names? Or should they charge the youths with disorderly conduct and arrest them? The officers' indecision will seldom be abated by reference to the statute book, since most statutory definitions of disorderly conduct are vague. Witness, for example, the Pennsylvania law:

> A person is guilty of disorderly conduct if, with intent to cause public inconvenience, annoyance or alarm or recklessly creating a risk thereof, he:
> (1) engages in fighting or threatening, or in violent or tumultuous behavior;
> (2) makes unreasonable noise;
> (3) uses obscene language, or makes an obscene gesture; or

(4) creates a hazardous or physically offensive condition by any act which serves no legitimate purpose of the actor.

How does one define *tumultuous behavior, unreasonable noise,* or *obscene language?* The ambiguity of the law provides the officers with flexibility of response. In some circumstances they might let the group off with a friendly warning, as when the boys are perceived as being "a bunch of good kids" who occasionally show poor judgment. If, however, the officers view the boys as "a bunch of troublemakers who need to be taught a lesson," they might resort to arrest. Because many laws are ambiguous, decisions are often made on the basis of extralegal factors, such as the person's age, race, socioeconomic class, and demeanor.

A second reason that people are treated differentially by agents of the criminal justice system is that a basic belief of many of its agents is that justice requires that each person be treated individually. Arrest and prosecution are likely to have different effects on a teenager with no previous arrests than on a teenager with a long history of arrests. Similarly, sentencing a habitual bank robber and novice bank robber by the same standards is clearly inappropriate. The kind of sentence that will deter the second is unlikely to deter the first.

A third reason for differential treatment is the recognition by agents of the system that the system is incapable of dealing with all law violators. Limited resources require that agents of the system, whether they be the police, the prosecutor, the judge, or the parole board, exercise their discretionary power so as not to overburden the system and thereby bring it to a virtual halt. Stories abound of overworked police officers, of crowded court dockets in which defendants must wait months for their cases to come to trial, and of overcrowded prisons. Not surprisingly, therefore, the police do not enforce all laws all the time, prosecuting attorneys do not prosecute all suspected offenders, and judges do not sentence all violators to prison. By exercising their discretionary powers, agents of the criminal justice system avoid overtaxing the system's facilities and human resources, thereby permitting the system to deal more effectively with the more serious offenders.

The fourth reason for differential treatment by agents of the criminal justice system relates to social pressures from fellow agents and from members of the community. Guided by their values and beliefs concerning the adminstration of justice, fellow agents formulate norms that influence the daily administration of the system. With regard to performance by the police, norms influence how vigorously certain laws will be enforced, what kinds of persons will be sought out as suspects and subsequently arrested, and how those arrested will be treated during and after arrest (Chambliss & Seidman, 1971). As Quinney (1970) has observed, "While the activities of the police are governed officially by procedural law, their actual behavior conforms to their own occupational code" (p. 123). Furthermore, attempts at vigorous enforcement of laws in opposition to the beliefs of important segments of the community will meet with strong resistance, resulting in significant social, economic, and political costs for those who operate the system. It is one thing for the authorities to arrest and punish an unemployed grocery clerk for gambling and drug violations, and it is another thing to arrest and punish the son or daughter of a powerful upper-class member of the community for the same violations. When a law is unpopular with important segments of the community—for example, a law making possession of marijuana a felony—then the law is likely to be liberalized.

Competing Values in the Operation of the Criminal Justice System

Naturally, we would not expect all agents to agree on how a system as vast and diverse as the criminal justice system should best operate. Although all agents would agree with the value of "fighting crime," they tend to disagree on how much weight should be placed on catching criminals and how much on protecting the innocent from abuse by agents of the system. Packer (1964) has identified two competing value systems, or models of law enforcement, and labeled them the "crime-control model" and the "due-process model." The first is based on the proposition that suppressing criminal behavior is by far the most important function of the criminal justice process. This model requires that a high proportion of criminal activity be punished. In order to accomplish this function, the system, with its limited resources, must operate efficiently and speedily. Thus, "The process must not be cluttered up with ceremonious rituals that do not advance the progress of the case. Facts can be established more quickly through interrogation in a police station than through the formal process of examination and cross-examination in a court" (Packer, 1968, p. 155). In effect, this model operates on the presumption that if a person is charged with a crime, he or she is probably guilty.

The due-process model, in contrast, takes as its central value the protection of noncriminals from abuses by agents of the state. Those who subscribe to this model are more concerned about mistakes that result in convicting the innocent than mistakes that allow the guilty to go free. The model operates on the presumption of innocence. Thus, speed and efficiency are less important than the goal of reliable fact-finding. Whereas believers in the crime-control model are prepared to tolerate a certain level of error in determination of guilt, believers in the due-process model are not. Subscribers to the due process model recognize the possibility of error when fact-finding is left in the hands of police and prosecutor and, therefore, place greater confidence in the process of examination and cross-examination in court. Whereas the crime-control model resembles an assembly line along which passes the accused, the due-process model resembles more an obstacle course, where each successive stage "is designed to present formidable impediments to carrying the accused any further along in the process" (Packer, 1964, p. 13).

With regard to the differential treatment of suspects by agents of the criminal justice system, subscribers to the crime-control model are very likely to accord differential treatment to various individuals and groups. Because suspicion by police is based in part on probabilities associated with previous occurrences of crime, members of certain ethnic, occupational, and age groups, because of their groups' high crime rate, are more likely to be processed by the system than others. In the United States such groups are likely to be blacks, Chicanos, Puerto Ricans, and youths between ages 15 and 20. As will become evident, although most police officers, prosecutors, and courtroom personnel give lip service to the due-process model, their behavior often more closely approximates the crime-control model.

In the preceding pages we have tried to show how the day-to-day conditions under which the criminal justice system operates result in a significant discrepancy between theory and practice. It should be abundantly clear that we are dealing not only with a criminal justice system but with a social system as well. Although much of the behavior of its agents is circumscribed by statutes, the system provides for a wide latitude of individual discretion. In exercising this discretion, agents of the criminal justice system must evaluate the individual characteristics of those who pass before them. Whatever decision is reached—to arrest or not arrest a suspect, to find a defendant guilty or not guilty— agents of the system usually consider the impact of their decision on the person being judged as well as how others within and outside the system will react to it. Consequently, if we are to gain an understanding of how the criminal justice system works in practice, we must adopt an approach that considers both the individual decision maker and the social context in which he or she must operate. The behavioral science that studies the behavior of the individual in the social context is social psychology.

SOCIAL PSYCHOLOGY AND THE CRIMINAL JUSTICE SYSTEM

Social psychology can be defined as the branch of psychology that studies how a person's thoughts, feelings, and behavior are influenced by the actual, imagined, or implied behavior and/or characteristics of others. This definition calls attention to the fact that "social" behavior does not necessarily require the physical presence of others. Thus, a prosecutor's decision whether to prosecute a particular case, made in the privacy of his or her office, would be considered a social event if he or she weighed the expected reactions of others, such as the victim, the defense attorney, or the jury. The definition of social psychology that we have chosen is quite broad. It permits us to study social situations ranging from the one described above to those encompassing two parties in a face-to-face setting actively trying to influence each other.

In further defining the social-psychological perspective, it is helpful to distinguish it from the sociological perspective. Each chooses to explain social phenomena at a different level of analysis. Whereas sociologists tend to explain social behavior in terms of factors external to the individual, such as social class, social structure, social organization, and social stratification, social psychologists prefer explanations that focus on intra-individual processes, such as those pertaining to perception, motivation, and learning. Further, the two disciplines differ with regard to the unit of analysis that each chooses to examine. Whereas sociologists usually study aggregates of individuals, such as collectivities and classes, social psychologists tend to focus on the individual. Where the *small* group is concerned, however, this distinction becomes somewhat blurred, since both disciplines maintain an interest in small-group behavior.

Over the years social psychologists have conducted research on a variety of topics, such as attitude formation and change, conformity, aggression, person perception, helping behavior, social influence, obedience, interpersonal attraction, and leadership. Throughout this period the concepts and methods of social psychology have been applied to a number of important societal issues, such as desegregation, education, health care, population control, the effects of crowding, sex roles, interracial aggression, drug use, and romantic attraction, to mention but a few. In recent years the criminal justice system has attracted the attention of a growing number of social psychologists (Tapp, 1976, 1980). This interest has led to the formation of the American Psychology-Law Society, whose membership consists primarily of psychologists and lawyers, and the establishment of a new division of the American Psychological Association—the Division of Law and Psychology.

Social psychologists have begun to examine the social processes involved in various phases of the criminal justice system. They have conducted research on eyewitness testimony, procedures used by the police to interrogate suspects, selection of jurors, and decision making by victims, bystanders, jurors, judges, parole boards, and prison guards. A wide assortment of methods have been used. These are discussed next.

Methods Used to Study Decision Making in the Criminal Justice System

In their efforts to study decision making in the criminal justice system, investigators have proved themselves to be anything but methodological snobs. Thus, they have used laboratory and field experiments to study how bystanders and victims decide to notify the authorities (for example, Bickman & Rosenbaum, 1977; Greenberg, Ruback, Wilson, & Mills, 1980). Other researchers have used simulation techniques that involve having participants play the role of decision makers, such as jurors (for example, Shaffer & Sadowski, 1979), judges (for example, Sigall & Ostrove, 1975), and prison guards (Haney, Banks, & Zimbardo, 1973). Field studies involving observation of real-life decision makers have been used to study police officers' decisions to make an arrest (for example, Reiss, 1971) and judges' decisions on setting bail (Ebbesen & Konečni, 1975) and sentencing the offender (Stewart, 1980). Surveys and interviews have been used to study victims' decisions to notify the police (for example, Law Enforcement Assistance Administration, 1977a) and prosecutors' decisions to charge a suspect with a crime (for example, Law Enforcement Assistance Administration, 1977c). In addition, data archives, such as court records, have been analyzed in order to study the sentencing decisions of judges (for example, Konečni & Ebbesen, 1979).

Each of the above methods has particular strengths and weaknesses. The laboratory-experimental approach allows investigators to exercise a high degree of control over the situation and to measure effects with a high degree of precision. However, the rigor and exactitude of laboratory experiments are often achieved at the expense of generalizability. Critics contend that experiments conducted in the rarefied atmosphere of the laboratory yield results that are of questionable application in the "real world." Further, it is claimed that participants' knowledge that they are participating in an experiment causes them to react unnaturally. For these reasons, some investigators prefer to conduct their experiments in natural settings where the real-life decisions ordinarily occur. Such field experiments are not only more generalizable, but they can be conducted without participants' knowing that they are participating in an experiment. Because control cannot be exercised as well in natural settings as in the laboratory, generalizability of results is often achieved at the expense of rigor. Moreover, critics question the ethics of this procedure, as it often involves testing participants without their consent.

One recourse for investigators is the simulation approach. Rather than leading participants to believe that they are faced with some real decisions, participants in simulation studies are asked to imagine themselves in a certain role and to render a hypothetical decision. The procedure has the advantage of permitting the study of a wider range of decision contexts than can be studied in either of the experimental approaches. However, critics contend that because participants in simulation studies know that their decisions are hypothetical (that is, they have no real consequences), the results may tell us little about real-life decisions. In contrast, field studies involve the observation of real-life decisions as they naturally occur. Reiss (1971), for example, accompanied police officers on their patrols and observed them as they confronted criminal suspects. Similarly, Ebbesen and Konečni (1975) observed judges in the process of setting bail. Although the data derived from this method are applicable to real-life settings, some major liabilities are associated with its use. First, because the investigator does not exercise control over the situation, it is difficult to draw firm conclusions about what caused decision makers to decide as they did. In addition, the observer's presence may influence the decision maker. This is why observers try to be unobtrusive. Finally, the method is limited to situations in which the observer knows the time and place of the decision in advance (for example, the bail-setting decision). When such prior knowledge is lacking, as when a victim must decide whether to call the police, the method is difficult, if not impossible, to use.

In such situations, the investigator can contact decision makers after the decision has been made and, by means of carefully planned questions, have them recount the basis for their decision. This is the reasoning behind the use of surveys, questionnaires, and interviews. Such procedures allow for an in-depth probing of beliefs and attitudes. However, they lack the exactitude and clarity of experiments. Moreover, by relying on self-reports, they make certain assumptions about respondents that might not always be true—namely, that decision makers know why they decided as they did, that they can recall the reasons when asked to do so some time later, and that they are willing to provide the questioner with this information.

To get around the fact that respondents may distort their answers either by accident or by design, investigators have sought information from a very different source—already existing data such as can be found in police files and court records. The major advantage of this archival approach is that the data-collection process is *unobtrusive*. That is, the collection process does not change the phenomenon being measured, as might occur when one observes the police as they are deciding whether to arrest a suspect. By using a statistical procedure called regression analysis, researchers can determine what information in the data archive best accounts for the particular decision. The major problem with this type of research is that records are often incomplete or contain misinformation reflecting the biases of the recordkeeper.

As you can tell from this brief overview, each method has its own unique combination of weaknesses and strengths. You will soon see in later chapters that sometimes the different methods produce conflicting results (for example, Konečni & Ebbesen, 1979). We will call such conflicts to your attention, and where possible, we try to resolve them. In other instances, results produced by different methods are in agreement (for example, Greenberg, Wilson, Ruback, & Mills, 1979; Van Kirk, 1978). When this occurs, you can have more confidence in the reliability of the findings. This conclusion is based on the assumption that all methods suffer from some weaknesses and that more reliable inferences can be made when there is agreement across several methods, each with differing weaknesses and strengths (Campbell & Stanley, 1963).

Ethical Issues

Involvement of social psychologists in the criminal justice system has led to increased concern with the ethical implications of this involvement (Monahan, 1980). One basic problem faced by investigators in planning research is how to design a study so as to maximize its theoretical and practical value while minimizing the costs and potential risks to participants. Among the many ethical issues are whether to use deception in one's research and whether one should always maintain the confidentiality of the data. There are no simple solutions to these issues. Participants have a right to know what to expect when they participate in a study, yet such knowledge may make it extremely difficult for them to provide the investigator with valid information. Consider the problem faced by an investigator who wants to conduct an experiment on decision making by bystanders to a crime. To study why bystanders decide to call the police, the investigator may stage a crime before an unwitting subject. If such subjects were told in advance that they would be observing a staged crime, their responses would probably not be very informative. Accordingly, ethical guidelines proposed by the American Psychological Association (1973, p. 37) recognize that deception in experimental research may be acceptable when

> (a) the research problem is of great importance; (b) it may be demonstrated that the research objectives cannot be realized without deception; (c) there is sufficient reason for the concealment or misrepresentation that, on being fully informed later on, the research participant may be expected to find it reasonable, and to suffer no loss of confidence in the integrity of the investigator or of others involved; (d) the research participant is allowed to withdraw from the study at any time, and is free to withdraw the data when the concealment or misrepresentation is revealed; and (e) the investigator takes full responsibility for detecting and removing stressful aftereffects.

A second illustration of the ethical dilemmas confronting those doing research on the criminal justice system concerns the confidentiality of the information provided by the participant. Say, for example, that in the course of interviewing prison guards, investigators discover that several guards are mistreating inmates. What should the investigators do with this information? Should they inform the proper legal authorities even though they promised the guards that their responses would be kept in strict confidence? According to the American Psychological Association's Task Force on the Role of Psychology in the Criminal Justice System (Monahan, 1980), investigators may violate their promise of confidentiality when the information concerns a "clear and imminent danger" to the individual or society.

As the Task Force's report indicates, in research on the criminal justice system there are many complicated issues that have no simple right or wrong answers (Monahan, 1980). According to the Task Force's report, "Following the Watergate scandal, the American Bar Association voted to make a course in professional ethics required in every law school" (p. 16). We agree with the Task Force's conclusion that "rather than waiting for a moral Watergate to occur in psychology, we should see that professional education in applied ethics becomes part of the curriculum in every graduate program" (p. 16).

A Social-Psychological Framework for Studying Decision Making

The methods and related ethical issues presented in the previous section are not the sole province of social psychologists. Indeed, much of the research reported in this volume has been conducted by non-psychologists, such as sociologists, criminologists, and legal scholars. What, then, is distinctively social-psychological about this book? The answer lies in the theoretical framework that we use to analyze decision making in the criminal justice system. The major purpose of this book is to bring this diverse literature together under one cover and to provide a meaningful social-psychological framework for its integration. Rather than run the risk of confusing you by using a wide array of social-psychological concepts and theories, we will offer a more limited but potentially more coherent theoretical focus. Our approach will be to analyze decision making in the criminal justice system by using two complementary social-psychological theories: attribution theory and social-exchange theory.

Broadly speaking, attribution theory focuses on the mechanisms by which people make sense out of their own and others' behavior. Social-exchange theory focuses on the benefits and costs that people derive from others in the course of interacting with them. The decision to use the "attribution/exchange" framework reflects our beliefs about the basic social processes that underlie decision making in the criminal justice system. More specifically, we assume that such decision making consists of two broad stages. In the first, the criminal justice agent forms certain impressions of the person he or she is dealing with—for example, the suspect, the prisoner, the parolee. In the second, the criminal justice agent evaluates the various response options with regard to their potential benefits and costs.

The attribution/exchange framework is described in the following pages. We begin this description by considering the attribution phase of the model.

ATTRIBUTION THEORY

What is meant by the term *attribution*? Very simply, "An attribution is an inference about why an event occurred or about a person's dispositions" (Harvey & Weary, 1981, p. 6). Let us see how this works by considering the example of a security guard for a large department store who has apprehended a young woman on suspicion of shoplifting. The decision to apprehend the suspect requires that the guard have evidence that the act was committed. He may acquire knowledge of the act by direct observation or by indirect observation, as when a fellow employee reports the incident to him. If no one observed the act, then the attribution process would not be initiated. Assuming that the act was observed, the guard must decide whether it was deliberate or accidental. Did she commit the act voluntarily, or was she coerced by a companion? If the guard decides that the act was accidentally caused or was caused by the coercive influence of another, he will attribute causality to external factors, and this step will abort the attribution process. In this case, the guard will have got an answer to his question "Why did the act occur?" If, however, the guard decides that it was a deliberate act uncoerced by others, he will then try to determine the woman's motive for committing the act. The assignment of a motive or disposition to the woman will terminate the attribution process because this assignment will explain why the act was committed. Attribution theorists generally assume that the kind of motive that the guard attributes to the woman will play an important role in determining his subsequent reactions, which may range from letting her off with a stern warning to calling the police.

Heider's Naive Psychology

The psychologist most closely associated with the birth and development of the attribution perspective is Fritz Heider (1944, 1958). Labeling his approach "naive psychology," he described how the average person accounts for the behavior of others. Heider argued that one can understand and predict another's behavior by identifying the relatively stable, or dispositional, properties of others, which include their motives, traits, and abilities. Identification of these relatively stable dispositional properties of others permits a person both to predict another's behavior with some degree of accuracy and also to plan counterstrategies. In effect, Heider suggested that people respond not to the overt behavior of others but rather to the dispositions or motives that underlie their behavior. Consider the following example. Imagine yourself leaving the supermarket carrying a sack of groceries. Without warning, a young teenager crashes into you, scattering your groceries on the pavement. In addition to your initial reaction of surprise, how do you think you would respond? Your response would probably be determined by your understanding of the teenager's behavior. Was it an accident, or did he do it on purpose in order to harm you? If you interpret it as an accident, you may let him off lightly, perhaps with a stern warning to be more careful in the future. If, however, you attribute some malevolent motivation to him, you are likely to respond very differently. Note that in these instances the overt act is identical; only the attributed reasons for it are different. In the first case it was an accident, and in the second it was a deliberate act motivated by a desire to cause you harm.

Heider reasoned that when analyzing the outcomes of others' behavior, people consider the relative contributions of environmental and personal forces. In a given situation the two forces can be perceived as working in the same direction, as when a batter hits a home run with the wind to his back, or in opposition, as when a batter hits a home run in the face of a strong wind. In the first case, the perceiver will have difficulty allocating responsibility for the outcome, because the perceiver cannot be sure whether to attribute the home run to the batter's skill (personal force), the wind (environmental force), or a combination of the two. However, in the second case, the contribution of the personal force will be enhanced, because the ball reached the stands despite the strong wind.

Heider further noted that personal force can be analyzed according to two contributing subfactors: a power (or ability) factor and a motivational factor. Together they determine the strength of the personal-force factor. Thus, persons can fail because they lack the requisite ability and/or because they are insufficiently motivated to succeed. How one allocates the blame for failure will determine how one responds to the failure. Usually people who are perceived as failing because they lack the requisite ability will be treated more leniently than those whose failure is ascribed to lack of motivation.

Another example, more closely connected with the functioning of the criminal justice system, will illustrate the utility of Heider's analysis. Suppose that the police have just been called to investigate the murder of John Q. Wealthy at his suburban estate. After a preliminary investigation, homicide detectives identify two key suspects—his wife and his business partner. Mrs. Wealthy is a prime suspect because she was with the deceased shortly before his death. She therefore had the *ability* to murder her husband, but being unable to identify a *motive* for the crime, the police must drop her as a prime suspect. In contrast, the police are aware that the deceased and his business partner had been feuding for some time, thereby providing the partner with a *motive* for the killing. The partner, however, produces proof that at the time of the murder he was at a business luncheon with several community leaders and therefore could not possibly have committed the crime (that is, he lacked the *ability*). Thus, unable to establish a motive in the first case and the ability in the second case, the police are forced to drop both as prime suspects. In order to have committed the murder, the suspect must, according to their reasoning, have had both a motive for the crime and the ability to commit the act.

Heider's ideas have stimulated a great deal of theoretical and empirical work on the attribution process. The theories that followed from Heider's insightful analyses were stated in a more testable form, thereby permitting a more rigorous examination of the attribution process. One such theory, developed by Harold Kelley, is discussed in the following section.

Kelley's Three Principles of Attribution

One of the major virtues of Kelley's (1972a) theory of attribution is that it reduces the attribution process to three basic principles. Although there are other formulations of attribution (for example, Jones & Davis, 1965; Jones & McGillis, 1976; Kelley, 1967), we have chosen

Kelley's 1972 formulation because of its simplicity and comprehensiveness. Important to the understanding of Kelley's three principles is the distinction between *facilitative* and *inhibitory* causes. Facilitative causes are those causes that are perceived to *increase* the likelihood of a given behavior or effect, and inhibitory causes are those that are perceived to *decrease* the likelihood of a given behavior or effect. The distinction between the two can best be illustrated by our example of a ball player hitting a home run. One plausible facilitative cause for the act (that is, the home run) is the batter's strength, which would be considered an *internal facilitative cause.* Another facilitative cause is the strong wind, which could have aided the ball in its flight. This would be viewed as an *external facilitative cause.* An *internal inhibitory cause* might be the batter's state of fatigue following an all-night party. An *external inhibitory cause* might be the high humidity in the air, making it difficult to hit the ball far enough. Using only these terms, Kelley proposed the *covariation principle*, which states that "an effect is attributed to the one of its possible [facilitative] causes with which over time it covaries" (Kelley, 1972a, p. 3). If the batter hits home runs only when the wind is blowing toward the stands and not at other times, the perceiver will most likely attribute the effect to the wind.

The second principle, which Kelley calls the *discounting principle*, states that the role of a given facilitative cause in producing a given effect is discounted if other plausible facilitative causes are also present. By "discounted" Kelley means that the perceiver will be less confident that the cause is the correct one or, if it is the correct one, will be less confident that it is of particularly great magnitude. Thus, if a home run is hit off a poor pitcher on a windy day, the perceiver will be less confident in attributing the home run to the batter's skill. Because the home run could have been facilitated by the pitcher's poor ability *and* by the wind, the perceiver will tend to discount the role of the batter's ability in contributing to the outcome. Similarly, when it is revealed during a trial that a government witness gave testimony in return for a reduction in charges, the jury may be less confident of the witness's trustworthiness because the testimony may have been motivated by the desire to escape punishment.

Kelley's third principle, which he calls the *augmentation principle*, states that when an action occurs in the presence of an inhibitory cause, the perceiver will view the existing facilitative cause as being of greater magnitude or strength. The central idea here is that the facilitative cause must have been particularly potent to overcome the resistance induced by the inhibitory cause. Thus, a batter who hits a home run despite his state of fatigue and despite the high humidity must be a particularly strong hitter. Similarly, when it is revealed that a government witness gave testimony in return for no tangible rewards and despite threats on her life, the jury is likely to conclude that the witness was strongly motivated by a desire to tell the truth (an internal facilitative cause). Jurors would likely ask "What other plausible reason could she have for testifying under those circumstances?"

Kelley (1972b) points out that although his model is appropriate for making attributions in certain circumstances, quite often people cannot collect enough information for a complete causal analysis. In such situations they combine learning from past experience with partial cues provided in the present situation to make attributions. Kelley calls this backlog of information gained from past experience, which enables people to make attributions based on incomplete information, a *causal schema*. A causal schema is likely to be used when a quick decision is demanded and the perceiver finds it too costly to acquire all the information needed for a thorough causal analysis. All too frequently agents of the criminal justice system are forced into situations in which they must make hasty decisions on the basis of incomplete information. Thus, both a police officer who must decide whether to arrest someone and a judge who must decide on the appropriate amount of bail often rely on their backlog of past experience in deciding the fate of those who come before them.

Weiner's Attribution Model

Attribution theorists such as Heider and Kelley assume that attributions are important in that they mediate our responses to our own and others' behavior. One attribution theorist who has looked at how attributions affect subsequent reactions is Bernard Weiner. Following Heider's lead, Weiner, Frieze, Kukla, Reed, Rest, and Rosenbaum (1972) proposed that the attributions that people make for success or failure can be classified on two dimensions: a locus-of-control dimension (internal versus external) and a stability dimension (stable versus unstable). The locus-of-control dimension distinguishes between causes that are believed to be "inside" the person, such as the person's ability, personality traits, and motivation, and causes that are "outside" the person (that is, are due to the environment), such as the difficulty of the task and the person's good or bad luck. The stability dimension distinguishes between causes that are believed to be relatively stable over time, such as a person's ability, personality traits, and the diffi-

TABLE 1–1. Classification of causal attributions for suspect's behavior according to locus-of-control and stability dimensions

Stability	Locus of Control	
	Internal	**External**
Stable	Criminal disposition—for example, "dangerous," "psychopathic"	Bad neighborhood—for example, deviant social norms
Unstable	Emotional state—for example, "angered," "frustrated"	Bad luck—"wrong place at the wrong time"

culty of the task, and causes that are perceived as rather temporary, or unstable, such as a person's motivation, emotional state, and good or bad luck. Weiner et al. reasoned that people will attribute a given behavior to a stable internal cause if that behavior is consistent with the person's past behavior. Thus, if a person has a long record of committing crimes, he or she is likely to be viewed as having a stable criminal disposition. In order to make attributions to a stable external cause, people will compare the person's behavior with the behavior of others in the situation. Thus, if a large percentage of adolescents in a particular neighborhood are involved in crime, the perceiver is likely to attribute such behavior to some feature of the environment, such as the deviant norms of those living in the neighborhood. An attribution will be made to an unstable internal cause if some internal state assumed to be unstable (such as a state of anger) covaries with the behavior. Finally, an attribution will be made to an unstable external cause, such as luck, if the person's behavior is part of a pattern of highly variable or random behavior.

Weiner et al. (1972) reasoned that the stability dimension is used in predicting future performance and that the locus-of-control dimension determines affective responses to the person, such as anger and dislike. Although Weiner et al. applied the model to achievement-related behaviors, it can also be used to illuminate decision making in the criminal justice system. For example, if a member of a parole board attributes an inmate's criminal behavior to a criminal disposition or to the crime-ridden neighborhood where the felon lived when he committed the crime (both highly stable causes), the parole-board member is likely to conclude that if the inmate is released on parole and returns to his old neighborhood, the causes of the criminal behavior will still be present. The parole-board member will conclude that if the inmate is released, he will probably resume his criminal career. This process of inference would lead to a refusal of the parole request. If, however, the parole-board member attributes the inmate's criminal behavior to unstable causes, such as his state of frustration or bad luck (that is, he happened to be in the wrong place at the wrong time), the parole-board member might be more optimistic about the inmate's chances for success on parole. In this situation, the parole-board member might reason that because the causes of the inmate's criminal behavior were highly unstable and thus short-lived, he is unlikely to return to his criminal career when released on parole.

How will the parole-board member feel about the inmate? He will probably harbor more negative feelings toward an inmate whose crime was due (he believes) to internal causes, such as a criminal disposition or a lack of motivation, than an inmate whose crime is attributed to external causes. Weiner (1972) notes that an attribution to an unstable internal cause will generate more negative affect than an attribution to a stable internal cause, probably because people are seen as being more responsible for unstable internal causes, such as lack of motivation, than stable internal causes, such as lack of ability.

Attributional Biases

Attribution theorists make no claims about the accuracy of perceivers' attributions, preferring instead to call attention to biasing tendencies in perceivers that often cause them to make incorrect attributions. Predictably, people seldom approach situations with the objectivity of a scientist. Frequently they are misled both by the environmental context and by their own motivational and cognitive orientations. The source of many biases, according to Kelley (1972a), is the need to feel that one can predict and control one's outcomes. For example, Jones and Nisbett (1972) document the tendency of observers to attribute others' behavior to internal dispositions, whereas these others tend to attribute their own behavior to external causes. By locating the causes of someone's behavior in stable internal dispositions, people can achieve a sense of predictability concerning that person's future behavior. Consistent with this theorizing, research shows that the tendency to view others as responsible for their behavior is exaggerated when these others experience negative outcomes. Lerner and Miller (1978) view this tendency as reflecting the perceiver's "need to believe in a just world." By making victims worthy of their fate, perceivers are better able to maintain their belief in a just, and therefore predictable, world. Moreover, by assigning responsibility to the victim, people can see themselves as dissimilar to the victim, thereby reassuring themselves that a similar fate will not befall them.

This brief review of the attribution process calls attention to the fact that although the causes of behavior are often subtle and complex, people are not deterred from making causal attributions. The need to predict and control one's outcomes provides strong impetus for making such attributions. By developing an understanding of the causes of others' behavior, people are better able to anticipate the reactions of others and thereby develop maximally efficient strategies of response. The examples provided here make it apparent that many of the critical decisions made by agents of the criminal justice system hinge on the attribution process. As will become more evident, the victim's and bystander's decision to report a crime, the police officer's decision to make an arrest, the prosecutor's decision to prosecute, the jury's decision of guilt or innocence, the judge's sentencing decision, and the parole board's decision to grant parole all involve the asking of attributional questions. To what extent was the act coerced by the environment? What motivated the accused to commit the act? Does the act reflect a criminal disposition, and if so, under what conditions will the disposition lead to similar behavior in the future? What is the best way to alter this disposition—a fine, probation, or imprisonment? The answers to questions such as these will help determine the fate of those who are processed by the system.

Yet the answers to these questions are not the only considerations weighed by those who operate the criminal justice system. They must often gauge the impact that their decision will have on those accused of a crime, on other agents of the system, and on society at large. To carry out their duties, decision makers in the system must, to some extent, depend on others inside and outside the system. That is, the police need cooperation from the community, the prosecutor cannot assemble an effective case without the assistance of the police and witnesses, and the judge cannot render a wise sentencing decision without the cooperation of the probation officer who prepares the presentence report. Often the dependence is mutual. Thus, not only are the police dependent on the community for cooperation, but the community is dependent upon the police for protection. Similarly, the police rely on the prosecutor to make their jobs easier by securing convictions, thereby removing troublesome persons from their jurisdiction. It is helpful, therefore, to think of the criminal justice system as a social-exchange system in which the various parties trade "social commodities." To examine the implicit rules that govern these exchanges, we now turn to a consideration of social-exchange theory.

SOCIAL-EXCHANGE THEORY

The theories of social exchange considered here are based on the assumption that people are hedonistic creatures—that is, they seek to maximize their pleasures and minimize their pains—and that they are dependent on others for accomplishing this. Exchanging (trading) with others helps people obtain rewards, usually at a cheaper price than they would have to pay if they did not exchange with others. Consider an infant trying to reach a toy on the opposite side of the playpen. Let us imagine what the infant might be thinking as she tries to crawl across the playpen: "This is going to be tough. I can't seem to get these arms and legs working together. Oops, I fell again. That hurt. If I keep up at this pace, it'll take me all day to reach that toy [that is, this activity is costing me too much]. There's got to be a better [less costly] way. Let me see . . . hmm, that big man is just sitting there reading the paper. When I needed help yesterday, he helped me. He's good at reaching for things. First, I'll have to get his attention . . . wa, wa, wa. That didn't seem to work. Waa, waa, waa, waa! He's heard me, he's coming over. Now all I have to do is point. He's getting it. Great, I got it! That was a lot better than doing it myself. I'm so pleased, I think I'll give him one of my biggest smiles. Look at his face light up. I think tomorrow I'll have him get me another toy."

Scenarios similar to this are probably enacted every day. The infant, wanting to minimize fatigue and pain, engages in a social exchange with her parent. In exchange for help she gives her parent approval. Both parties profit from the exchange: the infant receives needed help for the cost of a smile; the parent receives approval from the infant for the cost of a small amount of physical exertion. This example also illustrates one of the important functions of exchange, whether it be social or economic: by trading with others, people try to acquire some commodity at a lower price than they would have to pay if they were to produce the commodity by themselves. This would suggest that when people can produce some commodity more cheaply by themselves than by exchanging with others, no social exchange is likely to take place. Because we are dependent on others for so many of our satisfactions, however, we must usually enter into exchanges, some explicit and some implicit, with others.

Drawing on principles from economic theory and operant behaviorism, social-exchange theorists consider as "exchangeables" a wide range of commodities, such as approval, respect, and advice, as well as the more tangible commodities of money and goods. The two most widely cited approaches to social exchange are those of George Homans (1961, 1974) and John Thibaut and Harold Kelley (1959). Homans' and Thibaut and Kelley's exchange theories have so much in common that it is appropriate, in most instances, to use the label "exchange theory." Both views assume that what people receive in exchange is quantifiable. Whereas Kelley refers to what people get out of an exchange as *outcomes*, Homans uses the term *profits*. As the two are synonymous, for the sake of simplicity we will use the term *outcomes*.

A person's outcomes in an exchange can be calculated by subtracting the costs incurred from the rewards received. *Rewards* refers to the pleasures, gratifications, and satisfactions received in the exchange. *Costs* refers to any factors that operate to inhibit or deter the exchange, such as physical or mental effort, fatigue, boredom, embarrassment, and anxiety. Costs also include the rewards that one gives up when one chooses to exchange with one person rather than another. That is, by exchanging with Person A, the individual misses an opportunity to obtain rewards from Person B. Economists refer to such costs as "opportunity costs."

A person's outcomes are not assumed to remain stable when the exchange relationship exists for a long time, such as a relationship between coworkers. Assume, for example, that two persons have formed a mutually profitable relationship in which one gives help (the "helper") and the other (the "recipient") responds with statements of gratitude, approval, and respect. As the exchange relationship continues, the helper may begin to tire of the approval and respect. What was initially very rewarding now becomes only mildly rewarding. In the language of operant conditioning, the helper is becoming "satiated" with approval and respect; or, in the language of economics, the "law of diminishing marginal utility" is operating. That is, the value of an additional unit of reward declines as more and more units of approval and respect are received. To maintain the flow of help, the recipient will have to make it more rewarding for the helper to remain in the exchange relationship. Approval and respect may have to be supplemented with additional rewards. In effect, the price that the recipient has to pay for the help has increased. If another person asks the helper for assistance, the recipient will have to offer the helper even more rewards in order to outbid the other and thereby maintain the relationship.

As the preceding example indicates, social exchange can lead to asymmetry of power. In exchange terms, *power* refers to a person's ability to affect the quality of someone else's outcomes. A person will have power over another when (1) the person has something the other wants very badly, (2) the other cannot get it from anyone else, (3) the other cannot coerce the person to surrender it, and (4) the other cannot resign himself or herself to doing without it (Blau, 1964; Emerson, 1962). A judge, for example, would be said to have great power over the accused in that the judge controls the commodity of freedom.

Evaluation of Outcomes

That social interaction can be construed as an exchange of rewards and costs tells us little about how satisfied people will be with their outcomes and whether they will continue the relationship. In order to make these decisions, people must compare their perceived outcomes with some criterion, or standard. Two such standards have been described by Thibaut and Kelley (1959). The first of these, called the *comparison level for alternatives* (or CL_{alt}), is the standard of outcome level that people use in deciding whether to remain in or terminate a relationship. The CL_{alt} can be defined as "the lowest level of outcomes a member will accept in light of available opportunities" (Thibaut & Kelley, 1959, p. 21). Thus, if a person believes that his or her outcomes in a given relationship are worse (that is, lower) than what can be obtained through other alternatives, the person will probably decide to terminate the relationship. If, however, the person believes that his or her outcomes are better (that is, higher) than what he or she can achieve elsewhere, the person will remain in the relationship.

The mere fact that a person chooses to remain in an exchange relationship does not necessarily imply that the person is satisfied with that relationship. To assess the degree of satisfaction, we must refer to the second standard discussed by Thibaut and Kelley—the *comparison level* (or CL). If a person's outcomes fall above the CL, the person will find the relationship attractive, whereas if they fall below the CL, the person will find the relationship unattractive. By distinguishing between how people *feel* about a relationship and what they will in fact *do* about it, Thibaut and Kelley have developed an extremely useful tool for analyzing exchange relationships. Consider the following four possibilities. Imagine that a person's outcomes are higher than his or her CL_{alt} and CL. In this situation the person will remain in and be satisfied with the relationship. In contrast, if the person's outcomes are lower than the CL and the CL_{alt}, the person will be dissatisfied and will terminate the relationship. The two remaining possibilities are more intriguing. Consider a situation in which a person perceives that his or her outcome level is *above* the CL but *below* the CL_{alt}. In this situation, the person would feel satisfied with his or her outcomes but would probably terminate the relationship, because better outcomes could be obtained elsewhere. For example, a probationary officer may enjoy the working relationship with a particular judge but may still terminate the relationship because there are better opportunities elsewhere. The fourth possibility, which Thibaut and Kelley have labeled a "nonvoluntary relationship," occurs when a person's outcomes are *below* the CL but *above* the CL_{alt}. The person is dissatisfied with the relationship yet must remain in the relationship because it offers better outcomes than the available alternatives. The situation of a prison inmate is a good illustration.

Knowledge of the sources of the CL_{alt} and the CL is essential if social-exchange theory is to be used as a predictive tool. We have already noted that the CL_{alt} is determined by the person's beliefs about the best outcomes available from alternative opportunities. What are the sources of the CL? According to Thibaut and Kelley (1959), "The location of CL on the person's scale of outcomes will be influenced by all of the outcomes known to the member, either by direct experience or symbolically. It may be taken to be some modal or average value of all known outcomes, each outcome weighted by its 'salience,' or strength of instigation" (p. 21).

This general statement implies only that several sources may combine to affect the CL. Three possible determinants of the CL have been identified. People may compare their outcomes with their own previously experienced outcomes, the outcomes of others considered to be similar to themselves, and the outcomes of the person with whom they are currently interacting. Consider a prominent business executive who is convicted of bribery and sentenced to a minimum-security prison. How satisfied would we expect him to be with his interaction with the guards? If his own previous outcomes are salient, then he will probably be dissatisfied, because his former status and power would create a particularly high CL. If, however, he compares himself with others like him who have been convicted and sentenced on bribery charges, he might feel very satisfied with his present outcomes. These others may have received more severe sentences and may be serving their sentences in less desirable institutions. Alternatively, the outcomes of the guard with whom he is interacting may be the most salient, and he may therefore feel somewhat dissatisfied, because the guard's outcomes from the interaction may be higher than his own.

The source having the strongest impact on the CL will be the one that is most salient at the time of evaluation. Thibaut and Kelley maintain that the salience of a particular outcome is, in part, situationally determined—the more vivid the reminders of some outcomes, the greater will be the salience of those outcomes. Of the three sources of comparison, they attach greatest weight to a person's own experienced outcomes, particularly those previous outcomes over which the person believes he or she exercised some control. Because Thibaut and Kelley attach such importance to experienced outcomes in determining the CL, they predict that the CL will tend to shift as new outcomes are experienced. Favorable outcomes will push the CL upward, and unfavorable outcomes will push it downward.

In pursuit of maximal outcomes, individuals must often conform to norms created and enforced by the group. Failure to comply with normative expectations can lead to costs in the form of social rejection and refusal by others to engage in future exchanges with the norm violator. The significance of normative expectations for social exchange is examined in the next section.

Norms and Social Exchange

According to Thibaut and Kelley (1959), a norm is "a behavioral rule that is accepted, at least to some degree, by both members of the dyad [that is, a two-person group]" (p. 129). In large groups, however, acceptance by all members is not required, "a sizable number" being sufficient. Ordinarily norms take on the character of a moral obligation, so that people comply with a norm because it is the "right" thing to do, rather than because they fear what the other person in the exchange might do in retaliation. Norms thus provide a substitute for the exercise of personal power. Persuading someone to do something because it is morally correct and proper deemphasizes the value of the behavior to the person making the appeal and therefore evokes less resistance than the direct exercise of power. By depersonalizing social influence, norms reduce the interpersonal costs associated with power confrontations and thereby smooth social interaction.

Norms reduce the costs for both parties in an exchange in yet another way. Because norms are rules about behavior, they increase the regularity and predictability of social exchanges, thereby giving each participant some basis for predicting how the other is likely to react in a given situation as well as serving as a guide for the participant's own actions. Thibaut and Kelley suggest that this knowledge permits people in a social exchange to behave in a more routine, or automatic, fashion without incurring the costs of uncertainty associated with moment-to-moment decision making.

Two norms that have important implications for social exchanges are the norm of equity, or justice, and the norm of reciprocity.

Social Exchange and the Equity Norm

The idea that parties in a social-exchange relationship expect to receive fair outcomes was first expressed by George Homans (1961, 1974). Borrowing from Aristotle, Homans described *distributive justice* as a situation in which people in a social-exchange relationship perceive that their ratio of profits to investments is equal to their exchange partner's ratio of profits to investments:

$$\frac{\text{person's profits}}{\text{person's investments}} = \frac{\text{other's profits}}{\text{other's investments}}$$

Investments represent what people perceive they and others contribute to a relationship that entitles them to certain profits, or outcomes. Investments may consist of a person's skills, education, seniority, and effort. When a person perceives that the ratios are unequal, a state of *distributive injustice* obtains. The person who has the less favorable ratio may feel angry and disappointed, while the person with the more favorable ratio may feel guilty. The perception of injustice is unpleasant and therefore constitutes a cost in the exchange. Homans does note, however, that the person with the more favorable ratio will probably be less sensitive to the injustice than the person with the less favorable ratio. It is easy for the costs of injustice to become diluted by the overabundance of rewards.

Although Homans' ideas have generated a fair amount of research, mostly by sociologists, the theory of justice that has generated the most interest and research by social psychologists is equity theory (Adams, 1963, 1965; Walster, Berscheid, & Walster, 1973, 1976; Walster, Walster, & Berscheid, 1978). For this reason our discussion will focus on the equity norm. The theory was first developed by Adams (1963, 1965) and later reformulated by Walster et al. (1973). The most recent version of the theory employs a ratio very similar to one used by Homans. Whereas Homans uses the concepts of profits and investments, equity theory uses the parallel concepts of outcomes and inputs. Inputs are defined simply as "the participant's contributions to the exchange which are seen . . . as entitling him to rewards or costs" (Walster et al., 1976, p. 3). The inputs can be either assets, which entitle the person to rewards, or liabilities, which entitle the person to costs. The theory rests on four propositions: (1) that people will try to maximize their outcomes (that is, rewards minus costs) in interactions with others; (2) that groups recognize the value of treating others equitably and therefore will reward those who treat others equitably and punish those who do not; (3) "When individuals find themselves participating in inequitable relationships, they become distressed. The more inequitable the relationship, the more distress individuals feel" (Walster et al., 1976, p. 6); and (4) the greater the amount of inequity, the greater will be the person's distress and the harder the person will try to restore equity.

Equity can be restored to a relationship in two ways. One can restore *actual* equity by changing the other person's outcomes or inputs or by changing one's own outcomes or inputs. Thus, when a police officer decides to place a hostile suspect under arrest and let a friendly suspect off with just a warning, the officer is establishing equity between himself and each suspect by altering the suspects' outcomes. The hostile suspect's behavior (that is, inputs) make him more deserving of arrest (that is, lower outcomes). The opposite would hold for the treatment of the friendly suspect. The decisions of other agents, such as prosecutors, jurors, judges, and parole-board members, can be seen as attempts to restore actual equity by altering the outcomes of those who come before them. Alternatively, people can restore equity *psychologically* by distorting their perception of their own and the other person's inputs and outcomes. Thus, a bystander who failed to come to the aid of a victim may try to restore equity by distorting the victim's inputs ("She invited the attack by dressing as she did") or by distorting the victim's outcomes ("She wasn't hurt too badly, only one broken rib"). Victims, in turn, can reduce their feelings of inequity by actually changing their outcomes (that is, demanding compensation) or changing the outcomes of the other by retaliating. Victims can reduce inequity psychologically by changing their perception of their own inputs—for example, by justifying their victimization.

The motivation to reduce inequity has been the subject of extensive laboratory and field research, as indicated by a recent annotated bibliography (Adams & Freedman, 1976) containing 167 studies relating to equity theory.

Social Exchange and the Norm of Reciprocity

In addition to the norm of equity, social exchanges are guided by a second norm—the norm of reciprocity. According to Gouldner (1960), the norm of reciprocity states that "(1) people should help those who have helped them, and (2) people should not injure those who have helped them" (p. 171). The norm was given more precise meaning by Greenberg (1968, 1980) in his theory of *indebtedness*. Indebtedness is a state of obligation to repay a benefit. Like inequity, the state of indebtedness is assumed to have motivational properties such that the greater its magnitude, the more uncomfortable the recipient will be, and hence the greater will be the recipient's effort to reduce the debt. The norm of reciprocity is very salient to agents of the criminal justice system, and they frequently use it in their everyday practices. For example, the police sometimes grant favors to prostitutes by not arresting them when they have a legal basis for doing so. Later, when the police need information to solve a case, they ask the prostitute to repay the debt by supplying them with the information. It is perhaps out of respect for the power of indebtedness that there are strong regulations prohibiting agents of the criminal justice system from accepting "gifts" from those being processed or likely to be processed by the system. Such gifts are often called bribes or graft.

Distributive Fairness

Some theorists contend that people may use a broader conception of "fairness" than that implied by the equity and reciprocity norms (Deutsch, 1975; Lerner, 1975; Leventhal, 1976). One theory that argues this position is that of Gerald Leventhal. Leventhal (1976) contends that equity theory relies on a "contributions rule" (what one deserves depends on one's contributions), which is but one of several rules for determining fairness in social exchange. In his "justice judgment model" Leventhal proposes the existence of two additional rules—a "needs rule," which dictates that persons with greater need should receive higher outcomes, and an "equality rule," which dictates that all should receive equal outcomes regardless of their inputs or needs. A major tenet of the model is that the relative weights of these rules change from one situation to the next. The particular weight assigned to each rule depends on the social setting and the individual's role in that setting. Leventhal presents evidence that high weight will be given to equity considerations (that is, the contributions rule) in interaction settings in which task achievement and productivity are the primary concern. In settings where the welfare of others is the primary concern, high weight is likely to be assigned to the needs rule, and in settings in which good interpersonal relations and group solidarity are the primary concern, people are likely to assign high weight to the equality rule.

Perhaps the major virtue of this model is that it calls attention to the shifting criteria that people use in evaluating fairness in social exchange. Further, the model makes salient the fact that rules of fairness can have contradictory implications in a given setting. Suppose that an off-duty police officer apprehends a young mother stealing food for her children. Application of the contributions rule would dictate that she be arrested. Her inputs to the situation make her deserving of arrest. However, application of the needs rule would dictate a more sympathetic response. As we shall see in Chapter 7, at the sentencing hearing the defense attorney often tries to heighten the salience of the needs rule, whereas the prosecutor often tries to heighten the salience of the contributions rule.

OUTLINE OF THIS BOOK

Beginning with the next chapter, the attribution/exchange framework is used to examine decision making at each successive stage of the criminal justice system. Our examination starts with a consideration of the factors that influence the reporting of crimes by victims and bystanders (Chapter 2). Following notification of the police, we then examine the determinants of the police's decision to arrest a suspect (Chapter 3). After the suspect is arrested and booked, our focus of attention shifts to the judge and the prosecutor (Chapter 4). The judge must decide on the pretrial status of the defendant. Should the defendant be released on bail, and if so, what should the amount be? After examining the factors that influence this decision, we use the attribution/exchange model to describe the pretrial activities of prosecutors, including their decision to charge the suspect and their involvement in "plea bargaining." The next two chapters (Chapters 5 and 6) deal with the trial phase of the criminal justice process. Chapter 5 focuses on the selection of the jury, and Chapter 6 examines the strategies used by the attorneys during the trial and how the jury reaches its verdict of innocence or guilt.

If the defendant is found guilty, the judge must decide what the sentence should be. The dynamics underlying this decision are discussed in Chapter 7. For defendants sentenced to prison, the key decision maker who determines their fate is the prison guard. Guards' decisions about how to treat inmates are analyzed in Chapter 8. Our focus of attention then shifts to decisions about parole (Chapter 9). The key decision makers at this stage are members of the parole board and the parole officer. In the final chapter (Chapter 10), the findings are pulled together, and an assessment is made of the future of the criminal justice system and the role of social psychology in it.

Some common themes run through this book. Agents at various stages of the system have different types of information available to them for making attributions about suspected offenders, but there are certain factors that affect attributions made by most decision makers. They include (1) the seriousness of the offense, (2) the suspect's prior criminal record, and (3) the judgments made by other decision makers. Although social-exchange considerations vary from one type of agent to another, certain exchange relationships influence most decision makers in the system. These exchange relationships are with (1) the suspected offender, (2) peers, (3) other agents of the criminal justice system, (4) the victim, and (5) the community.

SUMMARY

The focus of this book is on decision making in the criminal justice system. There is an inconsistency between how the system is supposed to operate and how it actually operates. Persons and groups are not treated equally by those who operate the system because circumstances require agents to exercise personal discretion continually. Two important value orientations that guide the exercise of discretion in the criminal justice system are the crime-control model and the due-process model. This book will examine the role of social-psychological factors in the decision-making process. Social psychology is the branch

of psychology that studies how a person's thoughts, feelings, and behavior are influenced by the actual, imagined, or implied behavior
and/or characteristics of others.

There is a growing interface between social psychology and the
criminal justice system. Social psychologists use several methods to
study decision making—laboratory and field experiments, simulations,
field studies, surveys and interviews, and archival analysis. Each
method has its advantages and disadvantages. Several ethical issues are
raised when conducting research in the criminal justice system, including deception and confidentiality.

The theoretical framework that we will use to analyze the criminal
justice system consists of two major components—an attribution component and a social-exchange component. The first of these focuses on
the processes by which people infer the causes of their own and other
people's behavior. The model assumes that the attributions people
make about the causes of behavior determine to a large extent how they
will respond to others' actions. The social-exchange component of our
theoretical framework is based on the premise that decision making in a
social context represents a form of exchange in which the participants
weigh their outcomes (defined as rewards minus costs). The outcomes
that people receive or expect to receive from others are evaluated with
regard to certain standards. Social exchanges are bounded by rules, or
norms, such as the norms of equity and reciprocity. These norms can be
integrated under the more general concept of distributive fairness. According to this concept, people use a variety of rules in determining the
fairness of a given exchange, the rule of fairness chosen being a function
of the particular context and the person's role in that context.

CHAPTER TWO

Reporting of Crimes by Citizens

Although most citizens are not official agents of the criminal justice system, their decision on the reporting of possible crimes have a profound influence on decision making at all stages of the system. The impact of citizens' discretion is most evident in the activities of the police. Because police officers rarely view crimes in progress, they are greatly dependent on citizens for information about possible criminal events. Indeed, notification by citizens accounts for about 85% of the incidents investigated by the police (Black & Reiss, 1967). Because citizens—in particular, victims—play a primary role in determining the number of suspected criminals who enter the criminal justice system, they have been called the "gatekeepers" of the system (Hindelang & Gottfredson, 1976). Although citizens have been playing this role for centuries, social scientists have only recently recognized the importance of citizens' discretion in the functioning of the criminal justice system. Two key events occurred in the 1960s that called attention to the importance of reporting by citizens and led to an increase of research efforts on citizens' reactions to crime: the murder of Katherine ("Kitty") Genovese in New York in 1964 and the National Opinion Research Center survey of victims of crime.

THE UNRESPONSIVE BYSTANDER AND THE RETICENT VICTIM

On March 13, 1964, a barmaid named Kitty Genovese was murdered outside her apartment in the Kew Gardens section of New York City. Murder is not a particularly rare event in New York City, but one aspect of the incident elevated the crime from local to international prominence. Thirty-eight of Kitty's neighbors witnessed the killer stalking his victim or heard her desperate screams for help. Yet not one person completed even an anonymous call to the police or tried to intervene while the crime was occurring—an event that took *more than thirty minutes* to complete. The police detective in charge of the investigation of this incident provided the following description:

> So many eyes were on Kitty as she lay under the yellow street lamp that she might have been spotlighted on a stage. For some of her neighbors she really was. One woman went to the window to see what the screams were about, but could not quite make out the scene below. "Turn off the lights, dumbbell," her husband said, "*then* you can see." The woman did see better with the lights out. She and her husband pulled chairs up to the window to watch [Seedman & Hellman, 1975, p. 119].[1]

The failure of the 38 bystanders to intervene in some way was more shocking than the crime itself. It prompted two social psychologists, Bibb Latané and John Darley, to initiate a series of experimental studies of bystander reactions to criminal and noncriminal emergencies. The aim of their research was to account for the apparent apathy of Genovese's neighbors. The work of Latané and Darley (1970) encouraged others to investigate the determinants of bystander reactions to crimes.

Research focusing on decision making by *victims* was stimulated by the surprising results of a national survey conducted by the National Opinion Research Center (Ennis, 1967). This survey revealed that victims, like bystanders, are frequently unresponsive to crime. According to this report, only about half the crimes indexed by the survey in 1966 were reported to the police. The rate of reporting varied with the nature of the crime. Thus, only 35% of petty larcenies were reported, compared with 65% of robberies and aggravated assaults. The revelation that many victims fail to alert the police to their victimization spawned a series of continuing surveys of victims sponsored by the Law Enforcement Assistance Administration (LEAA) and conducted by the Bureau of the Census. These surveys have provided valuable information about the characteristics of victims of crime (both reporters and nonreporters) and about the circumstances of their victimization.

In this chapter we will review separately the decision-making processes of bystanders and victims. We have chosen to discuss them separately because bystanders and victims have different perspectives. One is the target of the offender's actions and the other is merely an onlooker. This difference in perspective influences the attributional considerations as well as the social-exchange considerations of each person. We will now proceed to examine just how bystanders go about deciding whether to call the police.

[1]Reprinted by permission of Raines & Raines, agents for Peter Hellman & Albert Seedman. Copyright © 1974 by Albert A. Seedman and Peter Hellman.

DECISION MAKING BY BYSTANDERS

Before applying the attribution/exchange model to bystanders' decision to call the police, we must first account for how bystanders detect criminal events. Victimization surveys (Law Enforcement Assistance Administration, 1976a) show that most crimes occur in public settings in metropolitan areas. The most common locations include streets, parks, playgrounds, and parking lots. In such settings, we can expect to find that many crimes occur in the presence of bystanders. The fact that bystanders are often in a position to observe a criminal event does not guarantee that the event will be reported to the police. Research has shown that bystanders often fail to notice criminal events. Let us see why this is so.

Detection of the Event

Why do bystanders often fail to detect crimes that occur in broad daylight in public? The answer probably lies in the fact that people can attend to and process only a limited number of stimuli. Research on human perception suggests that three variables can explain why some events are attended to and others are ignored. First, such characteristics of observers as their ability to see and hear and their state of mind can influence what they attend to. Second, certain features of the situation, such as its novelty, may attract bystanders' attention. And third, whether a crime is detected can depend on social-influence factors, such as the reactions of others on the scene.

Characteristics of the observer

Whether a suspicious event is detected depends very much on the quality of the bystander's sensory apparatus. If the bystander's vision or hearing is impaired, the event is less likely to be detected. Also important is the bystander's "set," or state of readiness, to detect a criminal event. The set may exist for any number of reasons. For example, as a result of a personal experience or learning about the experience of others, certain people may be highly sensitized to the possibility of crime. Thus, people who have been victimized in the past are likely to maintain greater vigilance and therefore are likely to detect a suspicious event. To increase the public's readiness to detect criminal events, the federal government has helped finance crime-prevention groups consisting of citizens all across the country. The major premise underlying the formation of such groups is that by increasing citizens' awareness of and concern about crime, vigilance and hence detection of crime can be increased (Bickman & Lavrakas, 1976).

Nature of the stimulus situation

An event is more likely to be detected if it has some characteristic that makes it stand out from other stimuli in the situation. One such characteristic is the intensity of the stimulus. If a stimulus is more intense (for example, louder, brighter) than other stimuli in the situation, it should be detected more readily. For example, a gunshot is more likely to be heard in the stillness of the night than amid the sounds of a rock concert.

Another stimulus characteristic that makes an event stand out is novelty. A novel event is more likely to be detected than one that inconspicuously blends in with the background. For example, the sight of a well-dressed man running in the street is more likely to attract attention than the sight of the same man walking at a leisurely pace. Studies have shown that if a person's appearance or demeanor deviates from normative expectations in a given setting, that person becomes a novel stimulus and is likely to attract a bystander's attention. Thus, college-age shoppers in a university bookstore were more likely to notice shoplifting by a middle-aged female "conventioneer" (who was in reality a confederate of the experimenter) than by a young female college student (Bickman, 1975). Similarly, middle-aged customers in two suburban drugstores were more likely to detect shoplifting by a female dressed in hippie garb (blue jeans, army jacket, blue work shirt) than by a female dressed more conventionally (Gelfand, Hartman, Walder, & Page, 1973). Bank robbers and burglars are usually aware that novel stimuli are more easily detected: many of their actions are directed at minimizing the novelty of the criminal act. For example, this can be done by inconspicuously passing a robbery note to a bank teller or by posing as movers or repairmen when burglarizing a residence. Robbers have also been known to plan their crimes for rainy days because running in the rain (after a robbery) does not appear unusual and is therefore unlikely to attract much attention (Letkemann, 1973). Similarly, robbers have donned jogging outfits to disguise their escape attempts. Passers-by are not likely to pay much attention to a stranger dressed in a jogging outfit running through their neighborhood. This disguise worked quite well for a Washington, D.C., man known as the "Robber Jogger," who committed numerous stickups and two murders while dressed in running gear (Keyes, 1980).

Sometimes thieves will purposely create a competing novel event to distract others from the theft. One such instance took place in a large suburban department store. Several female thieves deliberately entered into an argument with store employees. When the employee attending the cash register left the register to see what was causing the disturbance, an accomplice promptly emptied the register and fled. Although the theft occurred at midday in a crowded department store, it was not discovered until the employee returned and found the emptied register.

Social-influence factors

A number of anticrime campaigns have attempted to alert citizens to signs of possible criminal activity and to impress them with the important role they can play in preventing crimes and apprehending criminals. The campaigns have used impersonal forms of communication that can contact many people at one time, including newspaper, radio, and television advertisements, posters, window stickers, and pamphlets. However, available evidence seems to show that such impersonal influence attempts do not enhance detection by bystanders (Bickman, 1975; Bickman & Green, 1975).

In contrast to the failure of impersonal forms of communication, several studies have shown that detection can be increased by personal face-to-face communications. In one study (Moriarty, 1975) a series of thefts of a portable radio from an unattended beach blanket were staged. In half the instances, the experimental accomplice playing the role of "victim" asked the subject at an adjoining blanket to "watch my things" while he went to the boardwalk for a few minutes. In a second condition, the victim made no such request but instead asked for a match and then strolled away in the direction of the boardwalk. Several minutes later an experimental accomplice walked up to the victim's blanket, picked up the radio, and walked briskly away. An observer stationed nearby noted whether the subject noticed the theft. Results showed that bystanders who had committed themselves to watch the victim's possessions were more likely to detect the theft and stop the thief from escaping with the radio than bystanders whose help had not been requested. Similar results were obtained in a study involving a staged theft in a library (Shaffer, Rogel, & Hendrick, 1975). Those who were asked to watch a victim's possessions while the victim checked a reference were more likely to observe the theft of the victim's property than those who were not asked to do so. Taken together, these studies suggest that a face-to-face communication in the form of a request can influence a bystander's commitment to maintaining surveillance over another's property and thereby increase the likelihood of detecting future crimes.

Several crime-prevention programs initiated in the 1970s have tried to encourage citizens to commit themselves to watch their neighbors' homes as a means of combating increasing crime rates. The National Sheriffs Association, for instance, has sponsored an anticrime measure known as the Neighborhood Watch Program. Citizens in the program are brought together at home or community meetings, given information on crime detection and prevention, and told that much crime could be detected and prevented if citizens would keep an eye on their neighbors' homes and report any suspicious activity. These programs incorporate face-to-face communications, which experimental studies have shown to be effective. Although thorough evaluations of citizen crime-prevention programs have not yielded conclusive evidence of their effectiveness (Bickman & Lavrakas, 1976), research on the role of personal commitment suggests that such programs might be effective in increasing detection of suspicious events by citizens.

Having detected a suspicious event, bystanders must decide whether it may be a crime and, if so, what to do about it. To understand how bystanders make these decisions, we will apply the attribution/ exchange model.

ATTRIBUTION/EXCHANGE MODEL OF DECISION MAKING BY BYSTANDERS

As shown in Figure 2-1, the attribution/exchange model consists of two stages. First, after detecting a suspicious event, bystanders must interpret the incident as a criminal event rather than some form of noncriminal activity, such as an accident or a practical joke. This constitutes the attribution stage of the model in that it involves making attributions about the criminality of the actor's intentions. Whether criminal intent is assigned to the actor depends on the characteristics of the observer, the nature of the stimulus situation (such as the suspect's behavior), and the responses of others in the situation. Once an attribution of criminal intent has been made, the bystander must make a second judgment: what action, if any, should be taken. This represents the social-exchange stage of the model. It is assumed that in making this decision bystanders weigh the potential benefits and costs associated with each of their options and choose the one that seems most profitable. The main source of benefits and costs is expected exchanges with agents of the criminal justice system, the suspected offender, and significant others, such as the victim and co-bystanders. We will examine separately each phase of the decision-making process of bystanders.

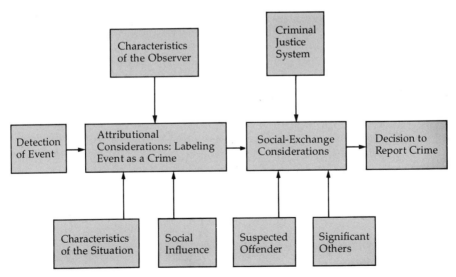

Figure 2-1. Attribution/exchange model of citizens' decision to report a crime

ATTRIBUTIONAL CONSIDERATIONS: LABELING THE EVENT AS A CRIME

After detecting an action, the observer must decide whether it is a criminal act. Yet this decision is not always simple, because of the ambiguity of many events and the observer's uncertainty of what constitutes a crime. Very few crimes are as blatant and easily defined as the ones portrayed in popular "cops and robbers" television shows. Consider the Kitty Genovese murder. Although the victim was crying out for assistance and was observed staggering along the street, some witnesses interpreted the incident as a "lovers' quarrel" rather than a violent, deadly assault. How does a bystander determine whether a particular event is an assault or a domestic argument, a burglary or a person locked out of his or her house, a robbery or a panhandler soliciting money for a cup of coffee? To answer these questions, we must first examine the factors that influence a bystander's definition of what constitues a crime, and we must then examine the factors that determine whether the observed action fits that definition.

Bystanders' Definition of a Crime

Although legal codes specify what acts constitute crimes and what acts do not, individuals may not always subscribe to such legal definitions (Quinney, 1970). An individual's beliefs about what behaviors are morally correct or appropriate in a given situation can be called "personal norms" (Kidd, 1979; Schwartz, 1977). Thus, a citizen may be aware of statutes prohibiting the possession of marijuana but may personally believe that possession of the drug is not a crime. Similarly, although physical attacks on one's wife or child may constitute criminal acts of wife or child abuse, an individual may personally believe that a husband or father, as head of the household, has a right—indeed, an obligation—to discipline family members when they get out of line.

Individuals' beliefs about what acts constitute crimes can be expected to vary over time in accordance with changes in social values. This is clearly shown in people's attitudes toward sexual offenses. Consistent with the liberalization in sexual attitudes (Hopkins, 1977) is the trend in recent years to view some sexual offenses, such as adultery and seduction, as minor offenses (Thurstone, 1927; Coombs, 1967; Greenberg, Wilson, Carretta, & DeMay, 1979). The impact of the social environment on how people define a criminal act can be seen in responses to white-collar crime. Media exposure of white-collar crimes committed by prominent public officials may lend some legitimacy to these actions. One is hard pressed to read a newspaper without noticing numerous examples of politicians and businesspersons involved in questionable practices such as receiving kickbacks, embezzling funds, and cheating on income tax returns. Citizens may feel that if prominent persons can do it, it must not be so bad (Sutherland, 1940).

When assigning criminal intent to others, bystanders probably take into account the role played by external causes. Actions that are provoked by external causes may not be viewed as criminal. Being the victim of injustice or inequity is one such cause. Employees may "look the other way" when a fellow employee is seen stealing from the employer because of their belief that they are inequitably paid. Such thefts may be viewed as legitimate means of correcting the inequity. Recently, a number of companies, recognizing that some employees perceive theft from an organization as a "just desert" rather than a crime, have accommodated themselves to such small thefts by redefining them as "reasonable pilfering." Similar reasoning can be applied to the actions of minority-group members living in urban ghettos. Feeling discriminated against, many of these persons may tend to view harmful actions committed against affluent whites as legitimate means for correcting inequity rather than as illegal acts. The urban riots of the 1960s and, more recently, the looting of stores during the 1977 New York City blackout were justified by many bystanders on the grounds that the store owners had exploited them in the past by charging unreasonably high prices. Rather than trying to stop the looters or assisting law enforcement officials, many bystanders simply stood around, watched, and sometimes even applauded the looters.

Fit between Observed Event and Bystanders' Definition of a Crime

Whether a bystander makes an attribution of criminality depends on the bystander's definition of a crime and how closely the observed act fits that definition. In the previous section we discussed some of the factors that determine how a bystander defines a crime. In this section we will examine some of the factors that determine whether an observed act fits this definition. As shown in Figure 2-1, there are three general determinants of how an act will be labeled: characteristics of the observer, nature of the stimulus situation, and social-influence factors.

Characteristics of the observer

Research on perception has generally shown that people's motivational states strongly influence what they perceive. Such states create a psychological set, or readiness to perceive an event in a particular way. For example, when hungry persons were asked to identify words flashed on a screen for a fraction of a second, food-related words were more readily identified than other words (Erdelyi, 1974). Studies such as these show that an observer's state of arousal may create a readiness to label an event in line with the observer's motivational state. The set to perceive an event may stem from nonmotivational sources as well. For example, the set to perceive an incident as a crime could result from training or from experience as a victim. Indeed, the purpose of much of the information given to neighborhood crime-prevention groups is to foster the appropriate set so as to make it easier for them to label suspicious acts as criminal. Thus, citizens are warned to be suspicious when they see strangers loitering, driving up and down their street, or carrying property that is not wrapped.

Nature of the stimulus situation

Whether a bystander attributes a criminal intention to someone depends very much on what act is observed. Few situations clearly present themselves as crimes to bystanders. Rarely does a bystander come across a robber pointing a gun at a victim with arms raised in the air. More typically, bystanders are confronted with an ambiguous event. Are the persons seen loading a television set into a pickup truck committing a burglary? Is the person seen using a coat hanger to open a car door in the process of stealing the car? When we witness two teenagers wrestling on the ground, are we observing an assault or a friendly scuffle? In such situations the bystander is confronted with the dilemma of determining whether the actor is criminally motivated—that is, whether the actor has a criminal intention. The bystander's task is an attributional one in that he or she is called on to identify the cause of the actor's behavior from among all the causes that are plausible in the situation. As stated in Chapter 1, it is very hard to make a causal attribution when many plausible facilitative causes are present. Criminals implicitly recognize this principle (the discounting principle) when they try to conceal their criminal intent by introducing a highly plausible facilitative cause for their actions. When burglars park their "repair truck" in front of someone's home during midday and proceed to remove the occupant's television set, few bystanders would assign criminal intent to this act. In contrast, it would be far easier to attribute criminal intent when a stranger is seen running from a house carrying a television set, because there are no plausible causes for this behavior other than a motive to commit a theft. The bystander's confidence in this attribution would, of course, be strengthened if, in response to the bystander's inquiry, the stranger refused to answer and instead quickened his pace.

In summary, with regard to the contribution of the stimulus situation, the attribution part of our model would predict that a bystander will find it easiest to label an incident as a crime when the stimulus situation presents few plausible causes for the target's behavior other than the intention to commit a crime.

Social-influence factors

Of the various factors that can determine whether a bystander will make an attribution of criminality, social influence appears to play a critical role. Social psychologists have shown that when people are uncertain about the correctness of their beliefs, they tend to rely on the opinions of others for confirmation (Festinger, 1954; Suls & Miller,

1977). Bystanders to an ambiguous criminal event often find themselves in the company of other eyewitnesses. We would expect bystanders in this situation to examine the verbal and nonverbal reactions of those present in order to resolve their uncertainty. For instance, if a person observes a fight in the presence of other citizens who ignore the event, the person may use others' inaction as a cue that the fight is not serious. If, however, the bystander observes another person shouting at the combatants, the bystander may view this reaction as a sign that the event should be taken seriously.

Research conducted by Latané and Darley (1970) shows that a bystander's definition of a noncrime emergency situation is powerfully influenced by the number of unresponsive bystanders who also witnessed the event. Latané and Darley found that the greater the number of unresponsive bystanders present, the stronger was the tendency *not* to define the situation as an emergency.

Evidence that the presence of unresponsive others affects the interpretation given to a possible criminal event was provided in a study conducted in Israel by Schwartz and Gottlieb (1976). Male subjects were led to believe that they were overhearing a scuffle in an adjoining room. (In reality, it was a tape recording of a staged event.) One group of subjects was led to believe that the incident was overheard by others as well and that these others were apparently taking no action. Another group was not given any information that would permit them to assess how others were reacting. The investigators hypothesized that subjects who were aware that others were unresponsive to the event would be less inclined to label it as a criminal emergency. Self-reports from subjects tended to confirm this reasoning. Most of those who had believed that there were other (passive) witnesses said that they had been inhibited by this belief, and many said it had led them to decide that taking action was inappropriate. In comparison, those who did not know how others responded tended to feel that it was more appropriate to take some action.

The studies by Darley and Latané and by Schwartz and Gottlieb show that a bystander's attributions about an ambiguous event can be influenced by nonverbal cues emitted by those present. But what about verbal cues? How important are they in determining attributions of criminal intent? Can someone's words have the same impact on the attribution process as someone's actions?

Two experiments conducted by Bickman and his associates support the idea that verbal statements by others on the scene affect how a bystander interprets a suspicious event. In the first of these, Bickman and Rosenbaum (1977) placed female subjects in a small cubicle with a female confederate and told them that they would be observing a live telecast (in reality a videotape) from a local supermarket. Their task was to record shoppers' reactions to a display located near one of the checkout lines. Several minutes into the tape, subjects observed a staged shoplifting of two packages of film from the display. The confederate then defined the incident either as a theft ("She's shoplifting") or as a nontheft. In the noncrime-interpretation condition she stated "Oh, no! She's not shoplifting. I'm sure she'll pay for it. She probably told the clerk she put it in her purse." When later questioned by the experimenter, subjects in the noncrime-interpretation condition were significantly less certain that a crime had occurred than other subjects. However, a second study by Bickman and Green (1977) yielded less clear results. A staged shoplifting incident was presented to subjects while they waited in a supermarket checkout line. A confederate standing in line behind the subject remarked in half the cases "Say, look at her. She's shoplifting. She put that into her purse." For the remaining half of the subjects, the confederate said nothing. More subjects who were cued by the confederate intervened, but they felt no more certain that the event was in fact a shoplifting than those who were not cued. They did, however, report feeling more obligated to intervene. Bickman and Green explained their failure to find a difference in perceived certainty that the incident was a theft by noting that the theft was so blatant that subjects may have felt no need to rely on the confederate's opinion. Overall, the above studies suggest that verbal and nonverbal cues provided by others on the scene affect the likelihood of bystanders' making attributions of criminal intent.

Having detected and labeled an incident as a crime, bystanders must decide what to do. Factors relating to this decision are discussed in the following section.

SOCIAL-EXCHANGE CONSIDERATIONS: TAKING ACTION

The bystander's decision about how to deal with the criminal incident can best be understood from a social-exchange perspective. This perspective views bystanders as making rough estimates of the rewards and costs associated with a few salient options and then choosing the option that they believe provides them with the best outcomes. This model does not imply that bystanders necessarily make these calculations in a cool and rational way. On the contrary, they often have to reach a decision under very stressful circumstances. More often than not the incident occurs without warning. If the act involves a physical assault, the victim's cries are likely to add to the bystander's arousal. Moreover, the bystander must decide very quickly what to do. In such highly arousing circumstances bystanders may sometimes act more on impulse than on a cool, rational calculation of the benefits and costs. The model assumes that insofar as possible, bystanders try to make a rational decision but that stress associated with the situation often prevents them from doing so perfectly.

The social-psychological literature suggests that bystanders have three salient options. First, they can intervene directly; second, they can notify the proper authorities; and third, they can decide to take no action. Of course, bystanders may choose both the first and second options. For example, a bystander may first intervene and restrain an assailant and later call the police. In choosing among these options, bystanders weigh the rewards and costs that they believe they will receive from one or more of the following: the suspected offender, agents of the criminal justice system, and significant others, such as the victim and other bystanders. We will discuss the social-exchange considerations associated with each option.

Direct Intervention

Social exchange with the suspected offender

The decision to intervene to stop a crime in progress or to apprehend a suspect poses several dangers to the bystander. The suspect's response to the bystander's intervention can range from passive surrender to violent resistance. Consider, for example, two incidents reported in the *New York Times:*

> Mr. Harris, a former Marine, was aboard a subway train in Manhattan the other morning when a man with a knife demanded money. As passengers obediently dropped coins, bills and wallets to the floor, Mr. Harris bristled. He threw down his newspaper, stood up to his full height of 5-feet-4, and told the robber in a no-nonsense voice: "Throw the money down on the floor— and give me your knife!"
>
> The startled holdup man complied, and some of the victims recovered enough to bind him with belts and sit on him until policemen took him away.
>
> "If you talk in a strong, authoritative voice," Mr. Harris said afterward, "you knock the bully out of them" ["He Didn't Sit Still . . . ," 1978, p. 6].[2]

A very different and sadder outcome awaited Charles Bivens when he and his wife and 9-month-old daughter saw two teenagers attack an elderly woman and grab her purse.

> Mr. Bivens, a caterer, stopped them. "She's an old lady," Mr. Bivens said. "Why pick on an old lady?" He took the pocketbook from the boys and returned it to the trembling woman.
>
> Then the boys, recovering from their astonishment, drew knives with six-inch blades.
>
> "Get the baby out of the street!" yelled Mr. Bivens to his wife, and Mrs. Bivens ran to their building. . . .
>
> When she got back to her husband he had been stabbed several times. He had staggered to Fifth Avenue, trying to escape the slashing blows, and there he collapsed [and died]. The street was full of people and no one had come to his aid ["Middle-Class Leaders . . . ," 1968, p. 46].[3]

[2]From "He Didn't Sit Still for Subway Holdup," June 4, 1978. ©1978 by The New York Times Company. Reprinted by permission.

[3]From "Middle-class Leaders in Harlem Ask for Crackdown on Crime," December 24, 1968. ©1968 by The New York Times Company. Reprinted by permission.

Incidents such as the one involving Mr. Bivens call attention to the tremendous costs that can be incurred when a bystander chooses to intervene. Some states, such as California, Nevada, Georgia, and New York, have enacted Good Samaritan statutes that provide monetary compensation to bystanders who are injured while trying to prevent a crime or catch a suspected offender. Commenting on the doubtful effectiveness of such laws to encourage intervention by bystanders, Culhane (1965) noted: "The fear of physical injury rather than the fear of uncompensated physical or financial injury would seem to be the major deterrent of citizen crime control participation" (p. 271).

Given the severity of the potential costs of intervention, what motivates bystanders to intervene in dangerous situations? An answer comes from interviews with Good Samaritans in California who were themselves injured in the course of aiding victims of crime (Huston, Ruggiero, Conner, & Geis, 1981). Compared with a matched group of "noninterveners," the "interveners" were described as being taller, heavier, and better trained to cope with crimes and emergency situations. Moreover, their self-perceptions were consistent with this description. They tended to describe themselves as physically strong, aggressive, emotional, and principled. Perhaps as a result of their feelings of competence and self-confidence, they were less likely to consider the possible costs of intervention. It is noteworthy that only one of the 32 interveners considered that he might be injured when he decided to intervene.

Similar findings were obtained in a study involving a simulated rape (Shotland & Stebbins, 1980). Those who directly intervened indicated that they had some physical-defense training and boasted afterward that they could "handle the situation." Several were varsity athletes, one was a police dispatcher, another was studying to be a police officer, and a third was armed with a pocketknife. What the interveners in both studies had in common was a high degree of capability and a strong sense of confidence in their ability to intervene successfully.

Other research shows that the perceived relationship between the victim and the offender can affect a bystander's beliefs about how risky it is to intervene. In one experiment subjects were exposed to a staged assault in which the victim indicated either that she was married to the assailant or that he was a stranger (Shotland & Straw, 1976). When the assailant was a stranger, 65% of subjects intervened; when he was the woman's husband, 19% intervened. When another group of subjects was shown a film of the episode, they indicated that they expected less resistance from the stranger than from the husband.

Social-exchange considerations involving the suspect affect not only the decision to intervene but the mode of intervention as well. Moriarty (1975) found that bystanders who intervened to prevent the theft of a portable radio from a beach blanket were more likely to use physical force when the thief was female. Whereas 73% of the interveners snatched the radio away from the female thief, only 17% did so when the thief was male. Presumably, bystanders believed that it would be less costly to use physical force in dealing with a female than a male. The same action applied to a male thief might meet with greater physical resistance and could result in the bystander's being harmed.

Social exchange with significant others

A bystander's social-exchange relationship with the victim appears to have a strong impact on a bystander's willingness to intervene in a crime. Numerous studies have shown that when bystanders commit themselves to watch a victim's belongings, they not only "watch" the victim's property but are more willing to intervene to prevent it from being stolen (Austin, 1979b; Moriarty, 1975; Shaffer et al., 1975; Schwarz, Jennings, Petrillo, & Kidd, 1980). From a social-exchange viewpoint the commitment to guard another's property increases bystanders' costs if they fail to intervene. The costs are likely to consist in having to deal with the victim's anger and disapproval as well as from others who may learn of the bystander's failure to act.

Is a commitment to watch someone's property by itself sufficient to cause a bystander to intervene? A study by Austin (1979b) suggests that male bystanders also consider the degree of harm suffered by the victim. When the victim's possessions were of high value (electronic calculator, folders), male bystanders were more likely to honor their commitment (69% intervened) than when the possessions were of low value (books, folders; 25% intervened). Female bystanders, however, showed a high rate of intervention regardless of the value of the property (high value, 82%; low value, 66%). Presumably, the amount of cost expected by male bystanders for not intervening varied with the value of the property, whereas for females it did not.

On certain occasions bystanders may be more likely to intervene because they expect that the victim will join them in confronting the suspect. This was shown in the study by Shotland and Straw (1976), in which bystanders witnessed an assault by a stranger or the victim's spouse. Subjects were more likely to intervene when the assailant was a stranger, in part because they expected more assistance from the victim in that situation than when the assailant was the victim's spouse.

In Shotland and Straw's study, many of those who witnessed the live assault by the stranger said that they felt that they should take some active role but were not sure just what to do. The uncertainty experienced by these bystanders suggests that if others had been present, the bystanders might have looked to them for guidance. A study involving bystanders' responses to a theft staged in a school library supports this reasoning (Shaffer et al., 1975). The presence of a passive bystander significantly reduced the percentage of those who intervened to stop the theft, compared with those who witnessed the theft alone. Shaffer et al. reasoned that the presence of another person decreased bystanders' sense of responsibility to intervene, which made them feel less guilty for not intervening and therefore reduced their costs. In this situation, then, bystanders may have believed that it was more costly to intervene than not to. When faced with such circumstances, bystanders may prefer to notify the proper authorities and let them deal with the situation.

Notifying the Authorities

Social exchange with the criminal justice system and with the suspected offender

The bystander's decision to notify the police or other authorities may produce such rewards as approval and recognition for "doing the right thing." Moreover, by summoning help and not intervening directly bystanders can avoid the risk of immediate injury at the hands of the offender. However, the decision to inform the police of the crime is not without its costs. If the police are called, the bystander may have to make a number of costly court appearances. Interviews with victims and witnesses in Milwaukee, Wisconsin (Knudten, Meade, Knudten, & Doerner, 1977), indicated that the most important costs were the loss of time and wages and the fear of retaliation by the offender. In addition, witnesses mentioned such costs as those associated with transportation to the hearings and with finding and hiring a babysitter. These problems were compounded by the fact that often witnesses would incur these costs only to learn upon their arrival that the case had been postponed. One can understand why many of the 38 witnesses to the Genovese murder gave "I didn't want to get involved" as their reason for not reporting. Similar findings were reported by Gelfand et al. (1973), who noted that 41% of their subjects who failed to report a staged shoplifting gave as their reason the desire to avoid the costs of a countersuit and court appearances.

A number of communities have attempted to reduce such system-related costs by making it easier for bystanders to give the police anonymous tips (National Advisory Commission on Criminal Justice Standards and Goals, 1974). The "Silent Observer" program initiated in Battle Creek, Michigan, is one such program. Cash awards ranging from $50 to $1000 are offered to residents who provide information leading to the arrest and conviction of an offender. Bystander/informants are permitted to remain anonymous simply by identifying themselves as "Silent Observers" and by giving themselves a code number for future identification. During the first eight months of operation, 24 convictions were obtained as a result of information provided by "Silent Observers."

A similar program was instituted in Tampa, Florida (National Advisory Commission on Criminal Justice Standards and Goals, 1974). Known as Turn In a Pusher (T.I.P.), the program offers cash awards of $100 to $500 to informants whose information leads to the investigation, arrest,. and conviction of a narcotics dealer. To keep informants anonymous and thus safe from reprisal, they are assigned code names from an out-of-state telephone directory, and the awards are made in cash to that name through general delivery mail or by arranging a secret "drop." Interestingly, nearly half the informants who were eligible for a cash award never tried to claim it. Apparently, the ability to provide the authorities with important information without becoming involved is reward enough for many bystanders.

Social exchange with significant others

The decision to call the police, like the decision to intervene, can be influenced by the exchange relationship with significant others. Whereas research on intervention by bystanders has focused on the exchange relationship with the victim, research on the decision to notify the authorities has focused on exchanges with other bystanders. In two experiments by Latané and Darley (1970) involving staged thefts of money from a receptionist's desk and of a case of beer from a beverage store, bystanders who observed the theft alone tended to report more often than bystanders who observed the theft in the presence of a passive other. Left unstated is the precise manner in which the other's presence inhibited reporting. Was the other's passivity a cue that the event was not a crime, or did the mere presence of the other person help to diffuse the responsibility of calling for help, or both?

Schwartz and Gottlieb (1976) conducted a study designed to clarify the nature of the social-influence process, using male Israeli students. During the course of an experiment subjects overheard a scuffle in a different room. Most subjects were led to believe that in addition to the victim, there were four other subjects present who were located in separate rooms connected by an intercom system. By leading subjects to believe that the microphone in each person's room was controlled by an automatic switching device, the experimenters manipulated subjects' awareness of the other bystanders' reactions to the attack (aware/unaware) and the other bystanders' awareness of the subject's reaction (aware/unaware). Also included was an "alone" condition, in which the subject was led to believe that he was the only bystander present. Three social processes were examined: diffusion of responsibility, negative social influence, and evaluation apprehension. Results supported the independent operation of all three processes. The diffusion-of-responsibility process was supported by the finding that 92% of the subjects in the "alone" condition sought help for the victim, compared with 45% of those in the "mutually unaware" condition (who did not know how the others were reacting, nor could the others know how they were reacting). Support for the negative-social-influence explanation was shown in the finding that just 48% of subjects who were aware of the other bystanders' unresponsiveness sought help, compared with 68% of those who were unaware how others were responding.

Finally, the evaluation-apprehension process was tested by comparing the reactions of subjects who believed and did not believe that the others were aware of how they were responding. The investigators assumed that because subjects probably believed that others would expect them to help the victim, those who believed the others could monitor their reactions would feel under greater pressure to help. This prediction was confirmed. Help was sought by 74% of subjects who believed that others were aware of their reaction, compared with 39% of those who believed they were not under the scrutiny of the other bystanders. The study suggests that when a bystander observes a criminal event, the presence of others may influence the bystander's decision to call the police by means of a number of processes.

When others are present or nearby during the commission of a crime, they may do more than silently observe the event. They may verbally remind the person of the responsibility or absence of responsibility to notify the authorities and may advise a particular course of action. The importance of such verbal advice was dramatically illustrated in the reactions of two bystanders to the murder of Kitty Genovese. According to Seedman and Hellman (1975), one eyewitness picked up the phone to call the police but was dissuaded from doing so by his wife, who said "Don't. Thirty people must have called by now." The decision of another neighbor who finally called the police clearly reveals the bystander's dilemma and how advice from others helped resolve it. Seedman and Hellman report that

> the first attack had come almost right under his [Harold Kline's] window. Now he didn't know what to do. He paced . . . went to the door . . . put his ear to it . . . unbelievable! He mustered his courage, opened the door, shut it quickly, went back to pacing. Should he call the police? Should he do nothing? He called a friend who lived in Nassau County who advised him to call the police. But from his own phone? He called old Mrs. Lucchese, who lived three doors down. She called Mrs. Morris, two more doors down. She called Evelyn Lozzi, who lived across the hall from Kitty. . . . But now what *should* they all do? Rather than take the stairs and confront the horror in the vestibule, Harold Kline hoisted himself out his window and scooted across the steep Tudor roof to Mrs. Lucchese's. From there, at 3:55, he called the 102nd Precinct to report that a girl had been attacked in the hallway in back of 82-62 Austin Street. From the time of Kitty's first scream in front of the card shop, thirty-five minutes had elapsed [1975, p. 120].[4]

Two experimental studies by Bickman and Rosenbaum (1977), mentioned earlier in this chapter, further demonstrate that advice from others can influence a bystander's feeling of responsibility, which, in turn, can have a strong impact on the bystander's tendency to report the crime. In the first study, shoppers were exposed to a staged shoplifting of some items from a checkout display while waiting in the checkout

[4]Reprinted by permission of Raines & Raines, agents for Peter Hellman & Albert Seedman. Copyright © 1974 by Albert A. Seedman and Peter Hellman.

line. At the start of the theft, a confederate bystander standing directly in line behind the subject called the subject's attention to the theft by saying "Say, look at her, She's shoplifting. She put that into her purse." The bystander then either discouraged reporting by adding "But it's the store's problem. They have security people here" or encouraged reporting by stating "We saw it. We should report it. It's our responsibility." Results showed that 72% of those encouraged to report did so, compared with just 32% of those who were discouraged from reporting.

In their second study Bickman and Rosenbaum exposed subjects to a videotaped shoplifting incident, which they thought was a live telecast. A female confederate either encouraged reporting by saying "We should call the store and tell them. It's really our responsibility" or discouraged reporting by saying "But it's not our responsibility. The store must have security people to take care of it." This study produced an even larger difference in reporting between those who were encouraged (72%) and those who were discouraged from reporting (8%). Presumably, encouragement to report increased the costs of doing nothing (for example, increased subjects' sense of guilt) and increased the benefits for reporting (for example, led subjects to expect approval from store personnel for doing the "right thing"). In a reverse manner, discouraging reporting by stating "It's not our responsibility" may have decreased the costs of doing nothing (by reducing the feelings of guilt). Further, the statement "The store must have security people to take care of it" may have led subjects to expect little gratitude from the store authorities, as they were probably already aware of the theft. The two studies by Bickman and Rosenbaum highlight the fact that a few comments from a fellow bystander may affect a bystander's expected costs/benefits ratio and thereby influence whether the bystander will report a theft to authorities.

Taking No Action

We have seen that when the costs of direct intervention and notifying the authorities outweigh the expected rewards, bystanders may find it more profitable to refrain from taking any overt action. In so choosing, bystanders can avoid the costs of direct intervention (such as being harmed by the offender) and of notifying the authorities (such as loss of time and wages). However, failure to act may subject the bystander to guilt feelings and disapproval from others because social norms dictate that people should help those who are dependent on them (Berkowitz, 1972; Schwartz, 1977). Although bystanders may try to justify their inaction by citing the obvious costs of intervention or reporting (for example, "If I had intervened, there would have been two victims instead of one"), they often find it necessary to reduce the costs associated with feelings of guilt by minimizing the inequity suffered by the victim. As Lerner, Miller, and Holmes (1976) have shown, this often takes the form of making the victim deserving of his or her fate. The bystander can rationalize that the victim deserved to be harmed because the victim provoked the offender ("She shouldn't have worn such a short skirt") or because the victim has dislikable personality characteristics, such as foolishness and carelessness. In addition, bystanders can minimize the harm done to the victim ("It was only $15"), thus reducing the amount of inequity suffered by the victim and thereby further justifying their failure to act.

Examples of such cognitive distortions abound in the literature. An anecdotal description provided by Latané and Darley (1970) shows how some subjects rationalized their failure to prevent the theft of money from an envelope on the receptionist's desk:

> "It looked like he was only making change," said several subjects. "I thought he took the money by accident," said one charitable soul. A number of subjects seemed to feel some conflict between their responsibilities to the receptionist and to law and order on the one hand and to the "obviously" poor (but well dressed) college peer on the other. Some decided that not much money had been in the envelope after all [p. 73].

Athough relabeling the event may help bystanders escape some of the costs of failing to help the victim, it can prove quite costly. Because relabeling the incident involves some distortion of reality, bystanders may find their perceptions challenged by other bystanders and by the victim, leading to social disapproval and possibly rejection by the bystander's peers. Making the victim worthy of his or her fate may be particularly costly when the victim is a friend of the bystander. Being likely to see the victim again, the bystander will have constant reminders of his or her distorted perceptions. Moreover, the social rejection that is likely to follow inaction and cognitive distortion is likely to be more painful when it comes from a friend.

In the case of property crimes, bystanders can resolve the dilemma between doing nothing and taking some overt action by *informing the victim* of the crime. In choosing this compromise solution, bystanders might reason that it is the victim's decision to notify the police and that their role is simply to provide the victim with information relevant to that decision.

Summary of Decision Making by Bystanders

In order for bystanders to decide to report a crime to the authorities, they must first detect the event and label it as a crime. We have seen that these decisions are subject to social influence. Others may call bystanders' attention to the event, help them define it as a crime, and influence their choice of response. The data suggest that others may influence bystanders' decision to act by focusing bystanders' attention on their responsibility to help the victim. The feeling of responsibility can be enhanced by the absence of others (Latané & Darley, 1970; Schwartz & Gottlieb, 1976), by securing a commitment from the bystander to watch the victim's property (Moriarty, 1975; Shaffer et al., 1975), and by verbally reminding bystanders of their responsibility (Bickman & Rosenbaum, 1977). As we will see in the following section, decision making by victims is also subject to social influence.

DECISION MAKING BY VICTIMS

Being the victim of a crime can be a very stressful event. Whether it is a property crime, such as burglary or theft, or a crime of violence, such as rape or assault, the victim is likely to feel violated and vulnerable. It is easy to imagine the victim of a violent crime having such feelings; it is somewhat more difficult to realize that burglary and theft victims have similar, though perhaps somewhat less intense, reactions to their victimization (Waller & Okihiro, 1978). Consider the reactions of two burglary victims:

> "It's a very, very funny feeling, the feeling you've been raped. They went through *everything*, including my dirty laundry. It's just like you have no privacy anymore. Everything had been looked through, cased out. I had bills I was going to pay sitting on the table; they went through that" [Barkas, 1978, p. 159].[5]

> "I felt violated, I felt people had been rummaging through things that were personal and very private. I consider my apartment personal and private. It's how I put things, how I do things, how I live; and somebody just came in and violated it. So I was really shaken up. I remember being very angry, upset, crying" [Barkas, 1978, p. 161].

These two examples illustrate that victims often have to make their decision about how to deal with the crime under great emotional stress. The victim's arousal is greater than the bystander's because it is the victim who is the target of the offender's actions (Austin & Hatfield, 1980). Consequently, victims may not be as rational as bystanders when deciding what to do about the incident. Nevertheless, we will assume that victims, like bystanders, try to make a rational choice on the basis of expected costs and benefits. It is further assumed that in order to make this decision, victims must first detect the incident and then label it as a crime.

Before we review the decision process of victims using the attribution/exchange model depicted in Figure 2-1, it is necessary to say a few words about how victims detect their victimization. With a few notable exceptions, our understanding of how victims decide to call the police is based on victimization surveys. Typically, participants in such surveys are asked whether they or any family members have been victims of a crime in the last six or twelve months. For each victimization experi-

---

[5]From J. L. Barkas, *Victims: Violence and Its Aftermath*. Copyright ©1978 by J. L. Barkas (New York: Charles Scribner's Sons, 1978). This and all other quotations from this source are reprinted with the permission of Charles Scribner's Sons.

ence, respondents are asked whether the police were notified and, if not, which reason(s) accounts for their failure to contact the police. These surveys of victims thus obtain information only from those who have both detected an incident and labeled it as a crime. Consequently, little is known about the conditions under which victims fail to detect an event or to label it as a criminal incident. For the most part, therefore, our discussion of detection and labeling by victims is speculative.

It can be reasonably assumed that detection poses no problem for victims of crimes of violence, such as assault, robbery, or rape. Crimes such as these are not likely to go unnoticed by their victims. However, this is not true of victims of property crimes, such as burglary and theft. Because property crimes are usually crimes of stealth, victims are rarely eyewitnesses to their victimization, and such crimes may therefore go undetected long after their occurrence. A variety of circumstances can lead to discovery of crimes by victims. Just as with bystanders, detection by victims depends on the quality of the victim's sensory apparatus and set. Obviously, those whose vision and hearing are not impaired and who enter a situation sensitized to the possible occurrence of a crime are more likely to detect a criminal event. In addition, some inconsistent or novel feature of the stimulus situation may call their attention to the crime. For example, on returning home, a burglary victim may find the front door ajar and his personal effects strewn about the house. When the criminal intends to victimize the person repeatedly, it may be in the criminal's interest to conceal the initial crime as long as possible. Successful white-collar criminals, such as embezzlers, are known to be adept at manipulating the stimulus conditions so as to avoid discovery of their actions. It is perhaps for this reason that officials estimate that white-collar crimes are among the least detected of all categories of crime (Edelhartz, 1970).

Many property crimes are not detected until the victim has a need to use the stolen property. The theft of a piece of garden equipment in the winter may not be discovered until the owner wants to use it the next spring. On other occasions, however, victims may be alerted to the occurrence of a crime by a friend, neighbor, or passer-by who either observed the crime taking place or discovered it afterward.

ATTRIBUTIONAL CONSIDERATIONS: LABELING THE EVENT AS A CRIME

Whether an incident is labeled as a crime depends on the victim's definition of a crime and how closely the incident fits that definition. The factors that affect the labeling process are assumed to be the same as those shown to influence labeling by bystanders. They include characteristics of the observer (in this case the victim), the nature of the stimulus situation, and social-influence factors. This is not to say that victims and bystanders will always label an incident the same way. Their perspectives are fundamentally different. Whereas bystanders are mere observers of the offender's actions, victims are also the targets of those actions. This difference in perspective may cause bystanders and victims to allocate responsibility for the incident in different ways. In order to maintain their belief in a just world (Lerner et al., 1976) and maintain the belief that the same fate will not befall them, bystanders may tend to view the victim as contributing to his or her fate. Consequently, they may be less inclined to attribute criminal intentions to the offender. For example, a fist fight between two men in which one (the victim) clearly comes off second-best may not be interpreted as a criminal assault by bystanders. However, as Jones and Nisbett (1972) have shown, actors (in this case the victim) tend to ascribe causality to the environment. The victim may view causality as residing primarily in the other person (an external cause) and therefore be more inclined to label the incident as a criminal assault. However, the attributions of bystanders and victims might not always differ. Recent evidence shows that certain classes of victims, such as victims of rape, tend to blame themselves for the incident (Janoff-Bulman, 1979). Presumably, such attributions help rape victims cope with the event by giving them a sense of control over their fate (Wortman, 1976).

As we have noted, the circumstances under which victims of property crimes discover that they have been victimized are decidedly different from the circumstances confronting victims of violent crimes. Whereas victims of assault and rape actually witness their victimization and can therefore more easily attribute a criminal intention to the perpetrator, victims of property crimes often cannot so easily label their victimization. Usually, after detecting the event, victims of property crimes go through a sequence of steps that results in labeling the incident as a crime or a noncrime. This sequence is shown in Figure 2-2. Consider, for example, a situation in which a student returns to her dormitory room and discovers that a check sent from home is missing. Immediately, she begins to search the room, looking in clothes pockets, under the bed, and behind the desk. When her roommate returns, the student questions her. She is, in effect, testing various causal hypotheses. After conducting this search, the student may conclude that she misplaced the check or that it blew out an open window. If so, she will have satisfactorily explained the event and will probably abandon the search. If, however, she concludes that another person is responsible for the occurrence, she will inquire further into the intention underlying the act. If she decides that the person acted unintentionally (for example, the cleaning person threw it out by mistake) or that the person took it intentionally but without intending to commit a theft (for example, her roommate was playing a practical joke), the student is unlikely to consider herself the victim of a crime. If, however, she decides that the check was taken

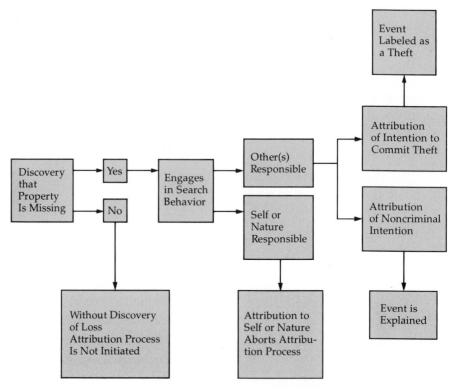

Figure 2-2. Stages in a victim's labeling an event as a theft

intentionally and that the intent was not to return it, she is likely to attribute criminal intention to the person who took it and, therefore, to label the incident as a crime.

SOCIAL-EXCHANGE CONSIDERATIONS: TAKING ACTION

Having labeled an incident as a crime, victims must then decide on what action, if any, to take. We will assume that in making this decision victims are strongly motivated to reduce the distress that accompanies being treated unfairly and to prevent its recurrence. Victims are likely to show greater concern with equity considerations than bystanders because they are the target of the offender's actions rather than mere witnesses to the crime.

There are two broad action strategies that victims can use to reduce their feelings of being unfairly treated. First, they can try to restore their original outcomes by obtaining *compensation* from the offender or from others. Second, victims can *retaliate* against the offender and thereby reduce the offender's outcomes to a level comparable to their own. As with the decision making of bystanders, it is assumed that victims will try to deal with the situation in a way that maximizes their rewards.

This does not mean that victims typically choose the wisest course of action. Because of their heightened state of arousal or because of insufficient knowledge or poor advice from others, victims may act in ways that do not optimize their outcomes.

Victims can obtain compensation or retaliate against the suspected offender and thereby reduce their feelings of being treated unfairly by doing one or more of the following: (1) seeking a private solution, (2) taking no overt action but instead dealing with the event by cognitively restructuring it, and (3) notifying the authorities. These actions may also provide victims with reassurance that they will not be victimized again. The remainder of this chapter will focus on the benefits and costs of calling the police. However, to understand better the conditions under which this is the preferred option, we must briefly review the two competing options—seeking a private solution and engaging in cognitive restructuring.

Seeking a Private Solution

To obtain compensation for loss of property due to theft or vandalism, victims can avail themselves of several private options. If the offender's identity is known, victims can confront him or her and, through the use of threats or actual force, retrieve the stolen property or its financial equivalent. For example, victims may threaten the offender with physical harm or threaten to reveal the theft to others, such as the police or the offender's family. Victims can increase the credibility of their threat to harm the offender by procuring a weapon or by enlisting the aid of others. Alternatively, if the offender's identity is not known, victims may motivate the offender to return the stolen property by advertising the offer of a financial reward for return of the property with "no questions asked." Further, they can enlist the aid of friends or hire a private detective to help identify the offender and retrieve the stolen property. Finally, rather than trying to obtain compensation directly from the offender, victims may try to obtain compensation *indirectly* by stealing from others, as sometimes occurs in communities where stealing is considered normative.

Regardless of whether the crime involves property loss, physical harm, or both, victims may try to reduce their feeling of being unfairly treated by personally punishing the offender, as was done by the hero in the movie *Death Wish*. In so doing, victims may strive for exact equivalence as exemplified by the ancient code of Hammurabi: "An eye for an eye, a tooth for a tooth." Often, however, the victim's retaliation exceeds the original offense and, as Wolfgang (1958) has shown, sometimes takes the form of homicide. An example of such excessive vengeance is shown in the following: "During a lovers' quarrel, the male (victim) hit his mistress and threw a can of kerosene at her. She retaliated by throwing the liquid on him, and then tossed a lighted match in his direction. He died from the burns" (Wolfgang, 1958, p. 253).

Ancient lawmakers recognized the dangers of unrestrained personal vengeance. Legal scholars are of the view that the injunction "An eye for an eye, a tooth for a tooth" was really an attempt to place limits on personal vengeance (Stone, 1965). What the code really meant was *no more than* an eye for an eye, *no more than* a tooth for a tooth. Modern-day courts have taken an increasingly dim view of persons who take private vengeance (often called "vigilantes") and have imposed harsh sentences on those who have done so. Such a sentence, for example, was meted out to Inez Garcia, who, after being raped, pursued her attackers and fatally shot one of them (Blitman & Green, 1975).

In addition to restoring equity, victims' private solutions are often aimed at preventing future victimizations. For example, retaliation may deter the offender from committing additional crimes against the victim and others. Another private solution for preventing future inequities may be to offer a financial reward to the offender in return for the promise not to commit any further crimes against the victim ("paying protection money"). Other private measures include increasing one's protective skills (for example, learning karate), buying a weapon or a watchdog, or installing a burglar alarm system. In addition, victims may hire a private guard or enlist the aid of friends or neighbors, which is what victims do when they join a neighborhood watch group. Finally, victims can attempt to avoid future victimization by changing their behavior pattern. The change can range from taking a different route home from work to changing one's residence or place of work. What the victim chiefly desires in taking these actions is not to reduce the present inequity but rather to minimize the likelihood of being victimized in the future.

Cognitive Restructuring

When victims conclude that trying to reduce the injustice through private means is not likely to be successful and may, in fact, prove too costly, they may decide to take no overt action, preferring instead to deal with the situation by restructuring their beliefs about the event. A measure of psychological compensation can be achieved by concluding that "come to think of it, little harm was done" and that, therefore, the victimization was not very serious. Interviews with crime victims (Fischer, 1977) show that victims do this by comparing their outcomes with worse outcomes that could have occurred. By so doing they can minimize the significance of their loss. Similarly, victims can sometimes convince themselves that the victimization provided them with compensatory benefits in that it taught them a valuable lesson, as the following example illustrates:

> "I'm probably farther ahead now than if it [the attempted rape] had never happened to me. When it happened, I was suddenly set back ten years emotionally and I acted like a child. Right afterwards, I started drinking heavily

and almost became an alcoholic. . . . Finally I decided I had to confront my-self. I had been stripped of all my defenses and realized how hard and mechanical I had become [before the attempted rape]. I think I'm in a better place now than I would have been" [Barkas, 1978, p. 127].

Victims can also obtain a measure of retaliation by subscribing to the adage "Crime doesn't pay," convincing themselves that eventually the offender will get his or her due.

Another mechanism victims often use to reduce their distress is to blame themselves for their victimization. Although self-blame may be painful, it may be less painful than believing that there is nothing they can do to prevent a recurrence of the incident (Wortman, 1976). By attributing their victimization to some controllable behavior of theirs (for example, "I shouldn't have been out alone at that hour"), victims can reassure themselves that the mistake will not be repeated and that it is therefore unlikely that they will be victimized again. These dynamics can readily be seen in the reactions of rape victims. Results of a questionnaire sent to 38 rape crisis centers by Janoff-Bulman (1979) indicate that three of four rape victims treated at these centers blamed themselves, in part, for their victimization. Of those who blamed themselves, 69% cited some modifiable behavior of theirs: "I shouldn't have let someone I didn't know into the house . . . I should not have hitch-hiked, I should not have gone to his apartment, I shouldn't have left my window open" (p. 1806). The function served by self-blame among victims of rape is succinctly summarized by Medea and Thompson (1974):

> If the woman can believe that somehow she got herself into the situation, if she can feel that in some way she caused it, if she can make herself responsible for it, then she's established a sort of control over the rape. It wasn't someone arbitrarily smashing into her life and wreaking havoc. The unpredictability of the latter situation can be too much for some women to face: If it happened entirely without provocation, then it could happen again. This is too horrifying to believe, so the victim creates an illusion of safety by declaring herself responsible for the incident [pp. 105–106].

Another "reward" that victims obtain by blaming themselves is that the incident does not appear as inequitable as it appeared originally. By making themselves "worthy of their fate," victims can restore their belief in a just world (Lerner et al., 1976).

Although psychological mechanisms such as these help victims reduce their distress without risking the costs of taking action, such mechanisms may be difficult to use when victims find themselves undeniably battered, bruised, and deprived of valuable possessions through no fault of their own. When this occurs victims are likely to consider notifying the police. The rest of this chapter will explore the conditions under which victims are likely to avail themselves of this option.

Notifying the Authorities

Notifying the police can reduce victims' distress in several ways. If the police are able to apprehend the offender, they may be able to recover the stolen property. Or, if the property is not found, the courts may force the offender to make restitution to the victim. Moreover, the conviction and sentencing of the offender to jail or prison could help satisfy the victim's desire for retaliation and, further, might deter the offender and others from committing similar acts in the future. Even if the offender is not caught, calling the police may lead to increased benefits for victims. It may cause the police to increase their patrols in the area and thereby provide victims with some assurance that the crime is less likely to recur. In addition, if victims want to receive compensation from their insurance company, they must first file a report with the police. Similarly, in order to be eligible for financial compensation from a state victim-compensation program, victims must report the crime to the police within 48 to 72 hours after the crime. In 1978, compensation programs for victims of violent crime existed in 24 states (Cain & Kravitz, 1978). Usually, such programs give victims cash awards to compensate them for medical expenses and loss of earning power. Several states even provide compensation for mental or nervous shock (Cain & Kravitz, 1978).

In recent years much knowledge has been gained about factors that influence victims' decisions to call the police. Most of this information has been obtained from victimization surveys involving interviews with crime victims. The surveys grew out of the survey of victims conducted by the National Opinion Research Center (Ennis, 1967). Using information gained from this initial survey, the Law Enforcement Assistance Administration and the Bureau of the Census have been conducting national surveys of victims since 1973. The surveys are designed to collect information on the incidence of criminal victimizations as well as a host of related variables, such as the time and place of occurrence, whether the incident was reported to the police, and the reasons offered by victims for not reporting. The surveys involve interviews with a random sample of the U.S. population about the extent of their victimization experiences during the preceding six- or twelve-month period. Although these surveys have not been immune from criticism (Levine, 1976; Skogan, 1976), it is generally assumed that they provide a more complete accounting of criminal victimizations than the FBI's *Uniform Crime Reports,* which reflect only the rate of *reported* crime.

The surveys, which have yielded remarkably consistent findings across time and geographical regions, have proved particularly useful in the study of such crimes as rape, robbery, assault, burglary, and theft. Whereas the surveys have revealed no racial differences in reporting, they have found that females tend to report more than males and that reporting tends to be greater among older victims (Hindelang, 1976). It appears, however, that the most important factors concern not the victim's race, sex, and age but rather the social-exchange relationship between the victim and (1) the criminal justice system, (2) the suspected offender, and (3) significant others, such as bystanders and covictims.

Social exchange with the criminal justice system

Whether victims will choose to notify the police depends on the net benefits expected from involvement with the criminal justice system. One fact remains clear: The more serious victims consider their victimization to be, the greater will be their feelings of injustice and distress and, consequently, the more they would have to gain from calling the police. Regardless of what benefits they hope to gain by calling the police—return of the stolen property, compensation for injuries, seeing the offender punished, or preventing future victimizations—victims of serious crimes have more to gain from calling the police than victims of less serious crimes. This fact has been extensively documented by the LEAA/Bureau of the Census surveys of victims (Law Enforcement Assistance Administration, 1976a, 1977a). These surveys have consistently shown that the most important determinant of victims' decision to call the police is the perceived seriousness of the crime. The more serious the crime, the greater the likelihood of its being brought to the attention of the police. This is true regardless of the criterion used for measuring seriousness. Thus, a crime is more likely to be reported if it is completed rather than attempted, if it involves a weapon, if it results in injury to the victim, and if the property loss is large (grand larceny) rather than small (petty larceny). Consistent with these findings are the reasons offered by victims for *not* calling the police. One of the most frequently cited reasons for not reporting is "Did not think it important enough." As expected, this reason was mentioned more frequently by victims of less serious crimes. For example, it was mentioned by 47% of victims of household larceny and 32% of victims of simple assault, compared with just 4% of rape victims. Similarly, 32% of victims of *attempted* auto theft cited this reason, compared with just 4% of victims of *completed* auto theft (Flanagan, Hindelang, & Gottfredson, 1980).

Even among victims who consider their victimization a very serious event, many may hesitate to report the incident because they believe that they have little to gain and much to lose by becoming involved with the criminal justice system. The LEAA/Bureau of the Census surveys of victims clearly show that many victims believe that the police either are unable to help them or lack the motivation to do so (Law Enforcement Assistance Administration, 1976a, 1977a). The belief that "nothing could be done" was the major reason mentioned by victims who failed to report property crimes, such as thefts, burglaries, and attempted auto thefts. This belief probably derives from victims' correct assumption that the police can focus only on the most serious crimes or on crimes for which they have good leads. Because property crimes are rarely witnessed by victims or bystanders, the police usually have little information on which to base an investigation. For example, a victim who has just discovered that his pocket was picked is likely to reason that the police have more important things to do than try to find the person who stole his wallet. In light of the limited resources available to the police and the high incidence of crime, such beliefs are probably realistic.

Not only do many victims hesitate to call the police because they believe that nothing could be done, many are reluctant because of real or imagined costs of involvement with the criminal justice system. There are numerous anecdotal accounts of rape victims' being treated in an insensitive manner by police officers, prosecutors, and defense attorneys (Barkas, 1978; Brownmiller, 1975). Such callous treatment represents just one type of cost that victims may expect. Recent research (Knudten, Meade, Knudten, & Doerner, 1976, 1977) documents additional costs of involvement with the criminal justice system. Interviews with victims of serious crimes in Milwaukee revealed that involvement with the criminal justice system caused them to suffer considerable losses of time and money. Many victims said that they lost time from work or school (63%), that they spent a "long time waiting" (56%), and that they had to make unnecessary trips to the police station or courthouse (33%). In addition, 87% said they incurred financial costs of transportation and parking, and 40% said they suffered a loss of income as a result of their involvement. Knudten et al. (1977) noted that "victims are victimized both as a result of the crime event and as a result of their entrance into the criminal justice system" (p. 4). The authors concluded that the major reason only 37% of the victims whom they interviewed called the police was that many had made a conscious decison to "cut their losses." Rather than lose time and wages making repeated trips to the police station and courthouse, they chose not to become involved in the system of justice.

The time costs that victims incur in their dealings with the criminal justice system often result from efforts by agents of the system to make efficient use of their *own* time. Overworked agents of the judicial part of the system try to economize on time by arranging their schedule so that they do not have to wait around idly for defendants, victims, and witnesses to appear. Like doctors and dentists, they often overschedule in order to maintain a ready supply of clients and cases. Although such practices can benefit the system by saving time, they may ultimately prove more costly to the system because the costs in time that victims incur may decrease their willingness to cooperate with the system.

The criminal justice system is not the only source of rewards and costs for victims. In deciding whether to notify the police, victims often consider the reactions of the suspected offender.

Social exchange with the suspected offender

Victims sometimes fail to notify the police because they fear that the offender will retaliate and make them a victim a second time. Consider, for example, an incident reported in *Time* magazine ("Scaring Off Witnesses," 1978, p. 41):

> Last December [1977] a man wearing a ski mask and carrying a shotgun broke into Richard Morgan's San Francisco Bay-area home. Morgan, a burly Teamster, managed to chase him away and get his license number. But after the suspect was arrested and released on bail, police say, he threatened Morgan over the phone, assaulted him in the courthouse hallway and stole one of his dogs. Finally, the suspect tried to blow Morgan up. Returning to Morgan's house late one night in mid-August bearing 75 sticks of dynamite, the suspect was scared off by barking dogs and fled, leaving the bomb to explode in the driveway. The blast rocked the neighborhood, shattering windows in nearby houses, but Morgan escaped unharmed. Now in hiding, Morgan says he will still testify.

Athough such incidents are uncommon, publicity given them reminds victims of the offender's ability to retaliate and may cause some to think twice about notifying the police. The LEAA/Bureau of the Census victimization surveys generally show that fear of reprisal is one of the major reasons that many rapes are not reported to the police (Flanagan et al., 1980). Further analyses of reasons offered by rape victims for not reporting in 13 cities (Chicago, Detroit, Los Angeles, New York, Philadelphia, Atlanta, Baltimore, Cleveland, Dallas, Denver, Newark, Portland, and St. Louis) reveal dramatic racial differences in reasons offered. Three of every four racial-minority victims of completed rape mentioned fear of reprisal as one of their reasons for not reporting (Hindelang & Davis, 1977). In comparison, only 12% of white victims of completed rape mentioned this reason. White victims tended to state instead their belief that it was a private matter (75%).

It is not only physical retaliation that some victims fear. Victims who are in an inferior economic power position with regard to the offender are particularly vulnerable to economic retaliation. The inferior power position may stem from the victim's continued dependence on the offender for needed financial resources. Thus, although many victims of wife abuse fail to report their victimization because they fear further physical abuse, many refuse to report because of their dependency on their husbands for financial support (Chapman & Gates, 1977).

On some occasions victims do not report an incident because of the belief that the criminal justice system would be "too efficient" in processing the suspected offender. Victims of petty larceny may hesitate to report a juvenile offender, particularly when they are acquainted with the offender, because they do not want to "get the kid in trouble with the police." The concern with the offender's welfare may stem from a desire to avoid giving the juvenile a criminal record or from concern about what might happen to the juvenile if he or she were sent to jail. For these reasons, victims of petty larceny and household burglary who can identify a juvenile suspect may prefer to seek a private solution, such as talking directly with the juvenile or with his or her parents or guardians.

Social exchange with significant others

Often victims are confused about how to deal with their victimization. The stress of the victimization sometimes makes it difficult for them to think clearly about the costs and benefits of the various alternatives. When confused, they frequently turn to others for advice. In their recent work *The Crime Victim's Book*, Bard and Sangrey (1979) observed that "a crime victim's entire structure of defenses becomes weakened under the stress of violation, leaving him or her unusually accessible to the influence of others. This characteristic response makes the behavior of other people unusually powerful in the period right after the crime" (p. 38). This statement is supported by recent field and laboratory research. Interviews with crime victims in Kansas City, Missouri (Van Kirk, 1978), revealed that victims' delay in reporting is the major reason for the delay in the police's arrival at the scene of a crime. Victims' delay in reporting stemmed from their seeking additional information or assurances from others that the incident required intervention by the police. This finding suggests that victims are similar to bystanders in that both appear to be highly dependent on others for advice and information.

A series of experiments conducted by Greenberg and his colleagues supports the role of social-exchange factors in decision making by victims and further clarifies the nature of this influence. The setting for the staged victimizations (a theft of $11) was a fictitious research organization, "Industrial Research Associates of Pittsburgh." A suite of offices was rented in a retail section of a middle-class neighborhood. The offices were furnished with all the accessories one would expect to find in a research organization, such as desks and file cabinets, as well as such human props as a "secretary," a "supervisor," and other "research participants." Participants were paid volunteers recruited through newspaper advertisements. On their arrival, they were paid the money promised them in the ad and told that they would be participating in a study of "clerical efficiency" with two other "participants" (in reality, confederates of the experimenter). After earning $12 for their performance on the first clerical task, they learned that they had performed poorly on a second task and therefore had to forfeit $11 of the $12 earned. Following the departure of one of the confederates (the "thief"), participants were presented with evidence that their poor performance on the second task had resulted from a theft of their work by the now-absent thief. The remaining confederate (the "bystander") then tried to influence participants' decision about what to do. Participants' willingness to call the police was measured by having the secretary prod them to report and then noting which, if any, of the secretary's prods they yielded to. For those who agreed to report the theft, no actual report was made, because the secretary's phone was not connected.

Results of five studies that used this general procedure will be summarized. The first study (Greenberg, Wilson, Ruback, & Mills, 1979) found that the bystander's advice to do nothing about the theft caused a significant decrease in reporting, in comparison with a control group that was given no advice. However, the advice to "do something about it" (that is, the theft) did not produce a significant increase in reporting. Interestingly, the study showed that the emotional state of victims strongly influenced their reporting. The greater their anger, the more willing they were to call the police. The second study (Greenberg, Ruback, & Wilson, 1981) showed that explicit advice by the bystander to "call the police" dramatically increased victims' willingness to report the theft. The third study (Greenberg et al., 1981) attempted to discover why victims went along with the bystander's advice to notify the police. Every participant was advised by the bystander to call the police. In half the instances, the bystander indicated her willingness to support participants in their dealing with the police by stating "I'll back you up. And, if anything happens later on, you can call me at work." She then wrote her phone number on a slip of paper and handed it to the participant. The remaining participants were led to believe that they could not count on the bystander's future support: "But don't use my name, I don't want to get involved." In half the instances, the bystander then either remained present during the secretary's prodding or left after the secretary said she could leave. Results showed that victims were most likely to follow the bystander's advice and call the police when the bystander offered to support them and remained at their side.

The persuasiveness of two types of supporting arguments used by bystanders was the focus of the fourth study (Westcott, Greenberg, & Ruback, 1980). In half the cases, the bystander advised victims to report because of "the principle of the thing." The bystander argued that what the thief did was wrong and that he "shouldn't be allowed to get away with it." In the remaining half of the cases, the bystander advised victims to report because of the effectiveness of the police: "The police will probably catch him. The secretary has that guy's address and phone number." Male victims were more easily persuaded by the "principle" argument, females by the "police effectiveness" argument.

Taken together, these four studies show that victims of a small theft attach great value to the advice and support of bystanders when deciding whether to notify the police. But bystanders are not the only people capable of influencing victims' decisions. Crimes sometimes involve the presence of covictims. The fact that covictims share the victim's fate might make their advice and support worth more than advice and support from bystanders. The fifth study (Westcott et al., 1980) compared the influence of bystanders and covictims and found that when a covictim was present, victims tended to follow the example of the covictim and ignore the bystander's advice.

These five studies suggest that just after their victimization, victims of a small theft are often uncertain about what to do. As a result of their uncertainty and confusion, the advice and actions of those present are highly valued in that they help resolve the victim's quandary. The data suggest that covictims' actions are of particular value to victims and that bystanders' advice is likely to have little impact in the face of such influence. However, when bystanders are the only others present, their advice to notify the police is most rewarding to victims when they (1) provide the victim with specific advice (for example, "Call the police") rather than diffuse advice (for example, "Do something"); (2) offer the victim assurances of continued support; and (3) after offering such assurances, remain at the victim's side until the report is made.

SUMMARY

In this chapter we have examined the factors that determine whether bystanders and victims will report a criminal victimization to the police. We have seen that in order for an incident to be reported, it must first be detected and then be labeled as a crime. The labeling process involves making attributions about the causes of the incident. The major factors contributing to such attributions are the characteristics of the observer (that is, bystander or victim), the stimulus conditions, and social-influence factors. After the event is detected and labeled as a crime, the observer must decide what action, if any, to take. For the bystander, the choice is among direct intervention, notifying the authorities, and taking no overt action. For the victim, the choice is among dealing with the incident privately, cognitively restructuring the situation, and notifying the authorities. The option chosen by both bystanders and victims depends on social-exchange considerations involving the criminal justice system, the suspected offender, and significant others.

Once the event has come to the attention of the authorities, the focus of attention shifts from the citizen to the police. In the next chapter, the attribution/exchange perspective will be used to examine how the police decide to deal with the incident.

CHAPTER THREE

The Police

The police are the largest and, for most citizens, the most visible segment of the criminal justice system. They are the agents of the system entrusted with preventing and detecting crime as well as identifying and apprehending those suspected of committing crimes. Therefore, when citizens seek official intervention to deal with a criminal matter, it is natural that they turn to the police.

Yet the popular image of police as acting mainly as crime fighters is a misconception. Although fictional detectives such as "Kojak" and "Starsky and Hutch" spend most of their time pursuing and arresting suspected criminals, in reality typical police officers, as represented by uniformed patrol officers, lead a far less exciting existence. Occasionally, a suspicious character may be detected in the act of "casing" a home, but most of the time police officers perform "service" and "order maintenance" functions in the community. For example, a study of all radio calls to police cars made by the Syracuse, New York, police department during a one-week period showed that 37% of the calls fell in the service category (Wilson, 1978). These included providing emergency medical aid, escorting ambulances, taking drunk persons home, and rescuing trapped or stranded animals. Order maintenance, the second-largest category of calls (30%), involved handling violent situations: police are often called to quell gang disturbances, calm family disputes, and break up assaults and fights. Only 10% of the calls could be classified as "crime fighting." Such incidents involved stopping a burglary in progress, investigating a suspicious car or an open window, or catching a prowler. Thus, catching criminals is but one of many jobs that the police are expected to perform. It is against this background of multiple and often contradictory roles that we will examine how the police deal with suspicious criminal events that come to their attention.

In this chapter we will use the attribution/exchange framework to examine how the police decide that a crime has occurred, how they identify a suspect, and how they decide to deal with the suspect: by making an arrest, by handling the matter informally, or by ignoring it. This last decision—how to deal with the suspect—will be the major focus of this chapter. Before we examine factors that influence these decisions, we will briefly review the historical and legal context in which these decisions are made. Because most police functions are performed by local or municipal police officers, they will be the major focus of this review.

A BRIEF HISTORY OF THE POLICE

Historians generally acknowledge that the form of policing used in the United States had its origins in medieval England. Before 1829, the English relied on a form of "self-policing." Police functions at the local level were performed by unpaid, elected constables who depended heavily on the support of the citizenry. In what was called the "hue and cry," all members of a community were expected to join in the pursuit of a felon. If a watchman or a constable had difficulty apprehending a suspect, he was to raise a "hue and cry," which obligated all citizens within earshot to stop what they were doing and assist him (Critchley, 1967).

This form of self-policing by the community lasted until the early part of the 19th century, when it became clear that something more was needed to deal with the problem of crime in the increasingly crowded cities that grew out of the industrial revolution. In 1829 this need for improved protection of citizens resulted in the formation in London of the first full-time, salaried police force. The force had as its main purpose the *prevention* of crime, to be accomplished by constantly patrolling the streets, both day and night. The headquarters of this police force looked out on a courtyard that had been the site of a residence used by the kings of Scotland and was therefore called "Scotland Yard." The officers were called "Bobbies" after the founder of the force, Sir Robert Peel.

As in England, early law enforcement in the American colonies relied on self-policing as exemplified by the constable/night-watchman system. Citizens were obligated to take turns as watchmen, crying out the time of night and the state of the weather (Fosdick, 1972). The night watch was instituted in Boston in 1636, in New York in 1658, and in Philadelphia in 1700. It was not until 1833 that the first paid, daytime police force was instituted, in Philadelphia. Boston followed suit in 1838. However, the existence of day and night shifts, each with its own separate administration, proved inefficient, and in 1844 New York City abolished this system and created the first unified, paid police force. By 1870, most cities had followed New York's example (President's Commission on Law Enforcement and Administration of Justice, 1967b).

Very often local police officials found themselves unable to cope with criminals whose activities extended beyond municipal boundaries, and state police units were created to deal with this problem. One of the first such units was the Texas Rangers, organized in 1835 to combat cattle rustlers and other outlaws. Other states, however, were slow in developing such agencies, and it was not until after World War I that similar units were formed in most states. By 1975 all states except Hawaii had such units. In about half the states, however, the duties of the state police are limited to enforcement of traffic regulations.

At the federal level various agencies were created to oversee the enforcement of federal regulations. For example, the Revenue Cutter Service was established in 1789 to prevent smuggling, and in 1836 Congress authorized the postmaster general to hire agents to investigate crimes involving the mail. Within the Department of the Treasury, the Secret Service was created during the Civil War to investigate counterfeiting and to guard the president. Perhaps the best-known federal enforcement agency is the Federal Bureau of Investigation, created in 1924 as a branch of the Department of Justice, with J. Edgar Hoover serving as its first head. The responsibilities of the FBI include investigation of all violations of federal laws except those explicitly delegated to other federal agencies. Among the offenses that the FBI is responsible for investigating are treason, espionage, robbery or theft from agencies whose funds are federally insured (for example, banks), and robbery or theft across state lines.

In the United States today there are 450,000 full-time municipal and county police officers distributed among 12,000 agencies varying in size from one person (for example, Maple Park, Illinois) to 28,000 in New York City (Webster, 1980). About 97% of these officers are male. Most departments are headed by a police chief or superintendent appointed by the mayor or head of the city government. The structure of local police departments varies with their size. Larger departments have a complex hierarchy of ranks, which include deputy chiefs, captains, lieutenants, sergeants, and patrol officers. Within larger departments there is also a high degree of specialization of function. Typical of such large city departments is the Pittsburgh, Pennsylvania, police department. Officers are grouped into several branches: an operations branch, which includes uniformed patrol officers located in nine precincts, a service branch, which is responsible for community relations, an administration branch, and a detective branch. The detective branch is further subdivided according to specialties. For example, separate divisions deal with homicide, robbery, sexual assault, burglary and theft, auto theft, organized crime, and narcotics. The operations branch is the largest, as it contains the uniformed beat patrol officers, who perform the everyday functions of order maintenance, service, and crime control.

In the eyes of many citizens, detectives occupy the glamour position in the department, as they fit the public's stereotype of the police officer as crime fighter. Unlike patrol officers, detectives work almost exclusively on solving crimes and catching criminals. Their job, in fact, begins where the patrol officer's leaves off. Thus, it is they who further investigate the "incident" or "offense" report turned in by the beat officer. Detectives are usually envied by patrol officers (Skolnick, 1975), not only because their work is often more interesting and exciting and the pay higher, but also because of their greater freedom to move about the city. Yet despite this relative freedom, detectives, no less than rank-and-file police officers, are subject to numerous legal restrictions.

Legal Restrictions on Police Practices

Law enforcement officers are instructed to practice their craft within legally prescribed boundaries. The most important source of such boundaries is the United States Constitution, the first ten amendments of which are known as the Bill of Rights. Three of these amendments are directly relevant to the police, as they provide the foundation for laws concerning search and seizure, arrest, questioning of suspects, and the right to counsel. The Fourth Amendment prohibits unreasonable search and seizure of persons or property. The Fifth Amendment lists safeguards for persons accused of a crime, providing, among other things, that no person "shall be compelled in any criminal case to be a witness against himself, nor be deprived of life, liberty, or property, without due process of law." The Sixth Amendment guarantees the accused "the right to a speedy and public trial" and "the Assistance of Counsel for his defense." The Bill of Rights was intended to apply only to the federal government, not to the individual states. It was not until 1868, when the Fourteenth Amendment was ratified, that the federal due-process provision contained in the Fifth Amendment became applicable to the states. This amendment explicitly stated that no state shall "deprive any person of life, liberty, or property, without due process of law."

The Supreme Court was left with the difficult task of "determining whether the due process provision of the Fourteenth Amendment protected those individual rights against the state in the same manner that the Bill of Rights protected them against federal action" (Klotter, 1977, p. 5). After more than 100 years of litigation involving over 300 cases, the Supreme Court determined that most of the rights included in the first ten amendments are applicable to the states. Thus, the search-and-seizure provisions of the Fourth Amendment, the self-incrimination provisions of the Fifth Amendment, and the right-to-counsel provisions of the Sixth Amendment are applicable to the states by way of the due-process provision of the Fourteeth Amendment. Impetus to comply with the court's decisions was provided by the "exclusionary rule," which states that evidence obtained in violation of a person's constitutional rights is inadmissible in court.

Several Supreme Court decisions have played particularly important roles in setting forth guidelines for dealing with criminal suspects. The

Mapp v. *Ohio* (1961) decision found that evidence obtained during an illegal search and seizure was inadmissible in state as well as federal courts. Another landmark decision was *Escobedo* v. *Illinois* (1964), in which the court ruled that suspects have a constitutional right to counsel when arrested and that they must be advised of their right to remain silent. In *McNabb* v. *U. S.* (1943) and in *Mallory* v. *U. S.* (1957) the Supreme Court barred the use of confessions resulting from an illegal delay in arraignment (that is, the appearance before a judge when the accused states how he or she wants to plead with regard to the charges). In one of the more controversial decisions, *Miranda* v. *Arizona* (1966), the Supreme Court ruled that persons taken into custody must be warned that they have the right to remain silent, that anything they say can be used against them, that they have a right to have an attorney present, and that if they cannot afford one, one will be appointed for them. Failure to give these warnings to persons taken into custody can result in their statements or confessions being declared inadmissible as evidence in court. However, recent Supreme Court rulings, such as *Michigan* v. *Tucker* (1974) and *Rhode Island* v. *Innis* (1980), have eroded some of the protections afforded citizens by the *Miranda* decision.

Legal Grounds for Arrest

An arrest can be defined as the decision to take a suspect into custody (LaFave, 1965). It usually, but not necessarily, involves taking the suspect to the station, where he or she is "booked." An officer is legally empowered to make an arrest with or without an arrest warrant. An arrest warrant is issued by a magistrate after the latter has determined that there exists *probable cause* to believe that the suspect committed the crime with which he or she is charged. What is meant by the term *probable cause?* The United States Supreme Court offered the following definition: "Probable cause exists where the facts and circumstances within their [the arresting officers'] knowledge and of which they had reasonable trustworthy information are sufficient in themselves to warrant a man of reasonable caution in the belief that an offense has been or is being committed" [*Draper* v. *U.S.*, 1959]. The key phrases are "reasonable trustworthy information" and "a man of reasonable caution." These terms are difficult to define, and their application depends on the circumstances of the individual case. All that can be said at this time is that the amount of evidence needed to demonstrate probable cause is somewhat more than that needed to produce mere suspicion and somewhat less than that needed to prove beyond a reasonable doubt that the person is guilty.

In most cases, the police do not have the luxury of first obtaining an arrest warrant. Criminal events usually occur without warning. Quick action is needed. Failure to act immediately may result in the escape of the suspect. In such situations the police are empowered to make an arrest without a warrant. The minimal legal criteria for making a warrantless arrest vary with the seriousness of the crime. Federal and state laws recognize two levels of crimes—misdemeanors and felonies. Misdemeanors are crimes for which the maximum penalty is usually no more than one year in jail. In this category are such crimes as petty larceny (that is, theft under $50), simple assault, loitering, jaywalking, and speeding. Felonies are more serious crimes that are punishable by a year or more in prison. This category includes such crimes as grand larceny (that is, theft over $50), aggravated assault (assault with a weapon), robbery, rape, and homicide. Most states limit misdemeanor arrests without a warrant to offenses committed in the officer's presence. "In presence" is usually defined as occurring when the officer gains direct knowledge of the offense through any of his or her five senses (sight, smell, hearing, touch, and taste). Where felonies are concerned, the requirements are less demanding. The officer does not have to be present during commission of the offense but merely must have "reasonable grounds," or probable cause, for believing that the suspect committed a crime.

As this discussion has shown, the courts have played an increasingly active role in defining the legality of various police practices. While legal factors no doubt have a strong impact on decision making by the police, their major function is to set boundaries for police behavior. Within these boundaries the police have a wide latitude of discretion. As we shall see, decisions made within these boundaries are strongly influenced by extralegal, interpersonal factors involving attributional and social-exchange considerations.

DETECTING SUSPICIOUS EVENTS AND IDENTIFYING SUSPECTS

Before we can apply the attribution/exchange model to the police's decision to arrest a suspect, we must first provide an account of how police typically come into contact with a suspect. The police sometimes simultaneously gain knowledge of the suspicious event and the suspect's identity, as when they catch a suspect in the act of burglarizing a home or a motorist speeding. Often, however, the two sets of information arrive in sequence. Thus, on some occasions the police first discover that a crime has occurred and later, after conducting an investigation, identify the suspect. Less frequently, the sequence of discovery is reversed. That is, the police may observe a person acting suspiciously, and only after detaining and interrogating him or her do they discover that a crime has been committed.

As noted in the previous chapter, the primary way in which the police learn about a criminal event is through notification by a citizen. Through direct observation of police activities in Boston, Chicago, and Washington, D.C., Reiss (1971) found that citizens were responsible for 87% of the instances in which the police were mobilized to deal with a criminal event. In the remaining 13%, the police discovered the event on their own initiative. Let us examine more closely these two modes of the police's becoming alerted to a criminal event.

Notification by Citizens

There are various categories of citizens. They may be victims of a crime, bystanders or eyewitnesses, paid informants, or suspects themselves. As noted in the previous chapter, the police are most frequently notified by victims and bystanders. In almost 90% of instances, the police are contacted by telephone. In the remaining instances citizens notify the police by flagging down a police car, approaching a foot-patrol officer, or walking into a police station (Reiss, 1971). Informants are an important source of notification in certain categories of crime, particularly victimless crimes, such as those involving narcotics, gambling, and prostitution. On rare occasions the police are alerted to the crime by suspects themselves. This may occur after a "crime of passion" when the suspect, feeling intensely remorseful, decides to inform the police about the crime. More frequently, the police are alerted to the occurrence of a crime by a burglar alarm system. Sophisticated alarm systems now in use in homes and businesses automatically alert the police to a suspected crime. However, the police in many communities are slow to respond to these alarms because usually the alarm has been inadvertently set off by a forgetful resident. For example, the police in Pittsburgh, Pennsylvania, estimate that nine of ten such alarms turn out to be false alarms (Gigler, 1976). To encourage quicker response by the police, citizens in some sections of Pittsburgh have offered a $20 reward to officers who respond quickly to such alarms.

Sometimes the suspect is still at the scene of the crime when the police arrive, and he or she can be identified and apprehended. However, for most cases in which the police are notified of a crime, the suspect has already fled the scene (Reiss, 1971). Identification of the suspect in such instances requires investigatory work by the police. This function is usually left to the detective branch. Because detectives have limited resources, they cannot search for the suspect in all known crimes. A study of the Kansas City, Missouri, police department (Greenwood, Chaiken, Petersilia, & Prusoff, 1975) revealed that a large percentage of reported crimes assigned to an investigator receive no more attention than the reading of the initial crime-incident report. The study showed that investigators worked on less than half the reported crimes and most of the cases they did work on received less than one day's attention.

Before the police will commit their resources in a search for the suspect, they must be highly certain that a crime has indeed been committed. This point is clearly illustrated by the police's decision to investigate allegations of rape. A national survey of 208 police departments (Law Enforcement Assistance Administration, 1977b) concerning factors that influence their decision to investigate rape cases showed that the most important factors were those having to do with the credibility of the victim's testimony. The following factors were cited most frequently: proof of penetration (80%), use of physical force (70%), promptness of reporting (49%), injury to victim (44%), relationship between victim and suspect (41%), use of weapon (32%), and resistance offered by victim (24%). To the extent that such evidence exists, the police are likely to infer that an involuntary sexual act took place.

The Kansas City study revealed that detectives tend to restrict their investigations to cases that have a higher probability of success (that is, good leads exist) and to the more serious crimes, such as homicide and rape, particularly those receiving notoriety in the press or in the community. Crimes not falling into these categories are usually not investigated. Cases receiving national prominence that have led to intense investigative activity by the police include the searches for the "Son of Sam" murderer and for the kidnapers of Patricia Hearst.

In addition to receiving information from ordinary citizens, the police are sometimes alerted by special informants to the occurrence of crimes. Informants are usually members of the "underworld," such as petty thieves, drug addicts, and prostitutes. The information they supply to the police pertains to crimes that have occurred or those being planned, as well as the identity of the suspects and the location of incriminating evidence. In order for the police to conduct a search or make an arrest on the basis of a tip supplied by an informant, they must first secure a warrant. To do so, they must establish probable cause; this is sometimes difficult, as there is more reason to doubt the credibility of an informant than an ordinary citizen. As one writer has noted, "'Stool pigeons' are neither Boy Scouts, princes of the church, nor recipients of testimonials" (Moylan, 1974, p. 758). Information supplied by typical informants is not given in the spirit of a concerned citizen, but rather is often given in exchange for some concession or payment. Informants' unsavory backgrounds convey an impression of unreliability. The police and the judge issuing the warrant are faced with the task of evaluating the credibility of the informant's information. They usually rely on three considerations to determine the credibility of such reports by informants (LaFave, 1978).

First, they examine the informant's past performance. If the informant supplied consistently reliable information in the past, the information presently conveyed is deemed more reliable. If the informant's track record cannot be shown, then it must be proved that the informant's information is reliable on this particular occasion. One form of proof, which is a second category of information used to determine credibility, is the presence of what Kelley (1972a) calls "inhibiting causes." In what is called "admission against interest," information supplied by an informant may implicate him or her in the crime. The fact that the informant offered the information despite the potential costs of so doing serves to "augment" the authorities' confidence in the informant's credibility. Finally, an informant's testimony is likely to be viewed as credible if the information supplied is sufficiently detailed and precise, the reasoning being that only one who had personally observed the facts could have such detailed knowledge. When any one or more of the above circumstances are present, the police are likely to receive a warrant to investigate further.

Of course, the police do not always need a warrant to act on an informant's tip. If the informant tells the police of a bank robbery planned for the next afternoon, the police can be there waiting and intervene when the attempted robbery occurs.

Discovery of crimes does not always depend on tips received from citizens. Occasionally, the police happen upon a crime during its commission, or they spot a person acting suspiciously, and after questioning him or her, they discover that a crime has been committed. Let us examine more closely this form of discovery by the police.

Discovery Initiated by Police Action

Most police officers believe that if they are to "fight crime" effectively, they must do more than passively wait for citizens to notify them of a crime. Police administrators encourage their officers to take an active stance toward detecting crime and identifying suspects. Officers are explicitly advised by their superiors to maintain vigilance and to stop and detain those judged to be acting suspiciously. The authority to detain and interrogate suspects short of placing them under arrest was confirmed in an important Supreme Court ruling (*Terry* v. *Ohio*, 1968). In that case the court ruled that "a police officer may in appropriate circumstances and in an appropriate manner approach a person for purposes of investigating possible criminal behavior *even though there is no probable cause to make an arrest*." The ruling upheld the authority of the police to "frisk" (pat down outer garments) and interrogate a person whose conduct leads them to conclude, in light of their experience, that a criminal act is about to be, is being, or has been committed. The authority to frisk a suspect is viewed as a self-protective measure designed to assure the officer that the person is not concealing a weapon. That there is a degree of risk in confronting suspects is shown by the fact that 1143 officers were killed in the line of duty from 1970 to 1979 (Webster, 1980).

As a result of questioning suspicious persons, police officers may discover that a crime has taken place. As mentioned above, this sequence of discovery is the reverse of that usually found when citizens notify the police of a crime.

The variables that lead the police to detect criminal incidents and identify suspects are similar to those that affect detection by citizens. They include (1) the characteristics of the observer (that is, the police officer) and (2) the nature of the stimulus situation, such as type of activity observed, characteristics of the person performing the activity, and surrounding circumstances.

Characteristics of the observer

The observer's set, or state of readiness, to detect a criminal event is a critical determinant of whether a suspicious incident or person will be noticed. In this regard police officers are very different from ordinary citizens. Officers are trained to be vigilant and suspicious of what goes on around them. The set to look for suspicious events derives in part from their initial training at the police academy and from police manuals. Officers are taught that the competent officer is always suspicious. Moreover, they are advised when and where to look for crime, what activities are deemed suspicious, and what kinds of persons to be suspicious of. Illustrative of such advice is the following excerpt from a Chicago Police Department training bulletin (cited in Tiffany, McIntyre, & Rotenberg, 1967, p. 39):

> Actions, dress, or location of a person often classify him as suspicious in the mind of the police officer. Men loitering near schools, public toilets, playgrounds, and swimming pools may be sex perverts. Men loitering near bars at closing time, or any other business at closing time, may be robbery suspects. Men or youths walking along looking into cars may be car thieves or looking for something to steal. Persons showing evidence of recent injury, or whose clothing is disheveled, may be victims or participants in an assault or strong arm robbery.[1]

The set to look for suspicious events and persons is reinforced by the presence of "wanted" posters in the station house, by advice from peers, and by rewards from police administrators. Indeed, the reward structure in police departments, whether it be praise and approval from peers or the possibility of a promotion by the police chief, serves to reinforce "nabbing" a suspected criminal or making a "good pinch." When these factors are combined with the police officer's everyday experience on the beat, the product is usually a person who is far more sensitive to suspicious activity than the ordinary citizen.

Nature of the stimulus situation

Events are more likely to be detected if they have characteristics that make them stand out from surrounding events. As noted in the previous chapter, stimuli that are intense or novel are more likely to draw an observer's attention. Police officers are trained to respond not only to such gross cues as the sound of gunshots, screams, or breaking glass but also to more subtle events that are distinguished from other occurrences

---

[1]From *Detection of Crime: Stopping and Questioning, Search and Seizure, Encouragement and Entrapment*, by L. P. Tiffany, D. M. McIntyre, Jr., and D. L. Rotenberg. Copyright 1967 by Little, Brown and Company. This and all other quotations from this source are reprinted by permission.

by their novelty or incongruity. A Milwaukee police-training-school bulletin describes a suspicious person as "one who, because of the peculiarity of his conduct, differs from the other persons an officer customarily meets during his tour of duty" (Tiffany et al., 1967, p. 39). In order to know what events are novel or unusual, the police officer must first know what is usual. According to a former patrol officer,

> The time spent cruising one's sector or walking one's beat is not wasted time, though it can become quite routine. During this time, the most important thing for the officer to do is notice the *normal*. He must come to know the people in his area, their habits, their automobiles and their friends. He must learn what time the various shops close, how much money is kept on hand on different nights, what lights are usually left on, which houses are vacant . . . only then can he decide what persons or cars under what circumstances warrant the appellation "suspicious" [Connell, cited in Skolnick, 1975, p. 48].

The most extensive investigation of the actual practices of police officers in stopping and interrogating persons on the street was a field study done in Chicago by Tiffany et al. (1967). The study spelled out the stimulus situations that were most likely to arouse the suspicion of the police. These situations can be classified according to (1) type of activity, (2) characteristics of the person performing the activity, and (3) circumstances under which the activity is viewed.

1. *Type of activity.* Persons seen loitering in an alley of a business district may be suspected of burglary, robbery, or purse snatching. Similarly, a car with no license plates or a non-illuminated plate may suggest to the police that the vehicle was stolen. Also suspected are persons who show undue concern at the sight of the police. Such persons may try to dispose of property or flee when sighted by the police. Suspicion of such activities is supported by the Biblical proverb "The wicked flee when no man pursueth, but the righteous are bold as a lion."

Attributional concerns are central to all the examples in the previous paragraph. In each case, officers view an action for which there is no *reasonable* legal cause. The fact that the police are not able to explain the behavior in reference to a legitimate cause prompts them to assume an illegal or illegitimate cause and, therefore, to interrogate the person. This point is well illustrated by the practice of the police in identifying drunk drivers. A study of the San Diego police (Cloyd, 1977–1978) showed that officers' suspicion was most likely to be aroused when the driver

> makes an irregular driving maneuver (swerves over the double line, does not negotiate a turn smoothly, etc.) that has no observable or ostensible explanation (e.g. swerves to miss an animal, the road is rough, making it hard to negotiate a smooth turn, etc.). Given that there are no observable external explanations for the irregular behavior, it is seen as "reasonable cause" to assume there are some internal factors determining this behavior, possibly alcohol or drugs [p. 391].

2. *Characteristics of the person performing the activity.* Certain types of people are more likely to arouse the suspicion of the police than others. Characteristics of a person deemed most relevant to the decision to stop and question include age, sex, race, appearance, and arrest record. Young people are more likely to be stopped than older people, because the police know that most crime is committed by people between ages 16 and 25. Likewise, males are more likely to be stopped than females, except in areas where prostitution is known to flourish. The general reluctance to stop females may reflect the police's belief that males are more likely to commit crimes or the police's fear that a woman is more likely to accuse the police of improper conduct. Police officers seem more inclined to stop minority-group members than whites. This may reflect their belief that minority-group members commit more crimes. It may also reflect the fact that more officers are assigned to high-crime neighborhoods—neighborhoods that are usually inhabited by minority-group members. Because of the higher concentration of police officers, people living in these areas are likely to be subject to closer scrutiny by the police and therefore more likely to be stopped for interrogation.

A person's appearance also affects whether he or she will be stopped and questioned. Those whose appearance suggests that they are of the lower socioeconomic class are most likely to be detained because police believe that poor individuals are most likely to commit crimes. Thus, a shabbily dressed person will arouse more suspicion than one whose appearance suggests relative affluence. However, this is true only in racially mixed or predominantly white areas. In black neighborhoods, dress, as a measure of respectability, is given less weight by the police.

Persons who are on probation or parole are more likely to be stopped by the police than persons who do not have a criminal record. The knowledge that these persons have been in trouble with the law in the past implies that they have a stable criminal disposition, which heightens the police's suspicion of them. As one officer stated,

> If you found a parolee whom you recognized out in an area late at night, you would certainly be entitled to frisk him. Parolees live under a different form of law because they have already proven that they have criminal tendencies. You would naturally suspect that most parolees who were out late at night were in violation of their parole or up to no good or both [Tiffany et al., 1967, p. 24].

As we will see in Chapter 9, the police's treatment of parolees affects their chances of successfully completing their parole period.

Not only are police officers more likely to stop persons convicted of crimes, they are also more likely to stop persons who have been arrested but not convicted. The fact that the police often do not distinguish between these two classes of persons reflects a view among officers that "the failure to prosecute or to convict a suspect does not necessarily indicate his innocence" (Tiffany et al., 1967, p. 25).

3. *Circumstances of the activity.* The time of day and the neighborhood where the action is observed are further situational factors that influence the police's decision to question someone. Officers are more likely to stop and question someone seen on the street late at night than during the day. This reflects a general belief among patrol officers that decent people are in bed at such hours and that those who are out in the street are probably up to no good. Similarly, persons seen in the street in high-crime areas are more likely to arouse the suspicions of the police than those seen in low-crime areas.

In summarizing the situational factors that contribute to an officer's suspicion, the reader should keep in mind that situational cues are judged in combination, not in isolation. That is, whether a situation is judged to be suspicious depends on the type of activity observed, the characteristics of the person performing the activity, and the surrounding circumstances. An activity that ordinarily might not arouse the police's suspicion may seem very suspicious when other cues are present. For example, seeing a black youth on the street might not cause the police to take notice, but when the youth is seen walking in an exclusively white area late at night, he is likely to arouse the police's suspicion and be interrogated. Likewise, a street-corner exchange of some substance for money will assume special significance if it occurs in a neighborhood where there is intensive drug traffic (LaFave, 1978).

After detecting a suspicious event and detaining a suspect, the police must decide whether to make an arrest. To understand how this decision is made, we will apply the attribution/exchange model.

ATTRIBUTION/EXCHANGE MODEL FOR THE DECISION TO MAKE AN ARREST

The knowledge that a crime has been committed, and that the suspect is likely to be responsible for it, establishes reasonable grounds for making an arrest. However, all that the existence of reasonable grounds or probable cause means is that it is legally permissible to take the suspect into custody. As shown in Figure 3-1, whether an arrest will occur depends, first of all, on the kinds of attributions the officer makes about the suspect. A suspect who is perceived as "blameworthy," "dangerous," "disrespectful," or "unrepentant" is more likely to be arrested than one who is perceived as "blameless," "not dangerous," "respectful," or "repentant." Whether an arrest will take place also depends on the expected outcome of social-exchange relations that the officer has with the suspect, the complainant, the community, the police administration and other agents of the criminal justice system, and fellow officers. It is assumed that in deciding whether to arrest the suspect, the officer chooses the response that at the time appears to yield the fewest costs and the most benefits. In the remainder of this

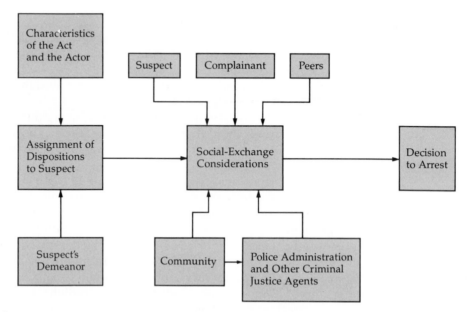

Figure 3-1. Attribution/exchange model of police's decision to make an arrest

chapter we will examine separately the attributional and the social-exchange phases of the model.

ATTRIBUTIONAL CONSIDERATIONS: ASSIGNING DISPOSITIONS TO SUSPECTS

How do police officers make attributions about suspects? What type of cues do the police tend to rely on? In this section we will discuss two sources of information the police use in attributing dispositions to the suspect: (1) the observable characteristics of the act and the actor (that is, the suspect) and (2) the suspect's demeanor when confronted by the police.

Observable Characteristics of the Act and the Actor

It is well known that the police are more likely to arrest persons suspected of committing serious crimes than those suspected of committing less serious crimes (Black, 1971; LaFave, 1965; Piliavin & Briar, 1964; Siegel, Sullivan, & Greene, 1974). One explanation for this practice is that the police attribute stronger criminal dispositions to those suspected of committing more serious offenses. The attributional principle at work here is Kelley's (1972a) augmentation principle. The police may reason that because there are strong moral and legal sanctions against committing serious crimes (that is, inhibiting causes), anyone who does so must have a particularly strong criminal disposition.

Seriousness is judged not only on the basis of the amount of harm done to the victim but on other bases as well. The police tend to consider more serious those crimes that are carefully planned, as opposed to offenses committed "on impulse" (Goldman, 1951). A premeditated offense provides the police with better evidence of a stable criminal disposition than one based on impulse. In the latter case, the offense is likely to be viewed as being due to an unstable disposition, such as a temporary state of excitement or anger.

The seriousness of a crime and therefore the type of disposition assigned to the suspect may also be influenced by the suspect's and victim's race. LaFave (1965) found in Detroit that assaults involving a black suspect and a black victim were not treated as serious offenses by the police. This tendency is strikingly illustrated by incidents of felonious assault on a spouse. What would normally be considered an aggravated assault was viewed by officers as just a family squabble. Similar practices by the police were observed in Albany and Newburgh, New York (Wilson, 1978). The accounts given by LaFave and by Wilson indicate that the police in these communities believe that settling disputes violently is normative behavior in the black ghetto community. Given such beliefs, the police are less likely to see assaultive behavior between blacks as indicative of a criminal disposition; they tend to view it, rather, as reflecting community norms. In such instances, the offense is not considered very serious, and an arrest, therefore, is not likely to be made. However, when the same crime is committed against a white person, it is likely to be viewed as very serious.

Besides the seriousness of the act, the police make attributions about the causes of suspected offenders' behavior on the basis of their observable personal characteristics, such as age, race, social class, record of previous offenses, and appearance. The police tend to view minor offenses committed by youths as reflecting "immature judgment" and "youthful exuberance" (LaFave, 1965). There is evidence that some officers view blacks and those living in slum neighborhoods as having stronger criminal dispositions than whites and those living in middle-class neighborhoods (Westley, 1970). Suspects having a record of arrests and convictions are more likely to be viewed as having a stable criminal disposition, and thus as posing a greater danger to the community, than those whose record is "clean." An illustration of this reasoning is provided by Westley (1970), who concluded from his interviews with police officers that "the man with a criminal record who has done time in prison, the patrolman sees as the 'pro' or 'hardened criminal.' Policemen feel that the previous record predicts the future" (pp. 134–135).

A person's appearance is another cue often used by the police to infer a criminal disposition. Through their experience on the beat, patrol officers come to associate certain modes of dress with criminality. Extensive observations of the criteria used by police to arrest juvenile suspects led Piliavin and Briar (1964) to conclude that "older juveniles, members of known delinquent gangs, Negroes, youths with well-oiled hair, black jackets and soiled denims or jeans (the presumed uniform of "tough" boys) . . . tended to receive more severe dispositions" (p. 210). Suspects who dress unconventionally are more likely to be viewed by the police as having criminal tendencies (Wilson, 1978). When observing persons whose dress is unusual, officers are likely to reason that anyone who "publicly flouts community mores is more likely than one who does not to break community laws" (Wilson, 1978, p. 40).

Suspect's Demeanor When Confronted by the Police

One of the key sources of attributions about a suspect is his or her demeanor when confronted by the police. Suspects who display hostile and disrespectful behavior toward the police are likely to be perceived as having a stronger criminal disposition and are therefore more likely to be arrested (Black, 1971; Pepinsky, 1975; Piliavin & Briar, 1964; Reiss, 1971; Siegel et al., 1974). Those who are cooperative and show respect for the police are more likely to be seen as having "good character" and therefore to be treated leniently. Data collected by Piliavin and Briar (1964) clearly illustrate this point. They observed how the police dealt with youths suspected of minor offenses. They noted that the police based their decision on their assessment of the youth's character. If the officer perceived the youth as basically "all right" or "good," then he was likely to receive a "break." However, if the boy was seen as basically "bad," he was likely to be arrested. Assessment of the youth's character, in turn, was based primarily on the youth's demeanor. Of the youths who displayed a "cooperative" demeanor, just 4% were arrested, while 87% were given an informal warning and released. In contrast, of the youths who displayed an "uncooperative" demeanor, 67% were arrested, while just 10% were informally warned and released.

A similar conclusion was reached by Pepinsky (1975), who observed officers' treatment of motorists who violated traffic regulations. Motorists were very likely to receive a ticket if they argued or got angry with the officer or just asked what they had done wrong. They were also likely to be ticketed if they asked the officer for his badge number or asked him why he had not stopped the person who had run the light before them. If motorists admitted running the light and expressed the belief that the officer had acted correctly in stopping them, they had an excellent chance of being let off with just a warning. Pepinsky (1975) summarized the rationale for the officers' actions in the following way:

> If a citizen behaves disrespectfully toward the officer, the citizen is not seen by the officer as merely showing disregard to the officer as an individual. The citizen is seen as disregarding the larger authority the officer believes he represents. This disrespect to the officer represents the best evidence the officer is apt to have of disrespect for the law itself—hence, of a citizen's determination not to adhere to the dictates of the law in the future [p. 37].

In this section we have seen that the police's attributions help determine how the police will deal with a suspected offender. Suspects most likely to be arrested are those who the police believe have strong criminal dispositions. They include persons suspected of having committed serious offenses. They tend to be older, black, or from the lower socioeconomic class, have a record of previous offenses, and have an appearance that sets them apart from the ordinary "law-abiding" citizen. They also include persons who, when confronted by the police, display a hostile and disrespectful demeanor.

The police do not arrest all suspects who they believe have criminal dispositions. According to the attribution/exchange model shown in Figure 3-1, an officer's belief about the suspect's criminality is but one factor that contributes to the decision to arrest or not arrest that person. Officers also compare the potential benefits and costs of making an arrest with the benefits and costs of alternative actions. As we will see in the next section, the expected rewards and costs derive mainly from the social environment.

SOCIAL-EXCHANGE CONSIDERATIONS

The police, like citizens, can deal with a suspected offender in a number of ways. First, they can take official action, such as making an arrest or issuing a summons; second, they can handle the situation informally, as by letting the suspect off with a warning; and third, they can simply ignore the offense. The decision about how to deal with the suspect depends on which option the police think will yield the most favorable outcomes. Like citizens, the police are not always able to calculate the costs and benefits in a cool and rational way. Often the decision must be made under very stressful circumstances. Typically, when responding to a call, the police are outnumbered by citizens (Reiss, 1971). Such situations may be stressful for the police—first, because they present a greater physical danger to officers and, second, because when onlookers are present, the police have to be on their best behavior lest they be accused of violating the constitutional rights of those involved. Moreover, as the President's Commission on Law Enforcement and the Administration of Justice noted in its report (1967a, p. 91), "Policemen deal with people when they are both most threatening and most vulnerable, when they are angry, when they are frightened, when they are desperate, when they are drunk, when they are violent, or when they are ashamed." Under such conditions, police may fail to meet the ideal of cool and rational decision makers. The same conclusion was reached by Skolnick (1975), who observed that "danger typically yields self-defensive conduct, conduct that must strain to be impulsive because danger arouses fear and anxiety so easily. Authority under such conditions becomes a resource to reduce perceived threats rather than a series of reflective judgments arrived at calmly" (p. 67). Although there are constraints on the police's ability to make rational decisions, we will assume that their decisions, insofar as possible, are guided by rational calculations, imperfect as they may be.

Many of the costs and benefits associated with each of the police's options derive from social exchanges with others. "Others" include those who are physically present, such as the suspect and the victim or complainant; those who are not present such as members of the community, the police administration, and other agents of the criminal justice system; and those who may or may not be present, such as fellow officers. Weighing the various benefits and costs from each of these sources poses something of a dilemma for the police, as Wilson (1978, p. 84) notes:

> [The officer's] actual decision whether and how to intervene involves such questions as these: Has anyone been hurt or deprived? Will anyone be hurt or deprived if I do nothing? Will an arrest improve the situation or only make matters worse? Is a complaint more likely if there is *no* arrest, or if there *is* an arrest? What does the sergeant expect of me? Am I getting near the end of my tour of duty? Will I have to go to court on my day off? If I do appear in court, will the charge stand up or will it be withdrawn or dismissed by the prosecutor? Will my partner think that an arrest shows I can handle things or that I can't handle things? What will the guy do if I let him go?[2]

In the following sections we will discuss the costs and benefits associated with each of the persons and groups with whom the police are in a social-exchange relationship. We will begin with the suspected offender.

Social Exchange with the Suspected Offender

The exchange relationship with the suspect has an important impact on how the police will handle a given situation.

Suspect's demeanor

A critical factor in the police's decision making is the suspect's demeanor. Demeanor not only conveys information about the suspect's criminal disposition but also constitutes a significant source of benefits and costs for the officer. To understand why, one must understand the "working personality" of the police. According to Skolnick (1975), a key element in a police officer's personality is the need to assert authority when dealing with the public. This need to take charge of the situation is reflected in officers' beliefs that everyone present should answer their questions and obey their commands, whether to raise his or her hands or to move to the other side of the street. Interestingly, Reiss (1971) has found that suspects are more likely to cooperate with the police when the police are summoned to the scene by another citizen than when the

---

[2]From *Varieties of Police Behavior* (2nd ed.), by James Q. Wilson. Harvard University Press, Copyright 1978.

police arrive on their own initiative. In the latter situation, the police are more apt to be viewed as intruders. Suspects who by their demeanor confirm the police's authority serve to reward the police, whereas those who challenge the police's authority impose a cost on the police. The police's response to those who refuse to defer to their authority is to treat such persons in "a hostile, authoritarian or belittling manner" (Reiss 1971). Another way of dealing with such challenges to their authority is to place the "offender" under arrest. By so doing, the police can convert any further challenge into a legal offense—that of resisting arrest. This response by the police is designed to reassert their authority and to make continuing such behavior costly for the suspect. In some respects the confrontation with the suspect in the street resembles a courtroom proceeding. In administering "curbstone justice," police officers have the same need as judges do to "maintain order in the court." Whereas challenges to a judge's authority are met by holding the offender in contempt of court, the police respond by making an arrest.

Additional evidence for the importance of the suspect's demeanor is provided by Black (1971), who observed encounters between police officers and suspects in Boston, Chicago, and Washington, D.C. Not surprisingly, he found that an arrest was more likely to occur in felony encounters (58%) than in misdemeanor encounters (44%), even though the police had sufficient evidence to make an arrest in all cases. What is surprising is his finding that "the police are more likely to arrest a misdemeanor suspect who is disrespectful toward them than a felony suspect who is civil. In this sense the police enforce their authority more severely than they enforce the law" (p. 1099).

The encounter between the police and citizens is, of course, a two-way exchange. If an officer initially treats the suspect in a rude and hostile manner, the suspect may reciprocate by refusing to cooperate. Observation of numerous encounters between police officers and citizens revealed that when an officer gave suspects no reason for stopping and questioning them, they were less willing to reward the officer by cooperating than when the officer provided a reason (Wiley & Hudik, 1974).

Differential power of suspects

Suspects can control the police's outcomes not only through their demeanor during their encounter with the police but through their ability to "make trouble" for the police in the future (Lundman, 1974). Such considerations often figure prominently in decisions by officers who encounter persons suspected of committing minor offenses, such as traffic violations. Wilson (1978) reported that officers in some of the communities he observed were reluctant to issue tickets to cars belonging to persons having political influence. He asked officers in several cities what they would do if they saw a car with a very low license number (for example, "N Y 2") speeding. Officers in two New York

communities (Newburgh and Amsterdam) responded unequivocally—
"Mind your own business."

In contrast to persons who can make trouble for the police are those
persons and groups who are politically powerless. Several studies provide evidence of police discrimination against persons of lower socioeconomic status and members of minority groups (Cochran, 1971; Skolnick, 1975; Westley, 1970; Wilson, 1978). Chambliss and Seidman (1971),
among others, contend that suspects of lower socioeconomic status are
discriminated against by the police because they wield less political
power than middle-class suspects. Chambliss and Seidman further contend that because the police associate minority-group membership with
lower socioeconomic status, minority-group members have become the
objects of police discrimination.

Westley (1970) provided evidence supporting this social-exchange interpretation. His interviews with and observation of patrol officers in
their everyday encounters with citizens confirmed that the police were
aware of social-class differences in political power and that this knowledge affected how they dealt with suspects. Wilson (1978) reported a
similar pattern of response by the police in some of the cities he studied.
However, he questioned whether the differential treatment accorded
suspects on the basis of their social class resulted from the police's
concern with suspects' ability to cause political trouble in the future or
from the police's belief that different types of treatment are needed to
deter members of each social class from committing future crimes. For
example, an officer might feel that a severe warning to a middle-class
youthful offender will prove as effective as having a lower-class offender
spend the night in jail. This reasoning is reflected in the following
statement from an officer interviewed by Westley (1970):

> "In the good districts you appeal to people's judgment and explain the law to
> them. In the south side the only way is to appear like you are the boss. You
> can't ask them a question and get an answer that is not a lie. In the south side
> the only way to walk into a tavern is to walk in swaggering as if you own the
> place and if somebody is standing in your way give him an elbow and push
> him aside" [p. 98].

The decision to treat suspects on the basis of what action will best
deter them from future crimes can be viewed from the social-exchange
perspective. The officer is trying to select a mode of treatment that will
reduce the probability of the future criminal conduct—conduct that
may cost the police valuable time and effort. The available evidence
does not permit us to determine how much weight the police give to
suspects' ability to cause them future costs, whether political costs or
the costs of having to deal with the criminal behavior in the future.

Another social-exchange explanation for the higher arrest rate of
black suspects was offered by Black (1971). His observation of encounters between the police and citizens yielded *no* evidence of discrimina-

tion against black suspects. Rather, he found that the higher rate of arrest for black suspects was due to "the higher rate at which black suspects display disrespect toward the police" (p. 1097). Among black and white suspects who showed a respectful demeanor toward the police, no difference in arrest rate was observed.

What conclusions can be drawn about the role of the suspect's race in the arrest decision? It seems fair to conclude that blacks and members of other minority groups are more likely to be arrested than members of the white community for committing the same crime. This difference may exist for a number of reasons. First, encounters with minority suspects may more often involve a hostile confrontation, which is perceived as costly by the police. One way for the police to handle such threats is to place the suspect under arrest. Further, the police often show little hesitancy in arresting minority suspects because they usually have less to fear from them in the way of political retaliation. However, the recent growth of organizations concerned with protecting the rights of minorities has increased the power of such persons. Consequently, the police have come to exercise greater caution in their treatment of minority-group members.

When the police believe that the suspect controls some valuable commodity, they are usually more than willing to bargain for the suspect's freedom regardless of the suspect's race or social class. This willingness is clearly shown in the police's dealings with suspects who double as informants. In some cases, the crucial factor determining the arrest decision is the suspect's ability to provide the police with valuable information or services. Those who have such resources can trade them for their freedom. For a better understanding of why the police are willing to engage in such exchanges, one must appreciate how the police—in particular, detectives—sometimes have to operate. In order to solve certain types of crimes, such as narcotics crimes and burglaries, police need tips from informants (Skolnick, 1975). Without a network of informants, there is very little the police can do to identify and apprehend those suspected of committing such offenses. A major problem for the police is how to motivate potential informants to supply them with information about the suspect's identity, where he or she can be found, and the location of the "merchandise." What the police have to offer potential informants is money and/or the promise of leniency for any offense that the informant might have committed. Leniency can be shown in several ways. It may involve overlooking a crime committed by the informant or promising to ask the district attorney for a lighter sentence (see Chapter 4). Of concern to us in this chapter is the decision to withhold arrest in exchange for the informant's cooperation.

Informants are likely to be people whose occupation or habits make them privy to information about dealings in narcotics and stolen merchandise and whose behavior often puts them on the wrong side of the law. They include drug addicts, petty thieves, prostitutes, and bartenders. Rubinstein (1973) observed that the patrol officer's "steadiest source of information is what he collects as rent for allowing [such] people to operate without arresting them" (p. 207). One officer clearly described the social-exchange relationship with prostitutes: "If you treat 'em right, they will give you what you want. They don't want to get locked up, and you can trade that off for information" (Rubinstein, 1973, p. 207). Skolnick (1975), who observed similar tactics used by narcotics detectives, reported that detectives may ignore a minor offense by an addict in exchange for information about more serious offenses. Indebtedness appears to be the mechanism that underlies this exchange (Silberman, 1978). By ignoring an addict's minor offenses, a detective builds up credit with the addict. Later, when the detective is in need of information, the debt can be called in. Effective narcotics detectives are those who have built up such credit with a number of persons who can give them information when it is needed. The police are willing to engage in such exchanges because the police administration reinforces them for making a "good pinch." A good pinch does not mean the arrest of an addict for injecting drugs, but rather the narcotics dealer who supplies the addict. The desire to make a good pinch, in effect, leads the police to follow the strategy of tolerating offenses committed by "smaller fish" in exchange for information that will lead to the arrest of "bigger fish."

As one would expect, being an informant can be quite costly. If word of the informant's identity should leak out, the informant might be physically harmed. Detectives who deal with informants are, of course, aware of such potential costs, and it is probably to balance such costs that detectives favor severe penalties for using narcotics. They often favor strict penalties not because they believe the penalties deter addicts from using drugs but because such penalties improve the police's bargaining position vis-à-vis the addict. An addict who must decide between the certainty of several years in prison and the possibility of being the object of a narcotics dealer's retaliation may conclude that more is to be gained by cooperating with the police than by not doing so.

In part, detectives are willing to overlook certain types of offenses in order to obtain information about more "important" offenses because they are often organized into units specializing in certain types of crimes. Thus, urban detectives may be grouped into a burglary and theft division, a homicide division, a narcotics division, and so on. This specialization determines what type of crime is most important to a particular detective. According to observations made by Skolnick (1975), detectives tend to ignore offenses not related to their specialization when dealing with informants. Skolnick summarized his observations as follows: *"In general, burglary detectives permit informants to commit narcotics offenses, while narcotics detectives allow informants to steal"* (p. 129).

Considerations of equity and fairness

In their dealings with suspected offenders, the police are frequently guided by considerations of fairness or equity. Police officers want to see suspects get what they deserve. What officers feel someone deserves may not correspond to what will be prescribed in a court of law. They do not always make an arrest even when the suspect is caught red-handed. Reiss (1971) found that in situations in which probable cause existed, police failed to make an arrest in 43% of the felonies and 52% of the misdemeanors. To the officer, what someone deserves depends not only on the nature of the evidence and the offense that the person is alleged to have committed but also on the circumstances, on who the person is, and on how he or she acts toward the officer. The police may hesitate to make an arrest because they feel that the punishment required by law is excessive. For example, they frequently voice the opinion that it is un-fair to give a youthful first offender a record and that the needs of justice are better served by letting the suspect off with a sharp warning. Con-sider the following illustration by LaFave (1965):

> A traffic officer stopped a car that had been going 15 m.p.h. over the speed limit. The driver was a youth, but he had a valid driver's license. Although the 15 m.p.h. excess was beyond the ordinary toleration limit for speeding violations, the officer only gave the youth a severe warning. The officer knew that the law required suspension of the license of a juvenile driver for any moving violation [p. 138].[3]

The police are also likely to show leniency toward consenting middle-class adults engaged in illegal sexual behavior. The arrest of such persons and the attendant publicity might cause them to suffer needless embarrassment or to lose their job or might harm their re-lationship with their family. In such situations the police are apt to let the offenders off with a warning or with a promise to seek psychological counseling (LaFave, 1965). That the police consider the excessive dam-age to a relationship that might result from an arrest is clearly shown in the following example:

> A woman returned home from work in a disheveled condition and told her husband that she had been kidnapped and raped. The husband called the police, and they began an investigation. Upon questioning the woman the following day, the police discerned some discrepancies in her story, and she finally admitted that she and a man had engaged in lovemaking by mutual consent, and that she had fabricated the story in order to explain her absence to her husband. Since proceeding against the woman for a false felony report would have endangered her marriage, the police decided to take no action [LaFave, 1965, p. 140].

In the cases above, the police's conception of justice dictated that an arrest would not serve the cause of justice. More than likely, officers in

[3] From *Arrest: The Decision to Take a Suspect into Custody*, by Wayne LaFave. Copyright © 1965 by Little, Brown, and Co., Inc. This and all other quotations from this source are reprinted by permission.

these situations gave considerable weight to Leventhal's needs rule (see "Social-Exchange Theory" in Chapter 1) when deciding what action to take.

The need to maintain fairness also dictates that certain suspects be arrested. Wilson (1978) described this aspect of the police's concern with justice in the following way: "A 'wise guy' deserves less than a 'good guy'; a man who does not accept police authority, and thus legal authority, deserves less than a man who does" (p. 37). This statement suggests that a suspect's demeanor in part determines what the police feel is the right thing for them to do. Justice *requires* that disrespectful suspects be punished by arrest and respectful suspects be treated more leniently.

The police also believe that certain people are deserving of arrest because of their past deeds as well as the present offense. If the police know that a suspect has got away with committing a serious offense in the past, they may arrest the suspect for a minor offense that can be proved even though persons committing the offense would ordinarily not be arrested (LaFave, 1965). It is the police's way of seeing that "justice" is done. Consider the following illustration:

> The police learned of a minor property theft. As the victim was not interested in prosecution, the police, in accord with their usual policy, decided not to arrest. However, when they learned that the offender was known to the police department as a "bad actor," and that the police had been unsuccessful in obtaining his conviction for other, more serious offenses, they arrested him [LaFave, 1965, p. 149].

Numerous examples can be found in the criminal justice literature of the police's use of arrest to correct for previous "injustices." Such examples can be found in the tendency to file charges of income tax evasion against notorious crime figures when hard evidence of more serious crimes is lacking. Similarly, in some communities the police arrest prostitutes for loitering when they cannot prove that the suspects were soliciting. At least in one city, prostitutes have found a way to deal with such harassment. Prostitutes in Madrid, Spain, threatened to name their better-known clients, publish their photographs, and "expose their sexual tastes." Harassment by the police immediately ceased (Walker, 1978).

Although the social-exchange relationship with the suspect is an important determinant of the arrest decision, it is by no means the only relationship that affects this decision. The social-exchange relationship with the complainant is also of critical importance to the police.

Social Exchange with the Complainant

When the police respond to a call from a citizen, the complainant is usually present when the police arrive on the scene (Black, 1971). The complainant, who in most cases is the victim (Law Enforcement Assistance Administration, 1974; Reiss, 1971), exercises considerable power over the arrest decision, as the complainant's testimony usually determines whether the arrest will lead to a successful prosecution in court, particularly when the offense is a misdemeanor. For a misdemeanor arrest to be made, either the offense must be committed in the officer's presence or a citizen/complainant must swear out a warrant for the suspect's arrest. Accordingly, when the officer has not personally observed a misdemeanor offense being committed, the complainant's preference largely determines the arrest decision. When the offense in question is a felony, the police are not nearly as dependent on the complainant's cooperation. As noted earlier in this chapter, the police may make a felony arrest without directly observing the offense; all that is needed is the belief of "reasonable" or "probable cause." Although the police may proceed with an arrest despite the complainant's wishes, they often do not, because they know that without the complainant's cooperation the case is not likely to be successfully prosecuted. Alternatively, if the officer ignores the complainant's desire to arrest the suspect, the officer runs the risk that the complainant will go over his or her head and report the incident to the officer's superiors. The outcome of these exchanges with complainants is that the police generally follow the complainant's preferences in the arrest action.

This outcome is clearly shown in a study of police/citizen encounters by Black (1971). Complainants were observed to make their arrest preferences clear in a majority of encounters (63%). Further, Black found that when the complainant wanted a felony suspect arrested, the police made an arrest in 72% of the cases. In comparison, when the complainant preferred that the police make no arrest, an arrest was made in just 9% of the cases. The police followed the complainant's preference in 78% of the felony encounters and 87% of the misdemeanor encounters. In addition, the data revealed that the complainant's preference overrode the suspect's demeanor in affecting the arrest decision. That is, when the suspect behaved antagonistically toward the police and the complainant was opposed to the arrest, just one out of five suspects were placed under arrest. In comparison, when the complainant expressed no preference regarding arrest, an arrest was made in four of five cases in which the suspect behaved antagonistically toward the police. These data led Black (1971) to conclude that "complainants have voices sufficiently persuasive in routine police encounters to save disrespectful persons from arrest" (p. 1108).

Although the police usually follow the complainant's preference, they do not do so unconditionally. Generally speaking, the more serious the offense, the less influence the complainant has on the arrest decision (Hall, 1975). The reason is that when the offense is serious, the officer knows that others, such as police administration officials, members of the community, and fellow officers will have greater interest in the decision and therefore will be more apt to use stronger sanctions to get the officer to comply with their wishes.

Complainants' demeanor is another factor that determines whether their wishes will be followed. The police are less likely to follow the advice of a disrespectful complainant than one whose demeanor is civil (Black, 1968). In addition, the police tend not to go along with the complainant's desire that a suspect be arrested for a minor offense if they expect that the complainant will not file a formal charge or is likely to withdraw the charge shortly afterward. Situations likely to elicit such beliefs by the police are those in which they believe that the victim/complainant is in a continuing relationship with the suspect (Black, 1971; Hall, 1975; LaFave, 1965) or is only interested in restitution (LaFave, 1965). Often, when the police are called to mediate a domestic dispute, the victim (usually the wife) expresses an initial desire to see the offender arrested. However, when passions have cooled, such victims often withdraw their charges. Rather than waste their time with an arrest, the police usually prefer to settle the matter privately. In such situations they view their role as primarily peacemakers (Hall, 1975). After quelling the initial disturbance, officers often counsel the participants themselves or advise them to seek professional help from a social service agency. Generally, the closer the relationship between victim and suspect, the less the likelihood that an arrest will be made.

The following example illustrates the police's reluctance to waste their time arresting a suspect when they believe the complainant is only interested in restitution:

> A merchant turned over a "no account" check to the police, requesting apprehension of the writer. The merchant was asked whether he was willing to appear in court when the offender was prosecuted, and he replied that he only wanted to collect the amount of the check. The police refused to take any action [LaFave, 1965, p. 117].

However, if the police have already expended considerable resources in investigating the offense, they are likely to ignore the victim's wishes. In such cases, they will probably try to persuade the victim to cooperate in the prosecution of the suspect.

Social Exchange with Members of the Community

It is clear that citizens are dependent on the police for law enforcement and service functions. The police are likewise dependent on the community in a number of ways. As we have seen, if the police are to do their job, they need the cooperation of the community. Without notification by citizens the vast majority of crimes would go undetected by the police. Moreover, information supplied by citizens usually determines whether a suspect will be identified and subsequently prosecuted. Additional leverage is exerted on the police by citizens acting in their role as voters and taxpayers. The influence exerted in these latter ways is, of course, indirect (see Figure 3–1). That is, if members of a community are dissatisfied with the performance of the police, they can put pressure on the mayor to order the chief of police to alter his policy. Mayors, being political creatures, usually are not eager to alienate the electorate and, therefore, are likely to comply with the community's wishes. The chief of police, ever mindful of the mayor's ability to hire and fire, is usually not in a good position to challenge the mayor's wishes. Similarly, patrol officers, conscious of the police adminstration's ability to control financial rewards, promotions, and duty assignments, are not in a position to do battle with the administration over a change in arrest policy.

Because of the community's control over resources needed by the police, officers are usually careful not to engage in actions that will alienate the community. In practice this means that the community's attitude toward an offense determines how vigorously the police will deal with that offense. Thus, when an offense, because of its notoriety, arouses public indignation (for example, the "Son of Sam" murder case), the police will go to extreme lengths to see that the suspect is apprehended. However, when the police perceive that the public does not desire that an ordinance be strictly enforced, an arrest is unlikely to be made. Consider the following example reported by LaFave (1965):

> A police officer came upon open gambling in a local tavern. The community was known as a "wide-open" town, and much of the revenue in the city came from operation of gambling and entertainment houses. A considerable majority of the community appeared to favor the continuance of such conditions. No arrest was made [p. 127].

That the police tend to follow what they perceive to be the will of the community does not imply that there always exists a single community or a single standard to follow. Often the police are confronted with different communities having different standards of enforcement, and they have to find compromise solutions. An example is the dilemma of the police in a small Wisconsin community. Local politicians were angry with the police because their cars were ticketed for meter violations while parked around the courthouse square. For the police to abstain from ticketing the cars of important political figures while ticketing cars of other citizens would have angered the less influential members of the community who received tickets. To avoid the appearance of showing favoritism, the police hit upon the solution of ticketing all cars for parking violations but later tearing up the tickets issued to the politicians (LaFave, 1965). By this action both "communities" were placated.

Another way to satisfy conflicting demands from different communities is for the police to apply different standards of enforcement when dealing with members of each community. Several studies found that the police tend to treat an offense involving black participants less seriously than the same offense involving white participants (LaFave,

1965; Wilson, 1978). Police officers who believed that violence is an accepted way of life in black ghetto communities were less likely to arrest a black suspect for stabbing her husband in a domestic quarrel than a white suspect believed to have committed the same offense. By arresting one and not the other, the police believed, they were only following the wishes of the respective communities. The importance attached to community reactions is reflected in the growth of community-relations divisions within most urban police departments. Their function is to foster improved relations between the police and the surrounding community. A variety of programs have been instituted, such as providing speakers for community gatherings, publishing pamphlets on how to prevent being victimized, and organizing tours of police facilities.

Social Exchange with the Police Administration and Other Criminal Justice Agents

Social exchange with the police administration exerts an even stronger influence on the arrest decision than social exchange with the community. The police administration, as personified by the police captain or chief, has an important impact on the decision to arrest, through control of duty assignments and promotions. Further, as Westley (1970) has observed, the chief of police's "control over the patrolmen arises from the fact that the disciplinary rules are so extensive and detailed that it is impossible for the patrolmen to abide by them," so that "the chief always has something he can pin on them" (p. 46). As a consequence of his superior power, the chief can set policy regarding how strictly certain types of laws will be enforced. He can, for example, keep officers out of gambling establishments and brothels and make them ease up on traffic violations. Alternatively, he may insist on strict enforcement of such laws. Although the chief's control over the officers' decisions is not absolute (he is not in a position to monitor all their behavior), his preferences greatly affect the style of policing in the community.

A detailed study of policing in eight communities by Wilson (1978) identified three general styles of policing, which are shaped by the community's and the police chief's expectations. Wilson labeled them the "watchman" style, the "legalistic" style, and the "service" style.

Watchman style of policing

The watchman style views the primary function of the police as maintaining order rather than law enforcement. Minor offenses are typically ignored, especially traffic and juvenile offenses and, to a lesser extent, vice offenses. Private disputes, such as assaults between friends or family members, are also ignored or, at most, treated informally. For minor violations, justice depends not only on what offense is committed but, in addition, on who the suspect is and the standards of the group with which the officer identifies the suspect. Thus, because juveniles are expected to misbehave, minor offenses committed by them are likely to be ignored or treated informally. Blacks are thought "to want, and to deserve, less law enforcement" (Wilson, 1978, p. 141) and are treated accordingly.

Although officers are expected to ignore the "little stuff," they are expected to "be tough" when a more serious offense is involved. Thus, arrests are likely to be made for serious crimes or when the public peace has been breached, as by offending current standards of propriety, creating a disturbance in a public facility, or endangering others.

Wilson notes that the reward structure in such departments gives officers little incentive for vigorous enforcement of the law. Watchman-style departments have a minimum number of special-duty squads, which means that there are few positions to which one can be promoted. The result is that there are few incentives for hard work. As one officer described it,

> "The motto is, 'don't rock the boat.' don't get the citizens upset, keep the taxes down, keep stories out of the newspapers, and keep things quiet. There's no reason and no incentive for writing a lot of traffic tickets. Nobody puts the pressure on you to write that kind of paper. The cops are low paid and they won't do it unless they are forced to do it and nobody forces them to do it" [Wilson, 1978, p. 149].

Legalistic style of policing

In contrast, the chief in legalistic-style departments induces officers to handle commonplace situations as if they were matters of law enforcement rather than order maintenance. Arrest is the preferred mode of dealing with minor offenses, rather than seeking informal solutions. Accordingly, departments that follow a legalistic style tend to issue many traffic tickets, to arrest a high proportion of juvenile offenders, and to make a large number of misdemeanor arrests even when public order has not been threatened. Officers act as if there were a single standard of community conduct rather than, as in the watchman style, different standards for juveniles, blacks, and drunks. That is, unlike officers in watchman-style departments, who define justice in terms of who the offender is, officers in legalistic departments define justice in terms of what the person has done. Hence, all offenders, regardless of who they are, are likely to be arrested.

Legalistic departments place a high value on the officer's productivity—whether it be the issuing of traffic tickets or the arrest of juveniles, drunks, or prostitutes. Unlike watchman-style departments, legalistic-style departments are organized into highly specialized divisions. The existence of these divisions provides officers with opportunities for promotion that act as an incentive for them to be productive—that is, to enforce the law vigorously.

Service style of policing

In service-style departments the emphasis is on providing services to the community. Consequently, a premium is placed on maintaining good community relations. Citizens in such communities expect the police to display the same qualities found in department-store sales personnel—courtesy, a neat appearance, a prompt response to requests for service, and a deferential demeanor. As a consequence, the police take seriously *all* requests for law enforcement and maintenance of order. In contrast to the watchman-style, no group's complaints are ignored. However, when the police in service-style departments intervene, they are less likely than in legalistic departments to do so by making an arrest. Although serious offenses are dealt with by arrest, minor offenses are more likely to be handled informally and by means of nonarrest alternatives (such as referral to family court). As one detective stated, "If we can possibly do it, we try to avoid an arrest. We don't want to send [juvenile suspects] into the courts. We try to handle it right here in the department. We bring the parents in here, and usually they're cooperative once we bring the situation to them" (Wilson, 1978, p. 210).

Service-style departments do, however, share several features with the two styles previously discussed. Officers in service-style departments are similar to those in watchman-style departments in that their definition of justice depends not only on what the suspect has allegedly done but also on who the suspect is. Thus, one officer told an interviewer that when dealing with traffic violations by doctors or members of the clergy, "we just like to warn [them] to slow down for their own good; they may be tired and in a hurry to get home from the hospital" (Wilson, 1978, p. 221). Service-style departments resemble legalistic-style departments in that both emphasize professional training and provide incentives for hard work by maintaining highly specialized divisions to which officers can be promoted.

Social exchange with court personnel

Wilson's identification of these three styles of policing calls attention to the joint role of the police chief and the local community in determining the police's decision to arrest a suspect rather than handling the matter in some other way. But the chief of police is not the only agent of the criminal justice system who can influence the decision to arrest a suspect. Social exchanges with other agents, such as the prosecutor and judge, may also influence this decision, although to a lesser extent.

Officers may decline to make an arrest because they expect that either the prosecutor or the judge will not support them and that the suspect will soon be back on the street. They may believe that the prosecutor will decide to drop the case for lack of sufficient evidence or that the judge will release the suspect either because the judge has a reputation for excessively lenient sentences in such cases or because the incriminating evidence was gathered illegally. Rather than waste their time making an arrest, officers will seek more profitable solutions, such as dealing with the situation informally or ignoring it.

Such "interference" by judicial officers often frustrates and angers the police. However, the fear that the judge will exclude the evidence because it resulted from an illegal search and seizure usually will not deter the police from arresting the suspect. Rewards in the form of approval from superiors and peers are usually sufficient to override any such costs. According to Skolnick (1975),

> The worst that can happen to the individual policeman for an illegal search is loss of a conviction as a result of the exclusionary rule. Superiors within the police organization will, however, be in sympathy with an officer, provided the search was administratively reasonable, even if the officer did not have legal "reasonable" cause to make an arrest [p. 223].[4]

Skolnick further observes that the police are wholly capable of "doctoring" the facts so as to meet the legal requirements of search and seizure. The same conclusion was reached by Oaks (1970), who studied the effects of the *Mapp* v. *Ohio* (1961) decision restricting the search and seizure practices of the police. Oaks found that in misdemeanor narcotics arrests in New York City after the *Mapp* decision, there was a dramatic increase in the number of instances in which police officers claimed to have seized the evidence because it was either dropped or thrown to the ground by the suspect. (The police can legally seize evidence that is "in plain view.") Oaks questioned the reason for the increase in such "dropsie" cases and concluded that officers were probably fabricating grounds of arrest in narcotics cases in order to legalize the seizure of evidence.

There are, of course, other ways for the police to legalize an arrest and thus avoid the cost of having the case dismissed by the judge. Because an arrest can be legally justified if the suspect resembles a wanted fugitive, one instructor in a police training school advised his students to always keep a 30-day accumulation of wanted-fugitive descriptions with them. The instructor explained that "an officer is a poor policeman if he cannot find a description to fit any suspect from the bulletins for thirty days" (LaFave, 1965, p. 146).

Social exchange with fellow officers

Although the decision to arrest can be influenced by those in positions of formal authority, much of this influence is usurped by informal influence exercised by fellow officers. This occurs because the police administration and the judiciary are not always able to monitor decision making by the police. Their monitoring capacity is limited to situa-

---

[4]From *Justice without Trial: Law Enforcement in Democratic Society* (2nd ed.), by Jerome Skolnick. Copyright © 1975 by John Wiley & Sons, Inc. This and all other quotations from this source are reprinted by permission.

tions that come to their attention—that is, those in which a suspect is placed under arrest. Only in such situations are they in a position to apply positive or negative sanctions to the arresting officer. Less visible to the authorities are decisions in which the police decide *not* to make an arrest (Goldstein, 1960). In these situations, the strongest influence is likely to be exerted by those physically present—the suspect, the complainant, and on some occasions, fellow officers.

In most occupations, the formal system of authority coexists with an informal social system complete with a set of norms and supporting sanctions. Numerous investigators have shown this to be true for the police profession (for example, Barker, 1977a, 1977b; Skolnick, 1975; Stoddard, 1968; Wilson, 1978). As in any profession, conformity to peer norms produces rewards for the individual, such as approval and respect, whereas noncomformity leads to such costs as disapproval and rejection by the group. The pressure to conform to peer norms is no more keenly felt than among police officers. Such commodities as approval and respect from peers are especially valued by the police because of their unique working conditions. Being in a position of authority and sensing danger about them, the police often feel isolated from the community (as do prison guards; see Chapter 8). This isolation draws them together and makes them highly dependent on one another for assistance and approval. Skolnick (1975) notes that because the police are entrusted with the job of enforcing public morality, as by telling a couple parked in a lovers' lane to do their lovemaking elsewhere, they become the target of citizens' hostility and resentment. The dangers of their work further isolate them from the public and increase their dependency on one another. According to Skolnick (1975),

> The policeman's responsibility for controlling dangerous and sometimes violent persons alienates the average citizen perhaps as much as does his authority over the average citizen. If the policeman's job is to insure that public order is maintained, the citizen's inclination is to shrink from the dangers of maintaining it. The citizen prefers to see the policeman as an automaton, because once the policeman's humanity is recognized, the citizen necessarily becomes implicated in the policeman's work, which is, after all, sometimes dirty and dangerous (p. 53–54).

Thus, the shared feeling of hostility from the community and the perception of danger isolate police officers from the citizenry and make them increasingly dependent on one another for rewards (Stotland & Berberich, 1979).

Although young officers are taught the rules and regulations and many of the technical aspects of police work at the police academy, most of the "real learning" occurs on the job under the direction of more experienced officers (Rubinstein, 1973). The rookie's first day on the beat usually produces what Niederhoffer (1967) calls "reality shock"—"the demoralizing realization of the vast discrepancy between idealistic expectations and sordid reality" (p. 49). The young officer quickly learns that "you can't go by the book." He or she also learns from senior officers the accepted ways, or norms, for handling different types of offenders. Above all, the police subculture requires that the officer show that he or she is in charge of the situation in confrontations with the public. The "police code" prohibits backing down. An officer who ignores challenges from citizens not only loses the respect of the citizenry but, more important, makes it more difficult for other officers to do their job. Rookie cops are needled by their more experienced colleagues when they ignore challenges or fail to assert their authority by making an arrest (Rubinstein, 1973). "Over and over again well-meaning old-timers reiterate, 'You gotta be tough, kid, or you'll never last' " (Niederhoffer, 1967, p. 53). In short, the young officer learns from more experienced peers when to ignore an offense, when to handle it informally, and when to make an arrest. An officer who brings too few cases into the station house is likely to be considered a "shirker," while one who brings in too many trivial cases is likely to be viewed as incompetent.

In some instances, peer norms support ignoring certain offenses in return for certain favors, as when an officer accepts a $5 bill for not issuing a traffic ticket. Documentation of such peer norms, which are in clear violation of the law, has been provided by Barker (1977a, 1977b) and by Stoddard (1968). One of the best-known instances of peer pressure to conform with illegal norms concerns a former New York City detective named Serpico. He was ostracized and finally "set up" by his fellow officers for failing to go along with the norm of accepting bribes from drug dealers in exchange for not arresting them. According to Stoddard's findings, to be accepted in the department, recruits had to accept the illegal practices of fellow officers. Negative social sanctions were applied against "goofs" who insisted on adhering to the official police ethic. The pressure to comply with peer norms is captured in Stoddard's interview of a former police officer. The officer was asked what he would do if he caught Sam, a restaurant owner who gave police officers free meals, committing an offense. The officer responded:

> "If I had run across Sam doing anything short of murder, I think I would have treaded very lightly. Even if I hadn't accepted his free meals. Say I had turned [the meals] down; still, if I stopped this man for a minor traffic violation, say I caught him dead to rights, I'd be very reluctant to write this man a ticket because I'd suffer the wrath of the other men on the force. I'd be goofing up their meal ticket. . . . I'd have been more ashamed, and I'd have kept it quiet if I'd stopped such a man as this, because I'd have felt like some kind of an oddball. I would have been bucking the tide, I'd been out of step" [Stoddard, 1968, pp. 208–209].

The above account also suggests that adherence to peer norms is mediated by attributional considerations. An officer is less likely to attribute blame to himself or herself for allowing an offender to go free when all the other officers in the department are doing the same thing. The knowledge that others are acting in the same way provides the officer with consensus information, which will probably induce him or her to make an external attribution for his or her activities. Alternatively, self-attributions are more likely to be made when the officer finds that his or her behavior differs from the group's. As the officer in the interview stated, by going against his fellow officers, he would have made a derogatory self-attribution—namely, that he was an "oddball." Thus, the combined weight of social-exchange and attributional considerations makes officers highly susceptible to peer-group influence.

In this section we have shown that the police's decision to arrest a suspect depends on the net balance of rewards expected from a variety of sources: the suspect, the complainant or victim, the community, the police administration and agents of the criminal justice system, and fellow officers. Only by considering the benefits and costs controlled by each of these parties can a full understanding of decision making by the police be achieved.

SUMMARY

In this chapter the attribution/exchange framework has been used to examine the factors that influence the police's decision to arrest a suspected offender. We have seen that for an arrest to be made, the police first must become aware of a suspicious event and identify a suspect. The actual arrest decision depends on two preliminary decisions. First, the police must decide what type of attribution to make about the suspect. That is, does the suspect have a criminal disposition, and if so, how strong is it? The attributions are made on the basis of characteristics of the offense and the actor and the suspect's demeanor when confronting the police.

Having decided what attributions to make about the suspect, the police weigh the benefits and costs associated with each of the following response options: (1) taking official action, such as issuing a summons or making an arrest, (2) handling the matter informally, and (3) ignoring the offense. The option chosen is a function of social-exchange considerations involving the suspect, the complainant or victim, the community, the police administration and other agents of the criminal justice system, and fellow officers.

CHAPTER FOUR

Pretrial Proceedings

Following arrest, suspects are usually taken to the local police station, or precinct house, where they are "booked." The booking process consists in making an official record of suspects' identity and involves, among other things, fingerprinting and photographing them. They are then thoroughly searched, and a record is made of any personal belongings taken from them. Before being sent to a cell to await their initial appearance before a magistrate, suspects are given an opportunity to notify one person of their detention. While awaiting the initial appearance, suspects may be taken from their cells and interrogated. Suspects, of course, have the right to remain silent or to postpone answering questions until their attorney arrives. After interrogation suspects may be released or returned to their cells to await the initial appearance. At this point the scene shifts to the pretrial stage, where the focus of attention is on the prosecuting and defense attorneys and the judge. In this chapter the attribution/exchange perspective is applied to pretrial decisions involving the setting of the bail, the filing of charges, and the plea-bargaining process.

From the time the suspect is taken to a jail cell to await an initial hearing until sentencing, the agent in the criminal justice system with the most responsibility for dealing with the accused is the prosecutor. The prosecutor—or an assistant in large cities—must (1) recommend an amount of bail to the judge to ensure that the suspect appears for trial, (2) decide whether to press charges against the suspect, and (3) decide how he or she will negotiate with the defendant and the defense counsel regarding a guilty plea in exchange for a reduction in charges or recommendation for a lenient sentence. Before examining these three prosecutorial decisions, we will briefly look at the role of the prosecutor and the social-exchange relationships that exist between the prosecutor's office and other individuals and groups. We will then look at each of the three decisions in terms of our attribution/exchange framework.

THE PROSECUTOR'S OFFICE

Under early English law, a person who suffered because of a crime could bring the wrongdoing to the attention of the authorities, who would submit the matter to God's judgment by requiring the defendant to undergo one of the ordeals (see Chapter 5). With the development of the common law in the 12th and 13th centuries, an alternative method was created. Presentment juries, presided over by the king's justices, would both give and hear evidence of alleged crimes. If a jury returned a "true bill," the accused was taken to trial on an indictment (Harding, 1966). Later, English law allowed the government to arrest offenders and bring them to trial on the "information" of private persons without obtaining an indictment from the grand jury. Eventually, each county had professional informers who would bring prosecutions to the court. The use of the information rather than a grand-jury indictment allowed the king, through his attorney in the appropriate court, to prosecute a wrongdoer directly (Harding, 1966). The position of public prosecutor in the United States is derived from these English roots as well as from the Dutch influence in New York (Reiss, 1975). By 1785, all states had established the offices of public prosecutor (McDonald, 1979).

Today, in almost all jurisdictions in the United States the prosecutor must be a lawyer (Nedrud, 1960), and the prosecutor is an elected official in all but five states (Jacoby, 1979). Most prosecutors are in the beginning or middle of their careers and are hoping for a higher political office or a more lucrative law practice in the future (Newman, 1974). In many smaller towns and counties, the prosecutor works only part-time. In larger cities the prosecutor's office consists of an elected district attorney, two or three deputy district attorneys, and many assistant district attorneys. In these large offices specialization often exists, either by duties or by type of crime. In some offices, certain assistants will be in charge of bringing charges, while others will do only trial work. In other offices, some assistants will specialize in certain kinds of crimes. For instance, some assistants might specialize in property crimes, others in drug crimes, and still others in white-collar crimes.

Because of the interdependence of agents in the criminal justice system and because prosecutors often have an eye toward political office or private practice, prosecutors are involved in a number of social-exchange relationships. Prosecutors are dependent on the police for the kinds of cases they receive and the quality of evidence they are able to use to prosecute these cases. In turn, the police depend on prosecutors to accept the cases and evidence that the police offer. If prosecutors reject too many cases, the morale, discipline, and workload of the police are affected (Cole, 1970).

Assistant prosecutors often develop close personal and professional relationships with the trial judges (Felkenes, 1973). There are two major reasons. First, the continuing daily contact between the two often leads to an understanding of the legal and administrative problems of processing routine cases. Second, because many criminal-court judges began their careers as assistant prosecutors, the judges are inclined to help inexperienced prosecutors. Because of the close working relationship between the judge and the assistant prosecutor, a number of types of social exchanges occur between the two. For example, if an assistant prosecutor expects that a judge will probably dismiss a case because the police used improper, although not illegal, methods or because the complainant in an assault case does not want to testify against the defendant, the prosecutor may decide not to bring charges against the accused (Felkenes, 1973). In addition, the assistant's expectations of the judge's probable decision regarding conviction in nonjury trials will affect the decision to charge, and his or her expectations of the probable sentencing decision will affect his or her decision to plea-bargain (Cole, 1970).

The prosecutor's staff also has social-exchange relationships with the defense attorneys in the community. Because most cases are processed by plea-bargaining, it is important that the defense and prosecuting attorneys have a good working relationship so that they will be able to discharge their responsibilities efficiently. The social-exchange relationship between the defense attorney and the assistant prosecutor will be discussed more fully later in the chapter.

The community is the final group that has an effect on the prosecutor's office. Citizens might want a crackdown on certain types of crimes (for example, drug crimes) and a lenient policy on other types (for example, gambling). Because the prosecutor is almost always an elected official, he or she must be aware of the wishes of the political leaders in his party. Finally, the prosecutor must be cognizant of the interests of business leaders in the community, who are also campaign contributors.

The prosecutor acts in four sometimes conflicting roles: administrator, advocate, judge, and legislator (Alschuler, 1968). As an administrator the prosecutor's task is to dispose of as many cases as quickly and efficiently as possible. Because the backlog of cases may be large (for example, the backlog in Chicago in 1968 was 2500 cases), the prosecutor has a strong interest in not increasing and trying to decrease the backlog. The major administrative factor in the decision on how to handle a particular case is the probable amount of time the case would require if it went to trial. As an advocate, the prosecutor's goals are to have a high proportion of convictions and to have severe sentences imposed for those convictions. As a judge, the prosecutor seeks to do the "right thing" for the defendant in light of his or her situation, with the proviso that the "right thing" will be done only if the defendant pleads guilty. As a legislator, the prosecutor may, if he or she decides a law is too harsh, grant concessions to all defendants accused of violating that law. Conflicts in these roles occur if the prosecutor must sacrifice the number of convictions and the severity of punishments in order to reduce the backlog of cases or to be fair to the defendant.

BAIL DECISION MAKING

Within a "reasonable time" after being arrested, a suspect must be taken before a magistrate, who is generally a judge of a court of limited jurisdiction, for a proceeding that is usually called the "initial appearance." For minor offenses, such as traffic violations, the magistrate may have authority to try the case, accept a plea of guilty, and levy a fine (Newman, 1974). For most misdemeanors and all felonies the magistrate's jurisdiction is limited to (1) reviewing the evidence against the accused to ensure that there is probable cause to suspect that the accused committed the crime and (2) determining whether the accused should be released from jail or maintained in custody while he or she awaits further judicial proceedings. Because probable cause almost always exists at this stage, the magistrate's major responsibility is to determine whether to release the accused while he or she awaits trial. This determination is usually called the "bail-setting decision," although bail is only one of several means by which the accused may be released. Retaining the accused in custody serves three functions. First, it ensures that the defendant will be at the trial. Second, it guarantees that he or she will not commit more crimes before trial. Third, this custody placates the public by jailing and thus punishing a suspected offender. This third consideration is particularly important when heinous crimes are involved.

According to medieval English law, a person accused of violating the law was allowed to be released from custody if a member of the community would vouch that the accused would be present at the trial. Originally, if the accused did not appear at the trial, the person who had guaranteed the accused's appearance would stand trial in place of the accused. Later, it became the practice for the person guaranteeing the accused's appearance, the "bailor," to forfeit money if the accused did not show up for trial (Vera Institute of Justice, 1972).

Types of Bail

Today, conventional bail is the setting free of persons arrested or imprisoned in exchange for (1) their promise that they will appear in court at a certain day and time and (2) an amount of money that will be forfeited to the court if they do not appear at the specified time. The type of bail often used for minor crimes such as drunken driving, domestic nonsupport, and disorderly conduct is called "cash bond." If released by cash bond, the defendant deposits with the court the entire amount of bail that was set. If he or she appears as required, the cash will be returned; if not, it will be forfeited. A second, and much more common, type of conventional bail is often called "bondsman release." Under this form of bail the defendant pays a fee to a professional bondsman, about 10% to 30% of the bond amount (often with collateral for the remainder), in exchange for the bondsman's acting as a guarantor for the entire bond amount (Clarke, Freeman, & Koch, 1976). That is, if the accused fails to appear, the bondsman is required to pay the full amount of the bond to the court. Naturally, the bondsman's desire not to forfeit the bail often results in his maintaining some type of surveillance over those for whom he has posted bail, particularly those whom he considers to be risks. A third type of bail being used in a few jurisdictions is something of a compromise between the first two. The accused must still pay cash to the court, but instead of paying the full amount, he or she pays only a percentage (often 10%) of the amount. If the accused appears, the payment is returned. In effect, the court is acting as a bondsman for the accused.

All three of these forms of bail use the loss of money resulting from bail forfeiture as a means of encouraging defendants to appear at trial. The main considerations involved in these forms of bail are the severity of the crime and the accused's criminal record. The assumption is that the more severe the crime and the longer the criminal record, the more a defendant will desire to escape punishment and, therefore, the less likely he or she will be to appear at the required time (Clarke, Freeman, & Koch, 1976).

In addition to these forms of bail, which require the accused to post at least some money as a surety for his or her appearance, there are two other types of pretrial release that do not require the posting of money. The first involves an "unsecured appearance bond." Defendants promise to pay a certain amount of money if they do not appear when required, but they do not have to deposit money or pledge property to guarantee their appearance. The second type of unsecured release is called "release on own recognizance." After an investigation of their background, defendants merely sign a promise to appear, but no financial penalty is involved if they do not show up. When these two forms of pretrial release are used, additional information about the defendant's "local ties" is also examined. Local ties are aspects of the defendant's life that link him or her to the local community, thus lowering the probability that he or she will flee if released before trial. These ties include the following: (1) the accused lives in the local area, (2) the accused is employed, and (3) responsible persons, including friends and relatives, can vouch for his or her reliability, reputation, character, and mental condition.

The emphasis on local ties in addition to the severity of the crime and the prior record is largely a result of the Vera Foundation's Manhattan Bail Project (Vera Institute of Justice, 1972). Earlier studies of bail practices had shown that judges almost always required bail bonds, that bail was usually set according to the crime committed rather than the person involved, and that when everything else was held constant, pre-trial detention was strongly related to both subsequent conviction and severity of sentence (Goldfarb, 1965). By providing the judge with more information about the accused and by using a point system (which included as factors prior record, family ties to the area, employment and schooling, and length of residence in the area), the Manhattan Bail Project found that many persons who previously would have been held in custody awaiting trial could be released safely on their promise to appear in court at the trial date. The most significant result, however, concerned the trial outcomes of the persons who were released before trial. Sixty percent of these persons were acquitted or had their cases dismissed during the first year, while only 23% of a control group of similar persons who were not released had similar outcomes. Additionally, only 16% of those released pending trial who were convicted were sentenced to prison, while 96% of the control group who were convicted were given prison sentences (Vera Institute of Justice, 1972). Clearly, then, the decision to release a defendant before trial can have important consequences at later stages of the criminal justice system.

Factors Affecting the Bail Decision

All jurisdictions grant the right of access to reasonable bail for most offenses, although there are a few capital offenses for which bail is not available. The only real limitation on the bail setting is the Eighth Amendment to the Constitution, which prohibits "excessive" bail. Aside from this proscription, the judge has a great deal of discretion in the bail-setting decision. The amount of guidance judges are given by statutes, rules of criminal procedure, and court rules varies from state to state (Goldkamp & Gottfredson, 1979). Ten states provide no criteria at all for the bail decision; two states list 16 factors to be considered. Both extremes—that is, the absence of guidelines and guidelines that list many factors—reflect ambiguity with regard to the function of bail. Furthermore, neither extreme provides much guidance to the judge. The factors used most often in bail-decision-making guidelines are the nature of the present charge (35 states), the defendant's prior criminal record (31 states), and the defendant's financial resources (29 states). Even though the judge may consider many factors in his or her determination of bail, research seems to show that the actual bail decision can be predicted from just a few factors.

Local ties

The most relevant studies on local ties were conducted in San Diego with court judges making decisions on both simulated and actual cases (Ebbesen & Konečni, 1975). Using simulated cases that manipulated the defendant's prior record, the defendant's local ties, the defense attorney's recommendation for bail, and the district attorney's bail recommendation, it was found that the judges set higher bail when the defendant had weak rather than strong ties to the community, when the defendant had a prior record, and when the district attorney recommended a higher bail amount. The factor that was most strongly related to the judges' decision was the presence or absence of local ties. As the authors noted, these results suggest that (1) the judges considered local ties the most important factor in the bail-setting decision, as the Manhattan Bail Project would suggest is an appropriate strategy, and (2) defendants with weak ties were required to post more bail than defendants with strong ties, which again is a reasonable decision-making scheme.

District attorney's recommendation

Although the local-ties variable was extremely important when judges made bail-setting decisions on simulated cases, in actual bail-setting decisions this variable did not prove to be important at all. Judges seemed to base their decisions primarily on the district attorney's recommendations and secondarily on the defense attorney's recommendations. Neither the defendants' prior record nor their local ties added any predictive ability once the other factors were taken into account. When homicide cases were ignored, the severity of the crime had a small influence on judges' decisions. Homicide cases were eliminated from the analysis because high bail was usually set for accused murderers regardless of prior record or local ties.

Judges' primary reliance on the recommendations of the district attorney emphasizes the importance of social-exchange relationships in the bail-decision process. By relying on the district attorney's recommendation, judges are acknowledging the district attorney's greater knowledge of the case and the defendant. A second reason that judges rely on the district attorney's advice is to divide the blame if the accused does not appear at trial. Often, the prosecutor will recommend a high bail setting with the expectation that the judge will reduce the amount. If the judge does reduce the amount and the accused does not appear in court, the blame must be on the judge rather than the prosecutor (Cole, 1970). The more closely the judge follows the district attorney's recommendation, the less the judge can be blamed for the defendant's failure to show.

Community sentiment

In addition to the recommendations of the prosecutor, judges must also consider community sentiment when they set bail. The amount of community controversy that can arise from a judge's bail-setting decision is evident from a New York case concerning whether Bruce Wright, a criminal-court judge, acted wisely in releasing on his own recognizance a defendant who had been charged with slashing a decoy police officer on the neck ("Many Queries . . . ," 1979). The mayor of the city and the Patrolmen's Benevolent Association, who called the judge "Turn 'Em Loose Bruce," attacked the judge's decision. In contrast, 21 black and civil liberties groups defended the judge's decision and suggested that he be called "Treat 'Em Right Wright."

The public is not aware of most bail decisions and therefore has no adverse reaction to them. However, when a case is made public and negative reactions follow, community pressure is likely to lead the judge to increase the amount of money required for bail or to refuse to release the suspect at all. For example, in Pittsburgh a magistrate who released on $5000 bail an accused robber charged with shooting a police officer was removed from the position of setting bail when the incident was made public. Later, bail was raised to $50,000 (Donalson, 1977). In New York, when a pretrial-services agency recommended that the accused murderer "Son of Sam" be released without bail because of his community ties, the mayor of New York City said: "Obviously no judge would accept such a recommendation in the 'Son of Sam' case, but it does make us wonder whether judges, confronted with busy court calendars, are accepting recommendations that could permit dangerous criminals to walk the streets on little or no bail" ("Probation Report Urged Freedom for Berkowitz," 1977). In the face of such community pressure, the judge did not release the accused murderer, and two days later the agency decided to stop making bail recommendations in murder cases ("Agency Stops Court Advice . . . ," 1977).

Severity of the crime

Given that judges tend to rely on the recommendations of the two attorneys, particularly the district attorney, the question is what factors these attorneys consider when they decide how much bail to recommend. Again excluding homicides because accused murderers seemed to be treated uniformly regardless of other factors, in the San Diego study the only variable that affected both district attorneys' and defense attorneys' recommendations was the severity of the crime (Ebbesen & Konečni, 1975). A simple attribution interpretation can explain attorneys' reliance on crime severity in their bail recommendations. Presumably, the more severe the crime, the more "criminal" must be the disposition necessary to commit that crime. That is, given the inhibiting causes against committing a crime (for example, moral strictures, fear of punishment) and the fact that these inhibiting causes increase with crime severity, one can conclude that the criminal disposition was of great strength. Furthermore, because a severe criminal act is very low in social desirability, attributing a criminal disposition to the offender is likely.

The major consequence of the attribution of criminality is that the inferred disposition is likely to be used as a basis for other dealings with the accused. Thus, persons to whom a criminal disposition is attributed will probably be mistrusted. If they are not trusted, then they are not likely to be released on bail before trial, because they cannot be trusted to return for the trial. In summary, the chain would appear as follows: (1) the more severe the crime, (2) the more criminal the accused is perceived, (3) the less likely he or she is to be trusted, and, therefore, (4) the less likely he or she is to be released from jail. Although this causal sequence probably reflects actual processes, the underlying incorrect assumption is that the accused is guilty. At this stage he or she is still *legally* presumed to be innocent. However, the attributions of actors at this stage of the criminal justice system belie that presumption.

In addition to the district and defense attorneys' reliance on crime severity as a basis for their bail recommendations, the San Diego study also found that district attorneys used a combination of crime severity and local ties in their decisions (Ebbesen & Konečni, 1975). Interestingly, district attorneys tended to recommend higher bail when local ties were strong or moderate than when the ties were weak. The authors explained this seemingly strange decision scheme by assuming that district attorneys relied on the information that would be relevant to a high bail recommendation. Thus, district attorneys would recommend high bail if they (1) focused solely on crime severity and ignored community ties, if those ties were strong or moderate, or (2) considered community ties, if those ties were weak, and relied less on crime severity.

In another study, which examined over 8300 bail decisions in Philadelphia, Goldkamp and Gottfredson (1979) found that the decisions to release on own recognizance and to detain without bail were influenced primarily by the seriousness of the offense charged. For the remaining cases, in which the setting of cash bail was needed, the existence of any weapons charges was an important determinant of the amount of bail set. Neither community ties nor demographic variables (race, sex, age) were significantly related to any of the three decisions (but see Nagel, 1981). In spite of including a number of factors in their analysis, Goldkamp and Gottfredson were able to explain only a moderate proportion of the variance in the decisions, suggesting that there is a large amount of inconsistency among decisions.

A study in North Carolina examining actual appearance rates at trial suggests that severity of offense, which both district attorneys and defense attorneys relied on heavily in San Diego, may not be very important (Clarke, Freeman & Koch, 1976; see Kirby, 1977). Of course, because defendants accused of more severe crimes were required to post higher bail amounts, it may be that the threat of bail forfeiture made these defendants perform as well as defendants accused of less severe crimes. Clarke et al. also found that sex, age, race, income, and employment status had little relation to whether the accused appeared at trial. The factors found important were the amount of time between release and trial, the defendant's criminal history, and the type of release he or she received. The longer the time between release and trial, the less likely the defendant was to appear at trial, particularly if he or she had two or more prior arrests. With regard to type of release, those defendants who received supervision during the release period had the highest rate of appearance, followed by those who were released on their own recognizance. Both groups generally had a better appearance rate than defendants who posted a cash bond or were released by a bondsman posting bail, even adjusting for prior arrests and amount of time between release and trial.

Once the judge makes a bail decision, the accused will, if he or she can, post the required amount of money. If the accused is released on his or her own recognizance, no bail needs to be posted. In some jurisdictions, the accused who is released without posting bail is required to report regularly to an officer who supervises his or her behavior during the pretrial release period. If the accused cannot post the bail set or if bail was denied, he or she will remain in jail until the trial date.

After the bail-setting decision, the prosecutor's next responsibility in the case is to charge the accused officially with a crime, a decision in which he or she has a great deal of discretion.

THE DECISION TO CHARGE

The prosecutor's most important responsibility is the charging decision. He or she must decide whether to file charges against the accused and if so, the nature and number of these charges.

Prosecutorial Discretion

For a number of reasons the prosecutor has a great deal of discretion in the charging decision (*Southern California Law Review*, 1969). First, many legislatures enact new penal statutes without revising earlier laws. Hence penal codes may be overlapping, somewhat inconsistent, and even archaic. These problems may allow a prosecutor to search the laws until he or she finds a statute that a given defendant has violated. A second reason that prosecutors have charging discretion is intentional legislative overgeneralization. For some kinds of crime the legislature intentionally outlaws all forms of the behavior in order to eliminate loopholes that the real targets of the law might use to escape prosecution. For example, in most states all forms of gambling, including small-stakes poker games, are made illegal, so that the law includes both persons in the numbers rackets and bookmakers. A third reason prosecutorial discretion exists is that some criminal laws were designed to serve social purposes rather than to prevent crime. In bad-check cases in which insufficient funds are involved and in nonsupport cases, the threat of prosecution is often used as a means of forcing payment of the debt. Fourth, some laws are written more to satisfy a sense of community decency than with the expectation that they will be enforced. Examples of laws that unrealistically prescribe moral behavior are the criminal statutes against fornication, homosexuality, and adultery. The final, and most important, reason for prosecutorial discretion is that all statutes are general mandates. How these general principles are applied to particular situations must be at the discretion of some criminal justice agency. In the United States, the prosecutor has most of this responsibility.

The prosecutor's need for discretion in the charging decision has been explicitly recognized by the American Bar Association in its *Standards for Criminal Justice* (1980a). According to these standards, "the public interest is best served and even-handed justice best dispensed not by a mechanical application of the 'letter of the law' but by a flexible and individualized application of its norms through the exercise of a prosecutor's thoughtful discretion" (p. 3–56). Among the factors that the prosecutor may consider in the exercise of his or her discretion are the following (p. 3–54):

   (i) the prosecutor's reasonable doubt that the accused is in fact guilty;
  (ii) the extent of the harm caused by the offense;
 (iii) the disproportion of the authorized punishment in relation to the particular offense or the offender;
 (iv) possible improper motives of a complainant;
  (v) reluctance of the victim to testify;
 (vi) cooperation of the accused in the apprehension or conviction of others; and
(viii) availability and likelihood of prosecution by another jurisdiction.[1]

The Grand Jury

In many jurisdictions the prosecutor is required to obtain an indictment from a grand jury in all felony cases. The prosecutor presents evidence to the grand jury regarding the crime in question. In proceedings that are kept secret, the grand jury hears this testimony and decides whether a "true bill" should be issued. A true bill, as in old English law, is a formal indictment that lists the specific criminal charges against the defendant (Newman, 1974).

The grand jury is usually composed of 16 citizens (in contrast to the trial jury or "petit" jury, which has 12 or fewer) and meets for a specified amount of time, often a term of court (Bopp & Schultz, 1972). Originally, the grand jury was designed to act as a shield against indiscriminate prosecution by the government. Today, however, it almost always follows the recommendation of the prosecutor, and for all practical purposes, it no longer serves as a constraint on the prosecutor's discretion (Felkenes, 1973).

Although the grand jury almost always follows the prosecutor's recommendations, one function it does serve is to shield the prosecutor from adverse public reaction in difficult cases (Felkenes, 1973). For example, a prosecutor who is reluctant to charge an influential politi-

---

[1]From *American Bar Association Standards for Criminal Justice*, Volume I, Chapter 3. Copyright 1980 by Little, Brown and Company. Reprinted by permission.

cian or businessperson may rely on the grand jury to perform the unpleasant task of indicting the person. Or, in doubtful cases in which the prosecutor's decision not to prosecute would probably result in adverse public reaction because of the heinous nature of the crime, a decision by the grand jury to prosecute allows the prosecutor to escape both public censure for not prosecuting and professional censure for prosecuting a doubtful case. Likewise, grand juries can refuse to indict in cases in which the evidence is clear. In such cases, the prosecutor can point to the grand jury as the reason the offender was not prosecuted. Such a case occurred in Honey Grove, Texas. There the grand jury refused to indict a woman who had killed her husband after he had started beating her and their 13 children ("Jurors Refuse to Indict . . . ," 1980).

The Information

In some jurisdictions the prosecutor can file felony charges without going to the grand jury. Under this alternative procedure, the prosecutor drafts the formal charge in an "information." The legal sufficiency of the information is tested before a judge at a preliminary hearing. Although the defendant can waive this hearing, generally defendants who plan to go to trial do not waive it. Because the prosecutor must present enough evidence to convince the judge that probable cause exists to believe that the accused actually committed the crime, the defense can use the preliminary hearing to discover the nature and strength of the prosecution's case. The defense can also use the hearing to cross-examine prosecution witnesses and sometimes to persuade them not to testify. In almost all cases, the judge will find that probable cause does exist and will bind the case over for trial (Newman, 1974).

The prosecutor's charging decision is influenced by the attributions the prosecutor makes about the suspect and the social-exchange relationships the prosecutor has with the victim, witnesses, the offender, and other agents in the criminal justice system, as summarized in Figure 4–1. Our discussion of the charging decision will examine the attributional considerations first and then the prosecutor's social-exchange relationships.

Attributional Considerations

The most important consideration in the prosecutor's decision to charge is his or her belief that the accused is guilty of the crime (Kaplan, 1965; Worgan & Paulsen, 1961). If the prosecutor does not believe the accused committed the crime, then to charge the accused is usually considered an abuse of discretion. Although prosecutors might determine that the accused is guilty on the basis of information that would not be admissible at trial, such as hearsay or illegally seized materials, the important consideration is not how they determine the accused is guilty but that they do make this determination before they charge the suspect with a crime.

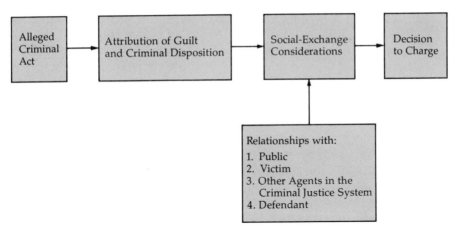

Figure 4-1. Attribution/exchange model of the prosecutor's decision to charge

Clearly, then, prosecutors must attribute a criminal disposition to the accused before they invoke their powers as agents of the criminal justice system. If the evidence against the accused is overwhelming, making this attribution is not difficult. However, if the incriminating facts are less certain, prosecutors must rely on other information to decide that the accused is guilty and therefore has a criminal disposition. One study asked deputies in the Los Angeles County district attorney's office whether they placed great weight, some weight, little weight, or no weight on each of eight factors when deciding to file charges: occupation, prior record, race, dependents, age, intelligence, sex, and residence (*Southern California Law Review*, 1969). Most of these factors were not considered important by these deputy district attorneys. This was particularly true of race; all said they placed no weight on race in their charging decision, although social desirability may have affected their answer. Prior convictions were given great weight by about 27% of the deputies and given some weight by almost 47%. Taking notice of a prior record would seem to violate the presumption of innocence, because a person found guilty of a crime in the past is not necessarily guilty of the present crime. Nevertheless, prosecutors seem to use a prior criminal record as evidence of a stable criminal disposition. Hence, if they are in doubt regarding the accused's guilt, they will probably be more inclined to file charges if the accused has a criminal record.

Almost half the deputy district attorneys in Los Angeles gave at least some weight to the occupation of the accused. For property crimes, a suspect who does not have a job might be seen as being more likely to be guilty than a suspect who does, since the former is more likely to need money than the latter. The type of occupation might also be important. The more money people make, the less likely they probably will be to commit a crime involving property.

Although a belief that the accused is guilty is a prerequisite for a decision to charge, even if the prosecutors are convinced that the accused is guilty, they may not file charges at all, they may file fewer charges than they could, or they may file charges of a less severe crime. The factors affecting the charging decision, given a belief that the accused is guilty, are subsumed in the many social-exchange relationships the prosecutor has.

Social-Exchange Considerations

Prosecutors have limited resources in terms of staff and money and cannot possibly prosecute every offense brought to their attention (LaFave, 1970). Therefore, they must allocate their resources so as to maximize their rewards. These rewards are a high rate of convictions for crimes that the public wants punished. Generally, the community desires that severe crimes be punished more than less severe crimes. In addition to their social-exchange relationships with the public, prosecutors have social-exchange relationships with the victim of the crime, with other agents of the criminal justice system, and with the offender.

Obtaining a conviction to satisfy the public and the prosecutor

An important consideration in the charging decision is the likelihood, given the habits of judges and juries in the jurisdiction, that the case will result in a conviction (Kaplan, 1965). A high conviction rate is important for several reasons. First, most prosecutors are elected, and a high rate of convictions establishes a record that the prosecutor's office is doing a good job. Prosecutors are therefore likely to try to achieve a high conviction rate so that they will be reelected. A low conviction rate brings public disfavor. For example, in one federal district attorney's office a high rate of acquittals was perceived by the press, judges, and defense bar as resulting from either staff incompetence or overzealous prosecution (Kaplan, 1965). A second reason assistants want a high conviction rate is for their advancement within the office. Because prosecutors are concerned with a high conviction rate, they are also likely to reward those working for them who provide what they want. These rewards are in the form of both salary increases and increased status and respect from coworkers. Third, a high conviction rate encourages guilty pleas (Kaplan, 1965). The more likely it is that defendants will be convicted for a certain crime, the more they will want to plead guilty to a less severe crime. A recent study of plea bargaining in the District of Columbia found, using a statistical model, that 16% of those who pleaded guilty after arrests for robbery, 34% of those who pleaded guilty after arrests for assault, 31% of those who pleaded guilty after arrests for larceny, and 32% of those who pleaded guilty after arrests for burglary would not have been convicted if they had gone to trial (Rhodes, 1978). Clearly, the fear of conviction can induce guilty pleas. Because a high rate of convictions is so important, prosecutors are likely to charge defendants only when they are reasonably certain that a conviction will result.

Because the charging decision is so important, one would expect that experienced prosecutors would perform this function. In most jurisdictions, however, inexperienced attorneys are assigned to decide which cases should be prosecuted, because it is believed that their inexperience will cause fewer problems in that role than in open court. And because the task does not have the excitement of trial work, it is usually given to those with the least seniority. The resulting problem is that the prosecution staff must often invest time and effort in cases for which prosecution is not warranted. Having experienced attorneys make the charging decision is thought to produce a more effective prosecution office (National District Attorneys Association, 1973) and is becoming a more common practice (for example, Merola, 1980).

Consistent with the importance attached to obtaining convictions, a prosecutor is likely to consider several factors before filing charges. These factors are almost always related to the strength of the evidence in the case, since the strength of the evidence is highly related to the prosecutor's willingness to pursue a case (Forst & Brosi, 1977). In a national survey of 150 prosecutor agencies (Law Enforcement Assistance Administration, 1977c), the following factors, most of which pertain to the strength of the evidence in the case, were cited most frequently in the decision to file charges for forcible rape: use of physical force (82%), proof of penetration (78%), promptness of reporting (71%), extent of the identification of the suspect (67%), injury to the victim (63%), circumstances of the initial contact between the victim and the suspect (61%), relationship of the victim and accused (61%), use of a weapon (58%), and resistance offered by the victim (54%). There was very high agreement between prosecutors' ranking of factors for their charging decision and their ranking of factors for obtaining a conviction of forcible rape. In addition, it should be noted that seven of the nine factors listed above were cited frequently by the police in their decision to investigate an alleged rape (see Chapter 3).

One of the factors prosecutors consider in their charging decision is the credibility of the witness, from which they try to predict the judge's and jury's likely reactions to the witness. Generally, a "bad" witness lowers the probability of a successful conviction. In a study of how prosecutors reacted to female victims, Stanko (1980) found that prosecutors were likely to reduce the charges if the victim could be seen as having brought on her own victimization (for example, the robbery of a prostitute) or if she knew the perpetrator (for example, if they had a common-law relationship). In the latter case, the crime would have to be understood in the context of the interaction, and hence the woman could be seen as being partly to blame. The ideal victim for the prosecutors, a "stand-up witness," was one who was "calm, articulate, consistent in her testimony, of neat appearance and credible" (p. 7). The same factors are probably used to assess the credibility of male victims.

There is some evidence that the race of the victim affects how credible he or she is perceived as being. Miller (1970) found from interviewing prosecutors that when the victim of an assault was black, the assailant was less likely to be prosecuted than if the victim was white. The reason was probably that black victims were more reluctant than white victims to testify in court. In a more recent and more sophisticated study, Myers and Hagan (1979) examined prosecutors' files in a sample of about 1000 felony cases in Indianapolis, Indiana. Results showed that cases were more likely to be prosecuted fully if the victim was willing to prosecute the case fully and, holding the amount of evidence constant, if the victim was white, regardless of the race of the defendant. According to Myers and Hagan, this latter finding suggests that "prosecutors may consider white victims more credible than black victims or their troubles more worthy of full prosecution" (p. 447).

Social exchange with the victim

In addition to the wishes of the public and the prosecutor, assistant prosecutors also consider the victim's desires when they are deciding whether to charge the accused. If the victim prefers that the offender not be prosecuted, frequently the assistant prosecutor will follow those wishes. The victim's desires are given weight in the charging decision for two reasons. First, especially in domestic assault cases, the victim's lack of interest in prosecution is evidence that the victim has forgiven the offender and does not place importance on the incident (Miller, 1970). Second, victims who are reluctant to testify at trial often make very bad witnesses because they are not likely to cooperate with the prosecutor. This lack of cooperation makes the prosecutor's task more difficult, lowering the probability that a conviction will result.

Social exchange with other agents of the criminal justice system

Social-exchange relationships between the prosecutor's office and other agencies of the criminal justice system also affect the decision to prosecute. One way the prosecutor can help the police and other prosecutors is to grant immunity to an offender in exchange for the offender's cooperation, which often consists in providing information about or testifying against other suspects and codefendants (Miller, 1970). Often, immunity from prosecution is granted to lower-level offenders so that they will testify against the "higher-ups" in a large operation, such as narcotics trafficking or prostitution rings. Particularly for narcotics policing, the absence of informants would make the police's task very difficult (Skolnick, 1975).

A second way in which the prosecutor cooperates with another agency concerns the disposition of a person who commits another crime while he or she is on probation or parole (see Chapter 9). Commission of a crime during a probation or parole period is grounds for revocation of the probation or parole. Revocation means that the offender will have to serve time on the original sentence, whether or not he or she is convicted of the offense committed during the probation or parole period. In some cases, if the amount of time the offender owes on the first offense is approximately equal to the sentence he or she would receive if convicted on the subsequent offense, the prosecutor may decide not to initiate prosecution in view of the revocation by the probation or parole authorities (Kaplan, 1965). In other cases, the probation or parole authorities may not revoke the release status because the prosecutor filed charges against the offender and a conviction was obtained. In still other cases, the prosecutor will initiate charges *and* the probation or parole will be revoked. The main point, however, is that for this type of offender the revocation decision and the charging decision are usually made with full knowledge of, rather than totally independent of, each other.

In addition to cooperating with other agents of the criminal justice system in his or her own jurisdiction, the prosecutor will often cooperate with agents in other jurisdictions in anticipation of any future cooperation he or she might need from them or to repay their past cooperation. Pressure can also be applied through the charging decision. For example, a local prosecutor might decide not to prosecute a narcotics offender, a prosecution that would be desired by the attorney for the federal government, in order to pressure the United States Attorney's office to cooperate on another case (Cole, 1970). The reverse is probably true as well, in that the most common reason federal prosecutors give for not prosecuting a case is that the state will prosecute (Frase, 1980). It is also possible that one jurisdiction will do something that another jurisdiction would prefer not occur. For example, a police officer in Dade County, Florida, was granted immunity from state prosecution in exchange for his testimony against other police officers accused of beating a man to death. After the unsuccessful state trial, a federal grand jury, at the insistence of federal prosecutors, indicted the officer for violating the dead man's civil rights ("How Safe Is Immunity?," 1980).

Social exchange with the defendant

The final social-exchange relationship the prosecutor has is with the accused. In contrast to the other social-exchange relationships, the prosecutor's relationship with the defendant is completely one-sided. The only constraint on prosecutors is their sense of fairness, which is manifested in several ways. As mentioned earlier, the most basic standard in prosecutors' decision to charge is their belief that the accused is guilty. The general feeling is that it is morally wrong to prosecute unless one is personally convinced that the accused committed the crime (Kaplan, 1965). A second way that prosecutors can demonstrate fairness is to decline to prosecute when the only sanctions available are too severe for the offense. Offenses in this category include drunken brawls and trivial squabbles between neighbors (Wright, 1959). Another example is a person who helps another person commit suicide. Although this is a crime, a prosecutor may be reluctant to send the accused to prison. For instance, a Milwaukee deputy district attorney decided not to prosecute an 83-year-old woman who had helped her 53-year-old daughter, paralyzed and in deteriorating health, commit suicide by hanging. The prosecutor believed that even though a crime had been committed, action by the criminal justice system would be inappropriate ("No Prosecution in Suicide," 1980).

A final way that fairness to the offender can be shown is the use of a noncriminal option that would be more helpful to the offender than would processing through the criminal justice system. Examples are the use of a detoxification facility for an alcoholic or of a mental-health facility for a mentally disturbed offender. In some pretrial diversion programs for narcotics addicts, the addict must enter a plea of guilty before entering the program. After the person successfully completes the program, the drug charges against him or her are dropped (Aaronson, Kittrie, & Saari, 1977).

It is clear that the various social-exchange relationships the prosecutor has can influence the charging decision to an important degree. In some cases, as a result of these social exchanges, the prosecutor may decide not to charge the offender with a crime even though he or she is convinced that the suspect is guilty. These social exchanges might also result in a reduction in the number or severity of the charges or both.

"Overcharging"

Most defense attorneys claim that prosecutors "overcharge"—that is, that they inflate the initial charges against the defendant so that they will be in a more advantageous bargaining position when plea negotiations begin. Two types of overcharging have been distinguished (Alschuler, 1968). "Horizontal overcharging" occurs when the prosecutor accuses the defendant of every possible crime he or she might have committed. One Boston defense attorney described the process in the following way: "Prosecutors throw everything into an indictment they can think of, down to and including spitting on the sidewalk. They then permit the defendant to plead guilty to one or two offenses, and he is supposed to think it's a victory" (Alschuler, 1968, p. 86). By filing a large number of charges against the defendant, the prosecutor can later appear to be making concessions by reducing the number of charges in exchange for the defendant's guilty plea, even though the prosecutor had no intention of proceeding to trial with all the charges. The second type of overcharging has been called "vertical overcharging," which is "charging a single offense at a higher level than the circumstances of the case seem to warrant" (Alschuler, 1968, p. 86). In other words, the prosecutor files the accusation against the defendant for the most severe crime that is even slightly supported by the evidence and for which there is even a slight possibility of conviction.

It must be noted that overcharging does serve purposes other than simply strengthening the prosecutor's position during plea bargaining (Alschuler, 1968). First, because the charging decision is usually made well before the prosecutor has fully prepared the case for trial, charging the defendant with as many crimes and at as high a level as supported by the evidence allows the prosecutor later flexibility. If the case is not strong enough to support the charges, they can subsequently be dropped or reduced. However, if the prosecutor later discovers that the defendant is probably guilty of a crime related to the original accusations for which he or she was not charged, and the defendant pleads guilty to the original charges, the prosecutor cannot then charge at the higher level. Thus, "overcharging" allows the prosecutor to be safe should additional evidence later appear. Second, overcharging makes a trial less attractive because for each charge the defense must prepare pretrial motions, arguments on the admissibility of evidence, and, later, arguments on the instructions to the jury. Third, because court rules and state statutes requiring speedy trials generally allow more time to dispose of a felony charge than of a misdemeanor charge, it is often to the prosecutor's advantage to charge at a felony level (Dodge, 1978). Fourth, a long list of charges has a psychological impact on the jury. The jury members may be overwhelmed by the length of the list and may feel that although the defendant may not be guilty of all the charges, he or she is probably guilty of at least some of them. Finally, overcharging in a murder case allows the prosecutor to require all jury members to consider inflicting the death penalty if the evidence shows that the defendant committed a capital crime. Even if the prosecutor seeks a conviction on a less than capital crime, the type of juror who is willing to impose capital punishment is generally thought to be more favorable to the prosecution than someone who opposes capital punishment (Bronson, 1970).

Once the defendant has been charged, at a hearing called an arraignment he or she must be notified of his or her constitutional rights, the formal charges must be read to the defendant, and the defendant is asked to plead to the charges. If the defendant pleads guilty and the court accepts the guilty plea, a presentence report will usually be ordered, which will be used at the sentencing hearing a few weeks later (see Chapter 7). If the defendant pleads not guilty, he or she is bound over for trial, which will be conducted at a later date. After the plea of not guilty, the judge reconsiders his or her bail decision and may modify it (Newman, 1974).

Even if charges are filed against the accused and he or she pleads not guilty to them, a trial based on these charges will not necessarily take place. Some of the charges may be dismissed because they are based on inadmissible evidence. At what is called a suppression hearing the defense counsel will try to show that the evidence against his or her client should not be admitted at trial because it was based on an illegal arrest, an unreasonable search, or a statement made by the accused before the proper warnings about the rights to remain silent and to have counsel were administered. If the defense counsel is successful in having important evidence suppressed, then a reduction in charges or even a dismissal of some or all of them is likely.

Another way in which charges may be dropped or reduced is through plea bargaining. During this process the defendant, the defense attorney, and the prosecutor negotiate some or all of the following: (1) the number of charges the defendant will plead guilty to ("count bargaining"), (2) the severity of the charges the defendant will plead guilty to ("charge bargaining"), and (3) the sentence that the prosecution will recommend after the defendant pleads guilty ("sentence bargaining").

PLEA BARGAINING

Depending on the jurisdiction, between 75 and 90% of felony cases are decided not by jury trials but by a process of negotiation between the prosecutor and the defense attorney. Because this negotiation process, called plea bargaining, serves a number of purposes for both sides, both the prosecutor and the defense attorney enter the bargaining situation with the hope that a mutually agreeable exchange can be made. Basically, in a plea bargain the defense gives up its right to contest guilt by demanding a trial in exchange for the prosecutor's concessions with respect to the criminal charge and probable sentence (Nimmer, 1977).

Legal Standards

In several decisions the Supreme Court has laid down certain rules of plea bargaining. The court has required that a defendant's guilty plea be "voluntary" as judged by "the totality of the circumstances," which includes the defendant's age, his or her prior experience with the criminal justice system, and his intelligence. One of the most important of these circumstances is the absence of coercion. Defendants have claimed that because their guilty plea was induced by concessions from the prosecutor (usually a reduction of the charge to a lesser offense), their confession was not "voluntary." That is, the promise of a measure of lenient treatment was a type of coercion and therefore invalidates their guilty pleas. Of course, such an argument would cast doubt on the legitimacy of plea bargaining in general. However, this argument has not been accepted by the Supreme Court. In *Brady* v. *U. S.* (1970), the court held that a bargained plea, at least for a defendant who was represented by counsel and therefore had "full opportunity to assess the advantages and disadvantages of a trial as compared with those attending a plea of guilty" (p. 754), was consistent with the voluntariness standard. Moreover, the court stated that guilty pleas serve both rehabilitative and administrative functions. Through the offer of a negotiated plea the state was extending a benefit to a defendant who in turn extends a substantial benefit to the state and who demonstrates by his plea that he is ready and willing to admit his crime and to enter the correctional system in a frame of mind which affords hope for success in rehabilitation over a shorter period of time than might otherwise be necessary [*Brady* v. *U. S.*, 1970, p. 753].

In a more recent case (*Bordenkircher* v. *Hayes*, 1978), the prosecutor offered the defendant a five-year prison sentence if he pleaded guilty but told him that if he did not plead guilty, he would probably face a life sentence under the state's "habitual criminal" statute. The defendant refused the plea bargain, was found guilty in a jury trial, and received a life sentence. On the basis of its earlier decisions, the Supreme Court held that the prosecutor's efforts to induce a guilty plea did not violate the Constitution.

A second circumstance relating to the voluntariness of a confession is that defendants must understand all the rights they waive when they plead guilty (*Brady* v. *U. S.*). Therefore, as a matter of federal constitutional law, defendants must understand the nature of the charges against them (*Boykin* v. *Alabama*, 1969). They must also understand all the requisite elements of the crime to which they are pleading guilty (*Henderson* v. *Morgan*, 1976). In *Henderson* the guilty plea was reversed because the defense counsel did not explain to the defendant that intent to kill was a necessary element of second-degree murder.

There are other rules pertaining to plea bargaining. The Supreme Court in *Brady* proscribed certain behaviors of prosecutors. For example, they must not threaten prosecution on a charge that is not justified by the evidence. Other types of threats are also prohibited. In addition, the court said that a guilty plea could not be accepted by the judge if the prosecutor had misrepresented his or her position by not fulfilling his or her promises. This last limitation on the prosecutor was strengthened in *Santobello* v. *New York* (1971). In that case the prosecutor recommended a sentence in violation of his earlier promise not to make a recommendation. The court, "in the interests of justice," remanded the case to the New York court either to permit withdrawal of the guilty plea or to enforce the plea bargain.

Although a judge does not have to accept a plea bargain between the defense and the prosecutor, judges usually follow prosecutors' recommendations without question (LaFave, 1970). Prosecutors have a strong interest in making sure that the judge does accept the plea bargain, because they must be seen as credible during the plea negotiations. If judges tend not to accept the bargains they negotiate, then prosecutors will have to take more cases to trial, thus consuming their own and the judges' time. Although there is a greater risk that a judge will not accept a sentence recommendation than that the judge will not accept a recommendation for reduction in charges, the risk is still slight, and both parties in the plea negotiations can feel relatively safe that the bargain they agree on will be accepted by the judge.

Power of the Prosecutor

An important factor in the plea-bargaining situation is the power differential that exists between the prosecutor and the defense counsel. That is, the prosecutor has greater influence over the defendant's decision to plead guilty than the defendant has over the presecutor's decision to reduce the charges. The difference in power is reflected in the "price" that the prosecutor can demand for a plea bargain. Even though a plea might be to the advantage of both the prosecutor and the defendant, it is the defendant who ultimately pays, in terms of a fine, prison term, or other restriction of his or her freedom. Prosecutors have to "pay" for a plea bargain only if there is adverse reaction from their superiors or the public or both. However, if they feel that they might have to pay a price because there is the slightest possibility of such negative reaction, they almost certainly will not make the plea bargain. The number of cases for which negative reaction is likely is, however, relatively small.

The prosecutor's superior power is evidenced in three areas. The prosecutor, representing the "people" and having the prestige generally associated with that office, is usually regarded with more esteem than the defense counsel and perhaps is more likely to be believed by a jury than a defense counsel is. In other words, the prosecutor may be seen as having higher investments than the defense counsel and therefore entitled to higher outcomes. In addition to this status differential, the prosecutor is in a better situation than the defense counsel because the jury is likely to know that in order for the case to reach the trial stage, the defendant must have already passed preliminary screening by a number of criminal justice agents. That is, the jury probably knows that the police believed there was sufficient evidence against the defendant to make an arrest, a magistrate believed there was enough evidence at the preliminary hearing to warrant the arrest, and a grand jury believed there was enough evidence to return an indictment against the defendant. The third area in which the prosecutor has more power than the defense counsel concerns resources. One important type of resource is information. Although defendants generally know whether they are innocent or guilty, they usually do not know the exact quality and quantity of evidence that the prosecution has against them. This ignorance forces them to negotiate from weakness, because they generally have to guess how strong the prosecution's case against them is. A second kind of resource is money. Usually the prosecutor, even with budget restraints, can spend more money on a case, for the salaries of attorneys, researchers, and investigators, than a defendant can. Finally, the resource of time is often to the prosecutor's advantage. Defendants, particularly if they are in jail awaiting trial, are unlikely to desire to postpone the resolution of the case much longer than necessary. If, however, defendants are released on bail, they might want to delay the trial, hoping that the prosecution's witnesses will change their minds about testifying, move away, die, or remember the circumstances of the crime less clearly.

Prosecutors also have power in that they can appear to be making an equitable exchange, which, when the entire situation is examined more closely, is less favorable to the defendant than to the state. For example, a multiple check forger who pleads guilty to only one forgery may still, as a condition of his or her sentence, be required to make restitution for all the forged checks (Newman, 1966). In addition, both sentencing judges and parole boards are likely to look at the *original* charges rather than the final convictions when they make their judgments regarding the defendant (Alschuler, 1968; Shin, 1973). Prosecutors may also make promises that, although they keep them, are hollow in the sense that the defendants gain nothing by a plea bargain that they would not have gained had they not entered into the plea bargain. For instance, if the usual practice is to grant probation to a first offender, then a promise of a probation recommendation from the prosecutor in exchange for a guilty plea is of no real benefit to the defendant. The same may be true when the prosecutor promises not to ask for application of habitual-offender laws or consecutive sentences when they are hardly ever invoked in the jurisdiction (Newman, 1966).

It is clear that the prosecutor has more power than any one defendant. However, several factors, including ethical and legal restrictions and self-interest, limit the degree to which prosecutors can give the impression that they have a stronger case than is warranted by the evidence. It is a clear violation of ethical standards to bring charges against a defendant unless there is evidence that would support a conviction (American Bar Association, 1971). Moreover, on the request of defense counsel, prosecutors must present the results of tests conducted by the police, such as chemical analyses, line-ups, and ballistics tests (*Brady* v. *Maryland*, 1963), and even without a request prosecutors must give all exculpatory evidence to defense counsel (*U. S.* v. *Agurs*, 1976), although there is some ambiguity about what constitutes exculpatory evidence (McDonald, Cramer, & Rossman, 1980). In addition to ethical and legal proscriptions against bluffing, another limiting factor is self-interest, because attorneys who have lost their credibility will find that cooperation with other attorneys and judges is difficult, if not impossible (McDonald et al., 1980).

Power of Defendants

Although the prosecutor's office is more powerful than any one defendant and his or her attorney, all defendants and their attorneys together have more power than the prosecutor's office. That is, if all defendants took their cases to trial, the prosecutor's office (as well as the courts) could not function. Thus, the defendant's power rests in being a member of a group that, if it used its power, could effectively shut down the system.

Alschuler (1975) has compared the power of defense attorneys to bring cases to trial to the power of unions to strike. If defense attorneys are generally dissatisfied with the actions of prosecutors and judges, they may decide to take all cases to trial (the equivalent of a general strike). If defense attorneys are dissatisfied with the plea bargains and sentences for one particular type of crime, they may decide to take to trial every case of that type (the equivalent of a strike on the craft-union principle). If defense attorneys are dissatisfied with the behavior of one particular judge, they may decide to take to trial all cases on that judge's docket (the equivalent of a strike on the industrial-union principle). According to Alschuler, general strikes are only rarely called, although the threat of them is always present. The "craft-union strike" and the "industrial-union strike" are used more often, usually by lawyers in the public defender's office who have both large caseloads to make the strike effective and a close working relationship to carry through with the strike.

Attributional Considerations

The prosecutor's decision to plea-bargain, like all the other decisions we have considered, is based on attributions about the defendant and a number of social-exchange considerations. Figure 4–2 shows the two stages of the decision and the relevant factors in the decision.

Basically, the same attributional issues are involved in the decision to plea-bargain as were involved in the decision to charge, since the two decisions are very closely related. As with the charging decision, prosecutors must believe that the defendant is guilty of the crime and has a criminal disposition. If they doubt the defendant's guilt or if they believe the defendant does not deserve the stigma and punishment of a felony conviction, prosecutors are more likely to plea-bargain (Silberman, 1978). Thus, concessions are likely to be granted "on the assumption that the law should not be fully invoked against otherwise 'good' persons" (Newman 1974, p. 118).

In addition to this belief that the defendant is guilty, prosecutors (and defense attorneys) are likely to engage in an attributional process based on their past experience. Using this accumulated experience, or causal schema, prosecutors engage in what is called "typification" (Myers & Hagan, 1979; see Sudnow, 1965). According to Sudnow, "typifying" a case is defining it in terms of the "normal" crime of that type. Thus, typification is based on "knowledge of the typical manner in which offenses of given classes are committed, the social characteristics of the persons who regularly commit them, the features of the settings in which they occur, the types of victims often involved, and the like" (Sudnow, 1965, p. 259). Once this typification is completed, prosecutors have established an attributional explanation for the crime, because the typification explains the crime in terms of the usual characteristics of

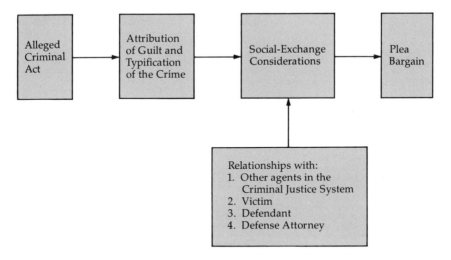

Figure 4-2. Attribution/exchange model of the prosecutor's decision to plea-bargain

the offender and the situation. Thus, typifying cases is an efficient means of dealing with a large caseload. A typification also includes the usual disposition of the typical case, including the plea concessions that are likely to be made. These concessions are part of the social-exchange considerations that exist at the plea-bargaining stage.

Social-Exchange Considerations

Prosecutors' decisions to plea-bargain are based to a large extent on their relationships with (1) other agents in the criminal justice system (including their superiors), (2) the victim, (3) the defendant, and (4) the defense attorney. We will examine each of these relationships in the following pages.

Social exchange with other agents of the criminal justice system

On the basis of their exchange relationships with other members of the criminal justice system, prosecutors are almost certainly motivated to obtain plea bargains. First, the prosecutorial staff is saved the time, work, and expense of proving the defendant's guilt at trial. It has often been argued that plea bargaining exists because of insufficient time and money to try every case. Undoubtedly, that is one reason, although there is evidence from Connecticut that even when caseloads are reduced, the percentage of cases going to trial does not increase, as would be expected if insufficient resources were the major reason that plea bargaining occurs (Heumann, 1978). Even when the prosecution has virtually unlimited resources, there are likely to be plea bargains. For example, the Watergate Special Prosecution Force, which probably could have taken every case to trial, settled most of its cases through plea negotiation (Silberman, 1978). One reason for this behavior is the uncertainty that always surrounds a trial. Even if the evidence of guilt appears overwhelming, there is always the possibility that the jury will find the defendant not guilty. Therefore, prosecutors are likely to plea-bargain because they can ensure that they will obtain convictions, which are necessary to achieve success in their position.

Other actors in the criminal justice system who benefit from plea bargaining are the police, judges, and the victim. Most of the complex corollary issues involving the legality of the search and the arrest and the exclusion of evidence are avoided by plea bargains (Newman, 1966), and thus police or other official misconduct is left unrevealed (Rossett, 1967). The police further benefit because they do not have to invest time attending the trial, and oftentimes the defendant, in exchange for pleading guilty, will admit other unsolved offenses, thereby allowing the police to clear their books of the now-solved crimes. Sometimes a plea bargain can result in the defendant's cooperation with the state in a case against a codefendant.

Judges who sentence benefit in several ways from a plea bargain. The bargaining arrangement gives them (1) psychological satisfaction, because their doubts about the defendant's guilt are reduced, (2) greater discretion in sentencing, especially when a plea bargain avoids a statutorily mandated sentence, and (3) a rationalization for leniency to defendants in a setting in which the publicity usually attending a trial is absent (Newman, 1966). Avoiding trial also spares the victim of the crime from being exposed to publicity and from having to testify. Finally, the plea bargain benefits the system as a whole by reducing the backlog of cases and by furthering the objectives of punishment through the prompt imposition of penalties following the admission of guilt.

Social exchange with the victim

Prosecutors have an important exchange relationship with the victim. Earlier we saw that the victim's credibility affects the prosecutor's decision to charge the defendant. At the plea-bargaining stage, it seems that the victim's characteristics affect the decision to try the case rather than to accept a plea of guilty. In the Indianapolis study mentioned earlier, Myers and Hagan (1979) found that, holding the amount of evidence constant, prosecutors were more likely to go to trial and refuse a guilty plea if the victim was male, older, and employed. Prosecutors may see such victims as being more credible and therefore as increasing the likelihood of winning at trial. Or, prosecutors may judge the cases of such persons to be more worthy of processing by the criminal justice system than the claims of women, youths, and the unemployed.

Social exchange with the defendant

A third social-exchange relationship the prosecutor has is with the defendant. In most cases, it is the prosecutor's task to persuade the defendant that pleading guilty is in his or her own best interest. The most obvious gain to the defendant is a reduction in the number and severity of the charges. Usually, this reduction results in a less severe sentence because plea bargaining can avoid conviction of felonies with statutory minima or maxima, nonprobationable offenses, and multiple offenses. Plea bargaining to a lesser offense can also circumvent the stigma attached to certain classes of crimes, particularly sexual offenses. In addition, a guilty plea following a plea bargain reduces the defendant's exposure to the public and eliminates the practical and emotional burdens of a trial. Finally, a plea bargain to fewer offenses may mean that the defendant will be in a stronger position if he or she is arrested, is convicted, and has to be sentenced again than if he or she had not negotiated a plea.

Defendants who committed the offense are probably more likely to plea-bargain than those who are completely innocent. To investigate how the defendant's guilt and the likely response of the criminal justice system to the defendant's alleged offense affect the defendant's decision to plea-bargain, Gregory, Mowen, and Linder (1978) used a role-playing study in which subjects were asked to imagine that they either had or had not committed a robbery. In addition, subjects were given information about the number of charges filed against them and the likely sentence they would receive if found guilty. Results showed that defendants, especially guilty defendants, were more likely to accept a plea bargain when the number of charges filed against them was high and when the likely punishment was severe. Moreover, consistent with results from this study, a subsequent deception experiment by Gregory et al. (1978) revealed that guilty defendants were significantly more likely to accept a plea bargain than were innocent defendants.

In sum, defendants are likely to plea-bargain because they believe it is in their best interest, a view that is reinforced by prosecutors. Guilty defendants are especially likely to plea-bargain, at least as suggested by studies using college students as subjects.

Social exchange with the defense attorney

Although some defendants waive their right to an attorney and negotiate directly with the prosecutor (Casper, 1972; Newman, 1956), in most cases the prosecutor and the defense attorney negotiate the guilty plea (Daudistel, Sanders, & Luckenbill, 1979). The prosecutor's exchange relationship with the defense attorney has been characterized by some as a competitive relationship and by others as a cooperative one.

Given the basic assumption of the criminal justice system that in most cases truth and justice are best served when an advocate for the state and an advocate for the defendant are locked in battle, one would presume that the plea-negotiation process is conducted as an adversary relationship (for example, Rothblatt, 1973). Using this characterization, the plea-bargaining situation has been considered in terms of decision theory (Nagel & Neef, 1976a, 1976b). Nagel and Neef assume that the defendant/buyer is looking for the lowest price possible (a light prison sentence) and the prosecutor/seller is looking for the highest price possible (near the statutory maximum).

Actually, there is some possibility that both parties can be satisfied (Alschuler, 1968). Defendants generally want a sentence with a low minimum term that must be served before they are eligible for parole, because the chances are fairly good that they will be paroled shortly after they become eligible. Thus, the lower the minimum sentence, the sooner the defendant can "hit the streets." The prosecutor, however, wants a high maximum sentence, because the longer the sentence, the more he or she will be perceived as being "tough on crime." And if the defendant is later released after serving only a short term in prison, the blame must be on the parole board rather than the prosecutor. In some instances, then, the preferences of both the defendant and the prosecutor can be met by a sentence that has a low minimum and a high maximum term. However, this form of plea bargain is not always possible. For example, in a particular case a prosecutor may want both a high minimum and a high maximum sentence.

Although the plea-bargaining situation is often characterized as an adversary relationship, it might be more accurate to conceive of the relationship between the prosecutor and the defense counsel as cooperative. Their relationship has often developed over a fairly long period, and their interaction is likely to continue long after the case in question has been settled. The relationship may have begun as early as law school, but usually it began when they were members of the prosecutor's staff. Many defense attorneys, especially the "regulars" who have the best contacts with the prosecutor's staff, worked in the past in the prosecutor's office. Moreover, because many current members of the prosecutor's staff are looking toward a defense practice on the "outside," they want to be on cordial terms with other members of the profession (Alschuler, 1968; Fishman, 1979). According to a report by the National District Attorneys Association (cited in Silberman, 1978), most assistant prosecutors stay in their jobs for less than two years. In Pittsburgh, assistants' salaries in 1979 ranged from $15,000 to $25,500, with about 25% earning only $15,000. Once they obtain some experience, many are inclined to leave after an average stay of two years because, according to the district attorney, they have the opportunity to earn in private practice two to three times what they earn as prosecutors (Maryniak, 1979).

There are two ways defense attorneys can be effective plea bargainers (Alschuler, 1968). If they are highly competent, they can gain concessions because the prosecutors are afraid that they will lose the case at trial. If defense attorneys act in a friendly and conciliatory manner, they can gain concessions because a climate of reciprocity and mutual obligation will be created. From the defense attorney's perspective, the easier of the two approaches is to have good personal relationships with the prosecutor's staff.

A guilty plea provides a number of advantages to the defense attorney. Generally, defense attorneys charge a single fee for handling a defendant's case, regardless of the amount of work that they may subsequently put into the case (Petty, cited in Alschuler, 1975). They can therefore maximize their rewards by reducing the amount of time they spend on each case. This time reduction can be accomplished by having the defendant plead guilty rather than go to trial. Even if a lawyer charges just $50 for each client who pleads guilty, the lawyer who pleads his or her clients guilty can earn a very comfortable salary, because five cases a day can easily be dealt with. Commenting on this practice, one prosecutor noted: "There are twelve to fifteen lawyers who hang around the courthouse day after day hoping to pick up cases. We refer to them as the _____ Street Bar. What they want to do is pick up a fee by pleading their clients guilty" (Newman, 1966, p. 74). In addition to considerations of time and money, plea bargaining allows the defense attorney to maintain good relations with the prosecutor, which is very important if he or she is to continue getting favorable plea bargains.

If a defense attorney enjoys good personal relations with the prosecutor's staff, he or she is likely to be an effective plea bargainer. Although the defense attorney must be in the good graces of the prosecutor's staff, the prosecutor's staff is not similarly bound. "A defense attorney ... knows, first, that he needs the prosecutor's office, and, second, that the prosecutor's office does not need him" (Alschuler, 1968, p. 68). This cooperation can be evidenced in several ways (Alschuler, 1975). First, the defense attorney may disclose to the prosecutor evidence or confidential information revealed by the client. Second, the defense attorney may refuse to use at trial information provided by the prosecutor that may embarrass the prosecutor. A third way that cooperation can be shown is the entry of guilty pleas rather than taking cases to trial.

A final form of cooperation between the defense attorney and the prosecutor's office is called a "trade-out." This is an agreement between the two, generally considered unethical, about the way the cases of two or more defendants will be handled (Alschuler, 1975). Generally, one or more of the clients will be treated harshly in return for lenient treatment of the remaining defendants. For example, one defendant may plead guilty and receive a severe sentence, while a second defendant may plead guilty and receive probation or have the charges against him or her dismissed. The two defendants may have worked together in the same crime, or they may not even be aware of each other's existence. The advantage of such an agreement to procecutors is that they can obtain a severe penalty for the defendant they are more interested in punishing. The advantage to defense attorneys is that by sacrificing one defendant they can obtain better treatment for other defendants.

The defense counsel and the prosecutor are more permanent in the courthouse scene than the defendant is. That is, the defendant usually enters and leaves the pretrial portion of the criminal justice system, while both the defense and prosecuting attorneys remain in the system. This relative permanence of the two lawyers in the system is a major factor in their cooperation and affects their exchange (the plea bargain), often to the detriment of the defendant. One author characterized the system as follows (Blumberg, 1967, p. 21; see also Cole, 1971):

> The client, then, is a secondary figure in the court system as in certain other bureaucratic settings. He becomes a means to other ends of the organization's incumbents. He may present doubts, contingencies, and pressures which challenge existing informal arrangements or disrupt them; but these tend to be resolved in favor of the continuance of the organization and its relations as before. There is a greater community of interest among all the principal organizational structures and their incumbents than exists elsewhere in other settings. The accused's lawyer has far greater professional, economic, intellectual and other ties to the various elements of the court system than he does to his own client. In short, the court is a closed community.

Given that the two attorneys must work together after the particular defendant has passed through their bailiwick, it is not surprising that their cooperation is valued more highly than the outcome to the defendant.

Thus far, the plea-bargaining relationship has been characterized in two ways: (1) as a competitive relationship in which the defense counsel and the prosecutor deal impersonally with each other and (2) as a cooperative relationship in which the defense counsel and the prosecutor work together to reach a mutually satisfactory solution. Although neither of these conceptualizations is wholly true, both raise a question regarding defense attorneys' loyalties. When will defense attorneys place the interest of their client above their relationship with the prosecutor? That is, which of the two relationships is more valuable to them? Exchange theory assumes that a person seeks to maximize his or her rewards and therefore predicts that defense attorneys will be "loyal" to the party who offers the most reward. The most important rewards offered by the prosecutor are (1) the continuing nature of the professional relationship between the prosecutor and the defense attorney and (2) their personal relationship. The most important rewards offered by the client are (1) rewards from meeting one's responsibility as defense counsel (for example, ethical demands, serving justice),

(2) money paid for services, and (3) a good reputation, which can be useful for attracting future clients.

As discussed earlier, the defense attorney's continuing relationship with the prosecutor, both professional and personal, is usually more important than either the rewards offered by the client or the rewards received from meeting ethical responsibilities. However, it is not difficult to conceive of situations in which the client's interests would be more important than the defense attorney's relationship with the prosecutor. For example, if the defendant offered a large amount of money to the attorney for his or her defense, the sense of obligation arising from feelings of indebtedness would probably motivate the defense counsel to work hard for the client. A second circumstance in which the defense counsel is likely to place the client's interest above his or her relationship with the prosecutor occurs when the defense attorney is fairly certain that in a trial the defendant will be found not guilty (whether or not the defendant is actually innocent). Generally, a defense attorney's reputation is better served by gaining an acquittal for a client than by obtaining a plea bargain. However, an attorney can enhance his or her reputation by defending a notorious client such as the "Son of Sam" or because of the legal issue involved, regardless of the outcome of the case.

Social exchange between defense attorney and judge

Not only must the defense attorney cooperate with the prosecutor, he or she must also cooperate with the judge, particularly if the attorney is a public defender or was appointed by the judge. Public defenders are lawyers paid by the government to defend accused persons who are too poor to hire their own counsel. Because of the large volume of cases the public defenders handle, smooth working and personal relationships are desirable. Should judges not like a certain public defender, their power over sentencing and other matters can be used against the particular defender and other defenders to express their displeasure and can influence the defender's being assigned future cases in the judge's court and even the defender's maintaining employment at the public defender's office (Alschuler, 1975). When the judge appoints defense counsel, his or her power is even greater than it is with public defenders. Appointed counsel, who earn a statutory fee (often $50) for handling a case, are often relatively inexperienced and usually need the fees they earn as appointed counsel. Should these appointed attorneys offend the judge by "unnecessarily" consuming the court's time, they are unlikely to be appointed again (Alschuler, 1975).

Attempts to Reform Plea Bargaining

Without question plea bargaining is one of the most criticized aspects of the criminal justice system. Within the past few years there have been several attempts to reform the plea-bargaining system. One of these efforts has been to bring parties who have an interest in the negotiations, besides the defense and prosecuting attorneys, into the negotiating process. These other parties include the defendant, the judge, the victim, and the arresting officer, none of whom are usually present during the actual bargaining process. In response to a proposal by Morris (1974) that judges should participate in the negotiation process and that defendants, victims, and arresting officers should be invited to attend the sessions, a field experiment was conducted in Dade County, Florida (Kerstetter & Heinz, 1979). In about 300 randomly selected cases, a pretrial settlement conference was held. The conference, which averaged about 10 minutes, was directed by a judge and attended in 83% of the cases by a lay participant (defendant, victim, or police officer) as well as by the two attorneys. Compared with various control groups, the pretrial conference appeared to reduce the amount of time a case was in the system.

The response of the participants varied. Two of the three judges did not believe the pretrial conferences were worth the increased time and effort involved. Police officers who attended the conference generally knew more about, and were more satisfied with, the disposition of their case than officers who did not attend. Although victims who attended the conference knew more than nonattenders about the disposition of their case, attenders did not feel more satisfied than nonattenders with the processing of the case (Heinz & Kerstetter, 1980). In summary, results from this experimental analysis of pretrial settlement conferences were not as positive as had been expected, although the mere fact that the negotiation process was opened up to the defendant, victim, and arresting officer may be enough of an advantage in itself.

A second effort to reform plea bargaining has been to abolish it. For example, El Paso, Texas, abolished plea bargaining in December 1975 and replaced it with a set of guidelines, based on points assigned for factors including the type of crime, the magnitude of harm, and the defendant's prior record (American Bar Association, 1977). The total points indicated, for defendants who pleaded guilty, whether probation was likely and, if a prison term was likely, the probable length of the prison sentence. After two years with this system, a very large backlog of cases was created, in large part because defendants believed the point system gave them little incentive to plead guilty (Daudistel, 1980). The backlog became so great that civil-court judges had to begin hearing felony cases. Defendants who expected to receive long sentences were not likely to plead guilty, because by going to trial they increased the delay until their cases would be heard and thus made it more probable that victims and witnesses would forget facts or be unable to testify, thereby increasing the likelihood of acquittal.

Plea bargaining was also abolished in Alaska in 1975 by an order of the state attorney general. An evaluation of the effects of Alaska's ban on both charge and sentence negotiations revealed that across all three major cities in Alaska the number of guilty pleas was not significantly different than before the ban (Rubinstein & White, 1980). The authors concluded that most defendants decided to plead guilty because most of the cases were "dead-bang losers" and conviction was very likely if the case went to trial. Thus, the increase in the number of trials was much smaller than expected. Furthermore, the average time required to dispose of a case was significantly reduced, following a trend that had begun before the ban on plea bargaining. Generally, prosecutors spent more time screening cases before the charging decision, and as a result the percentage of cases at trial in which the defendant was found guilty increased. Finally, the researchers found that explicit plea bargaining in Alaska was virtually nonexistent two years after the ban had been imposed and had not been replaced by covert or implicit bargaining. Contrary to the results in El Paso, the experience in Alaska suggests that plea bargaining can be abolished with only relatively minor effects on the criminal justice system.

SUMMARY

At the pretrial stage, the most important agent of the criminal justice system is the prosecuting attorney. Prosecuting attorneys make bail recommendations, charging decisions, and decisions about plea negotiations. Their bail recommendation, which they base primarily on the severity of the crime, seems to be the most important factor in the judge's bail-setting decision. Prosecutors have a great deal of discretion with regard to the decision to file charges against the accused and, if charges are filed, the nature and number of these charges. In most cases, the prosecutors' recommendation to the grand jury to charge the accused with a crime is followed. Prosecutors charge defendants only if they genuinely believe that the defendant is guilty. The charging decision is also influenced by prosecutors' social-exchange relationships with the public, the victim, other agents of the criminal justice system, and the defendant.

Prosecutors are in a much more powerful bargaining position than any one defendant, although all defendants together have more power than the prosecutor's office. From the prosecutors' position of strength, they can often negotiate a plea without giving up as much as the defense. Furthermore, the judge will usually accept the terms of this negotiated plea. Prosecutors' decision to plea-bargain is based on their belief that the defendant is guilty, and the decision is made after "typifying" the case. The plea-bargaining decision is also based on social exchanges with other actors in the criminal justice system, such as the victim, the defendant, and the defense attorney.

If, as in almost all cases, a guilty plea is entered, the defendants will be sentenced within a few weeks after they enter their plea. However, if they plead not guilty, then a trial must be held. The next two chapters discuss the social-psychological aspects of the trial situation.

CHAPTER FIVE

The Trial: Overview and Jury Selection

Of the various stages of the criminal justice system, it is the trial that is perhaps most likely to capture the interest of the public. The public's fascination with trials is shown by the prominence given such proceedings in the press and by the popularity of fictionalized television trial dramas, such as *Perry Mason*. As portrayed in the mass media, most of those accused of a crime are eventually brought to trial, where their innocence or guilt is decided by a jury of 12 citizens. The trial is usually depicted as a contest, refereed by a judge, between opposing attorneys, each of whom tries to convince the jury of the defendant's innocence or guilt. Having heard the evidence, the jury retires to deliberate its verdict. According to this popularized version, after acrimonious debate lasting many hours or days, the jury emerges, haggard and fatigued, to announce either that it has reached a verdict or that it is hopelessly "hung."

Although such a characterization of the trial process makes for interesting reading or viewing, it is not an entirely accurate portrayal. As we saw in the previous chapter, hardly anyone accused of a crime is ever brought to trial. Only about one out of ten persons accused of a serious crime will stand trial; the remaining 90% will plead guilty in return for concessions from the prosecutor. Moreover, of those who prefer that their innocence or guilt be decided by a trial, many choose to be tried by a judge rather than a jury. Only about 60% of felonies brought to trial are decided by a jury (Kalven & Zeisel, 1966). Furthermore, over 95% of those charged with misdemeanor offenses are tried by a judge. It is understandable that Kalven and Zeisel (1966) should conclude that the jury trial "is the mode of final disposition for only a small fraction of all criminal prosecutions" (p. 14).

Not only are jury trials a rarity in the criminal justice system, but the amount of time that the typical jury spends deliberating is much shorter than is commonly believed. Popular conceptions about the length of jury deliberations probably derive from highly publicized and sensationalized trials, which are by no means representative. In reality, the median deliberation time for the typical jury is less than one and a half hours, and for trials lasting up to two days the median deliberation time is less than one hour (Kalven & Zeisel, 1966). Moreover, the typical jury almost always manages to reach a verdict, only about 5% being deadlocked, or hung.

Nevertheless, the trial is an exceedingly important stage of the criminal justice process. The mere possibility of a public trial and the opportunity it presents for cross-examining witnesses influences the decisions made earlier by the police and the prosecutor, as well as the defendant and his or her attorney. As we have seen in Chapter 3, the threat of excluding illegally gathered evidence can have an important impact on decision making by the police. Moreover, the time that prosecutors must spend preparing a case and presenting it in court is a strong incentive for them to engage in plea bargaining. Similarly, defendants' uncertainty about how the jury will respond to the evidence often prompts them to plead guilty in return for a reduction of charges. Thus, by merely existing as an option, the trial casts its shadow over the system and exerts influence well beyond the frequency of its occurrence.

Because much more is known about decision making by juries than by judges, this chapter will focus on the jury trial. Kalven and Zeisel (1966) conducted what is probably the most comprehensive examination of decision making by juries, the University of Chicago Jury Project. Judges across the United States were sent a questionnaire asking them to compare their own hypothetical verdict on trials over which they presided with the actual verdict of the jury. The 555 judges who responded provided information on 3576 trials. The study found that the judge agreed with the jury's verdict 78% of the time. When they disagreed, the jury tended to be more lenient than the judge. That is, the jury voted for acquittal in 19% of the cases, whereas the judge did so in just 3%. The reasons for the disagreement concerned juror's reactions to the evidence and their feelings about the law. The fact that the judge and jury agree in almost four out of five cases suggests that much can be learned about trial outcomes in general by focusing on the jury trial.

In this chapter, we will present a brief overview of the historical antecedents of the modern jury trial along with a summary of relevant Supreme Court decisions. Next we will briefly summarize the sequence of stages of a typical jury trial. Then we will use the attribution/

exchange model to examine some of the strategies used by attorneys during the selection of the jury.

HISTORICAL DEVELOPMENT OF THE JURY TRIAL

It is to 11th- and 12th-century England that historians turn for the relevant antecedents of the modern jury trial. The proper place to begin is with the method of determining guilt and innocence before the jury was established. In 10th- and 11th-century England, disputes in criminal matters were settled not by a rational examination of evidence and witnesses but rather by appeals to the supernatural. Through the ordeals of fire and water, the elements of nature were "interrogated" in order to determine guilt and innocence. In the ordeal of fire, a party in a criminal case, usually the defendant, would have to carry heated stones a certain distance. The person's hand would then be bandaged and several days later inspected. If infection was present, a verdict of guilty was pronounced. If the wound was clean, the person was declared innocent. The ordeal of water called for the defendant or plaintiff to be bound and dropped into a nearby body of water. If the person sank, he or she was removed and presumed innocent, because water—an element of nature—accepts only "pure souls." If, however, the person floated, a verdict of guilty was declared. With the conquest of the Normans in 1066, trial by battle was introduced as an ordeal. Here the two parties in a dispute usually hired champions, and right was seen as being on the side of the victorious. Despite the Norman taste for battle, the ordeals of fire and water remained the common means of proof in criminal cases, it being widely believed that God himself settled disputes by intervening directly in human affairs.

Beginning in the 12th century, the ordeals came under increasingly severe attack from several quarters. First, the Church, which had previously supported and actively participated in the ordeals of fire and water, began to question this method of proof because theologians argued that it was "tempting God" to insist on his constant intervention into human affairs (Van Caenegem, 1973). Eventually the Church, at the Fourth Lateran Council in 1215, prohibited the participation of clergymen in the ordeals.

A second reason for the growing distrust of the ordeals was the doubts that 11th- and 12th-century English kings came to have about their validity. King William Rufus (1087–1100), for example, suspected that local priests often collaborated with the accused in the ordeal of fire, permitting them to carry stones that were only lukewarm. And, indeed, there is some evidence from a later period to support such suspicions. Thus, during the early years of the 13th century, 308 trials by ordeal ended with just 78 verdicts of guilty (Van Caenegem, 1973). Distrust of the traditional methods of proof led Henry II (1154–1189) to decree that even persons who had been accused of a serious crime and had successfully undergone the ordeal of water were to be banished from England if they were of "bad reputation."

The demise of the ordeals owned much to the new rationalist spirit that was increasingly evident in the 12th century. Still, some method of proof in criminal cases was clearly needed. If the ordeals were now in disrepute, what would take their place? How could guilt and innocence be determined? In England, the vacuum left by the demise of the ordeals was filled by a rather peculiar institution called the jury, a body of 12 men "good and true" that decided guilt and innocence, right and wrong. The voice of the people had replaced the voice of God.

The emergence of the modern jury can be traced to attempts by 11th- and 12th-century English kings to bring law and order by offering their subjects more efficient justice than was then available. Beginning with William the Conqueror, royal officials visited the counties and inquired into the affairs of the community. These visits, called inquests, had been occasional under the Anglo-Saxons, but with the reigns of Henry I (1100–1135) and Henry II (1154–1189) they became frequent and regularized. Significantly, Henry II authorized his officials during their visits to call before them a certain number of men, 12 or 16, and to inquire of them about serious criminal offenses committed in the vicinity. This body, which also told the king's official the names of notorious persons who were likely to have committed these offenses, was the forerunner of the modern grand jury.

Soon these bodies of neighbor-witnesses, summoned because they were knowledgeable about local affairs, were "presenting" certain suspected felons to the court. That is, if the presenting jury, as this body was called, thought the evidence pointed to someone, it brought a "true bill" against that person. To put it in more modern terms, the presenting jury set in motion a criminal prosecution upon indictment.

Once indicted, the defendant had to undergo a trial. Although the old ordeals lingered on as a means of determining guilt and innocence, the institution of the trial jury became increasingly popular. Initially, the trial jury consisted of many of the same men as the presenting jury. Soon it became common to add new members to the trial jury, so that by 1352 the presenting jury and the trial jury were functionally separate bodies. The presenting jury focused on indictments, whereas an entirely new body, consisting not of neighbor-witnesses but of 12 men who had little or no knowledge of the crime, heard the arguments and brought forth a general verdict of guilt or innocence. With slight changes, it was this system that was carried across the Atlantic Ocean and transplanted in the American colonies.

The framers of the United States Constitution provided for a trial by jury. This right is guaranteed by the Constitution in two places. First, in Article III Section 2, it is stated that "the Trial of all Crimes . . . shall be by Jury." Second, the Sixth Amendment states that "in all criminal prosecutions, the accused shall enjoy the right to a speedy and public trial, by an impartial jury." However, this right has not generally been viewed as applying to minor offenses. Such cases are usually tried by a judge. The right to a jury trial was deemed applicable to state trials, through the Fourteenth Amendment, in a 1968 Supreme Court decision (*Duncan* v. *Louisiana*).

In *Williams* v. *Florida* (1970) the Supreme Court allowed for a jury in a state trial to have fewer than 12 members, but the court later ruled in *Ballew* v. *Georgia* (1978) that the jury must consist of least 6 members. In addition, the Supreme Court allowed nonunanimous verdicts in state trials (*Johnson* v. *Louisiana*, 1972; *Apodaca* v. *Oregon*, 1972). Despite these recent decisions, most state trials continue to use a 12-person jury operating under a unanimous-decision rule.

The framers of the United States Constitution provided to defendants two additional rights that affect modern trial proceedings. The right against self-incrimination was guaranteed in the Fifth Amendment, which states that "no person shall be . . . compelled in any criminal case to be a witness against himself." The right to be defended by an attorney in a criminal trial was guaranteed by the Sixth Amendment: "In all criminal prosecutions, the accused shall enjoy the right . . . to have the Assistance of Counsel for his defence." In *Gideon* v. *Wainwright* (1963) the Supreme Court extended to felony defendants in state trials this right to be represented by counsel, by means of the due-process provision of the Fourteenth Amendment. Left unanswered by the *Gideon* decision was whether defendants in misdemeanor cases have a right to an attorney as well. The issue was settled in *Argersinger* v. *Hamlin* (1972), in which the Supreme Court held that a person could not be *sentenced to prison or jail* without being represented by an attorney. However, the decision allowed defendants to be given a suspended sentence or fined without representation by an attorney.

What can defendants expect when their case comes to trial? Despite slight regional variations, the following description is a reasonable portrait of the sequence of events in a typical jury trial.

SUMMARY OF THE TRIAL PROCESS

After the arraignment in which the accused pleads not guilty, the attorneys for the defense and prosecution may file a number of motions with the court. The defense may file the following motions: for dismissal of the charges, for a delay in the trial date (called a "continuance"), for a change of the site of the trial (called a "change of venue"), for suppression of certain evidence at the trial, or for disclosure of certain information (called "discovery"). Further, the defense may request that the prosecution make available the following information: (1) any evidence favorable to the accused, (2) any written or oral confession by the accused, (3) the defendant's prior criminal record, and (4) results of scientific tests, opinions of experts, and physical evidence, such as fingerprints, photographs, and electronic recordings. Similarly, in some states the prosecutor may file a motion requesting that the following information be disclosed: (1) a notice of the defendant's alibi (if one is to be used) and the names and addresses of witnesses whom the defendant intends to call in support of such a claim, (2) a notice of the intention to offer at trial the defense of insanity, and (3) results of reports of physical or mental examinations that the defense intends to introduce at the trial. Although both sides can file motions, most motions are likely to be presented by the defense.

After the judge's resolution of the pretrial motions, the jury is selected by a procedure called *voir dire* (Old Norman French, which can be loosely translated as "to tell the truth"). The procedure allows for the questioning of prospective jurors and the removal through "challenges" of those judged to be biased. After selection of the jury but before the commencement of the trial, the judge will instruct the jury on the basic rules of conduct. These rules usually include prohibiting discussion of the case among jurors before deliberation, prohibiting viewing, reading, or listening to accounts of the case as reported by the mass media, and prohibiting visits to the site of the crime.

The prosecution then presents its opening statement, which summarizes the prosecution's view of the case and the way the prosecution intends to prove the defendant's guilt. The defense is then permitted to present its opening statement to the jury. However, the defense usually waives this opportunity, preferring to include its opening statement with the presentation of its case. By law, the prosecution must present its case first. Drawing upon physical evidence (for example, photographs, fingerprints, blood samples) and testimony from experts and other witnesses, the prosecution tries to to prove "beyond a reasonable doubt" that the defendant committed the crime. The prosecutor elicits testimony from witnesses by *direct examination*. After the direct examination by the prosecutor, the defense is given the opportunity to discredit the testimony by *cross-examination* of each witness.

After the prosecution has "rested" its case, it is the defense's turn to present evidence showing that there is some reasonable doubt about the defendant's guilt. The defense begins its case with the opening statement, which had previously been deferred until this moment. Like the prosecution, the defense will try to prove its case by presenting physical evidence and testimony from witnesses. After each witness has been directly examined by the defense attorney, the prosecutor is given the opportunity for cross-examination. When the defense has rested its case, the prosecution is permitted to present witnesses in rebuttal. So, too, may the defense.

Subsequently, through *closing arguments*, each side summarizes what it has proved and what the other side has not proved. With some exceptions, the usual procedure is for the defense to present its closing arguments first, followed by the prosecution. Thus, in most jurisdictions, the prosecution is allowed to begin the trial with its opening statement and to conclude the trial with its closing arguments. On completion of the closing arguments, the judge will instruct, or *charge*, the jury. (In some jurisdictions, however, the judge may do so before the closing arguments.) The judge's instructions summarize the charges, explain the relevant laws, and define the standards for reasonable doubt. On receiving these instructions, the jury retires to a separate room, where it deliberates its verdict. When a verdict has been reached, the jury returns to the courtroom, where the *foreperson* (the elected or otherwise chosen leader of the jury) reads the verdict. The jury is then dismissed by the judge, who releases the defendant (if the verdict is not guilty) or sets a date for sentencing (if the verdict is guilty).

METHODOLOGICAL NOTE ON THE STUDY OF DECISION MAKING BY JURORS

How can one collect information on the process by which a jury reaches a verdict? One solution would be to observe the deliberation process directly. This was the strategy used in an early phase of the Chicago Jury Project. The deliberation of a federal jury meeting in Wichita, Kansas, in 1954 was recorded by means of a microphone concealed in the jury room, with the knowledge and consent of the judge and the attorneys but without the knowledge of the jury. Several months later, the public learned of the recording through a story in the *Los Angeles Times*. The story set off a nationwide outcry against such "bugging." According to Burchard (1958), "Within a few days, editors, columnists, and radio commentators from coast to coast had condemned the use of concealed microphones in making such studies; and in a short time a Senate subcommittee had investigated the matter" (p. 687). The result was Public Law 919, which provides for a fine of not more than $1000 or imprisonment of not more than one year, or both, for anyone not a member of the jury to record, observe, or listen to the proceedings of a United States jury while it is deliberating or voting.

With this avenue of investigation blocked, researchers turned to another method—the use of a simulated, or "mock," jury. In this procedure subjects are asked to play the role of jurors and to render a verdict or a sentence on the basis of information provided them. This technique has become increasingly popular, and over 100 jury-simulation studies have been conducted between 1964 and 1975 (Weiten & Diamond, 1979). Simulation affords investigators an opportunity to control relevant variables (for example, nature of the evidence, defendant characteristics) and monitor the deliberation process. Many, however, have criticized its generalizability to juries deciding real cases (for example, Vidmar, 1979; Weiten & Diamond, 1979). We will postpone a discussion of these criticisms until after reviewing the findings.

We are now ready to examine the first major stage of the jury trial—

selection of the jury. In the next chapter we will examine the second major stage—presentation of evidence and deliberation by the jury.

SELECTION OF THE JURY

Selection of the jury takes place in two steps. First, a pool of potential jurors is identified. Typically, such persons are selected from voter registration lists, although in some jurisdictions additional names may be gathered from other listings, such as tax rolls and driver registration lists. Next, a number of persons selected randomly from the pool are sent a questionnaire to identify those who are qualified to serve and those who should be exempted. Most jurisdictions require that eligible persons be United States citizens, be at least 18 years of age, have resided in the jurisdiction for a certain length of time, be able to read, write, and understand English, have no felony record, and be free of physical or mental disability. Most jurisdictions provide exemptions for mothers of small children, officers of the criminal justice system, and certain professionals (for example, doctors, teachers).

Those who survive the initial screening in the selection process are summoned to appear in court. On a given day as many as 300 persons may be summoned to appear for this second step of the jury-selection process. From this larger group, a smaller group, or "panel," of about 20–30 persons is randomly selected for voir dire examination for a given trial. From this small group, 12 jurors and 2 alternate jurors will be selected. The voir dire proceedings are the final selection process designed to weed out biased or prejudiced persons. Present are the two attorneys and the judge. The voir dire may be conducted in several ways. The judge may conduct the questioning after the defense and prosecuting attorneys have submitted questions that they want asked of members of the panel. This procedure is used in the selection of jurors in federal trials and in some state trials. More commonly, the questioning is done by the opposing attorneys. This questioning of jurors may be conducted individually with only one juror in the room (known as "individualized" voir dire), or it may take place in front of the other prospective jurors (known as "group" voir dire). In state trials, group voir dire is by far the more common because of its greater efficiency.

Prospective jurors can be removed, or "stricken," through two forms of challenge. A prospective juror's presence on the jury may be challenged for *cause*, as when one of the attorneys offers the judge reasons that the person should be stricken. If the judge accepts the reasons, the person is excused. The second form of challenge is called a *peremptory* challenge. Such challenges require neither justification nor the judge's consent. The number of peremptory challenges is limited and varies from one jurisdiction to another. Often, the defense is allotted more peremptory challenges than the prosecution, though in many states the two are allotted the same number.

ATTRIBUTION/EXCHANGE MODEL OF JURY SELECTION

As shown in Figure 5-1, our model of jury selection consists of two stages—an attribution stage and a social-exchange stage. The initial stage of the model focuses on the strategies used by attorneys to choose jurors whose characteristics predispose them to make attributions about the defendant consistent with the wishes of the competing attorneys. It is also a time when the attorneys actively try to manipulate prospective jurors' attributions about the defendant's guilt or innocence. This is done by creating certain dispositions, or sets, in prospective jurors toward the evidence to be presented and toward each of the attorneys. Finally, the voir dire gives the opposing attorneys an opportunity to initiate a social-exchange relationship with prospective jurors, the purpose of which is to influence them to render a favorable verdict. In the following pages we will show just how attorneys try to achieve these goals. We will begin by discussing the attributional factors involved in the voir dire.

ATTRIBUTIONAL CONSIDERATIONS

Characteristics of the Juror

How does an attorney decide, on the basis of questioning prospective jurors, that they have characteristics that predispose them to make attributions consistent with the attorney's wishes? After all, people are very often unaware of their prejudices, and when they are aware, they may be unwilling to disclose their true feelings in the presence of an

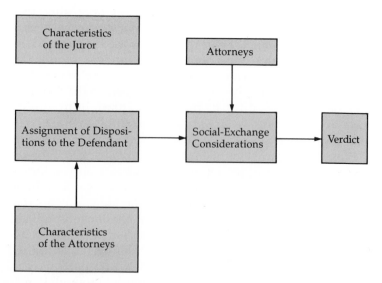

Figure 5–1. Attribution/exchange model of decision making by jurors during the voir dire

audience, especially when such feelings or attitudes are socially undesirable (Broeder, 1965; Suggs & Sales, 1981). Thus, in selecting a jury, attorneys are faced with an attributional problem of identifying prospective jurors' hidden predispositions. The lawyer's task is made more difficult by the fact that in some courts, such as federal courts, it is the judge, rather than the lawyer, who questions prospective jurors. Other obstacles to accurate assessment of prospective jurors' dispositions derive from the time constraints imposed by the judge and the fear of antagonizing other prospective jurors by a lengthy questioning session (Suggs & Sales, 1979). As we have seen in previous chapters, when agents of the criminal justice system have to make quick decisions about others, they often rely on ethnic, racial, sexual, and socioeconomic-class stereotypes. Such stereotypes play a particularly strong role in the selection of the jury. It is to these stereotypes that we now turn.

Attorneys' stereotypes about prospective jurors

Attorneys tend to view the composition of the jury as critical to success in the courtroom. To facilitate juror selection, a folklore has developed among attorneys concerning what types of persons make the best jurors. This folklore is based on personal experience, hunches, intuition, and common sense. Since it has not been subjected to scientific verification, this folklore is often uncritically passed on from one generation of attorneys to the next. Part of the folklore is illustrated in the following passage:

> As a rule, clergymen, school teachers, lawyers and wives of lawyers do not make desirable jurors. They are too often sought out for advice and tend to be too opinionated.
> Retired businessmen are usually fair but disinclined to render wild verdicts. A reasonably well-educated laboring man is not to be despised. Generally railroad men and their wives are excellent jurors. They are solid, substantial citizens who work hard, are frugal in their personal living, yet have the opportunity to travel and to play more than their fellows [Simon, 1967, pp. 103–104].

Clarence Darrow, the noted criminal defense lawyer, was explicit in stating his beliefs about the ideal juror. The prospective juror's nationality and religion figured prominently in Darrow's reasoning (1936, pp. 37, 211):

> An Irishman is called into the box for examination. There is no reason for asking about his religion; he is Irish; that is enough. We may not agree with his religion, but it matters not; his feelings go deeper than any religion. You should be aware that he is emotional, kindly, and sympathetic. If he is chosen as a juror, his imagination will place him in the dock; really, he is trying himself. You should be guilty of malpractice if you got rid of him, except for the strongest reasons.

An Englishman is not so good as an Irishman, but still, he has come through a long tradition of individual rights, and is not afraid to stand alone; in fact, he is never sure that he is right unless the great majority is against him. The German is not so keen about individual rights except where they concern his own way of life. . . . If he is a Catholic, then he loves music and art; he must be emotional, and will want to help you; give him a chance.

If a Presbyterian enters the jury box and carefully rolls up his umbrella, and calmly and critically sits down, let him go. He is cold as the grave; he knows right from wrong, although he seldom finds anything right. He believes in John Calvin and eternal punishment. Get rid of him with the fewest possible words before he contaminates the others. . . .

If possible, the Baptists are more hopeless than the Presbyterians . . . you do not want them on the jury, and the sooner they leave the better.

The Methodists are worth considering; they are nearer the soil. Their religious emotions can be transmuted into love and charity. . . . If chance sets you down between a Methodist and a Baptist, you will move toward the Methodist to keep warm.

Beware of the Lutherans, especially the Scandinavians; they are almost always sure to convict. Either a Lutheran or Scandinavian is unsafe. . . . He learns about sinning and punishing from the preacher, and dares not doubt. A person who disobeys must be sent to Hell; he has God's word for that.

As to Unitarians, Universalists, Congregationalists, Jews, and other agnostics, don't ask them too many questions; keep them anyhow; especially Jews and agnostics.

You may defy all the rest of the rules if you can get a man who laughs. . . . A juror who laughs hates to find anyone guilty.[1]

Hegland (1978) offers the following tongue-in-cheek advice to young lawyers: "As a prosecutor try for 12 infuriated Prussians; for the defense, 12 drunken buffoons" (p. 87). In a more serious vein, Hegland advises: "Look at the prospective juror and ask 'Do I feel comfortable with this person? Will this person give me a fair shot?' It is primarily a matter of chemistry and intuition" (p. 89).

Intuition is not the only guide for predicting dispositions of prospective jurors. Attorneys have long attempted to acquire information about prospective jurors that would aid them in deciding whether to challenge a prospective juror. There are several ways of gathering such information. In several states (for example, California, New York, Pennsylvania, and West Virginia) there are commercial organizations that sell "jury book" information to attorneys. These organizations compile demographic, credit, police, reputational, and previous-trial-experience information on prospective jurors who form the jury pool at a particular time (Winick, 1979). Recently, psychologists have provided attorneys with an additional set of systematic procedures for selecting a jury. The use of these procedures is called scientific jury selection.

[1]Excerpted from "Attorney for the Defense," by Clarence Darrow (*Esquire*, May 1936). Copyright © 1936 by Esquire Publishing Inc. Used by permission.

Scientific jury selection

Instead of relying on hunches and intuition to select unbiased jurors, lawyers are now able to rely on "scientific" procedures. Scientific jury selection, first used in the 1971–1972 conspiracy trial of Father Philip Berrigan and several other anti–Vietnam War protesters (known as the "Harrisburg Seven"), involves a series of techniques long known to social psychologists. First, a questionnaire is devised that assesses attitudes toward the case and the defendant and asks about a number of demographic characteristics of respondents, such as age, sex, race, occupation, and education. Also solicited is information about the type of newspapers respondents read and news shows they listen to, political affiliations, and organizations to which they belong. The questionnaire is given to a random sample of people in the community where the trial will take place and from which the juror pool was drawn. Of course, the questionnaire is not given to any of the *actual* prospective jurors selected for this trial but rather to other members of the larger pool from which they were drawn.

The respondents to the questionnaire are then interviewed, and the resulting data are analyzed by computer. The result is a profile, or portrait, of the kinds of persons who are likely to have the most favorable or unfavorable attitudes toward the defendant. Thus, it might be found that the type of person most favorable to the prosecution is a white middle-class male with a college degree, over 40, in a managerial occupation, who votes Republican, reads the *New York Times*, and belongs to the Kiwanis Club. Armed with this information, attorneys need not worry about the truthfulness of responses given during the voir dire. They can simply look for a prospective juror whose demographic characteristics best match those of the ideal juror. Naturally, an attorney can never be completely certain that a particular person will be sympathetic or hostile to the defendant. All that the procedure ensures is that *on the average* persons having certain characteristics are likely to have certain attitudes.

Another procedure in the arsenal of scientific jury selection is the construction of an informal community network consisting of (in the case of the defense) the defendant's friends, family, and other supporters. By having each of these people contact others, who contact others, an informal network of informants is set up. When the list of prospective jurors is made known, it is distributed among the network in the hope that members know something about the prospective juror and can thereby aid in identifying the juror's relevant predispositions. Saks and Hastie (1978) point out that government attorneys have long used this method, and Schulman (1973) has estimated that information on 70–80% of prospective jurors can be produced from a network consisting of about 400 people.

To increase the accuracy of the selection procedure, the questionnaire and network data are supplemented by observational data collected during the voir dire questioning. During such questioning, prospective jurors' nonverbal behavior (for example, eye contact, head nods, facial expressions, posture) is observed in order to provide an additional source of attributions about their dispositions and attitudes. Presumably, because nonverbal behavior is less subject to conscious control, it is a more reliable indicator of prospective jurors' attitudes than is their verbal behavior, such as their responses to questions. The results of these observations are then compared with the questionnaire findings, and only when they agree is the prospective juror viewed as a favorable candidate for selection.

Jurors are selected not only on the basis of their predisposition toward the defendant but also on the basis of how their presence will influence the deliberation process. Thus, in the trial of the Harrisburg Seven, the defense felt that it would be desirable to place at least one Catholic on the jury because most of the defendants were Catholic. The defense believed that the presence of a Catholic juror would inhibit the expression of anti-Catholic sentiment during the jury's deliberation (Schulman, Shaver, Colman, Emrich, & Christie, 1973). Similar concern for the dynamics of social interaction during jury deliberation was shown in the selection of the jury in the conspiracy trial of two former members of President Nixon's cabinet—former attorney general John Mitchell and former secretary of commerce Maurice Stans. The defense managed to have appointed as an alternate juror a person who was of considerably higher socioeconomic status than members of the jury. As it turned out, this person later became a member of the jury and was instrumental in persuading other jurors to acquit the defendants (Zeisel & Diamond, 1976).

How effective is scientific jury selection? Judging by the outcomes of the trials in which it has been used, one would have to say that it is very effective. The side that has used it has usually emerged the victor. However, the matter is not that simple. The procedure has been used solely by the defense and primarily in cases in which the defendant was charged with conspiracy, a charge that is notoriously difficult to sustain in court (Saks, 1976). Hence, the successful outcomes for users of scientific jury selection may derive more from the type of case and the relevant evidence than from the method used to select the jury. Results from two simulated studies further call into question the advantage of scientific jury selection.

In the first of these (Penrod, 1980), volunteers from actual juror pools were asked to render a verdict in four simulated trials presented by audiotape. Attempts to predict the verdicts on the basis of jurors' demographic characteristics, such as age, sex, and occupation, and their attitudes on a range of legal issues proved unsuccessful. A simulated-*lawyer* study (Horowitz, 1980) comparing the scientific method of juror selection with the intuitive, or conventional, method for four criminal cases revealed that the scientific method was superior in predicting jurors' verdicts in two cases, inferior in one case, and equally effective in the remaining case. Overall, the scientific method was not found to be superior to the conventional method of juror selection in predicting jurors' verdicts. Even if future research demonstrates the greater effectiveness of the scientific procedure, its cost in time and money will prohibit its frequent use. For example, in the Joan Little murder trial, in which the defendant was accused of murdering her jailer, the defense spent almost $40,000 on this procedure (Tivnan, 1975). With the assistance of a considerable number of volunteers, however, the cost can be cut significantly. In the trial of the Harrisburg Seven, the cost was only $450 when volunteers (including social scientists) were used (Schulman et al., 1973). Such assistance is not, however, always available or easily obtained.

Importance of jurors' characteristics

Although trial attorneys attach great importance to the proper selection of a jury, either "scientifically" or intuitively, there is little hard evidence that the "type" of juror significantly affects the outcome of the trial (Penrod, 1980; Saks & Hastie, 1978). More often than not, the results of studies on the predispositions of jurors have been inconsistent. Consider, for example, the personality variable of "authoritarianism." Authoritarians are described as conservative, rigid, and punitive toward those who violate conventional values (Adorno, Frenkel-Brunswik, Levinson, & Sanford, 1950). We would expect such persons to vote for conviction more often and to recommend harsher punishment. Although the literature indicates that authoritarians do indeed recommend more severe punishment (for example, Berg & Vidmar, 1975; Jurow, 1971), only a single study has shown that they are more likely to vote for conviction (Bray & Noble, 1978). More typically, the reactions of authoritarians depend on the nature of the case. Thus, Mitchell and Byrne (1973) found that authoritarian mock jurors were less certain of the defendant's guilt than nonauthoritarians only when they were led to believe that the defendant was attitudinally similar to themselves. The authoritarians also attributed lower morality to the dissimilar defendant than the similar defendant. In another study mock jurors identified as having "harsh" attitudes toward criminals gave higher guilt ratings than "lenient" jurors when the testimony was characterized as unreliable or when no characterization was made but not when the information was reliable (Kaplan & Miller, 1978).

To illustrate further that the way a particular "type" of juror votes depends on the nature of the case, consider another characteristic—the juror's sex. No sex difference in guilt attributions was found in two studies involving negligent homicide (Griffitt & Jackson, 1973) and incest (Simon, 1967). However, fairly consistent sex differences have emerged when the defendant is charged with rape. In such cases females are more likely to judge the defendant guilty than males (Davis, Kerr, Stasser, Meek, & Holt, 1977; Selby, Calhoun, & Brock, 1977; Ugwuegbu, 1979). Conceivably, the sex differences in rape cases are mediated by differences in the kinds of attributions made by actors and observers. As we pointed out in Chapter 1, actors tend to attribute responsibility for outcomes to external factors, whereas observers tend to attribute responsibility to dispositions of the actor. Females and males may have taken the perspective of different actors in the situation. Females may have taken the perspective of the rape victim and assigned greater responsibility to external factors, such as the actions of the accused rapist. Males, in turn, may have taken the perspective of the rapist and therefore attributed greater responsibility to the victim. Indeed, recent evidence shows that male simulated jurors tend to attribute greater responsibility to rape victims for their fate than female simulated jurors (Calhoun, Selby, Cann, & Keller, 1978; Selby et al., 1977).

In summary, the evidence on juror predispositions tends to show that such predispositions are predictive of guilt attributions only when additional features of the trial are taken into account—the type of crime, the reliability of the evidence, and the defendant's characteristics. As the next chapter will show, the nature of the evidence is the best predictor of a juror's attributions. Only when the evidence is evenly balanced or ambiguous will the juror's predispositions and personality make a difference. Considering, moreover, that the evidence in most trials is clear and unambiguous (Kalven & Zeisel, 1966; Lempert, 1975), initial dispositional differences among jurors probably contribute little to the outcome of most jury trials.

One possible exception to this generalization is what is known as the "death qualification" of a jury. In cases in which capital punishment is a possible penalty, jurors must state that they personally could impose a sentence of death on a convicted capital felon. This death qualification might result in a jury that is "conviction-prone." That is, jurors who are not opposed to the death penalty and therefore may serve in capital cases may be more likely to find defendants guilty. Several studies suggest that there is a relation between death qualification and conviction (for example, Bronson, 1970; Goldberg, 1970; Jurow, 1971). There is also evidence that the process of death qualification tends to exclude a disproportionate number of blacks and women.

Strategies for influencing jurors' attributions

The acknowledged purpose of the voir dire is to make a reliable *assessment* of prospective jurors' predispositions and attitudes so as to ensure an unbiased jury. However, the voir dire also provides attorneys with an opportunity to actively shape the direction of jurors' attributions about the defendant, hoping to enhance the likelihood that jurors will make attributions favorable to the attorney's cause. One such strategy is called "indoctrination" (Blunk & Sales, 1977), the purpose being to indoctrinate, or "educate," prospective jurors about the lawyer's view of the case. This "education" is accomplished under the guise of questioning jurors about their prejudices. By phrasing questions in a certain way, lawyers can introduce beliefs about the case that serve as a set, or filter, through which evidence presented during the trial can later be interpreted. As an illustration, consider the following questions posed to prospective jurors by the noted defense attorney William Kunstler (Phillips, 1978, pp. 137–138).

> "Can you accept the possibility that the government, the police and the district attorney's office could try to frame an innocent black man for a crime they themselves committed? Can you accept the possibility that a police officer could come into this court, swear an oath before God to tell the truth, and then lie to you? Can you accept the possibility that a conspiracy exists to send James Richardson [the defendant] to jail?"

Apparently, this practice is quite common. Observations of voir dire questioning in a federal district court led Broeder (1965) to conclude that attorneys used about 80% of the voir dire time in attempts to indoctrinate the jury.

Attorneys who use this strategy are usually not content merely to introduce their view of the case. They prefer, in addition, to elicit some sign of commitment from the prospective juror. As Bem (1972) has shown, such commitment can lead people to infer that they really believe in the position to which they have become committed. Often lawyers will try to elicit a commitment from prospective jurors to set aside personal prejudices and not to rely on certain damaging information in reaching their verdict. Consider the following example:

> "Now the evidence will show that my client has previously been convicted of a crime. . . . But, will that fact, in and of itself, prejudice you against him so that you assume him to be guilty of the crime he is currently charged with?"
> Juror grunts "No."
> "I take it from your response that your view is that everyone is entitled to a second chance. And that once someone has paid their debt to society they should be treated like everyone else; that the fact that a person has made one mistake doesn't mean he'll make another" [Hegland, 1978, p. 92].[2]

Later, when presenting their closing arguments, the attorneys may remind the jurors of their commitment made during the voir dire proceedings.

Characteristics of the Attorneys

In addition to the characteristics of the jurors, the characteristics of the attorneys also affect the attributions jurors make about the defendant. It is a truism among trial lawyers that the jury tries the lawyer as much as the defendant. Whereas the defendant may or may not take the stand, the opposing lawyers almost always occupy center stage. They

[2]From *Trial and Practice Skills in a Nutshell*, by Kenney F. Hegland. Copyright © 1978 by West Publishing Company. This and all other quotations from this source are reprinted by permission.

usually conduct the voir dire examination, present opening and closing arguments, examine and cross-examine witnesses, raise objections, and in general, command much of the jury's attention. As Bailey and Rothblatt (1971) point out in their influential book *Successful Techniques for Criminal Trials,*

> Jurors are not machines, they are human beings. They do not see only the evidence. They also see two rivals, you [the defense attorney] and the prosecutor, each vying for their friendship. If they like you, it will probably be reflected in their verdict; if they dislike you, the road will be uphill all the way [p. 86].[3]

Further, lawyers are aware of the importance of first impressions and recognize that the voir dire examination is the first opportunity jurors have for appraising the opposing attorneys. Moreover, as Bailey and Rothblatt note, the voir dire offers yet another advantage:

> During the selection process you are able to chat with each juror individually. This will be your only occasion to address him as a person rather than merely a member of a unit. It is at this stage of the case that you must achieve rapport between yourself and the jury. Make them like you.
> One way to build up this friendship is to question and speak to each juror as if he or she is the most important person in the room [p. 86].

Because the voir dire questioning often takes place before an audience of prospective jurors, lawyers have to be extremely careful lest their treatment of a prospective juror induce those in the audience to make negative attributions about the lawyer. Cohen (1961) provides a good example of how a prosecutor's attempt to dismiss a prospective juror can alienate other prospective jurors.

> It developed during the examination of the proposed juror that she was of the same religious faith as the defense counsel. The prosecutor promptly excused her, leaving the impression that her religion was the only reason why he did not want her on the jury. Unfortunately, the girl wore steel braces on both legs as the result of polio. Moreover, because of her warm personality, she had become well liked by the other jury members. From the inside of the jury box she had to stumble over the legs of five jurors in order to get out. The remaining members of the panel were indignant at the prosecutor for humiliating the girl in the courtroom. This incident created a fertile field in which the defense attorney could plant his testimony and other evidence [p. 57].

Given the importance of the voir dire, it is not surprising that attempts to influence the jury's perceptions of the opposing attorney begin at this time. Two strategies sometimes used by lawyers have been described by Blunk and Sales (1977) as (1) the grandstand play and (2) questioning to discover prejudices.

---

[3]From *Successful Techniques for Criminal Trials,* by F. L. Bailey and H. B. Rothblatt. Copyright © 1971 by Lawyers Co-operative Publishing Company. This and all other quotations from this source are reprinted by permission.

Grandstand play

In this strategy the attorney declines, with a "grand gesture," to question prospective jurors. While doing so, the attorney stresses his or her faith both in the jury system and in the particular prospective juror's ability to render a fair and just verdict. The strategy is designed to create a favorable attribution toward the lawyer and toward the lawyer's case. Prospective jurors may view the lawyer's refusal to question them as a sign of his or her confidence in the case. Jurors may reason that a weaker case requires a specially handpicked jury, whereas a lawyer with a stronger case need not worry about the makeup of the jury because "the facts speak for themselves." The grandstand play is not, however, without its risks, and it may backfire. Prospective jurors may view the tactic as a transparent attempt to manipulate them or as a sign of carelessness or laziness.

Questioning to discover prejudices

Sometimes lawyers use a strategy directly opposite to the grandstand strategy. Rather than declining to question prospective jurors, they vigorously pursue the voir dire examination. By questioning jurors about possible prejudicial attitudes, they hope that they will be perceived as being honest, candid, and frank—that is, as "straight talkers." They assume that in-depth questioning will lead prospective jurors to attribute positive dispositions to them, thus enhancing their credibility. Furthermore, prospective jurors who undergo a severe examination and "pass the test" may make very favorable self-attributions. After seeing peers challenged or excused while they themselves have succeeded, prospective jurors may come to view themselves as objective, fair-minded, and unbiased. As a result, the jurors may develop positive attitudes toward the person responsible for producing these self-attributions—namely, the examining attorney (McConahay, Mullin, & Frederick, 1977). This strategy, like the previous one, can backfire on its user, because prospective jurors may resent the time-consuming nature of such questioning and the lack of trust that it implies (Broeder, 1965).

SOCIAL EXCHANGE BETWEEN ATTORNEYS AND PROSPECTIVE JURORS

During the voir dire, attorneys try to involve prospective jurors in subtle social exchanges that they hope will produce a favorable verdict. Such an attempt is nicely illustrated by the grandstand strategy. When the attorney declines to take advantage of the opportunity to question prospective jurors, a message is being sent to the jurors—"I trust you!" In leading prospective jurors to believe they are trusted, it is the lawyer's intention that they will feel obligated to trust the lawyer. In effect, the lawyer initiates an implicit "deal": "I am willing to take a chance and trust you, and therefore you should be willing to reciprocate and trust me." This "deal" is a form of social exchange in which the commodity being exchanged is trust. Of course, the ultimate reward sought by the attorney is the juror's vote when the time comes to consider the evidence and render a verdict.

Not all the exchanges with prospective jurors during the voir dire are intentional, nor do they necessarily involve benefits or rewards. Occasionally, attorneys slip up and inadvertently become involved in costly exchanges with jurors. Texts on trial techniques tell lawyers how to phrase questions so as not to embarrass jurors and incur their hostility, since such jurors may retaliate by rendering a verdict unfavorable to the lawyer. Rather than keep a prospective juror whose anger has been aroused and thereby risk retaliation, attorneys are advised to excuse such persons in as pleasant a manner as possible (Bailey & Rothblatt, 1971).

Despite the great amount of lip service given to the various strategies for influencing the attitudes and beliefs of prospective jurors during the voir dire questioning, there is, in fact, little corroborative empirical evidence. With the selection of the jury accomplished, the cast of characters necessary for the trial to begin is complete.

SUMMARY

In this chapter we presented an overview of the jury-trial procedure and then applied the attribution/exchange framework to the selection of the jury. Although a jury trial is a rarity in the criminal justice system, its existence as an option for the defendant causes it to exert an influence on the system well beyond its frequency.

After discussing the historical antecedents of the modern jury trial and summarizing the sequence of stages that it involves, we used the attribution-exchange framework to examine some of the tactics that attorneys use to select as well as influence jurors. During the attribution phase, attorneys try to select persons who are inclined to make attributions about the defendant consistent with their case and to eliminate, through challenges, those who they feel are unfavorably disposed toward their case. Although attorneys often rely on common sense and folklore to select jurors, some have used a new procedure called scientific jury selection. However, the advantages of the scientific procedure over the traditional procedure have yet to be convincingly demonstrated.

Attorneys are not content merely to select jurors who are favorably disposed toward their side of the case; rather, they use the voir dire questioning to actively influence jurors' attributions. During the voir dire, attorneys also try to initiate social exchanges with jurors in order to influence the verdict. Such tactics carry risks, and there is presently little empirical evidence for their efficacy.

CHAPTER SIX

Trial Presentation and Deliberation by the Jury

A criminal trial is very much like a stage performance. Although trials differ in the amount of rehearsal time and the length of the performance, they all share certain features with a stage play. There are an audience, represented by the jury, and a cast of characters, consisting of witnesses, the opposing attorneys, and various courtroom personnel, the most important of whom is the judge. However, the key figures in this drama are the attorneys. They serve as producers, directors, actors, and costume designers, and they orchestrate the script.

One feature of a criminal trial, however, makes it very different from a typical stage performance. Each attorney labors to produce a different ending—the prosecutor strives for a guilty verdict, whereas the defense attorney strives for acquittal. Because the prosecutor must prove the defendant's guilt beyond a reasonable doubt, he or she must use a different strategy than the defense. What the prosecutor aims for is *simplification* and *clarity* of the facts related to the defendant's guilt. Since the defense attorney's goal is to create reasonable doubt about the defendant's guilt, he or she tries to make the facts of the case appear *complex* and *uncertain*.

ATTRIBUTION/EXCHANGE MODEL OF DECISION MAKING BY JURORS

As shown in Figure 6–1, our model of jurors' decision making consists of two stages—an attribution stage and a social-exchange stage. In the initial stage, jurors assign dispositions to the defendant. Such dispositions might consist of "guilty," "dishonest," "cruel," or "crazy," or they might consist of "innocent," "honest," "kind," or "sane." The disposi-

149

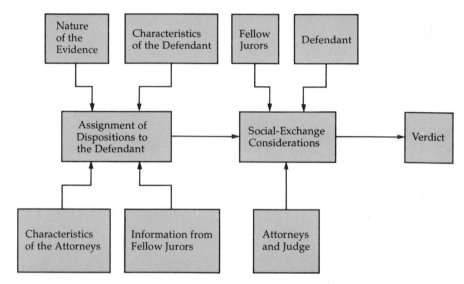

Figure 6–1. Attribution/exchange model of decision making by jurors

tions attributed to a defendant are based in part on the nature of the evidence; the defendant's characteristics, such as appearance, demeanor, and demographic characteristics; the attorneys' demeanor and appearance; and information provided by fellow jurors. Having decided on the defendant's attributes, the model assumes, jurors will reach a verdict that rests on the expected outcomes of social exchanges with the defendant, fellow jurors, the attorneys, and the judge. We will now proceed to examine each stage of the model.

ATTRIBUTIONAL CONSIDERATIONS

General Strategies

The elements of criminal responsibility are (1) commission of a criminal act *(actus reus)* and (2) a criminal state of mind *(mens rea)*. These elements correspond to the basic attributional strategies of the prosecution and defense. The prosecutor tries to convince the jury that the defendant had both the *ability* and the *motivation* to commit the criminal act. The defense attorney tries to show that either or both were lacking. If the defense can show that when the crime was committed, the accused was somewhere else, this would provide convincing proof that the accused lacked the ability to commit the act. As Bailey and Rothblatt (1971) note, "An alibi is the most perfect, physically conclusive evidence of the accused's innocence. An alibi precludes the possibility of guilt" (p. 212). If the evidence shows that the defendant had the ability to commit the criminal act, then the defense attorney can sow the seeds of reasonable doubt by pointing out that many others also had ability to commit the crime (for example, "My client was not the only person in the house").

Another defense strategy is to focus on the accused's state of mind. This is often done by showing that the defendant lacked a motive for committing the crime ("He loved her. Why would he want to harm her?"). Alternatively, the defense can try to discount the importance of a criminal motive by showing that there were other plausible facilitative causes for the defendant's actions. Thus, the defense attorney might try to attribute the act to forces beyond the accused's control. Such causes might be *external* ("It was an accident"; "She was only trying to defend herself"; "She was forced to commit the act") or *internal* ("She was insane"; "She was 'high' on drugs"). The prosecutor's purpose, of course, is to challenge the plausibility of these alternative causes and to show that the defendant chose to commit the crime for criminal reasons.

Given the different attributional strategies of the prosecution and defense, the most important question now remaining is what determines attributions of guilt made by jurors. A growing body of literature has addressed this question.

Nature of the Evidence

By far the most important determinant of jurors' attributions is the nature of the evidence. Results from the Chicago Jury Project, described in Chapter 5, revealed that "issues of evidence" accounted for 54% of the reasons that the jury's verdicts differed from the judge's (Kalven & Zeisel, 1966). In effect, jurors are far more objective in their judgments than critics claim. Mock-juror studies consistently show that judgments of a defendant's guilt are directly related to the strength of incriminating evidence (for example, Kaplan & Simon, 1972; Kaplan & Kemmerick, 1974; Kaplan & Miller, 1978; Myers & Kaplan, 1976; Sue, Smith, and Caldwell, 1973; Ugwuegbu, 1979). Moreover, as indicated earlier, the strength of incriminating evidence determines the influence that other trial factors will have on evaluations of guilt. Only when the incriminating evidence is ambiguous or weak do other trial factors affect attributions of guilt. For example, during the trial, evidence is sometimes introduced that the judge subsequently declares inadmissible. The jurors are told to act as though they had never heard the information. Defense attorneys sometimes say that asking jurors to ignore inadmissible incriminating evidence is like "throwing a skunk in the jury box and asking them not to smell it." Many have wondered whether the jury is really capable of ignoring such information. One study showed that mock jurors' verdicts were influenced by incriminating inadmissible evidence only when the case against the defendant was weak. When the prior evidence was highly incriminating, the incriminating inadmissible evidence had no impact on verdicts (Sue et al., 1973). Generally, when researchers want to study the effect of factors other than evidence on jurors' guilt attributions, they provide simulated jurors with a moderate amount of incriminating evidence.

According to Kalven and Zeisel's (1966) findings, witnesses are the major sources of evidence in criminal trials. Of the various types of witnesses called to the stand, the most thoroughly investigated is the eyewitness (Clifford & Bull, 1978; Loftus, 1979; Yarmey, 1979).

Eyewitness testimony

Eyewitnesses testify for the prosecution or defense in about 30% of criminal trials (Kalven & Zeisel, 1966), with the prosecution relying more often on such testimony (25%) than the defense (11%). Often such evidence constitutes the core of the prosecution's case against the defendant. Despite the unreliability of such testimony (Clifford & Bull, 1978; Loftus, 1979; Penrod, Loftus, and Winkler, in press; Yarmey, 1979), lawyers' reliance on it is not misplaced, because this type of testimony has sometimes been found to have a powerful and dramatic impact on jurors' attributions of guilt. Loftus (1974) gave mock jurors a written description of a grocery-store robbery in which the owner and his granddaughter were killed. Jurors in one condition were told that no eyewitnesses were present. Jurors in a second condition were told that an eyewitness saw the defendant shoot the victims. In a third condition, jurors were told of the eyewitness testimony but were also informed that the defense attorney discredited the testimony by showing that the eyewitness had very poor eyesight (20/400) and was not wearing his glasses on the day of the robbery. Results indicated that when no eyewitness was present, only 18% of the jurors judged the defendant guilty. In comparison, of the subjects who learned of the eyewitness testimony, 72% judged the defendant guilty. Most important, of those jurors in the third condition, who heard testimony from the discredited eyewitness, 68% voted guilty. The fact that the witness's testimony was discredited apparently made no difference to the mock jurors. If the eyewitness believed he was correct, then that was all the evidence jurors needed to convince them of the defendant's guilt. However, attempts to replicate this finding have met with mixed results. Whereas one study (Cavoukian, 1980) obtained findings similar to Loftus', two studies failed to replicate Loftus' findings (Hatvany & Strack, 1980; Weinberg & Baron, 1980). A plausible explanation for the inconsistent results is offered by Penrod, Loftus, and Winkler (in press). They reasoned that the outcome seems to depend "on the type of discrediting." They suggest that

> in Loftus (1974) the testimony seemed to have been only partially discredited so that jurors could still believe it if they chose to. In the Hatvany and Strack study, on the other hand, not only did the witness recant the testimony and apologize for even having taken the stand, but proof was actually provided that the original testimony could not possibly have been correct.

What attributes of eyewitnesses account for their influence on the jury? Several studies suggest that important factors include eyewitnesses' likability, whether they maintain eye contact with the person questioning them, and how confident they appear to be. Thus, in one study (Garcia & Griffitt, 1978) mock jurors were made to form likable or unlikable impressions of a witness to an auto accident. The likable witness was perceived as more credible. Moreover, attributions about the defendant's guilt depended on whose side the likable witness testified for. More guilt was attributed to the defendant when the likable witness testified for the prosecution and less guilt when he testified for the defense.

An eyewitness's failure to make eye contact with a lawyer was shown to have a strong impact on mock jurors' attributions (Hemsley & Doob, 1978). Subjects were shown a videotape of a defense witness who offered an alibi for the defendant. During questioning, the witness either looked the questioner in the eye or looked downward. Witnesses who averted their gaze were perceived as less credible. Consequently, greater guilt was attributed to the defendant for whom they testified.

Two recent studies demonstrated the impact of an eyewitness's confidence on the attributions of jurors. In the first of these (Erickson, Lind, Johnson, & O'Barr, 1978), mock jurors were exposed to testimony from a witness who used either a "powerful" or a "powerless" speech style. Compared with the powerless style, the powerful style involved less frequent use of *hedges* (for example, "kinda," "I think," "I guess"), *hesitation forms* (for example, "uh," "well," "you know"), *polite forms* (for example, "please," "thank you"), *intensifiers* (for example, "very," "surely," as in "I surely did"), *gestures* (for example, the use of hands and expressions such as "over there"), the use of bookish or *formal grammatical sentences*, and *questioning forms* (the use of rising, questionlike intonation in declarative contexts). Those who were exposed to the powerful speech style perceived the witness as more attractive and credible and were more likely to accept the testimony. The investigators hypothesized that "listeners may believe that a powerful style, by virtue of its succinctness and lack of hedging, indicates that the communicator is confident about the positions stated in the communication" (p. 268).

In the second study (Wells, Lindsay, & Ferguson, 1979), mock jurors observed a witness under cross-examination who had made either a correct or a false identification of a suspect after a staged theft of a calculator. At the end of the cross-examination, the witness was shown several mug shots and asked "For the benefit of the jury, would you please re-identify the photograph of the person you think you saw. How certain are you that the photograph you just identified is a photo of the person who presumably committed the theft?" (p. 443). After observing the cross-examination, jurors were asked to evaluate how confident they thought the witness appeared, whether they believed the witness, and how confident they were in judging the correctness of the witness. The results of this intriguing experiment showed that the greater the amount of confidence attributed to the witness, the more likely jurors were to believe the witness, and the more confident jurors were in the correctness of their decision.

Thus, both studies provide evidence that the greater the confidence exhibited by an eyewitness to a crime, the stronger will be the impact of that witness's testimony on jurors' attribution of guilt. An interesting question can be raised: Are jurors correct in assuming that a confident eyewitness is an accurate eyewitness? The answer appears to be no. Indeed, most studies show that the relation between eyewitnesses' confidence and their accuracy tends to be low or nonexistent (for example, Brown, Deffenbacher, & Sturgill, 1977; Greenberg, Wilson, & Mills, 1982; Leippe, Wells, & Ostrom, 1978; Wells et al., 1979).

Strategies for examining eyewitnesses

When examining one of their own witnesses (called "direct examination"), attorneys try to create an impression of someone who is competent, confident, and trustworthy. The attorney will try to show that the eyewitness's sensory apparatus was intact and that he or she was ideally situated to observe the criminal event. To impress the jury with the witness's confidence, the attorney will ask the witness: "Mr. Johnson, do you see the person who robbed you in this room?" "Yes, I do." "Will you please point him out to us?" (Witness points to defendant.) "That's the man. I'm absolutely certain that he is the person who robbed me." To forestall a challenge to the witness's trustworthiness, the attorney will try to bring out that before the crime the two had never met (so that the witness had no ulterior motive for identifying the defendant), that the witness is of good character (a minister and father of three small children), and that on previous occasions he has given trustworthy testimony (that is, he has a stable trustworthy disposition).

Not to be outdone, the opposing attorney in his or her cross-examination of the witness can try to discredit such testimony by challenging the witness's character, competence, motives, and confidence in his or her testimony (Whobrey, Sales, & Elwork, in press). As Bailey and Rothblatt (1971) have noted, the witness's competence can be questioned by pointing out contradictions in the testimony and by showing that the passage of time and suggestions of others may have colored or exaggerated the witness's recollection of the facts. One interrogation technique suggested by Bailey and Rothblatt is to inquire of the witness what persons have interrogated him or her since the case started and then to ask for a complete description of each person. The witnesses's inability to answer completely may cause jurors to question the witness's competence and may shake the witness's own confidence in his or her testimony. The opposing attorney can also challenge the witness's motives by suggesting ulterior motives, such as financial compensation or promises of immunity or leniency in return for the witness's testimony. The attributional principle operative here is Kelley's discounting principle. The greater the number of plausible reasons for the witness's testimony, the less certain jurors will be of the witness's true motives.

Questioning by attorneys can cause errors to be introduced into the eyewitness's testimony. A series of experiments by Loftus and associates shows how the use of leading questions can affect the accuracy of eyewitnesses' recall. In one study (Loftus, 1974) students were shown a short film segment depicting a multiple-car accident and then were asked several questions to test their recall. The questions differed in whether they used the indefinite article *a* or the definite article *the*. Use of the definite article more strongly implies that the object referred to exists. Compare "Did you see *the* broken headlight?" and "Did you see *a* broken headlight?" The results showed that witnesses who were asked "the" questions were more likely to report having seen something, whether or not it had been shown in the film, than those who were asked "a" questions.

In another study (Loftus & Palmer, 1974) subjects were shown films of auto accidents and then asked how fast they thought the cars were going when they "hit" each other. For other subjects the verb *hit* was replaced with *smashed, collided, bumped,* or *contacted*. The verbs differed with regard to how fast they implied the two cars were going when they came together. As expected, subjects in the "smashed" condition believed that the cars were going the fastest, whereas those in the "contacted" condition estimated that they were moving the slowest. The other verbs elicited estimates of intermediate speeds. In yet another demonstration of how misleading questions can impair the accuracy of an eyewitness's recall, Loftus (1975) showed subjects a film of an auto accident followed by a misleading question, "How fast was the white sportscar going when it passed the barn while traveling along the country road?" In reality, there was no barn in the film. When asked one week later whether they had seen a barn, 17% answered affirmatively. Fewer than 3% of control subjects, who were not asked the misleading question, said that they had seen a barn. The series of studies conducted by Loftus and associates suggests that questioning by attorneys can lead to false or inaccurate reports from eyewitnesses.

Evidence about the victim

The nature of evidence about the victim also affects attributions of guilt. The noted defense attorney Percy Foreman once remarked that "the best defense in a murder case is . . . that the deceased should have been killed, regardless of how it happened" (Smith, 1966, p. 96). In one case Foreman was so effective in vilifying the victim that he felt "the jury was ready to dig up the deceased and shoot him all over again" (p. 96). The opposite may be true for likable and defenseless victims.

Kalven and Zeisel (1966) report several cases in which jurors were more likely to find a defendant guilty in trials involving young or helpless victims. Similarly, analysis of actual trial records found that "jurors were more likely to convict if the victim was young or married rather than divorced, separated, or single" (Myers, 1980, p. 412).

If jurors believe that victims, because of their actions or personal characteristics, contributed to the occurrence of the crime, they will attribute less guilt to the defendant. In attributional terms, such characteristics of victims constitute plausible facilitative causes for the criminal act and thus may lead jurors to discount the defendant's guilt. One crime for which illustrative evidence exists is rape. Kalven and Zeisel (1966) were led to conclude from their data that the jury "closely, and often harshly, scrutinizes the female complainant and is moved to be lenient with the defendant whenever there are suggestions of contributory behavior on her part" (p. 249). One such contributory factor is the victim's physical attractiveness. Whereas psychologists have found that more positive characteristics are usually attributed to physically attractive people (Berscheid & Walster, 1974), in the case of rape, a physically attractive victim was judged in one study to have played a greater role in her victimization than an unattractive victim (Calhoun et al., 1978). Supposedly, the victim's attractiveness was viewed as eliciting the attack. A second study provides an alternative explanation of why less guilt is attributed to defendants who rape a physically attractive victim. Dermer and Thiel (1975) found that males and females alike harbor negative stereotypes about *extremely* attractive women. Such women are viewed as being more vain, egotistical, adulterous, and likely to request a divorce. Given such psychological and behavioral attributions, subjects in the study by Calhoun et al. (1978) may have believed that the attractive rape victim acted in such a way as to encourage the rapist.

This is not to say that physically attractive victims will always be blamed more for their victimization. Much depends on the type of crime. Whereas a victim's physical attractiveness may be perceived as a facilitative cause for rape, for other types of crimes physical attractiveness may be viewed as an inhibiting cause, leading to greater attribution of guilt to the defendant rather than less. That this statement has some validity is suggested in a recent study by Kerr (1978a). Mock jurors read a description of an auto-theft case in which the victim's physical attractiveness and care in preventing the theft were systematically varied. The most guilt was attributed to the defendant who victimized the "beautiful and blameless" victim.

Other characteristics of rape victims that affect perceptions of the defendant's causal role are whether the victim had been raped before, marital status, acquaintance with the defendant, and sexual history. A rape victim was seen as being more causally responsible (and the defendant less) when the victim was described as being divorced

(Feldman-Summers & Lindner, 1976) or as having been raped before (Calhoun, Selby, & Warring, 1976). In addition, greater blame was attributed to the victim when she was acquainted with the defendant and when she was described as being either a nonvirgin or promiscuous (L'Armand & Pepitone, 1977). Recently, laws restricting the admissibility of evidence about a rape victim's sexual history have been passed in several jurisdictions.

Evidence about the defendant's alleged confession

According to Kalven and Zeisel (1966), the defendant's confession is introduced as evidence by the prosecution in 19% of criminal trials. The very fact that there is a trial indicates that the defendant disputes the validity of the confession. The prosecutor, of course, will claim that the confession was freely made and therefore reflects the defendant's guilt; the defense attorney will try to discredit the confession by showing that it was induced by external causes. To the extent that jurors can be convinced that external causes played a contributory role in the confession, they will be less confident in using the confession as a measure of the defendant's guilt.

Kassin and Wrightsman (1979) gathered evidence bearing on jurors' acceptance of disputed confessions. They give simulated jurors information indicating that the defendant had freely confessed (no-constraint condition), had not confessed, or had confessed under one of two types of constraint. In one constraint condition, subjects were told that the confession had been made under the threat of harm or punishment (negative constraint); in the second constraint condition, subjects were told that the confession had been elicited by a promise of leniency (positive constraint). As expected, results showed that the confession in the two constraint conditions was perceived as being clearly less voluntary than the confession in the no-constraint condition. Consistent with this judgment, the confession in the negative-constraint condition was discounted, just 22% judging the defendant guilty, compared with 78% in the no-constraint condition. Although subjects in the positive-constraint condition acknowledged that the defendant had confessed involuntarily, they were unable or unwilling to dismiss the prior confession and tended to perceive him as guilty anyway (50% doing so).

Characteristics of the Defendant

Although the nature of the evidence plays a dominant role in affecting jurors' attributions of guilt, there are other important sources of attributions, such as the defendant's personal and behavioral characteristics. The noted trial attorney Clarence Darrow once remarked that "jurymen seldom convict a person they like, or acquit one they dislike. The main work of a trial lawyer is to make a jury like his client, or at least to feel sympathy for him" (Sutherland & Cressey, 1966, p. 442). Data collected by Kalven and Zeisel (1966) suggest, however, that Darrow may have overstated his case. They found that jurors' sentiments toward the defendant influenced verdicts in just 11% of the 1200 actual cases examined, and they concluded that "sentiments about the defendant are seldom powerful enough to cause disagreement with the judge by themselves; rather they gain their effectiveness only in partnership with some other factor in the case" (p. 114). Elsewhere they concluded: "We find no cases in which the jury convicts a man, so to speak, for the crime of being unattractive" (p. 385). They further noted that in two-thirds of the trials studied, defendants did not evoke particularly strong feelings among jurors one way or the other. Thus, their data ascribe a rather limited role to jurors' feelings about the defendant as a source of guilt attributions. Kalven and Zeisel's conclusions received additional support from an observation study of defendants in a criminal court (Stewart, 1980). No relation was found between observers' ratings of the physical attractiveness of 74 defendants accused of a broad range of offenses and jurors' verdicts.

Findings from simulated-juror studies have accorded a more important role to the characteristics of the defendant and the sentiments they evoke than have the results of nonexperimental studies of actual jurors and defendants. With some few exceptions, simulation studies show that certain types of defendant characteristics produce weaker guilt attributions than others. Less guilt is attributed to defendants who are physically attractive (for example, Efran, 1974), have positive character traits (for example, Izzett & Leginski, 1974; Kaplan & Kemmerick, 1974), and have attitudes similar to those of jurors (for example, Griffitt & Jackson, 1973).

The inconsistency between the findings from actual courtroom cases and simulated-juror experiments may reflect some of the criticisms of the mock-jury paradigm discussed later in this chapter. The differences in results may be due, in part, to the fact that simulated-juror studies typically present an abbreviated version of a trial. The omission of certain key elements in such simulations may cause the defendant's characteristics to exercise greater influence on jurors' guilt attributions than they would ordinarily. Thus, a recent mock-juror study found that the attractiveness of the defendant's character had a strong impact on guilt attributions when there were no instructions from the judge on the criteria of guilt. However, when such instructions were included, the attractiveness of the defendant's character had no impact on guilt attributions (Weiten, 1980).

What attributional mechanisms might account for the general tendency of simulated jurors to attribute less guilt to defendants who are physically attractive, have positive character traits, or have attitudes similar to their own? The favored interpretation is that defendants who have these characteristics are better liked and that jurors tend to attribute less guilt to those whom they like or find attractive. This is the liking/leniency, or disliking/harshness, interpretation to which Clarence Darrow and Kalven and Zeisel made reference.

Another attributional interpretation is that rather than affecting jurors' liking for the defendant, these characteristics may elicit a stereotypical image of the defendant that does not fit jurors' conceptions of what a guilty person is like ("He looks like such a clean-cut boy. I just can't believe he would do a thing like that"). However, the physically attractive defendant may not always be treated more leniently than the unattractive defendant. As we have seen to be true of victims, whether a person's physical attractiveness is viewed as a facilitative or an inhibitory cause depends on the type of crime. Just as a rape victim's physical attractiveness may make her appear more culpable, so might a defendant's physical attractiveness lead to harsher treatment by jurors. Subjects in one study (Sigall & Ostrove, 1975) read an account of a burglary or a swindle committed by an attractive or an unattractive female. In the swindle account, the defendant was described as ingratiating herself to a middle-aged bachelor and inducing him to invest money in a nonexistent corporation. Jurors reacted more negatively to the attractive defendant accused of the swindle than to the unattractive defendant, presumably because she used her attractiveness to commit the crime. However, when the defendant's attractiveness was unrelated to the crime, in the burglary case, the attractive defendant was viewed more positively than the unattractive one.

The best opportunity that jurors have for evaluating the defendant occurs when the defendant takes the stand, which happens in 82% of criminal trials (Kalven & Zeisel, 1966). Jurors can observe the defendant during the trial, but only when he or she elects to take the stand can they both see and hear the accused present his or her version of the facts. The defendant's appearance and demeanor are important because people tend to place great faith in their ability to size up others when given the opportunity to observe them firsthand. Because for many "seeing is believing," defense attorneys do well to give attention to the appearance of the accused. A management consultant who has specialized in studying the effects of a defendant's appearance advises defense lawyers to have defendants dressed "quietly"—particularly in cases in which a violent crime is at issue. "Clean 'em up, cut their hair and . . . No shiny suits or pinkie rings" ("What to Wear in Court," 1974, p. 52). Taking this advice to heart, defense attorneys often coach their clients on how to dress and act before the jury. The coaching sometimes involves a videotaped rehearsal, which gives defendants an opportunity to see themselves as the jury might.

Although trial attorneys accept as a matter of faith the importance of the defendant's demeanor, there is very little systematic corroborative evidence. A study by Parkinson (1979) examined the effect of defendants' speech style on jurors' guilt attributions. Transcripts from 38 actual trials, half of which resulted in acquittal and half conviction, were studied. Several differences were found between the speech styles of successful and unsuccessful defendants. Defendants who were acquitted displayed more courtesy and deference, made fewer references to themselves, and spoke in more grammatically complete sentences than defendants who were convicted.

The substance of the defendant's answers to questions may also have an effect on the jury. Defendants who take the stand in their own behalf do not have to answer all the questions put to them, being protected by the Fifth Amendment privilege against self-incrimination. Defendants use this privilege in about 20% of criminal trials (Kalven & Zeisel, 1966). Although the withholding of information by defendants is not a legal basis for a guilty verdict, evidence exists that simulated jurors are more likely to attribute guilt to those who invoke the privilege than to those who give the appearance of answering all questions in a straightforward manner (Hendrick & Shaffer, 1975). However, a later investigation (Shaffer & Sadowski, 1979) found that mock jurors did not make negative attributions about the defendant when the decision to invoke the Fifth Amendment privilege was attributable to an external source—the defendant's attorney.

Mock jurors also appear to base their attributions of guilt on the defendant's pretrial status. In one study, jurors were given a written description of a hypothetical court case involving the charges of breaking and entering and theft (Koza & Doob, 1975). During his testimony the defendant indicated either that he was in pretrial custody or that he was released on bail, or he said nothing about his pretrial status (control condition). Thus, in the pretrial-custody condition, the accused complained on the stand that the real criminal was walking around free, "while I'm the one who's been kept in jail for the past month since I got arrested." In the released condition, the accused testified that "since I was arrested, I've been walking through the park every day on my way to work." Jurors were more likely to view the accused as guilty when he was detained in custody than when he was released or when no such information was provided. The defendant's pretrial detention may have mediated guilt attributions for one or more of a number of reasons. Subjects may have inferred that the defendant was denied bail because he was less trustworthy or more dangerous than the ordinary defendant. Alternatively, the defendant who remained in pretrial custody may have been less able to prove his trustworthiness than the defendant who was released and therefore may have been more likely to be judged guilty. As we shall see in the next chapter, the defendant's pretrial status also affects the judge's sentencing decision.

Although evidence of a defendant's prior criminal record is inadmissible in court, such evidence can be introduced when the defendant elects to testify. The justification for the admissibility of this information is that it has some bearing on the defendant's credibility as a witness though not on the defendant's guilt. However, as Doob and Kirshenbaum (1972) have shown, jurors find it very difficult to ignore such information once it is introduced. Mock jurors either were given no information about the defendant's prior convictions, were told about seven previous convictions for the same kind of offense, or were told about the seven prior convictions but were, in addition, instructed by the judge not to use that information in deciding the defendant's guilt or innocence. Results showed that jurors attributed greater guilt to the defendant when information about previous convictions was introduced, regardless of the judge's instructions. Jurors apparently used the information about the defendant's background to attribute a stable criminal disposition to him.

That defense attorneys are very much aware of such tendencies in jurors is reflected in Kalven and Zeisel's (1966) finding that the defendant's record is an important determinant of whether he or she will testify. Defendants with no prior record testified in 91% of the trials, whereas those with a prior record took the stand just 74% of the time. Although the defendant's taking the stand does not assure that the previous record will be brought to the jury's attention, Kalven and Zeisel found that the jury discussed the defendant's record in 72% of the trials in which the defendant testified. In contrast to Doob and Kirshenbaum's findings, a follow-up study by Hans and Doob (1976) failed to find any effect of the defendant's prior record on mock jurors' guilt judgments. This difference may be due to the weaker manipulation of the defendant's prior record in the second study. In the earlier study, the defendant's prior record consisted of seven convictions; in the later study, only one.

Characteristics of the Attorneys

In addition to relying on the defendant's appearance, demeanor, and past record, jurors scrutinize the attorneys for possible clues about the defendant's guilt. As we have shown many times in the preceding pages, the prosecutor and defense attorney play critical roles in the conduct of the trial—selecting jurors, planning strategy, orchestrating the appearance of witnesses, conducting the direct and cross-examination of witnesses, and presenting final arguments. Although such trial skills undoubtedly affect jurors' attributions about the defendant, this section will not focus on them, as they have been discussed throughout this and the previous chapter. Instead, we will concentrate on yet another source of influence by attorneys—the kinds of characteristics attributed to them, such as their likableness, sincerity, candidness, credibility, attitudes toward the defendant, and confidence in the strength of their case.

Trial manuals are full of advice to lawyers concerning how jurors scrutinize their behavior for clues about the defendant's guilt or innocence. Hegland (1978), for example, reminds defense attorneys that during the trial, jurors are prohibited from talking about the case. "So what do they talk about," he asks? "You. Your client's not the only one on trial" (p. 83). According to Hegland, "The jury's main interest is whether or not you believe your client. The jurors are convinced that you know the truth. They also know that your job is to throw dust in their eyes" (p. 83). Elsewhere, Hegland cautions attorneys that their treatment of their client in the courtroom can influence jurors' attributions about the defendant.

> The jury's verdict will not rest solely on the evidence "from the box"—like it or not, part of the decision will turn on what the jury thinks you think of your client. Even if you believe 100 percent in your client, if you are cold toward him during the trial the jury may conclude that you think he's a liar [p. 84].

Thus, defense attorneys are well advised to "manage" displays of liking, respect, sympathy, and understanding toward their client.

Prosecutors, in contrast, try to prove to jurors that they are convinced of the defendant's guilt by not showing any signs of friendliness or sympathy toward the defendant. Thus, they often display contempt for the defendant and maintain a consistently aggressive attitude toward him or her. When referring to the defendant, prosecutors will avoid using his or her first name or a title of respect, such as *Mr.* Instead, the defendant is likely to be referred to as "Defendant Brown." Moreover, this behavior carries over outside the courtroom. During recess prosecutors are advised to avoid any friendly contact with the defendant lest a juror use that information to conclude that the prosecutor is not convinced of the defendant's guilt. This point is well illustrated by a case in which the jury surprisingly voted to acquit a defendant for an unusually vicious crime. According to Cohen (1961), "One of the jurors said afterward, 'Well, when I saw the prosecutor with his arm around Jim's shoulder (Jim being the defendant) out in the corridor, I figured he must not have done anything or the prosecutor wouldn't be chatting with him so friendly like' " (p. 64).

Although much of this advice to attorneys about the impact of their demeanor is based on anecdotal evidence, at least one study offers supporting empirical evidence. Parkinson (1979) analyzed written transcripts from 38 actual trials in order to compare the speech styles of successful and unsuccessful attorneys. Successful prosecutors showed more verbal aggression than their unsuccessful counterparts. They spoke longer and asked more questions referring directly to the witness, whereas unsuccessful prosecutors tended to use more polite forms of speech and more conditional statements.

Although prosecutors are advised to show jurors that they are convinced of the defendant's guilt, they must also avoid being too aggressive lest they be perceived as unfair. This point is nicely illustrated by a mock-juror study that manipulated the courtroom demeanor of the attorneys (Kaplan & Miller, 1978). In one variation the prosecutor acted obnoxiously and badgered witnesses. In another condition it was the defense attorney who acted this way, and in a third the judge and the experimenter acted obnoxiously. Finally, in a fourth variation none of the participants displayed obnoxious behavior. Mock jurors' beliefs about the defendant's guilt were affected by such displays, the least guilt being attributed to the defendant when the prosecutor behaved obnoxiously.

Further, it is likely that such displays by the prosecutor will prompt the defense attorney to call them to jurors' attention and to suggest that the prosecutor's real motive is not justice but simply adding another conviction to his or her record. It is perhaps for this reason that prosecutors often save their harshest indictment of the defendant for the final argument, when the defense attorney can no longer respond. A prosecutor will try to convey the impression to jurors that until the end of the trial he or she has tried to present the facts dispassionately—but the juror must be forgiving if, by the time of the final argument, the prosecutor can no longer contain his or her revulsion and disgust for the defendant.

If attorneys are to exercise any influence over jurors, they must work to establish and maintain their credibility. As has been noted, this effort begins with the voir dire examination, and, as we shall see, it continues throughout the duration of the trial. Attorneys try to enhance their credibility by "managing" their appearance and their behavior in court.

One consultant who studied the impact of attorneys' attire on jurors advised attorneys to vary their dress according to geographic region and the composition of the jury ("What to Wear in Court," 1974). For example, before a rural jury he suggests that attorneys avoid dressing like "a wise-guy city slicker." When practicing before a black middle-class jury, white male attorneys are advised that the most effective dress is a "modified Johnny Carson"—a plaid or other light suit with a paisley tie.

One trial tactic used by attorneys to enhance their credibility is to introduce damaging evidence themselves rather than have it dragged out during cross-examination by the opposing attorney. This tactic relies on Kelley's (1972a) augmentation principle and is likely to cause jurors to make a number of favorable attributions about the attorney. Jurors are likely to reason that the attorney's willingness to mention the damaging evidence is a sign of fairmindedness and honesty. They may see the attorney as trying to present "the truth, the whole truth, and nothing but the truth" rather than a one-sided version of the facts. Recall that this same mechanism could be seen at work in Chapter 3, in which we saw that informants' credibility with the police is enhanced when the information supplied is an admission against their own interest.

Not only will this tactic enhance the attorney's credibility, but it may also cause jurors to perceive the attorney as being very confident of the defendant's guilt (or innocence). Jurors may reason that only a very confident person would risk introducing information damaging to his or her side of the case. By such tactics, the prosecutor hopes to persuade jurors that if someone so fair-minded, honest, and trustworthy is convinced of the defendant's guilt, then the defendant must indeed be guilty.

We have seen that many of the jurors' attributions about the defendant are shaped in the courtroom by the evidence, the defendant's personal characteristics, and the characteristics of the attorneys. However, new attributions may be formed and others changed when jurors retire to deliberate the verdict. We consider these in the next section.

Influence of Peers on Jurors' Attributions

After the prosecutor has presented his or her final arguments and the judge has instructed the jury about the charges and the definition of reasonable doubt, the jurors retire to the jury room, where they deliberate the verdict. During deliberation, jurors review the evidence, raise questions, express opinions, introduce supporting arguments, and challenge the attributions of others. This is the first legitimate opportunity that jurors have to influence the attributions of fellow jurors, because they are prohibited from discussing the case before this point.

The first order of business for the jury is the selection of a foreperson. Research suggests that this choice is related to the juror's sex, the matter of which juror initiates conversation, the juror's location on the occupational status scale, and where the juror is seated at the jury table. Thus, a simulated-juror study using mock jurors drawn from actual jury rolls (Strodtbeck, James, & Hawkins, 1958) found that only one-fifth as many women were chosen as forepersons as would be expected by chance. This study also found that the person who "opened the discussion and sought either to nominate another, or to focus the group's attention on their responsibility in selecting a foreman, was himself selected foreman" (p. 382). Persons located higher on the occupational status scale (that is, proprietors, managers, professionals) were also more likely to be chosen than persons with lower occupational status (for example, laborers). Finally, persons seated at the ends of the rectangular jury table were more likely to be chosen (Strodtbeck & Hook, 1961). Davis, Bray, and Holt (1977) concluded from these findings that "a jury foreman is likely to be a male proprietor who begins conversation and sits at the end of the traditional rectangular table" (p. 342). A content analysis of forepersons' verbalizations during deliberations (Strodtbeck et al., 1958) revealed that rather than taking a partisan role in the deliberations, forepersons adopted a more neutral regulatory role.

At some point, usually early in the discussion, the jury takes its first vote. There is some evidence that by this time jurors have already made up their minds about the defendant's guilt. For example, on the basis of posttrial interviews with jurors, Kalven and Zeisel (1966) reconstructed the first-ballot votes in 225 actual trials. They found that the majority opinion on the first ballot predicted the eventual verdict in almost 90%

of the cases. Moreover, in only 4% of the trials was the minority successful in persuading the majority during the deliberation. These data led Kalven and Zeisel to conclude that

> *with very few exceptions the first ballot decides the outcome of the verdict.* And if this is true, then *the real decision is often made before the deliberation begins.* . . . The deliberation process might well be likened to what the developer does for an exposed film: it brings out the picture, but the outcome is pre-determined [pp. 488–489].[1]

This is not to say that the attributions of *individual* jurors are not affected by the deliberation process. Studies in which mock jurors make private judgments of the defendant's guilt before and after deliberation show that such change does occur. For example, Simon (1967) presented mock jurors drawn from a real jury pool with a trial involving either housebreaking or incest. After hearing the testimony, jurors rendered private predeliberation verdicts. After deliberation they rendered a group (public) verdict and then were asked once again to render private verdicts. About 25% of the jurors voted differently in the group situation than in the private predeliberation vote. Were their attributions of guilt actually changed by the group discussion or were these 25% merely going along with the majority in order to win their approval? This question can be answered by examining their private postdeliberation judgments. Such an examination showed that in most instances (65%) the private postdeliberation judgment agreed with the group verdict, suggesting that these individuals privately accepted the group's verdict. The remaining jurors (35%) rendered a private postdeliberation judgment that differed from the group's, suggesting that their attributions about the defendant's guilt had not changed, only their public behavior. In another study, Bray and Noble (1978) gave student mock jurors information about a murder trial and then collected pre- and postdeliberation private verdicts from them. About 20% of the jurors changed their beliefs about the defendant's guilt as a result of the group deliberation.

In addition to showing that jurors' attributions about the defendant's guilt are sometimes altered as a consequence of group discussion, recent studies provide information about the direction of these changes. Because of communications directed at them by the majority, most jurors who hold a minority position eventually accept the attributional judgment of the majority. Studies in which mock jurors make private judgments of the defendant's guilt before and after deliberation show that group discussion moves jurors in the direction in which the group is initially leaning. The predominant attribution among jurors, whether guilt or innocence, will become even more predominant after discussion (Bray & Noble, 1978; Hans & Doob, 1976; Kaplan & Miller, 1978; Myers

---

[1]From *The American Jury*, by H. Kalven and H. Zeisel. Copyright 1971 by Little, Brown & Company. This and all other quotations from this source are reprinted by permission.

& Kaplan, 1976). This has come to be known as the "group polariza-tion" phenomenon (Myers & Lamm, 1976).

Several investigators have found that group discussion "corrects" for certain attributional biases. For example, Izzett and Leginski (1974) reported that after group discussion the attractiveness of the defen-dant's character had no impact on guilt attributions. Jurors tended to be less biased against the unattractive defendant after group delibera-tion than before. Similarly, the tendency for an obnoxious attorney's behavior to influence jurors' guilt attributions disappeared after group discussion (Kaplan & Miller, 1978). Contrary to the previous two studies is the finding of Hans and Doob (1976), who reported that after group discussion *greater* bias was shown toward a defendant whose criminal record was made known.

The seeming disparity between these findings can be reconciled when one considers the function served by group discussion. Such discussion serves to highlight certain aspects of the case. Research has shown that people tend to attribute greater causal efficacy to salient features of their environment than to nonsalient features (Taylor & Fiske, 1978). In this context, group discussion serves to increase the salience of certain information about the case, thus enhancing the likelihood that such information will influence jurors' attributions. In Kaplan and Miller's (1978) study, discussion focused on matters of evidence to the exclusion of references to the attorney's obnoxious behavior. Because the salience of the attorney's behavior was decreased, less weight was given to such behavior when making attributions about the defendant's guilt. In con-trast, jurors in Hans and Doob's (1976) study accorded a greater role to the information about the defendant's record as a result of group dis-cussion. According to Hans and Doob, "The fact that the defendant has a record permeates the entire discussion of the case, and appears to affect the juror's perception and interpretation of the evidence" (p. 251).

What conditions are likely to increase peer influence? Several studies have suggested factors that might increase jurors' willingness to accept information from peers. One such factor is the size of the jury. Mock jurors participating in 6-person groups rated fellow jurors more favor-ably with regard to "reasonableness" and their contribution to the jury's work than mock jurors in 12-person groups (Saks, 1977). Jurors also appear to be more susceptible to influence by fellow jurors who occupy high occupational status positions. Strodtbeck et al. (1958) ob-served that such persons participated more actively in the deliberations and were, accordingly, perceived by jurors as more helpful. In addition, the previously noted willingness of jurors in the minority to accept information from the majority depends, in part, on the attributions they make about the cause of the majority's position. Research by Wilder (1978) yielded data consistent with the hypothesis that when agreement among majority members is perceived to stem from their membership in a single group, it is easier to discount their opinions, because their agreement can be accounted for by mutual influence or similar personalities. According to Wilder, "This attributed lack of independence among the majority provides a dissenting juror with an adequate explanation for his/her disagreement with the others, enabling the dissenter to resist conformity pressure from the majority" (p. 373). The opinions of a heterogeneous majority will be more persuasive, because such opinions are more likely to be perceived as independent of one another and therefore more difficult to discount.

In this section we have discussed the attributional stage of our model. We have seen that by far the most important source of attributions about the defendant's guilt is the nature of the evidence. Only when the evidence is ambiguous or evenly balanced will the remaining factors be important. Moreover, we have seen how the characteristics of the defendant and the attorneys influence jurors' attributions. Finally, we have discussed how information from fellow jurors provided during the jury's deliberation can cancel attributions formed earlier in the trial.

Yet jurors' attribution of guilt is but one determinant of the decision to find the defendant innocent or guilty of the charges. Jurors also weigh the anticipated rewards and costs of their verdict. It is to these social-exchange considerations that we now turn.

SOCIAL-EXCHANGE CONSIDERATIONS

Jurors typically have several verdict options among which to choose. They can find the defendant guilty on all charges or on some of the charges, or they can acquit the defendant on all charges. The fact that jurors attribute guilt or innocence to a defendant for a particular charge does not guarantee that their verdict will mirror this attribution. The verdict chosen will depend on which one jurors believe will yield them the best outcomes. As we have seen in previous chapters, other people can have an important impact on a decision maker's outcomes. For the juror, these others are those closely associated with the trial, including the defendant, fellow jurors, the opposing attorneys, and the judge. Presumably, the final decision represents a weighing of the benefits and costs expected from each. This analysis suggests several interesting possibilities. For example, jurors may believe that the defendant is guilty of the charges but may vote for acquittal because of social-exchange considerations. Alternatively, they may believe that the defendant is not guilty but vote to convict because they think it will prove more profitable to do so. This is not to say that jurors ignore their beliefs about the defendant's guilt. Rather, it suggests that attributions of guilt are but one factor in the juror's calculus. Further, we are not assuming that jurors are always correct in their calculations. Although jurors are usually not under as much pressure for quick action as the police or bystanders, they are nevertheless pressured by their fellow jurors and the judge to reach a verdict. The stress attending their decision may interfere with a perfectly rational calculation of costs and benefits. However, as with the decision making of bystanders and police officers, we will assume that, insofar as possible, jurors' decisions are guided by rational calculations.

We will examine the costs and benefits associated with each of the persons with whom jurors are in a social-exchange relationship, beginning with the defendant.

Social Exchange with the Defendant

Kalven and Zeisel (1966) provide a wealth of evidence showing that jurors strive to treat defendants equitably. Presumably, failure to do so constitutes an important cost for jurors. The concern for equity is reflected in jurors' failure to vote for conviction when they believe that the defendant has already been punished enough or when they judge that the punishment for the crime committed is too severe. Jurors' interest in justice is also reflected in their willingness to vote for conviction when they find the defendant's actions very offensive though not actually illegal. Evidence bearing on each of these situations is described below.

Defendant has been punished enough

Jurors tend to acquit defendants who appear to have paid for their crimes by suffering remorse, by enduring a lengthy pretrial detention, or by suffering misfortunes connected or unconnected with their crime. Several examples will illustrate this point. In one case reported by Kalven and Zeisel (1966) the jury acquitted a high school senior who had killed a 10-year-old while negligently using a rifle. According to the judge in the case, "The jury felt that having the charge and killing on his conscience was sufficient punishment" (p. 303). Another jury acquitted a defendant who had spent two months in pretrial custody on charges of stealing two pieces of lumber. Perhaps the most extreme case involved acquittal of a defendant charged with income tax evasion. The judge reported that

> during the years in question, his home burned, he was seriously injured and his son was killed. Later he lost his leg, his wife became seriously ill and several major operations were necessary. . . . These, however, are only a portion of the calamities the defendant suffered during the years he failed to file his income tax return [p. 305].

In each of these cases, jurors probably felt that the application of additional punishment would be excessive and therefore inequitable.

Threatened punishment is too severe

Kalven and Zeisel (1966) report a number of instances in which the judge believed that the jury failed to convict because the prescribed penalty was too severe and therefore did not fit the crime. Several such cases involved drunken driving, a penalty for which is loss of one's driver's license for one year. Jurors apparently believed that suspending the driver's license of a working man for one year was too severe a punishment, as it could seriously interfere with his livelihood. This "severity/leniency hypothesis" is the basis for the practice of excusing from capital-offense trials prospective jurors who oppose capital punishment, producing the so-called death-qualified jury. In rejecting such persons, it is assumed that those who object to such a severe penalty may be unwilling to vote for conviction even when the evidence favors that verdict (Jurow, 1971).

Three simulated-juror studies provide additional support for the severity/leniency hypothesis. In the first of these (Vidmar, 1972), subjects were given an abbreviated written description of a murder trial that had actually taken place. They were asked to return individual verdicts on the defendant's guilt under one of several conditions that varied the number and severity of decision alternatives. Subjects were made to choose from two, three, or all four of the following: first degree (25 years to life imprisonment), second degree (5–20 years imprisonment), manslaughter (1–5 years imprisonment), and not guilty. The highest percentage of acquittals (54%) occurred when subjects had to choose between the severest alternative (first degree) and not guilty. In comparison, when the alternatives were second degree and not guilty, the percentage of acquittals dropped to 17%, and when the choice was between manslaughter and not guilty, the percentage of acquittals was even lower (8%). Similar results were obtained by Kaplan and Simon (1972). Jurors given just two sentencing options, first-degree murder and not guilty, produced a higher percentage of acquittals (76%) than those given four options, including second-degree murder and manslaughter (43%).

A more tightly designed study by Kerr (1978b) using the same case materials as Vidmar (1972) and only two levels of penalties yielded essentially the same results as the previous two studies: there were fewer convictions in the severe-penalty condition than in the mild-penalty condition. One practical implication noted by Kerr is that if defendants are given a choice, they should prefer to be charged with the offense with the more severe prescribed penalty.

Kalven and Zeisel also note other circumstances in which defendants are acquitted because the threatened punishment is too severe. One such circumstance occurs when the jury is aware that the defendant's accomplice has received lenient treatment. A second such circumstance occurs when the jury fears that finding the defendant guilty would punish his or her innocent family. Often the defendant's family will appear in court, and its presence cannot be ignored. Kalven and Zeisel eloquently described family members who appear in court as "a gallery of patient and long suffering mothers, tearful wives, pregnant wives, wives with babies in their arms, and finally, a large array of small children . . . [who] appear as silent and suffering bystanders" (p. 205). Such scenes serve to remind us of a certain commonality between jurors and other persons who have to make decisions within the context of the criminal justice system. Just like victims and the police, jurors are reluctant to punish an offender if the expected punishment is overly harsh and is likely to create inequity.

Punishment to restore equity

Jurors' desire to maintain equity sometimes causes them to convict a defendant on the basis of legally insufficient evidence. Kalven and Zeisel (1966) show that those accused of sexual offenses against children generate so much outrage among jurors that they sometimes vote for conviction even when the act does not fit the legal definition of a crime. Another example of what Kalven and Zeisel call "pro-prosecution equities" occurred in an auto-accident case in which the defendant's car had knocked down a female pedestrian. The jury found the defendant guilty of reckless driving, whereas the judge would have found him guilty of the lesser offense of leaving the scene of an accident. According to the judge, "I believe the jury was imbued with the thought that the defendant had little regard for the rights of others and that he was inclined to wholly disregard all laws which in any way interfered with personal activities" (Kalven & Zeisel, 1966, p. 399). Kalven and Zeisel's interpretation is that the jury was "so incensed at the defendant for leaving the scene of the accident that it is not satisfied to find him guilty of the very crime that angers them but must go on to find him guilty of reckless driving as well" (p. 399). It would seem, then, that jurors have the capacity—indeed, the willingness—to disregard the law in pursuit of what for them is often a more important goal, the equitable treatment of the defendant.

Social Exchange with Fellow Jurors

Like any work group, the jury has a task to accomplish—in this instance, to reach a just verdict. By the time the jury retires to deliberate, jurors have participated in the voir dire examination, listened to the lawyers present their view of the facts, heard a parade of witnesses, and received instructions from the judge. Kalven and Zeisel (1966) found that when jurors are ready to participate in this final phase of the trial, most of them have already made up their minds. If they all agree, then there is no need to deliberate. They can return to the courtroom and announce their verdict. However, when there is not a sufficient number of votes to acquit or convict the defendant, jurors must engage in a sometimes lengthy process of negotiation and influence designed to achieve the requisite number of votes.

It is the exceptional jury that is equally divided (4%, according to Kalven & Zeisel, 1966). More often, the jury is divided into majority and minority factions, each with its core of spokespersons. One cost of the disagreement between the two factions is what we referred to in Chapter 1 as an opportunity cost. The time spent deliberating is time that jurors could spend engaging in more rewarding activities with family and friends. Moreover, as time drags on, jurors in the majority experience mounting costs associated with fatigue and frustration. As such costs increase, jurors' outcomes are likely to drop below their comparison level (see Chapter 1), but since there are no avenues of escape, their comparison level for alternatives remains low. Trapped in this situation, majority members are likely to direct their attack at the source of their frustration—the minority.

Minority members, too, find the passage of time increasingly costly. As a result of growing pressure from the majority to conform, they are also likely to experience outcomes below their comparison level. One way for them to eliminate these costs of being in the minority is to conform with the majority's wishes. However, this yielding to majority pressure is not the same type of yielding that we referred to earlier when we discussed how jurors' attributions are influenced by group discussion. Whereas that type of yielding implied some change in private beliefs or attributions, the type of influence discussed in this section involves changes in voting (that is, public conformity) *without* private acceptance. Psychologists call this type of influence *compliance*. Jurors who yield to this form of influence exchange their vote for approval or absence of disapproval from fellow jurors.

How can we determine what type of influence has occurred when we learn that a juror has switched his or her verdict? That is, how can we tell, when jurors change their vote, whether they are making a new attribution about the defendant's guilt or merely complying to avoid the costs of disagreement? To distinguish between the two situations, we need information about jurors' private predeliberation beliefs, their publicly expressed vote in the jury room, and their private postdeliberation beliefs. When jurors' votes in the jury room differ from their predeliberation choice, we have evidence that they have been influenced by the group in some way. To find out which type of influence is operative, we can compare the public vote in the jury room with jurors' private postdeliberation beliefs. If the two agree, we can assume that jurors privately accept the group's position. If they disagree, we can assume that jurors voted the way they did in order to win approval or avoid disapproval from their peers.

Two studies that have met these design requirements show that a small percentage yield because of compliance. In the first of these, Simon (1967) found that 10% of her mock jurors expressed a private postdeliberation opinion that differed from their vote in the jury room. A reanalysis of similar mock-juror data presented by Davis, Kerr, Atkin, Holt, and Meek (1975) revealed a 6% difference between the public vote expressed in the jury room and the private postdeliberation opinion. These data would suggest that somewhere between 6 and 10% of jurors yield to majority influence not out of conviction but in order to win the approval of peers and/or avoid their disapproval.

The nature of the intense pressure on jurors to conform with the majority is graphically depicted in two books describing deliberations in real trials. The first (Villasenor, 1977) dealt with the trial of Juan Corona, who was charged with the murder of 25 drifters and derelicts in California. On the basis of numerous interviews with each of the jurors, Villasenor was able to reconstruct much of the jury's deliberation. Near the end of the sixth day of deliberation, the lone holdout juror, Naomi, said to a juror who had just walked by her without speaking:

> "Jim, don't just walk by me without saying a word! Please, I'll change my vote. Just don't hate me. I'll change my vote so you can go home to your wife."
>
> "Naomi," said Jim, soothingly, "I don't hate you. I like you. Now, calm down, and think. This is a murder trial and you can't change your vote unless you've changed your mind."
>
> "Why not? That's what you all want me to do so you can go home to your wives. Here, I'll vote guilty right now" [pp. 241–242].

The fellow jurors would not accept her change of vote, because it did not represent her true beliefs. Rebuffed by her fellow jurors, she wrote a note to the judge asking whether she could change her vote but keep her own opinion. The note was never sent. Unable to win acceptance from her peers, Naomi returned the next day and told the assembled jurors, "I think I've changed my mind. Yesterday you gave me a day's rest and I relaxed and I saw things differently" (p. 265). Yet we can but wonder whether this action represented a change in her attribution about the defendant's guilt or whether it was instead a desperate ploy to win approval from her peers.

The second book (Zerman, 1977) was written by one of the jurors in a murder trial in New York City. The lone dissenter, having just been reduced to a minority of one,

> made it immediately clear that *he* was not planning to change *his* vote, now or in the future. Anger burst around him. He was being totally unreasonable.
>
> . . . Silence again and then a barely audible remark from Juror 6: "Let me sleep on it."
>
> . . . Around us indignation was boiling. The surrender of Juror 5 had proved to be like the dropping of a single shoe. Everyone had waited for the second to fall and now frustration was more intense than it had ever been, for it appeared that the shoe would not fall tonight.
>
> Somehow, by offering the faint suggestion that he might *eventually* change his mind, Juror 6 seemed more stubborn, quixotic, and self-indulgent than he had when he was proclaiming that he would never vote for acquittal. Shouts of abuse and personal hostility were coming from jurors who for hours had said almost nothing.
>
> . . . Was what followed the most sustained barrage of the evening? Had some sort of climax been reached? Yes, the voices were rising again, but were they actually louder and sharper than ever before? Perhaps Juror 6 only thought they were. How much pressure can one man take? Suddenly, he broke.

"All right," he said, almost softly. "I've come to respect all of you too much. I can't do this to you and I won't continue any longer. I change my vote" [pp. 135–138].[2]

Anecdotal evidence such as this, though not conclusive, nevertheless reveals the intense costs that dissenting jurors experience and why they often comply with the majority's will.

What conditions are likely to increase compliance with the majority? Several recent simulated-juror studies provide some clues. As the above excerpts show, compliance is very likely when jurors find themselves in the position of the lone dissenter. Research by Asch (1952) has shown that a unanimous majority of just three persons is often sufficient to cause the lone dissenter to conform. Increasing the size of the majority beyond three does not substantially alter this effect. However, the presence of just a single ally fortifies the dissenter and severely weakens the majority's influence. Interestingly, the recent Supreme Court decision permitting juries to consist of fewer than 12 members (*Williams* v. *Florida*, 1970) misinterpreted this classic finding of Asch. The court stated that what matters is the *proportion* of minority members rather than their absolute number. The justices reasoned that a jury split 5:1 was likely to reach the same verdict as one split 10:2. Yet on the basis of Asch's results we would expect that a jury split 10:2 would be more likely to hang. Most studies that have compared the verdicts of 6- and 12-person mock juries did not find support for Asch's position. Instead, they found no effect of group size on verdicts (for example, Davis et al., 1975; Saks, 1977).

However, Valenti and Downing (1975) did obtain a jury-size effect consistent with Asch's results when they used a case in which the evidence was highly incriminating. They reasoned that when the evidence is highly incriminating, it is to the defendant's disadvantage to be tried by a 6-person jury rather than a 12-person jury. A 12-person jury is more likely to have two dissenters than a 6-person jury, and a jury split 5 to 1 in favor of conviction is more likely to find the defendant guilty than one split 10 to 2—the latter being more likely to produce a hung jury. The same reasoning would suggest that if the evidence against the defendant is weak, it would be to the defendant's advantage to be tried by a 6-person jury, because a jury of this size is less likely to hang. Valenti and Downing's study showed that jury size had no effect when the evidence against the defendant was weak, but when it was strong, 6-person juries were more likely to convict (90%) than 12-person juries (20%). Moreover, regardless of how incriminating the evidence was, 12-person juries were more likely to hang (40%) than 6-person juries (0%).

A second condition likely to increase compliance with the majority

[2]From *Call the Final Witness*, by M. B. Zerman. Copyright ©1977 by Harper & Row Publishers, Inc. Reprinted by permission.

occurs when the dissenter's vote is needed for the group to render a verdict. Recent Supreme Court decisions (*Apodaca* v. *Oregon*, 1972; *Johnson* v. *Louisiana*, 1972) allowing nonunanimous verdicts in state trials permit the majority to tolerate a small minority of dissenters. That is, when only a majority is required for a group verdict, there is no need for all jurors to conform with the majority. Mock-juror studies have consistently found that once the required number of jurors has been achieved, little if any pressure is brought to bear on the remaining minority members (Davis et al., 1975; Kerr et al., 1976; Nemeth, 1977). For example, of 43 majority-rule juries without initial unanimity that eventually reached a verdict, 56% stopped deliberating when the required majority was achieved (Kerr, Atkin, Stasser, Meek, Holt, & Davis, 1976). Further evidence shows that majority-rule juries deliberate for a shorter time and conduct fewer polls than juries having to reach a unanimous verdict (Kerr et al., 1976; Nemeth, 1977). Analyses of interaction patterns during deliberation indicate that juries required to deliberate until a unanimous verdict is reached show more disagreement, show more friendliness and unfriendliness, and give more information and opinions than juries that have only to achieve a majority (Nemeth, 1977). These studies suggest that in unanimous juries, where every juror's vote is needed, greater pressure is placed on dissenters to conform than in juries that require only a majority.

Compliance with the majority is also more likely when the dissenting minority highly values the majority's approval. Although the value of social approval has not been studied in the context of jury deliberations, research on small groups suggests that greater value is placed on others' approval when the group is very cohesive and when the others are of high status. Cohesive groups are those in which there is a high degree of mutual attraction. Because members of such groups place a high value on social approval from the group, they are more likely to find disagreement painful and therefore tend to comply with the group's wishes (Festinger, Schachter, & Back, 1950). Similarly, approval from a high-status person has more reward value than approval from a low-status person (Homans, 1974) and therefore elicits more compliance. Of course, high-status persons are also likely to be perceived as more credible sources of information, which further adds to their influence. In group-pressure situations such as jury deliberations, high-status persons probably exert influence because of their higher credibility as well as the higher value placed on their approval. Therefore, it is difficult to separate the two forms of influence.

Finally, jurors are more likely to comply when they feel obligated to do so because of benefits received from fellow jurors. During the short lifetime of the jury's existence, members have occasion to perform all sorts of favors for fellow jurors, particularly if the jury is sequestered overnight. In addition to deliberating together, members eat as a group and share hotel rooms. In the course of these interactions, numerous occasions arise in which jurors provide peers with emotional support, advice, and sympathetic understanding. Benefits such as these may generate feelings of indebtedness, which can be repaid by altering one's vote in the jury room. Although this argument has some intuitive appeal, systematic empirical data are lacking. However, there is anecdotal support for this hypothesis. In the Mitchell/Stans conspiracy trial one juror was responsible for shifting an initial 8-to-4 majority for conviction into an acquittal. How did he do this? The juror, Andrew Choa, was vice-president of a bank and was clearly a person of high status. According to Zeisel and Diamond's (1976) account of this trial,

> During the many and long evenings, Choa had helped to break the monotony. Occasionally, he took his fellow jurors to the movies in the private auditorium of the bank. When the jurors asked to see the St. Patrick's Day parade and were told they could not go since this meant mingling with the street crowds, he arranged for them to watch it from one of the bank's branch offices. On one or more occasions when money was not readily available for minor jury expenses such as for entertainment, 'Andrew paid and then the Government paid him back.' Choa's bank also loaned baseball bats to the jury. He became, as the *New York Times* reporter put it, the jury's 'social director.' His fellow jurors could hardly help being obliged to the man who had used his high social position to make their sequestration more bearable [p. 165].

Choa's influence was no doubt supplemented by the fact that he was a high-status person.

In this section we have shown that exchange relations with fellow jurors have some impact on the juror's final vote. In addition, it was suggested that a juror is most likely to feel conformity pressure from peers when the juror is a lone dissenter, when the juror's compliance is needed for the group verdict, when the juror places great value on the approval of fellow jurors, and when the juror feels indebted to fellow jurors because of prior help. Before we conclude our discussion of social-exchange considerations, we will examine two additional sources of rewards and costs—the attorneys and the judge.

Social Exchange with the Attorneys and the Judge

Trial manuals caution attorneys not to alienate jurors lest they retaliate by returning an unfavorable verdict. In the previous chapter we called attention to the advice given attorneys on how to treat prospective jurors during the voir dire examination. We have seen how lawyers use the grandstand play to involve jurors in a social-exchange relationship: "I am willing to trust you; therefore you should be willing to trust me." Throughout the trial, the attorneys have many opportunities to continue this exchange. For example, because listening to the presentation of evidence can be very tiresome and boring for the most motivated of jurors, efforts by the attorneys to enliven the proceedings can sometimes be highly rewarding to jurors. Vivid presentations of evidence, such as showing slides or a movie, help to break the monotony of a trial. Similarly, attorneys who display a lively wit or sense of humor during examination of witnesses may be accumulating "credit" with jurors.

However, attorneys can make it costly for jurors when they delay the start of the session by not arriving on time. The same negative effect can be obtained by attorneys who badger witnesses and constantly interrupt the proceedings with objections. Although such displays may well leave their impression on jurors when they begin to deliberate, there is, unfortunately, very little documentation of such common-sense wisdom. In the lone previously cited investigation of the impact of attorneys' demeanor on jurors' predeliberation judgments, Kaplan and Miller (1978) found that when the defense attorney acted obnoxiously, jurors were more inclined to vote guilty. Similarly, when the prosecutor acted obnoxiously, jurors were less inclined to vote guilty. However, after a ten-minute deliberation, the biasing effects of the attorneys' behavior wore off completely. Apparently, the group discussion diminished the significance of the attorneys' behavior and enhanced the salience of the evidence.

Even less is known about the impact of the judge on jurors' verdicts. Newspaper accounts such as the following suggest that jurors are sometimes pressured by the judge to yield to the majority. After eight hours of deliberation, a judge told the jury:

> "I am not entitled to keep you here all night but if you can't reach a verdict then you will have to stay at a hotel overnight and start again in the morning. . . .
> "I don't want to pressure you, but I would like very much if you did reach a verdict. . . .
> "I feel one or more of you are holding out and you certainly have the right to disagree, but on the other hand you have a duty to reach a verdict on which you all agree" ["Jury Acquits Man . . . ," 1980, p. 3].

After one and a half hours of further deliberation, the minority yielded and the jury returned a verdict of acquittal.

Interviews with jurors who served on real juries suggest that jurors tried to guess which way the judge was leaning in order to return a verdict that would win the judge's approval (O'Mara, 1972). Additional evidence comes from Kaplan and Miller's (1978) study. In one condition, the judge and the experimenter acted in such a way as to annoy the jurors. The judge "interrupted the trial at predetermined intervals to ask pointless questions, to scold both attorneys, to give obscure points of law, and once to leave the room for a phone call" (p. 1451). Jurors' judgments of guilt before and after deliberation fell between the ratings obtained with the obnoxious defense attorney and the obnoxious prosecutor. Data on the impact of social exchanges with the attorneys and the judge are meager, but there is some suggestion that outcomes from such exchanges are considered by jurors when they weigh their verdict.

In discussing the social-exchange stage of our model, we have seen that there is fairly strong evidence that jurors weigh the potential outcomes from their exchanges with the defendant and fellow jurors in reaching a verdict. It was suggested that exchanges with the attorneys and the judge are also likely to be considered by jurors, though there presently exists very little confirming evidence.

Criticisms of Juror-Simulation Studies

Most of the evidence reported in this chapter is based on studies using simulated jurors. A number of criticisms have been leveled at this method of research. Four such criticisms cited by Weiten and Diamond (1979) are noteworthy. First, jury-simulation studies tend to rely on college students to play the role of jurors. Of 45 mock-juror studies surveyed by Bray (1976), 62% relied exclusively on college or high school students. College students differ from real jurors in several ways. Students tend to be younger, better educated, and more intelligent and to come from higher-socioeconomic-class homes than the typical juror. Second, simulations tend to be poor reconstructions of what is presented to jurors during a real trial. According to Bray's (1976) survey, evidence is presented to simulated jurors mainly through written summaries (51%) and audiotape summaries (42%). Only 10% of the studies used live presentation of the evidence. The importance of the mode of presentation is underscored by a recent finding that the mode of presentation influences the verdict and perceptions of the effectiveness of attorneys' presentations (Juhnke, Vought, Pyszczynski, Dane, Losure, & Wrightsman, 1979). Moreover, because the case material is drastically condensed to as little as 400 words (for example, Landy & Aronson, 1969), the variable being manipulated is likely to be more prominent, and therefore it is hardly surprising that this variable usually has an impact on jurors. One can only wonder whether the impact would be the same if the variable being studied were embedded in a trial proceeding of much longer duration than 15–20 minutes.

A third criticism is that juror-simulation studies use inappropriate dependent variables. Rather than asking subjects to render a guilty or not guilty verdict, as real jurors are asked to do, most simulated-juror studies ask subjects to judge the probability of the defendant's guilt or to recommend a sentence for the defendant. Yet only in capital offenses and felonies in 13 states are real jurors asked to sentence the defendant. Moreover, the factors that influence the sentencing decision may *not* be identical to those that affect judgments of innocence or guilt (for example, Stewart, 1980).

The final criticism of using simulated jurors to understand the decision-making process of real jurors is that simulated jurors know that no real person will be affected by their decision. In contrast, real jurors are acutely aware of the important impact that their decision will have on the defendant's life. In short, the argument is that hypothetical decisions are not the same as real decisions. Three studies that have compared the verdicts of real jurors with those of simulated jurors have produced inconsistent results. One has shown that simulated jurors are *more* likely to render a guilty verdict (Diamond & Zeisel, 1974), another found that simulated jurors are *less* likely to judge the defendant guilty (Wilson & Donnerstein, 1977), and a third found no difference (Kerr, Nerenz, & Herrick, 1979).

The criticisms of the simulated-juror paradigm do not mean that the results of such studies are invalid or that simulations should be abandoned. The proper conclusion to be drawn is that one should not uncritically accept the applicability of mock-juror findings to real jurors. As Bray and Kerr (1979) note, "The very existence of differences between typical jury simulations and actual trials does *not* make it implausible or impossible that results *will* generalize. Identifying such differences only raises the question of generalizability, it does not settle it" (p. 115). A major advantage of the continued use of the simulation procedure is that it allows study of trial practices and procedures not currently in use. As Elwork, Sales, and Suggs (1981) contend, "If we are to make improvements, we need to have the freedom to 'experiment' with variables that do not presently exist in the real world" (p. 53).

SUMMARY

In this chapter the attribution/exchange framework was used to study the factors that influence jurors' decision to find the defendant guilty or not guilty. As in the previous chapters, it was proposed that the final decision is a joint product of the kinds of dispositions assigned to the defendant and the expected outcomes of social exchanges with key others. We saw, too, that the dispositions assigned to the defendant depend on (1) the nature of the evidence, (2) characteristics of the defendant, (3) characteristics of the attorneys, and (4) information supplied by fellow jurors. The nature of the evidence is by far the most important determinant of jurors' attributions about the defendant. Only when the evidence is ambiguous or evenly balanced do the other factors come into play.

Having decided on the defendant's dispositions, jurors must decide on their verdict. Belief in the defendant's guilt or innocence does not necessarily imply that jurors will vote accordingly. Instead, the final decision is also a product of the balance of benefits and costs derived from social exchanges with the defendant, with fellow jurors, and with the attorneys and the judge.

Having rendered its verdict, the jury has completed its task. If the defendant is found not guilty of the charges, he or she leaves the courtroom a free person. If found guilty, and about 75% of felony defendants are (Brosi, 1979), the defendant can appeal the decision. However, appeals are limited to legal (that is, procedural), as opposed to factual, considerations. Few defendants appeal their convictions, and most of those who do are not successful (Saks & Hastie, 1978). In those rare cases in which a convicted defendant wins an appeal, the case is sent back to the trial court, where the state is given the option of retrying the accused. Convicted defendants who choose not to appeal may be released on bail or held in custody to await sentencing by the judge. In the next chapter, the attribution/exchange model is used to analyze the judge's sentencing decision.

CHAPTER SEVEN

Sentencing

According to the popularized view of the courtroom, the most tension-filled moment in the entire judicial process occurs when the defendant faces the jury, the jury foreperson rises and slowly reads the verdict, and the defendant then breaks down either in joy or in sorrow, depending on the plot of the story. Although this conception of a criminal trial makes for good drama, it is unrealistic in the extreme. As we have seen, defendants usually plead guilty to some crime, even if it is not the crime or crimes with which they were originally charged. Hence, in most cases the drama in the courtroom comes not from the finding of guilt or innocence but from the sentence that the judge imposes on the defendant.

In recent years the public has become aware of how judges exercise their sentencing power. Judge John Sirica, for example, used the threat of a longer sentence to try to get the Watergate burglars to cooperate in the government's investigation to discover the masterminds of the break-in. An indication of Sirica's power is that Howard Hunt, who cooperated with the government, was given a shorter sentence than Gordon Liddy, who refused to cooperate.

Within the past few years social psychologists have focused much attention on the sentencing decision. Their interest in this aspect of criminal justice derives from several sources. First, the decision involves a significant real-world problem that had not yet been systematically investigated. Second, a number of important factors (for example, race, sex, attitude of the criminal toward his or her crime, prior criminal record) can be conveniently investigated in questionnaire studies using college students as subjects. In addition to being easily administered, questionnaire studies have the advantage that the dependent variable—length of sentence—is easily understood by subjects and is, by its nature, quantifiable. A third source of interest in the sentencing decision is that the process by which the decision is reached involves issues raised by a number of prominent theories in social psychology, such as attribution theory, exchange theory, and information-integration theory. Finally, because of the interest of legal, academic, and governmental communities in the sentencing decision, social psychologists have been able to obtain resources, including money, research facilities, and, most important, cooperation, which are necessary for a study of this particular aspect of the criminal justice system.

This chapter will examine several aspects of the sentencing decision. First, the history of sentencing will be briefly surveyed, followed by an examination of the general pattern of sentencing in the United States today. Relevant social-psychological research will then be discussed, and an attempt will be made to integrate this material using the attribution/exchange framework.

A BRIEF HISTORY OF SENTENCING

In medieval and early modern Europe, criminal law was influenced by such theological conceptions as free will, moral responsibility, and a belief in the need for harsh and degrading penalties. By the late 18th century, however, many traditional beliefs had come under severe attack by philosophers such as Bentham, Beccaria, and Montesquieu, who were especially critical of inequitable penalties that resulted from judicial discretion. Consequently, in 1795 the Revolutionary government in France formulated a new code that specified the length of incarceration for every offense (Tappan, 1960).

In the United States, sentencing followed a similiar historical pattern. During the colonial period, Americans were subjected to the unbridled discretion of English judges who were unsympathetic to the colonists. After Independence, state legislatures severely restricted judicial discretion in sentencing. Because the laws generally specified the penalty for each offense, the judge's task was limited largely to presiding over the trial proceedings. After a person was found guilty of a crime, the statutorily prescribed penalty for that crime was imposed (Gaylin, 1974).

As years passed, state legislatures gradually drew distinctions between different types of what had been considered the same offense, thus creating "degrees" of each crime, depending on both the intent of the offender and the severity of the harm. Despite the creation of these grades of felonies, the sentences required by the legislature did not always fit the circumstances of every case, and therefore more discretion was given to judges. Judges were given a range of sentence lengths for each crime, from which they could allot the appropriate punishment for the particular criminal (Goldfarb & Singer, 1973). With the creation of the indefinite sentence in 1869 in Michigan, and by 1900 in most states, the actual power to determine the length of incarceration for many offenses had passed into the hands of an executive agency known today as the parole board.

This transition—from fixed penalties set by the legislature to the allowance for judicial discretion in setting sentences to the actual determination of sentence length by parole boards—has followed the corresponding change in the public's beliefs about the purpose of sentences. That is, sentences have come to serve less purely punitive functions and are viewed as also having rehabilitative goals.

The Sentencing System

The sentencing of criminals is designed to serve one or more of a variety of goals. One function is *individual deterrence;* it is expected that punishing an offender will keep that person from committing other crimes in the future. Individual deterrence is often compared with a second function—*general deterrence.* That is, the judge expects that the punishment of a law violator will discourage others who are considering breaking the law from doing so. *Incapacitation* is a third function served by sentencing. By sending a convicted felon to prison, the judge can ensure that the felon will not be committing crimes on the streets during the period of incarceration. In most cases the judge also wants to punish the criminal for having broken the law. This function, *retribution*, holds that the felon should not benefit from a law violation. A fifth function of sentencing is that it serves as an expression of *moral outrage.* That is, by sentencing the offender, the judge is reflecting society's values and telling the offender and others that breaking the law is wrong. *Rehabilitation* is also viewed as a goal of sentencing. Often the judge prescribes a certain sentence in the hope that the offender will receive some kind of treatment, which will enable him or her to live in society without breaking the law. Whether the purpose of the sentence and the sentence length are determined legislatively, judicially, or administratively—or by some combination of the three—depends on the jurisdiction and on the type of crime involved (Dershowitz, 1976). Individual deterrence, general deterrence, incapacitation, retribution, moral outrage, and rehabilitation are probably all included to some extent in the intent of the people who determine the sentence, regardless of who makes the actual determination.

In only seven states does the jury have the responsibility of making the sentencing decision for some or all noncapital crimes (American Bar Association, 1980b). Since the clear majority of jurisdictions give this power to the judge, the rest of this chapter will concern itself with the judge's sentencing decision.

Depending on the jurisdiction and the legislatively defined alternatives for the particular crime in question, judges generally have one or some combination of six sentencing options available to them. Judges may impose a *suspended sentence*, which means that the felon is released and is not under the supervision of the court. However, the judge has the power to reimpose the sentence if the offender gets into trouble during the period of release. A sentence of *probation* usually requires that the felon report regularly to a probation officer and have some program of rehabilitation for a specified period. A third sentencing alternative is to impose on the defendant a *fine* payable to the government. Requiring that the felon make *restitution* to the victims of the crime, usually by paying money to the victims to compensate them for their loss, is a fourth alternative. The fifth option is a term of *imprisonment.* Violators of minor laws (misdemeanants) may be sentenced to a term of imprisonment usually less than one year in length and often serve their sentences in county jails. Violators of major laws (felons) may be sentenced to a term of imprisonment in excess of one year and are usually sent to prisons controlled by the state. Finally, a sentence of *capital punishment* is sometimes available when the crime is particularly reprehensible, such as premeditated murder or murder of law enforcement officers. However, the use of this option is severely limited by recent Supreme Court decisions.

Proposals for Reform

Perhaps the major criticism leveled at judges is that their sentencing decisions are inconsistent from one judge to another. And, indeed, there is truth to this charge of "sentencing disparity." Such inconsistency has received a great deal of publicity, whereas the exercise of discretion at other stages of the criminal justice system is either ignored or minimized. This distinction in amount of publicity probably exists because it is much easier to quantify the existence of disparity at the sentencing stage (for example, by the percentage of probation sentences or the average length of prison terms) than at the arrest and prosecution stages (Dawson, 1969).

Disparity in sentences is evident not only from statistics on sentence lengths but also from more tightly controlled studies (Partridge & Eldridge, 1974). In Partridge and Eldridge's study, 50 federal judges were given identical sets of 20 files drawn from actual cases, with the crimes ranging from embezzlement to robbery. The results showed "glaring disparity" in judicial sentencing decisions. In one case, for example, the judges were presented with a male offender over age 40 who was found guilty of nine counts of extortionate credit transactions and related income tax violations. The offender's prior record included six other arrests, three convictions, and two periods of imprisonment. The sentences recommended by the judges ranged from three years in prison with no fine to 20 years in prison and a $65,000 fine. This example is just one of several that illustrate how reasonable persons in the same role can receive the same information and yet come to widely variant conclusions.

Recently, there has been a trend toward limiting judges' discretion in sentencing decisions. In some states, this trend is evidenced by mandatory sentences for certain crimes. For example, Massachusetts adopted a law that requires a mandatory sentence of one year in prison for carrying a firearm without a license. Supporters of this law have argued that assaults and homicides with guns have been reduced since the law became effective in 1975 (Stevens, 1980). In other states, there have been calls for a "presumptive sentence" for each offense (Twentieth Century Fund Task Force on Criminal Sentencing, 1976). This presumptive sentence, fixed by the legislature, would be the sentence imposed on the typical first offender who committed the crime in a typical manner. For repeat offenders, the presumptive sentence would be increased in some fashion specified by the legislature. If there were extraordinary circumstances, the judge could depart from the presumptive sentence after stating in writing his or her reasons for doing so. Another proposal to limit judges' discretion is the use of sentencing guidelines, similar to those developed for the U. S. Parole Commission (see Chapter 9). Under such guidelines, a narrow range of sentences is specified for a particular type of crime and criminal history. A judge may go outside the guidelines if he or she writes an explanation giving the mitigating or aggravating factors that justify doing so. With both presumptive sentencing and sentencing guidelines, the focus is on the usual case rather than the exception. Because a written explanation is required only in the exceptional cases, it seems reasonable to assume that the exceptions will be made only with some thought and only in cases that are unusual (Silberman, 1978).

Although proposals for sentencing reform have received support, there are critics of the suggested procedures. Some have suggested that sentencing guidelines pose legal and constitutional questions of due process and cause problems in administering sometimes very complex statutes (Crump, 1980). Moreover, because consistency in sentencing may produce sentences that are longer than present ones, the result may be even more crowding in prisons and greater likelihood of nullification by virtually all agents of the criminal justice system, who may believe that the penalties prescribed by the guidelines are too harsh (Schulhofer, 1980). Thus, as we saw in Chapter 3, if police officers believe the sentence for a certain crime is too harsh and are faced with choosing either a penalty that is too severe or no penalty at all, they sometimes choose not to inflict any penalty. The same considerations are probably even more true of prosecutors and judges (Alschuler, 1978).

Although several states are experimenting with sentencing guidelines, most states still grant judges a great deal of discretion in the sentencing decision. Given this discretion, judges are very likely to give different sentences to criminals who committed similar crimes and have similar backgrounds.

The question to be asked is not so much "Does disparity exist?" but rather "Why does it exist?" The report on corrections by the National

Advisory Commission on Criminal Justice Standards and Goals (1973) offered several answers to the latter question: "legislative inaction or inattention to sentencing statutes"; "lack of communication among judges concerning the goals and desiderata of sentencing"; "lack of communication between sentencing courts and the correctional system, and the insularity engendered thereby"; "most judges are unfamiliar with the institutions to which they sentence offenders"; and "lack of information about available sentencing alternatives" (pp. 146–147). Because statutes generally give judges little guidance about what objectives are to be accomplished through the imposition of a prison sentence, judges may have different objectives and accordingly may give different sentences for the same crime (see Bottomley, 1973; McFatter, 1978). The combination of lack of communication and ambiguity of purpose in sentencing allows "the intrusion of extralegal and specifically psychological considerations" (Pepitone & DiNubile, 1976, p. 448).

To understand these psychological and, more particularly, the social-psychological considerations involved, we will examine the sentencing decision in two stages: first, it will be viewed in terms of the attributions the judge makes about the defendant, and second, it will be viewed in terms of the social-exchange considerations that enter into the sentencing decision. The two stages and the relevant informational inputs are shown in Figure 7–1.

ASSIGNING A DISPOSITION OF CRIMINALITY

As discussed earlier, attribution theory tries to explain the general principles by which a disposition is assigned to an actor on the basis of an act or series of acts. In the sentencing decision, the act involved is the crime (or crimes) for which the defendant was found or pleaded guilty. The actor involved is the defendant, the observer is the judge, and the disposition in question is the criminality of the defendant.

Judges have a great deal of information about the defendant—much more, in fact, than they could possibly use (Wilkins, 1975). In such a situation they are likely to rely on their past experience to simplify their attribution-making task. Otherwise judges would have to spend more time on each case than they have. Because time is limited, judges rely on stored information about the characteristics of certain types of cases and the criminals who are likely to commit certain crimes. This stored information, which Kelley (1972b) termed a "causal schema," allows judges to assign a disposition to a defendant on the basis of his or her past behavior, according to rules that have worked for them in the past (see Fontaine & Emily, 1978). Thus, the disposition that judges assign to a defendant depends on the information about the defendant that is available to them and also on their schemata for attributing dispositions for the offense in question.

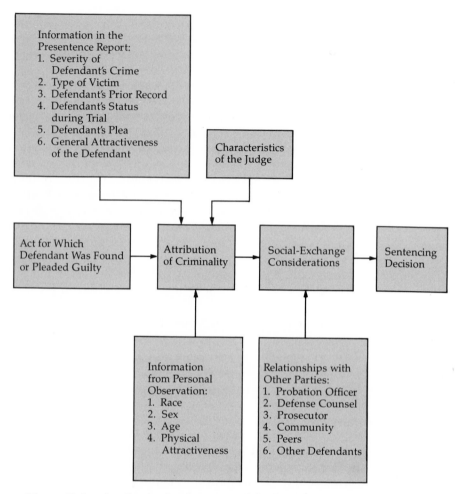

Figure 7–1. Attribution/exchange model of the judge's sentencing decision

The Presentence Report

Most of the information judges use to assign dispositions comes from the presentence report. This report usually includes a description of the original charges against the defendant, the final charges to which he or she pleaded guilty or of which he or she was found guilty, the defendant's general background (such as education and employment history), an evaluation of his or her chances for success on probation, and a recommended sentence. Although only about one-fourth of the states make a presentence report mandatory for felonies, we would estimate that over 85% prepare some kind of presentence report in such cases.

The presentence report is usually written by a probation officer assigned to the court. This officer interviews the defendant and tries to discover the defendant's attitude toward his or her crime (that is, whether or not the defendant is repentant). In addition, the officer examines the arrest report and the defendant's criminal record and generally tries to learn as much as possible about the defendant's employment history and prospects, education, drug and alcohol use, and family stability. Frequently, much of this information consists largely of hearsay and unreliable testimony (National Advisory Commission on Criminal Justice Standards and Goals, 1973). Although hearsay information is considered inadmissible when deciding the guilt or innocence of the defendant, it is admissible at the time of the sentencing decision. As the Supreme Court has stated,

> Highly relevant—if not essential—to [the judge's] selection of an appropriate sentence is the possession of the fullest information possible concerning the defendant's life and characteristics. And modern concepts individualizing punishment have made it all the more necessary that a sentencing judge not be denied an opportunity to obtain pertinent information by a requirement of rigid adherence to restrictive rules of evidence properly applicable to the trial [*Williams* v. *U. S.*, 337 U. S. 241, 246 (1949)].

At the end of the presentence report, the probation officer usually summarizes the case and then makes a specific recommendation based on the applicable law and, where appropriate, estimates the defendant's likelihood of a successful probation.

Severity of the crime

The central factor in the presentence report is the crime of which the defendant was convicted or to which he or she pleaded guilty. Perhaps the best measure of the perception of crime severity is the specified penalty for the crime in the jurisdiction's penal code. As one would expect, the more severe the crime, the more severe the sentence. A harsher sentence is more likely to be meted out for murder than for robbery. Indeed, studies relating the ranked seriousness of crimes with statutorily mandated sentences do seem to show the expected relation (Bullock, 1961).

There are a number of reasons that legislatures have set higher penalties for more severe crimes. First, longer sentences for severe crimes probably better serve all the purposes of a sentence previously described: individual and general deterrence, incapacitation, retribution, moral outrage, and rehabilitation. Attribution theory can also help explain why severe crimes carry higher penalties. The more severe the crime, the more likely the criminal is to be judged responsible for the crime (Carroll & Payne, 1975). The perceived correlation between responsibility and severity probably results from the inhibiting forces, such as social norms, that accompany more severe crimes. That is, the more severe a crime, the more obstacles there are to its commission. For a person to have committed a severe crime in the face of such obstacles would seem to require that he or she have really desired to commit the act—that is, that the person have a criminal disposition.

It is possible, however, that the way in which a crime was committed will affect the attributed responsibility for the crime, independent of crime severity. For example, multiple offenders might diffuse the responsibility of any one offender, and, therefore, the offender might receive less punishment. This notion was tested by Feldman and Rosen (1978), using college students as subjects. Results showed that the greater the number of participants in a nonnormative act, the less responsibility attributed to any single participant. This result was consistent with Feldman and Rosen's finding that jail sentences given robbers in Richmond, Virginia, were significantly longer when the robbery was committed by one person than by a group.

Nature of the victim

A second kind of information contained in the presentence report that influences the attribution process is the type of victim. One study bearing on this subject examined the proportion of prison sentences imposed by criminal judges for several types of crime, broken down by the following factors: (1) the specificity of the victim—that is, whether the victim was an identifiable person or persons, as opposed to the public; (2) personal contact between the offender and the victim; and (3) the extent of bodily harm (Green, 1961). Results showed that the more specific the victim, the more severe the sentence. Crimes against the public in general—that is, crimes in which there was no specific, identifiable victim, such as liquor and gambling violations—received the lowest penalties. Among cases involving personal contact between the defendant and the victim, crimes that included bodily harm received higher penalties than those that did not. Predictably, crimes in which the intention of bodily harm was the primary motive, such as murder, were judged more severe than those in which bodily injury was presumed to be an incidental by-product of the criminal act, such as robbery.

All three of the factors described above are directly related to the perceived criminality of the defendant. If the defendant singled out a specific victim, if he or she came in contact with the victim, and if he or she harmed the victim, it becomes more difficult for a perceiver to find a noncriminal explanation for the behavior. Consequently, as the level of each of these factors increases, the judge becomes more likely to attribute a criminal disposition to the defendant.

Another aspect of the victim that is likely to influence the judge's attribution about the defendant is the victim's defenselessness. A defendant who victimizes someone who is perceived as defenseless, such as someone who is very old, a child, or physically handicapped, will be seen as more blameworthy than a defendant whose victim is not so defenseless. A weak victim is seen as less likely to provoke the criminal act and thus as less blameworthy than a victim who could be perceived as having provoked the crime. In addition, a defenseless victim is less likely to be seen as deserving of his or her fate than one who is not defenseless, for there is more injustice in the former than the latter case. A severe sentence for the defendant in the first case would correct the injustice. Another reason that a defendant whose victim was defenseless might be perceived as more criminal is that there are stronger inhibiting causes against victimizing a defenseless person. These inhibiting causes derive from societal norms prescribing special treatment of the very young, the very old, and the physically disabled. To commit a crime against a weak victim in the face of these norms would suggest that the defendant has a very strong criminal disposition.

One observational study of the relation between the victim's characteristics and the actual sentence given to the defendant (Denno & Cramer, 1976) found that such characteristics of the victim as age, ethnicity, appearance, demeanor, and sex did not significantly affect the defendant's sentence. However, the overall impression reflected in the judge's reaction to the victim had a fairly high correlation with the sentence given to the defendant. That is, the more favorable the judge's impression of the victim, the longer the defendant's sentence. Interestingly, the factor of provocation by the victim was only moderately related to the sentence.

Questionnaire studies using college students as subjects have also been used in an effort to determine the influence of characteristics of the victim on the defendant's sentence. In one study, subjects tended to give a longer sentence to a defendant when the victim of an automobile homicide was of high status (a noted architect and prominent member of the community) rather than low status (a notorious gangster and syndicate boss) (Landy & Aronson, 1969). Results of a second study appeared to reflect subjects' need to believe in a just world in that there was a tendency to make the victim worthy of her fate (Jones & Aronson, 1973). More specifically, subjects blamed a rape victim more if she was married or a virgin than if she was divorced. However, even though subjects blamed the more attractive victims for their fates, contrary to expectations, subjects sentenced the defendant to a longer period of imprisonment for the rape of a married woman than for the rape of a divorcee. One would expect that shorter sentences would be given when the victim is more blameworthy. Yet it may be that when the crime is severe and the locus of causality is ambiguous (that is, both the defendant and the victim were somewhat to blame), subjects take two actions to defend themselves against future victimizations. First, they blame the victim for the crime, thus, in effect, saying that it could not happen to them. Second, they recommend more severe sentences, perhaps in an effort to incapacitate the offender or to deter others from committing such crimes in the future. It should be noted that other studies (for example, Zuckerman & Gerbasi, cited in Gerbasi, Zuckerman, & Reis,

1977) have found that more respectable rape victims were held less responsible for their victimization. Taken together, these studies show that the more positive the general impression of the victim, the more severe the sentence given to the defendant. This finding suggests that a stronger criminal disposition will be assigned when the victim is attractive.

One final feature of the victim that appears to affect sentence length is whether there was a prior relationship between the victim and the offender. Generally, sentences are more severe when the offender and victim were strangers than when there was a prior relationship. In a study by the Vera Institute in New York looking at the sentences given arrested robbers, it was found that when the victim and offender were strangers, 65% of the robbers were incarcerated, whereas when the two knew each other, only 21% of the robbers were incarcerated. Similarly, nearly half of arrested burglars were incarcerated when there was no relationship, whereas only 6% were incarcerated when there was a prior relationship (cited in Silberman, 1978). Attribution theory can help us understand these results. If a prior relationship existed between the victim and the offender, it is possible that the offender may have committed the crime in response to some action by the victim. If so, the offender would be perceived as less responsible for the crime and less deserving of punishment. Although the victim may not have precipitated the crime in every case, the possibility that such precipitation occurred does exist, and this doubt may cause judges to give more lenient sentences.

Defendant's prior record

Another important type of information in the presentence report concerns the defendant's prior criminal record. If the defendant has a history of prior convictions, a judge is likely to infer that the defendant has a stable criminal disposition because he or she has performed criminal acts in different situations and at different times. When behavior is consistent across varied circumstances, the likelihood of making an internal attribution to the actor is increased. In this case, the more crimes a person has committed in the past, the more likely a criminal disposition is to be assigned.

Not unexpectedly, therefore, the greater the number of prior felony convictions, the less the likelihood of a probation sentence (Dawson, 1969) and the more severe the prison sentence (Ebbesen & Konečni, 1976; Green, 1960). Judges seem to focus mainly on prior felony convictions. At the sentencing stage, a defendant with only prior misdemeanor convictions or arrests not followed by conviction is generally regarded as a first offender (Dawson, 1969; Green, 1960). Violations of the juvenile code, in many jurisdictions, are not included in the prior record, because by statute the juvenile's record is required to be sealed when he or she becomes an adult. However, the judge may take into account any felonies the defendant admitted committing but for which, as a result of plea bargaining, he or she was not charged (Dawson, 1969).

The judge is also likely to examine, where applicable, the defendant's prior success or failure on probation. A defendant who seriously violated probation in the past is unlikely to be placed on probation again (Dawson, 1979). The fact that a defendant committed a crime *despite* being on probation would increase the judge's confidence that the defendant has a strong criminal disposition.

Another type of information about defendants that often affects the sentencing decision is use of drugs. Defendants who have been addicted to narcotics are considered a bad risk for probation because it is deemed likely that they will violate the law again (Dawson, 1969). Judges' past experiences lead many of them to believe that there is little hope for rehabilitation of drug addicts. As Kelley has noted, reliance on stored information in the form of causal schemata greatly simplifies the attribution process. The application of particular labels, such as "drug addict" or "alcoholic," in combination with the commission of certain crimes, often results in the assignment of a stable criminal disposition—which inevitably yields a more severe sentence.

Defendant's status before and during the trial

As discussed in Chapter 4, the bail-setting decision is contingent on the defendant's likelihood of appearing for the trial. Not only does the decision to release the defendant on bail or on personal recognizance affect the defendant's freedom before and during the trial, but, more important, it influences the length of the sentence. Available evidence indicates that sentence leniency is highly correlated with having been released on bail (Ares, Rankin, & Sturz, 1963; Ebbesen & Konečni, 1976; Rankin, 1964). Conceivably, the criteria used for bail setting are similar to those used for the sentencing decision, so that those persons who are the best risks for the bail decision are also the best risks for the sentencing decision. However, when one controls for the factors that judges believe affect their bail-setting and sentencing decisions, such as the defendant's previous record, family stability, and employment stability, the mere fact of having been released on bail or on personal recognizance still results in a lighter sentence.

A number of reasons might account for differential sentencing based on the defendant's status before and during the trial. First, it could be argued that persons released on bail or on personal recognizance are more likely to have committed less serious crimes and therefore to receive shorter sentences. However, when researchers statistically controlled for seriousness of crime, they found that the defendant's pretrial status still had a substantial effect on the sentencing decision (Ares et al., 1963; Rankin, 1964).

Attribution theory supplies a second explanation. More trustworthiness is likely to be attributed to a defendant who maintains good behavior while released on bail on his or her own recognizance than is attributed to a defendant who spends his or her pretrial time in jail. As Strickland (1958) has shown, less trustworthiness is attributed to one who performs well when under surveillance (this is analogous to a jail setting) than to one who performs well when not under surveillance (this is analogous to being released on bail). Simply stated, the non-criminal behavior of a person under surveillance is more likely to be attributed to environmental constraints than is the noncriminal behavior of a person not under surveillance. In the latter case, the perceiver is more likely to view the defendant's behavior as reflecting a change in disposition from one labeled "criminal" to one labeled "non-criminal." Thus, a defendant who is released on bail or on personal recognizance is in a more advantageous position than one who remains in jail because he or she has a better opportunity to prove that the criminal disposition is no longer present.

A third explanation for the influence of the defendant's pretrial status on sentencing derives from the setting in which the probation officer interviews the accused. As the National Advisory Commission on Criminal Justice Standards and Goals (1973) reported,

> It is not unreasonable to assume that the attitude of a person detained prior to trial is markedly different from that of a person who was at liberty. The man who has met with the indecent conditions typical of jails is likely to have built up considerable animosity toward the criminal justice system and the society that perpetuates it [p. 99].

If such negative attitudes are reflected in the interview with the probation officer, then the officer's perceptions and recommendations, as reflected in the presentence report, are likely to be less favorable. The jail setting may also be disadvantageous for the defendant in that its atmosphere may heighten the salience of cues associated with criminality, which might bias the probation officer's perception in the direction of attributing greater criminality to the defendant.

The powerful effects that an institutional setting can have on evaluators' perceptions of its inmates were dramatically illustrated in a study involving patients in a psychiatric institution (Rosenhan, 1973). A group of pseudopatients, supposedly suffering from auditory hallucinations, gained admittance to several psychiatric hospitals. Once admitted, they proceeded to display normal behavior. Yet despite this unexceptional behavior, the staff continued to perceive them in terms of their psychiatric label. In several instances normal behavior was perceived as furthur support for the psychiatric diagnosis. In one example provided by Rosenhan, a bogus patient kept written notes of his experiences in the institution. Later it was learned that the patient's notetaking was described as compulsive and pathological. In view of the ways institutional settings can bias others' perception of an inmate, it is likely that defendants interviewed in jail are more negatively evaluated by probation officers than those who are interviewed in a noninstitutional context.

It should be noted, however, that there have been several criticisms of the Rosenhan study. For example, there is disagreement over whether the auditory hallucinations were the only symptoms of mental illness shown by the pseudopatients. After all, the pseudopatients had sought admission to mental hospitals, a behavior that is unusual among those who are not mentally ill (Ostrow, 1973; Spitzer, 1975). Weiner (1975) gave an attributional interpretation to the results of the study, arguing that because the pseudopatients and their hallucinations were consistent over time and because hallucinatory behavior is rare, it was quite rational to make an internal attribution of mental illness.

Konečni and Ebbesen (personal communication) suggest that the jail setting may bias the probation officer's report in yet another way. They note that in San Diego, where their research was conducted, most probation officers are female. These female officers, they suggest, may find it particularly aversive to interview male defendants in a jail context, mainly because of verbal and nonverbal reactions of fellow inmates. The discomfort experienced by these women may be reflected in less favorable probation reports.

Nature of defendant's plea

In most cases the probation officer notes in the presentence report whether the defendant *pleaded* guilty or was *found* guilty by a jury or by a judge. This factor undoubtedly influences the sentencing decisions of many judges. Within our attribution/social-exchange framework, it could be argued that a guilty plea is evidence of a change in disposition, particularly if there are inhibiting causes against the plea, such as the possibility of retaliation by other criminals. Yet this interpretation does not have as much explanatory power as one might expect, because there usually are more compelling reasons, having to do with social exchange, for pleading guilty. As discussed in Chapter 4, many people have argued that the criminal justice system could not function without the guilty plea. There simply are not enough prosecutors, judges, or courtrooms to accommodate all those who would need to stand trial. Many judges feel that by pleading not guilty, the defendant forces particular burdens on the system and the taxpayer, and that if the defendant is found guilty, he or she should be punished for creating this added expense. Thus, in terms of exchange theory, the guilty plea is merely one part of a prearranged bargain in which the defendant pleads guilty (usually to a lesser crime) in the expectation of being rewarded with a reduced sentence. Because of the salience of this reward, no change in disposition need be inferred from a guilty plea (National Advisory Commission on Criminal Justice Standards and Goals, 1973). The literature seems to suggest that most judges operate on the exchange model, assigning a more lenient sentence in exchange for a guilty plea. Moreover, they believe that other judges operate similarly (*Yale Law Journal*, 1956).

General attractiveness of defendant

The presentence report often contains a summary of the defendant's positive and negative traits. Although there is no direct evidence that this information influences the sentencing decisions of judges, there is experimental evidence that such information influences the sentencing decisions of college students when they are asked to make such judgments. In one study (Kaplan & Kemmerick, 1974) subjects read information about eight traffic felony cases in each of which (1) the evidence was either very incriminating or not very incriminating and (2) the defendant was characterized with positive, negative, or neutral traits. Regardless of the level of incriminating evidence, the pattern of punishment that subjects meted out was the same: negatively characterized defendants received more punishment than neutrally characterized defendants, who, in turn, received more punishment than positively characterized defendants. In yet another study (Landy & Aronson, 1969) the defendant in an automobile negligent-homicide case was made to appear either attractive (a friendly, hard-working insurance adjustor on his way to spend Christmas with his family) or unattractive (a janitor, twice divorced and with a criminal record, who was on his way to visit his girlfriend). Not surprisingly, subjects gave the unattractive defendant a longer sentence than the attractive one.

Subsequent studies have used modified versions of these descriptions from Landy and Aronson's study and have produced results that qualify those of the original study. In one study, for example, it was shown that when subjects were permitted to deliberate among themselves before making their sentencing decision, no significant difference was found between the sentences assigned to the attractive (high-status) and unattractive (low-status) defendants (Izzett & Leginski, 1974).

Judges' Personal Observation of Defendant

In addition to information contained in the presentence report, the judge has the opportunity to collect further information through personal observation of the defendant during the trial. Although some judges feel that the unique opportunity for personal observation of the defendant under stress gives them sufficient familiarity with the defendant's character, clearly the amount of reliable information that judges can obtain through personal observation is limited. Three limiting factors can be identified: (1) The great majority of defendants plead guilty, and therefore the judge's personal confrontation with the defendant is brief, perhaps only 10–15 minutes at the time of sentencing. (2) Even if the case goes to trial, the judge may be limited to visual cues because not all defendants testify at the trial. (3) Even when the defendant does testify, he or she may fail to present a reliable picture of himself or herself because of situational stress arising from the trial proceedings (Weiger, cited in Goldfarb & Singer, 1973). Given these limitations in their observations, it is not surprising that judges must often rely on stereotypes associated with gross observable characteristics, such as the defendant's race, sex, age, and physical attractiveness.

Defendant's race

A number of studies have investigated the importance of the defendant's race in the sentencing decision. Some of these studies have shown that blacks are given shorter sentences than whites in homicide cases but longer sentences than whites for other offenses (Bullock, 1961; Sellin, 1938). This result was explained by the fact that blacks usually committed murder against other blacks but usually committed property crimes against whites. It has also been suggested that during the period in which these studies were conducted, the criminal justice system was more concerned with deterring the latter type of crime. Other studies have found that in interracial capital cases (such as rape or murder) in the Southern United States, blacks tend to receive more severe sentences than whites (Wolfgang & Riedel, 1973).

Unfortunately, most studies of sentencing in noncapital cases have not controlled for both the type of offense charged and the offender's prior history, so as to see whether the defendant's race has an independent effect on sentencing. In a review and reanalysis of studies on sentencing, Hagan (1974) argued that for noncapital cases in which crime type was held constant and only offenders with no prior record were examined, there were no differences in sentences given blacks and whites. However, for noncapital cases in which crime type was held constant and only offenders with "some" prior record (one or more previous convictions) were examined, there was some evidence that blacks received longer sentences than whites (Lemert & Rosberg, 1948; Nagel, 1969). A similar study, however, found no significant differences (Green, 1961).

Hagan made several suggestions about interpreting results from studies investigating the effect of race on sentencing. First, he counseled caution in interpreting the findings showing black offenders with criminal records appearing to fare worse than white offenders with criminal records, without further research controlling for the number of previous convictions. Second, Hagan recommended that readers keep in mind the difference between statistical significance, which is heavily influenced by the number of cases in a study, and "substantive" significance, which he defined to be the strength of the relationship. Most of the studies on sentencing use very large samples so that if a significant effect is discovered, the researcher can be fairly confident that the relationship was not due to chance. However, in virtually all 20 of the studies Hagan reviewed, the relationship was substantively relatively weak. Third, Hagan argued that studies finding differences in sentencing of blacks and whites in capital cases should be viewed critically, because these cases differ in several important ways from noncapital cases (for example, more likely to be tried before a jury, more likely for the case to take a long time before sentence is imposed).

On the basis of the available data, it is too early to conclude whether the defendant's race directly affects the sentencing decision, although it does seem likely that if the effect exists, it is not very strong. However, it may be that the defendant's race *indirectly* affects sentencing in that blacks and other minority-group members are more likely to be arrested and prosecuted and therefore are more likely to have a criminal record (Black, 1971; Chambliss & Seidman, 1971). And it is this prior criminal record that, in turn, affects the judge's sentencing decision.

Defendant's sex

A second observable characteristic that conceivably affects the length of the sentence is the sex of the defendant. Generally, women receive smaller fines, receive less severe sentences, and are more likely to be placed on probation than men (Moulds, 1980; Nagel, 1969). As is true with race, however, there is some disagreement whether sex has an independent effect on sentencing after other variables have been controlled for. In an analysis of cases in Philadelphia, Green (1961), considering only offenders with no prior record and holding type of crime constant, found no significant differences between sentences given men and women. On the basis of the study by Green and one by Judson, Pandell, Owens, McIntosh, and Matschullat (1969), Hagan (1974) tentatively concluded that the defendant's sex is only a minor factor in the sentencing decision. In a more recent study, Nagel, Cardascia, and Ross (1980) examined almost 3000 sentencing decisions in a city in New York State and found that females were less likely than males to receive severe sentences and that this advantage appeared to be independent of the seriousness of the crime. Convicted females were also less likely than males to spend any time imprisoned, and again this result appeared to be independent of crime seriousness.

As with race, there is insufficient evidence to conclude that sex has an independent effect on the sentencing decision. Overall, women probably commit less serious crimes than men and are probably less likely to have a prior record than men, possibly because they receive greater leniency at earlier stages in the criminal justice system. Until further research is conducted in which these variables are controlled, no firm conclusions can be drawn.

Defendant's age

Most studies of judges' sentencing behavior seem to show that youthful offenders receive lighter sentences than older offenders, although, as with race and sex, there is some question whether the effect is independent of other factors (Hagan, 1974). In California 20-year-olds are two and a half times as likely to be sent to prison as 19-year-olds for the same offense (Silberman, 1978). Young defendants also seem to be sentenced less severely than older defendants in experimental studies using college students (Smith & Hed, 1979).

Young offenders may receive lighter sentences for several reasons. First, younger offenders are very likely to have shorter criminal records. Second, many judges may be reluctant to expose youthful offenders to what they know to be the destructive environment of the prison. Third, many judges feel that younger offenders have a better chance of being rehabilitated than older offenders (Dawson, 1969). The optimism shown by many judges concerning the rehabilitation of younger offenders probably reflects their belief that the dispositions of younger defendants can be changed more easily than the dispositions of older defendants. Interestingly, although judges seem to be more lenient with youthful offenders partly because youthful offenders are expected to have a better chance of being rehabilitated, recidivism studies show that this is not usually the case. Youthful offenders are much more likely to commit a new offense than older offenders (Flanagan et al., 1980).

The defendant's age is the most prominent of several factors that together compose the defendant's "rehabilitation potential" (Dawson, 1969). These factors include family stability and family support, employment stability and skills, and education. As an aggregate, these factors affect how stable the judge perceives the defendant's criminal disposition to be. The less favorable these factors, the more likely a stable criminal disposition is to be assigned, and the more likely the defendant is to receive a severe sentence.

Defendant's physical attractiveness

A number of social-psychological experiments have investigated the role of a fourth observable characteristic of the defendant—physical attractiveness. It has been consistently shown that physically attractive people are viewed as possessing more positive traits and are evaluated more favorably than unattractive people (Berscheid & Walster, 1974). Although college subjects in one study expressed the belief that physical attractiveness should not be taken into account in the sentencing decision, other subjects in the same study judged physically attractive defendants to be less guilty and therefore assigned them less severe sentences (Efran, 1974). An observational study of real criminal defendants also found that more attractive defendants were given less severe sentences (Stewart, 1980). Assuming that this finding can be generalized, it provides another explanation of why defendants detained in jail while awaiting trial are given more severe sentences than those released on bail, since jailed persons are likely to be "unshaven, unwashed, unkempt, and unhappy" (Wald, 1964, p. 632).

Although attractive defendants seem to be given less severe sentences than unattractive defendants, one can easily imagine situations in which a physically attractive person would receive a more severe sentence than an unattractive person. Consider, for example, a situation in which defendants used their physical attractiveness to aid them in committing a crime. One would expect that such defendants would receive more punishment than if they were unattractive. As discussed in the previous chapter, this prediction was tested in a study using college students as subjects (Sigall & Ostrove, 1975). Subjects read that the female defendant had either broken into an apartment and stolen merchandise worth $2200 or induced a middle-aged bachelor to invest $2200 in a nonexistent company. Accompanying the description of the crime was a picture of the woman, who was made to look either attractive or unattractive. The experimenters found the predicted interaction between type of crime and attractiveness. When the crime was unrelated to attractiveness (a burglary), subjects gave more lenient sentences to the attractive defendant than to the unattractive defendant. When, however, the offense was attractiveness-related (a swindle), the attractive defendant received harsher treatment. These findings suggest that although a criminal disposition is generally less likely to be attributed to an attractive defendant than to an unattractive defendant, when the crime is related to a defendant's physical attractiveness, a criminal disposition is more likely to be attributed to the attractive defendant.

Characteristics of the Judge

The backgrounds of judges vary tremendously. Some have come from lower-socioeconomic-class homes, have attended public schools, and have received their law training at a city university, often while holding down a part-time job. Other judges have been raised in well-to-do homes, have attended private schools, and have received their law training at an exclusive Ivy League school. There is little doubt that the early socialization experiences of judges leave lasting impressions on them, having shaped their values, attitudes, beliefs, and ideologies. In this section we will explore some of these personality factors and their impact on the sentencing decision.

Several investigators have examined the correlation between personality variables and the sentencing decision. One personality variable that has been well studied is "authoritarianism," as measured by the California F Scale. People who score high on this scale show a general tendency to accept conventional values, to submit to those in authority, and to reject those who violate society's standards. Using college students as subjects, Mitchell and Byrne (1973) found that subjects who scored higher on the F Scale ("authoritarians") recommended significantly more severe punishment for a law violator than those who scored low on this test ("egalitarians"). A significant statistical interaction was also found between authoritarianism and the subject's attitudinal similarity to the defendant. Authoritarians were more influenced by their similarity to the defendant —that is, the more similar they were to the defendant, the less severe the recommended punishment. Other studies (for example, Boehm, 1968) have obtained similar results.

Another personality factor relevant to the sentencing decision is Rotter's (1966) locus-of-control construct. Rotter constructed a scale to measure the degree to which people feel that they control the rewards in their environment, "internals" believing that they control their rewards and "externals" believing that their rewards are controlled by the environment. Using this scale, Carroll and Payne (1976) found that internals showed a stronger preference for examining internal causes of the defendant's behavior, such as previous parole and probation difficulties, crime committed, and the defendant's educational level. Externals preferred to examine information pertaining to external causes, such as alcohol and drug use. Other evidence (Phares & Wilson, 1972) shows that internals are more likely to believe that people are responsible for their own outcomes and therefore show greater willingness to apply sanctions to another's behavior.

Differences in beliefs about locus of control may be related to political ideology. Miller (1973) has proposed that people who subscribe to a conservative political ideology are likely to focus on the internal responsibility of the criminal, while those who subscribe to a liberal political ideology are likely to focus on such external conditions as societal inequality and discrimination. This proposed difference does seem to have some basis in fact, as shown by a number of studies relating demographic characteristics of the judge to sentencing decisions (for example, Nagel, 1962). Most of these studies have correlated length of sentence imposed with such factors as religion, economic status, occupation before becoming a judge, and types of organizations to which the judge belongs. Generally, these studies show that Republicans give longer sentences than Democrats, that Protestants give longer sentences than Catholics and Jews, that members of the American Bar Association give longer sentences than nonmembers, and that former district attorneys give longer sentences than former defense attorneys. In a related study Hagan (1975) found that judges strongly favoring "law and order" sentenced defendants primarily on the basis of legal definitions of the seriousness of their offenses. Although judges less concerned with the maintenance of law and order also emphasized the seriousness of the offense, they were more likely to consider other variables, such as the defendant's race, prior record, and number of charges against the defendant. The latter group of judges also gave more lenient sentences to offenders from minority groups.

It would appear, then, that persons giving longer sentences tend to be part of the political right. These data suggest that persons who are internals or who are politically conservative tend to focus responsibility on the defendant and therefore give longer sentences than persons who focus responsibility on the environment.

Implicit in our examination of individual differences among judges is the assumption that there is a linkage between the causal attributions for a criminal act and the sentence imposed. A study by Carroll and Payne (1977a) used a modification of Weiner's attribution model (see Chapter 1) to examine systematically some of the sentencing consequences of certain causal attributions. College students read brief descriptions of crimes, each of which was accompanied by a single attributional cause (for example, the offender was in a depressed mood, had been drinking, was overcome by impulse). There were eight causes, each representing a particular combination of three attributional dimensions: (1) the locus-of-control dimension (internal/external), (2) the stability dimension (stable/unstable), and (3) a dimension not represented in Weiner's original model, the intentionality dimension (intentional/ unintentional). Because the last dimension yielded weaker findings than the first two, we will summarize the results pertaining only to the first two dimensions. Carroll and Payne hypothesized that the locus-of-control dimension would relate to the general question of punishment for the crime, while the stability dimension would be more relevant to the question of recidivism risk. In general, their results supported these hypotheses. Carroll and Payne found that attributions to internal causes (for example, the offender had an aggressive nature) led to higher ratings of crime severity and responsibility for the crime as well as to recommendations for longer prison sentences. Attributions to stable causes (for example, the offender had thought about the crime for some time) produced higher ratings of criminality and higher expectations for recidivism, as well as higher responsibility for the crime, greater desire to remove the criminal from society, and longer recommended prison sentences. However, when Carroll and Payne replicated this study using actual parole-board members as subjects, the attributional dimensions of stability and locus of causality were unrelated to sentence length. However, they did find a relation similar to that obtained with their college sample between the attributional dimensions and other types of judgments, such as those relating to perceived criminality, responsibility, and crime severity.

Tentatively, it appears that making an attribution to either an internal or a stable cause, especially to an internal *and* stable cause, results in a longer sentence. This result is understandable in view of the fact that a judge who attributes behavior to an internal, stable cause is concluding, in effect, that the criminal justice system cannot change the criminal's disposition and that it should, instead, try to prevent the criminal behavior that results from that disposition. In other words, a judge making an internal, stable attribution will probably feel that the criminal justice system should change its focus from rehabilitating the offender (changing a stable disposition) to keeping the defendant in prison so that he or she cannot commit more crimes against the public (preventing the consequences of that disposition).

The conflicting result emerging from the college sample and the parole-board sample is particularly troublesome because it raises once again serious questions about the generalizability of findings based on college students (see Chapter 6). This is not to say that the results from the parole-board members are a more reliable indicator of how judges would respond in a similar situation. The issue of judicial reaction is an empirical question best answered by replicating the study using a sample of real judges.

SOCIAL-EXCHANGE CONSIDERATIONS

In addition to the factors related to attributions about the defendant's criminality, other considerations have an important effect on the sentencing decision. Judges do not make their decisions in a social vacuum. As we have seen in previous chapters, decision makers in the criminal justice system must deal with other agents in the system, with community sentiment, and with their own notions of fairness to all concerned. These social-exchange considerations, similarly, have a decisive impact on the sentencing decision. Judges, no less than others in the system, depend on other agents for information, advice, and material and social rewards.

Judges are required to make a number of sentencing decisions with little time to deliberate on all the relevant factors. Earlier we stated that this situation causes judges to rely on their past experience, which Kelley (1972b) has termed "causal schemata," when they make decisions. A second consequence of the hasty deliberation process is that judges must rely on the advice of other agents in the criminal justice system.

Social Exchange with the Probation Officer

The most important adviser to the judge at the sentencing stage is the probation officer. It is this person's duty to write the presentence report, at the conclusion of which the probation officer recommends an appropriate sentence for the defendant. This advice provides the basis for the most important exchange at the sentencing stage.

Using data furnished by the Administrative Office of the United States Courts, Carter and Wilkins (1967) found that the percentage of agreement between probation officers' recommendations for *probation* and those of judges in the ten federal judicial circuits ranged from 90 to 99%. Agreement on recommendations for *imprisonment* was somewhat lower—68 to 93%. The same general proportions of agreement were observed in the California courts (Carter & Wilkins, 1967). More recently, Ebbesen and Konečni (1976) found that the best predictor of the judge's sentencing decision was the probation officer's recommendation. When the defendant had a prior record, judges agreed with the probation officer 93% of the time.

Ebbesen and Konečni also asked the judges in their sample to rate the importance of the probation officer's recommendation in their decisions. Interestingly, rated importance of the recommendation was virtually *unrelated* to the actually observed agreement. That is, judges who rated the recommendation of the probation officer as a very important determinant of their decision making were no more likely to agree with the probation officer's recommendations than were judges who said they placed less weight on the probation officer's recommendation.

In trying to explain the high percentage of agreement between probation officers and judges, Carter and Wilkins (1967, p. 508) suggested four possible reasons:

1. The court, having such high regard for the professional qualities and competence of its probation staff, "follows" the probation recommendation—a recommendation made by the person (probation officer) who best knows the defendant by reason of the presentence investigation.
2. There are many offenders who are "obviously" probation or prison cases.
3. Probation officers write their reports and make recommendations anticipating the recommendation the court desires to receive. (In this situation, the probation officer is quite accurately "second-guessing" the court disposition.)
4. Probation officers in making their recommendations place great emphasis on the same factors as does the court in selecting a sentencing alternative.[1]

The authors concluded that although the four factors probably operate simultaneously, the first is probably the most important.

That judges seem to follow the recommendation of the probation officer is not surprising, given the small amount of time they have in which to arrive at a sentencing decision. What is surprising, however, is that some judges do not realize the extent to which they rely on the probation officer. This situation can be characterized as an exchange, although it may not be acknowledged as such by the two parties. By providing the presentence report, the probation officer controls a valuable commodity in that the report saves the judge a great deal of time. In return for this service, judges often feel somewhat obliged to accept the probation officer's recommendation. The exchange relationship between the judge and the probation officer is not, however, an exchange between equals. The judge has a distinct power advantage. Thus, if the judge feels that the probation officer has not written a useful presentence report, he or she can ask the probation department not to have that particular officer write any more presentence reports for him or her. The power that the judge has over the probation officer is even more explicit in the federal system, where the probation officer is hired by the judge to conduct inquiries and to write the presentence reports. The existence of this power differential suggests that the high percentage of agreement between probation officers' recommendations and judges' sentencing decisions may be affected by the officer's desire to please the judge and thereby be assured of continuing favorable outcomes from the exchange.

[1]From "Some Factors in Sentencing Policy," by R. M. Carter and L. T. Wilkins. In *Journal of Criminal Law, Criminology and Police Science*, 1967, *58*, 503–514. Copyright 1967. Reprinted by special permission of the publisher, Northwestern University School of Law.

In addition to the information given by the probation officer at the sentencing hearing, the judge is provided with information by the defense attorney and by the prosecutor. The defense counsel's "primary duty is to ensure that the court and his client are aware of the available sentencing alternatives and that the sentencing decision is based on complete and accurate information" (National Advisory Commission on Criminal Justice Standards and Goals, 1973, p. 19). Defense counsel must be ready to present information to explain or contradict information that might be present in the presentence report, and if the defense counsel believes probation is an appropriate disposition for his or her client, the counsel should be prepared to suggest a program of rehabilitation. At the hearing, the defense attorney will try to present the defendant in the best possible light by introducing letters or affidavits from members of the community who can attest to the good reputation of the defendant. In addition, witnesses are sometimes called to testify about the defendant's good character. Judges, however, place less weight on the presentation of character witnesses than on the presentence report, because they know that the testimony of such witnesses is motivated more by a desire to present the defendant in the most favorable light than by a desire to present an objective picture of the defendant. In attributional terms, the testimony of witnesses is discounted because of the presence of other facilitative causes (for example, the witness is a close friend of the defendant). Although sentencing judges' professional and social relationship with the defense counsel is important to some judges (Chambliss & Seidman, 1971), it in no way compares with judges' need to preserve their working relationship with the probation officer.

Social Exchange with the Prosecutor

Whereas the prosecutor plays a central role as adviser to the judge at the bail-setting stage (see Chapter 4), the prosecutor plays only a peripheral role at the sentencing stage. Here prosecutors supply information about the defendant's prior record and outline the facts from which the case arose. Because most guilty pleas are arrived at through plea bargaining, prosecutors present their information objectively, since any departures from objectivity would jeopardize their plea bargain with the defendant.

An important consideration that affects judges' exchange relationships with other agents of the criminal justice system is the amount of crowding in the entire system. As discussed in Chapter 4, a plea bargain is encouraged in order to avoid overcrowding of trial dockets and long delays. But the problem of overcrowding is not limited to the pretrial phase; it also occurs in prisons, thus necessitating probation for some offenders simply because there is no room for them in prison (Twentieth Century Fund Task Force on Criminal Sentencing, 1976). For three reasons, however, the pressure to reduce overcrowding in prisons does not always result in fewer inmates' being sent there. First, judges are not always, or even usually, sympathetic to the problems engendered by overcrowding; second, in many jurisdictions at least some term of imprisonment is fixed by statute; and third, public opinion would probably be against a felon's receiving probation simply because of overcrowded prison conditions (Hawkins, 1976).

Social Exchange with the Community

This last reason is suggestive of the exchange that judges make with the voters of their communities. Community interest in sentencing varies, of course, with the type of crime. Certain categories of crime—for instance, sensational murders or sex offenses—arouse community interest and force judges to take account of public opinion (Dawson, 1969). That judges are particularly mindful of community sentiment as election day approaches can be observed from their media campaigns. In addition, judges are exhorted by their peers to consider public opinion. For example, the National Probation and Parole Association has stated in its *Guides for Sentencing* (1957) that

> the judge must use public opinion constructively as an aid in sentencing, but not be dominated by it; he must respect it, but not be enslaved by it; he must lead the community toward higher standards of justice and treatment, but not be so far ahead of it that it will lose sight of him [p. 46].

In virtually every jurisdiction, trial-court judges are elected. In return for their satisfactory performance, which in many communities means being "tough" on criminals (Gallup, 1978), the voters will reelect them. Hence, it is not surprising that sentencing decisions usually reflect the attitudes of the communities where the courts are situated. Hogarth (1971), for example, found that the attitudes and penal philosophies of Canadian magistrates reflected the types of communities in which they lived and seemed to be those that were most appropriate to the problems they faced in their local communities. The fact that sentences often reflect the local community helps explain why there are regional differences in severity of sentences. Thus, courts in the South tend to give more severe punishments than those in the North (Harries & Lura, 1974). Although there are probably many reasons that together explain such regional variations in sentencing, one is almost certainly the unwritten "deal" that judges make with their communities when they are elected to serve.

Social Exchange with Peers

Judges are also concerned with the rewards given by their peers—other judges and lawyers. These rewards are mainly social in that they consist in approval, prestige, and respect. The influence of peer opinions can be seen, for instance, in a trial judge's relationship with the appellate court. The possibility of being reversed on appeal is an important factor in judges' behavior. If the appeals court reverses them, they have been corrected in front of the entire legal community of the state—justices, other judges, and attorneys. If the reversal is on a matter as basic as a sentencing decision not being within legislative guidelines, they are quite likely to lose the respect of their peers. A second example of peer influence comes from those few cases in which several judges sentence the defendant. Although sentencing councils are rare in the United States, Frankel (1972) reported that peer pressure from council members tempers individual extremes in sentencing. The overall effect of this moderating influence seems to be a shortening of prison terms and an increased use of probation.

Another way in which judges are measured by their peers is by the number of cases the judges process. "Quality judges" are those who dispose of a relatively large number of cases, which is the usual result of imposing reasonable sentences. If judges give unreasonable sentences, defendants will be more likely to go to trial, as there is no incentive to do otherwise. Thus, "hanging judges" end up disposing of fewer cases and are seen as less competent than "quality judges" (Silberman, 1978). This result is the other side of the "strike on the industrial-union principle," discussed in Chapter 4.

Still other exchange considerations are sometimes involved in the sentencing decision. Judges, for example, may be lenient with an informant as a reward for cooperating with the police, particularly if the informant's services led to the conviction of an important criminal. Further, even though the chances of a successful probation are slight, judges sometimes grant probation to a known addict if his or her information led to the conviction of a drug dealer (Dawson, 1969). Leniency may also be granted to defendants who testify against their codefendants, the exchange in this case consisting in sacrificing one case in order to obtain convictions in others. In situations involving cooperative informants and codefendants, keeping these persons out of prison is a particularly important reward because their safety in prison cannot be guaranteed, a fact of which judges are well aware.

Equity Considerations

If all the forces in an exchange situation operated in the same direction, sentencing would be a fairly simple matter—for example, if everyone agreed either that the defendant should be imprisoned or that the defendant should be allowed on probation. Seldom, however, are cases so clear-cut. On the contrary, often the forces in a given case move in opposing directions. Compounding the problem of balancing the exchanges is the maintenance of equity.

The exchanges that judges make with others within and without the criminal justice system are moderated somewhat by equity considerations. Although most empirical and theoretical work has examined the notion of equity as it applies to the relationship between two persons (for example, a victim and a harmdoer), it is also possible to examine the concept of equity from an observer's perspective (Austin, Walster, & Utne, 1976). The observer in our situation is the judge, who has the power to restore equity in (1) the relationship between the defendant (the harmdoer) and the victim and (2) the relationship between the defendant and society.

According to equity theory, observers of an inequitable exchange experience distress very much like that experienced by the participants in the exchange. The major difference between the reactions of the observer or judge and the victim is the intensity of the feelings of distress and the desire to restore equity; obviously, victims react much more intensely than impartial observers to inequitable relationships. Given that judges are likely to be distressed when they see inequity and that their role is to correct it, how will they deal with that inequity? Equity theorists such as Walster, Walster, and Berscheid (1978) maintain that inequity can be resolved in two ways: restoration of *actual* equity and restoration of *psychological* equity. With certain property crimes, such as check forgery and minor larceny, judges sometimes require the defendant to make restitution to the victim as a condition of probation or a reduction in the prison sentence imposed (Hager, 1977). In this way the relationship between the defendant and the victim is restored to what it was before the crime occurred. To put it differently, actual equity is restored. If the judge did not require restitution, the victim would be forced to use a civil remedy, an unlikely alternative in many cases, because the amounts involved are not worth the time and expense of a civil suit. Judges will often grant probation in these cases to force the defendant to make restitution to the victim, even though such offenders are likely to violate probation. Compensating the victims in these cases—that is, restoring actual equity—appears to these judges to be worth the risk that the defendant will commit future crimes.

With regard to restoring equity in the relationship between the defendant and society, the judge generally has a range of sentencing options available. Probation, fines, imprisonment, and some combination of the three are the means by which actual equity is restored to the relationship between the defendant and society. Although actual equity usually requires active intervention by the criminal justice system, sometimes harm to the defendant independent of the legal system is perceived as restoring actual equity. For example, in one study subjects (college students) read a brief description of a crime in which the defendant merely took the victim's purse or both took the purse and beat the victim. The description of the crime further stated that the defendant, in the process of trying to escape the police, suffered either no harm, moderate harm, or excessive harm. The major finding of this study was that the more the defendant suffered while trying to escape, the less severe was the recommended punishment (cited in Austin, Walster, & Utne, 1976).

In a more recent series of studies, Austin (1979a) also found that college students gave less severe sentences the more the offender had suffered. Further, Austin found that the offender's suffering did not reduce punishment equally across all types of crimes. For a crime of low severity (purse snatching), the more the offender had suffered, either through physical pain or through personal tragedy, the less punishment he received. However, for more serious crimes (assault, rape), the offender's suffering reduced his punishment only if his suffering was perceived to be far greater than the victim's. Moreover, consistent with Kalven and Zeisel's (1966) anecdotal data, Austin found that physical suffering did not have to result from the criminal event to be effective in reducing punishment. Finally, Austin found that although subjects gave less severe sentences to offenders who had suffered, they did not believe that the offender should be acquitted merely because he had suffered. This last finding suggests that judges are willing to consider the fairness of a punishment in light of other information but that some moral blameworthiness is attached to the offender that is not erased by any suffering he or she may have endured.

That actual judges consider the extent of the defendant's suffering when deciding on a sentence is illustrated by an incident that occurred in a Pittsburgh courtroom. The sentence of a convicted rapist was reduced from 5–10 years to 11½–23 months after the judge observed that the defendant "cried like a baby. . . . He just went to pieces" ("Woman Jailed . . . ," 1978).

Undoubtedly, judges would like to restore equity to the relationships between the defendant and the victim and between the defendant and society. Sometimes, however, actual equity cannot be restored to these relationships. If, for example, the defendant irreparably injured the victim, actual equity could be very difficult to restore. Similarly, if the defendant stole a large amount of money from the victim but was unable to repay it, actual equity could not be restored. It is in order to rectify inequities such as these that several states have enacted victim-compensation legislation (see Chapter 2).

Considerations of equity are not always of paramount concern to judges. Often their conceptions of fairness are guided more by the needs rule than by the contributions rule (see Chapter 1). Thus, although equity considerations might dictate that a judge sentence a young male offender to prison, the needs rule might dictate otherwise. Considerations pertaining to overcrowding in prisons and the likelihood of homosexual assault cause many judges to place such offenders on probation. The dependence of the defendant's family on the defendant is another important determinant of the sentencing decision. The judge weighs the needs of the family and the impact that imprisonment would have on the satisfaction of these needs. If the defendant's family is likely to be placed on welfare should the defendant be sent to prison, the judge may show leniency in sentencing. This consideration may help explain why female defendants with dependent children are often not sentenced to prison. In basing their sentencing decision on the needs rule, judges do little to rectify the inequity between criminals and their victims. In fact, many vocal critics of the criminal justice system complain that until recently the needs rule was more likely to be applied to the offender than to the victim.

If actual equity cannot be restored either because of the nature of the crime or because factors exist that inhibit a prison sentence, then the judge, like the victim, will try to restore *psychological* equity. This can be achieved in one of three ways: derogation of the victim, minimization of the victim's suffering, or denial of the defendant's responsibility for the act. Derogation of the victim is an effective means of reducing inequity because it allows the judge to reason or conclude that the victim deserved to be harmed. Thus, a judge in Wisconsin achieved notoriety when he used derogation of the victim as a reason for granting probation to a juvenile convicted of raping a high school girl. The judge felt that rape was a "normal" reaction to the way many young women dress (Begley, 1977). Additional evidence is provided in a previously discussed questionnaire study that showed that observers tend to derogate rape victims (Jones & Aronson, 1973). The second means of achieving psychological equity is for judges to minimize the harm to the victim—to conclude, for example, that the theft of a car did not unduly inconvenience a family that owned three vehicles. Judges can also achieve psychological equity by placing responsibility for the crime somewhere other than on the defendant or the victim—for example, on the defendant's peers and home environment. Restoration of equity through psychological means almost always implies that the judge will show greater leniency in sentencing the defendant.

Thus far we have spoken about restoring equity between the defendant and the victim and between the defendant and society. It is also possible to conceive of an equity relationship existing between the defendant and other defendants. A judge would want to treat similar defendants, in terms of crimes committed and rehabilitative potential, in similar ways. One study investigating fairness to the defendant examined the effect of the defendant's accomplice being free or in custody (DeJong, Morris, & Hastorf, 1976). Subjects (college students) recommended less punishment for the defendant when the accomplice had escaped from custody than when the accomplice was in custody. In terms of equity theory, subjects felt that imposing a severe sentence on the defendant while his accomplice received no punishment at all would be inequitable. It is unlikely, however, that the effect of an escaped accomplice would be as important in a real courtroom, because most judges would probably assume that the accomplice would be captured sometime.

One can also study the need to maintain equity among defendants by examining the impact of a prior sentencing decision on one that follows it. After sentencing one defendant, a judge would want to treat a similar defendant in a manner consistent with the way the first defendant was treated. Similarly, judges would expect to treat differently defendants from different backgrounds and those who were guilty of different crimes. Both these assumptions lead to the conclusion that a judge who wanted to sentence consistently would use a sentence given to one defendant as a reference for making subsequent sentences. A laboratory experiment using college students as subjects suggests that this is indeed the case (Pepitone & DiNubile, 1976). It was found that when a recommended punishment for a first crime was "anchored"—that is, overtly recorded and thus publicly committed—the recommended punishment for a second offender's crime was increased or decreased as a function of the contrasted seriousness of the crimes. Thus, a homicide following a homicide received a mean sentence of 21.8 years, whereas a homicide following an assault received a mean sentence of 33.4 years. However, this difference in recommended punishment must be considered in the light of two factors: (1) the subjects were undergraduates rather than judges, and (2) the "anchor" for a judge who has made hundreds of sentencing decisions is probably not the previous case but some sort of weighted combination of all the earlier cases similar to the one under consideration.

SUMMARY

The sentencing decision is not an easy one for the judge to make, as it involves a great deal of information that must be processed quickly. In this situation, judges rely on two simplifying mechanisms: they rely on causal schemata formed by their past experience, and they use the advice of other agents of the criminal justice system.

The sentencing decision process can be seen as consisting of two stages. First, judges assign a disposition of criminality based largely on the information in the presentence report and what they observe personally of the defendant. This attribution stage focuses on such factors as severity of the crime, type of victim, defendant's prior record, defendant's status before and during the trial, nature of defendant's plea, and defendant's race, sex, age, and physical attractiveness. How these various factors are integrated depends largely on the judge's personal beliefs about the causes of criminal acts. The particular attribution assigned to the defendant has a major impact on the sentence assigned.

The second stage of the sentencing process deals with the exchanges judges must consider when they determine a sentence. The sentencing decision is influenced by exchanges with other actors in the criminal justice system, such as probation officers, defense attorneys, prosecutors, and other judges. In addition, judges are involved in important exchanges with members of their community that also affect the sentencing outcome. Judges are guided by considerations of equity between the defendant and the victim, between the defendant and society, and among defendants. The major dilemma for the judge is to decide which of these relationships should receive priority in establishing equity.

In some cases, equity demands that the defendant be sentenced to prison. Decision making in the prison will be examined in the next chapter.

CHAPTER EIGHT

Prisons

When we think of prisons, a number of conflicting images come to mind. First, prison life has been romanticized to some extent by motion pictures. Invariably in these movies the prisoners are independent, virile, intelligent, and heroic, while the prison staff members are mean and petty men whose sole function is to punish the inmates. A second image is the "country club" type of prison to which most of the former government officials in the Watergate scandal were sentenced. Still another image that comes to mind is the devastation and death of riots, such as the one at Attica, New York, in 1971. No one of these images completely captures what prison systems in the United States are like. Prison systems differ among the states, and, even within the same prison system, prisons are of different types and have different programs. Nevertheless, all prisons have certain factors in common: an expensive physical facility, a population of convicted persons who desire to leave, and a much smaller number of guards who must try to maintain order and prevent escapes.

In the United States on any given day, over 320,000 offenders are housed in American prison systems. The median age of these offenders is about 30, and 96% are male (Carter, McGee, & Nelson, 1975). About two-thirds of these offenders are in the almost 600 state correctional facilities. In 1978, states and local governments spent over $5.1 billion on corrections, including both salaries and maintenance (U.S. Department of Justice, 1980).

Our consideration of prisons will begin with a brief history of prisons in the United States and a discussion of the two major types of prisons in the country today. Because most prisoners are male, we will focus on men's prisons. We will look primarily at the most important criminal-justice-system agent in the prison, the guard. The guard's treatment of an inmate is determined by his or her attributions about the inmate and the many social-exchange relationships the guard has.

Finally, we will examine the prison as a mini–criminal justice system, where inmates must decide whether to report crimes, guards must decide whether to file reports of inmate misconduct, and a disciplinary board must determine an appropriate punishment if the inmate is found guilty of the misconduct.

A BRIEF HISTORY OF PRISONS

Before the 19th century, imprisonment for crimes was virtually unknown. The two most common penalties for violations of the law were the fine and the whip (Rothman, 1971). The use of the fine presumed that forfeiture of offenders' property would be sufficient punishment to discourage them from committing another crime. The use of the whip, in contrast, did not assume that offenders owned any property. It merely presumed that offenders would desire to avoid pain in the future. A punishment for minor crimes often used as an alternative to the fine was the stocks, which were devices that confined the offender to a cramped and uncomfortable position. When confined to the stocks, offenders had to endure not only a painfully cramped position for several hours but also the ridicule of their fellow citizens, a particularly painful psychological punishment in closely knit communities. Another punishment that focused on the offenders' reputations was branding on the flesh or making the offenders wear a letter on their clothes indicating their offense. For example, Hester Prynne in Hawthorne's novel was forced to wear a scarlet letter *A* for her crime of adultery. Often, offenders who were not residents of the community received thirty to forty lashes of the whip and were then expelled from the community. Whipping and expulsion were preferred as penalties for vagrants because such punishment was inexpensive and efficient and could be used on offenders who did not own property (Rothman, 1971).

If fines, whippings, and public ridicule did not deter an offender from committing more crimes, capital punishment was the usual solution. The criminal codes of the colonies included a large number of crimes that were punishable by hanging, and judges did not hesitate to impose the death sentence on offenders who were a danger to the community by reason of their continued failure to obey the laws.

Only rarely did imprisonment constitute a form of punishment in 18th-century America. Jails were used to hold persons before and during the trial, those who were awaiting sentence, and those who were unable to pay debts (Rothman, 1971). Jailing was not used to punish criminals, for two reasons: a number of alternative punishments were available, and because jails resembled household arrangements and were easy to escape from, they were not intimidating to offenders (Rothman, 1971). It was in the 19th century that the use of imprisonment as a form of punishment became common. The reason for this change was that the newly free states "reformed" their criminal codes by eliminating the death penalty for all but the most serious crimes and by instituting incarceration instead (Rothman, 1971).

In the early part of the 19th century, there were two opposing designs of prisons, reflecting different penal philosophies. One philosophy was represented by the Eastern State Penitentiary, built in 1828 in Philadelphia. It was designed so that each prisoner would do penance for his sins through separate and solitary confinement. Prisoners were brought into the medieval, fortresslike structures with black hoods over their heads. They were led to solitary cells, where the hoods were removed. Locked into individual cells, behind two thick doors, they were left for years with only a Bible for reading. Each prisoner had a back door and a tiny walled-in courtyard where he could step outside (see Figure 8-1). Prisoners never left their solitary areas or saw anyone other than a minister. Guards would push bread, water, or mush under the small opening beneath the cell door (Burkhart, 1973).

The second type of prison design was used in the Auburn Penitentiary, built in 1818 in Auburn, New York. The philosophy behind this design was that prisoners should work at hard labor to reform their character and make the prison economically sound. In this design, the cells were built back to back, each cell facing a corridor (see Figure 8–1). Since the cells in this prison design were small, all meals and work activities had to take place outside the cell in large rooms designed especially for the particular activity. Because the Auburn plan of prisons was cheaper to build ($91 per cell) than the Pennsylvania system ($1650 per cell), it was the design that was used in most subsequent prisons (Sheehan, 1978). Today, most prisons are of the Auburn type. Cells are relatively small, and inmates eat and work in large rooms designed expressly for those purposes.

Very recently, the Federal Bureau of Prisons and a few states have built "open prisons." In these buildings, designed usually for inmates who are minimum security risks, bars are noticeably absent, and the structure does not look like the traditional prison. Because this type of prison is atypical in the United States today, it will not be examined here. What will be discussed is the standard prison and its effects on prisoners and guards.

A final, very important piece of information concerns the location of the early prisons. The first penitentiaries were generally located in urban areas—Philadelphia, Pittsburgh, Columbus, Trenton, Baltimore, and Richmond. However, prisons built during the last two-thirds of the 19th century were placed in rural settings, because it was felt there could be no better place in which to isolate the inmates than a remote part of the state (National Advisory Commission on Criminal Justice Standards and Goals, 1973). Over 50 of these isolated prisons, housing approximately 75,000 of the 110,000 felons in maximum-security

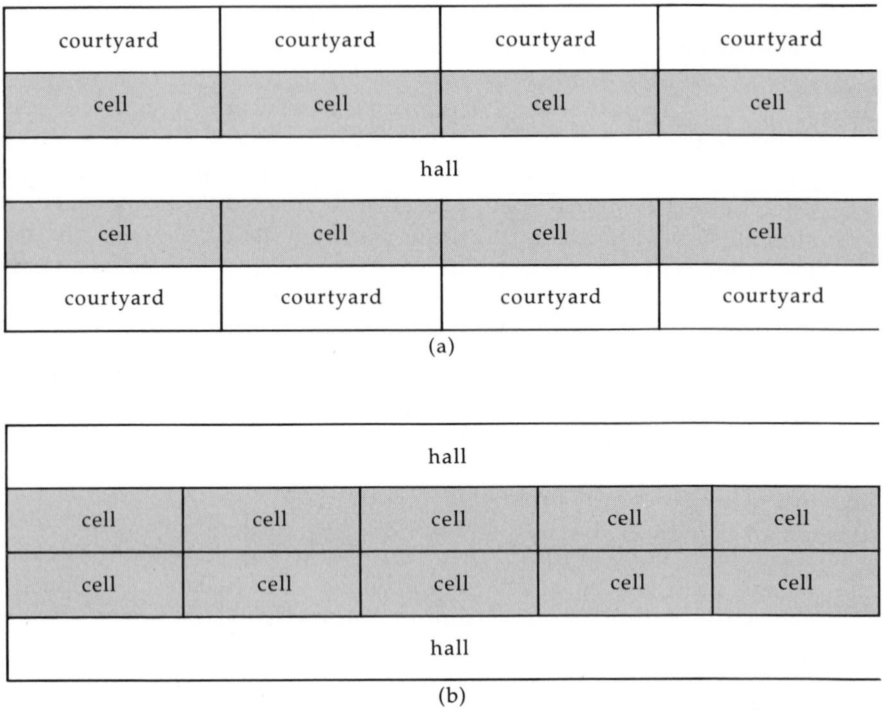

courtyard	courtyard	courtyard	courtyard
cell	cell	cell	cell
hall			
cell	cell	cell	cell
courtyard	courtyard	courtyard	courtyard

(a)

hall				
cell	cell	cell	cell	cell
cell	cell	cell	cell	cell
hall				

(b)

Figure 8–1. Design of cellblocks used in (A) the Eastern State Penitentiary, Philadelphia (1828), and (B) the Auburn Penitentiary, Auburn, New York (1818). (Drawings not to scale.)

facilities, are still in operation. As will be shown, the location of such institutions has an important impact on social interaction between inmates and their guards.

TYPES OF PRISONS

As discussed in Chapter 7, the sentence imposed on an offender may have one or more purposes: individual deterrence, general deterrence, incapacitation, retribution, expression of moral outrage, and rehabilitation. When prisons are viewed in terms of what they are supposed to accomplish, there are really only two kinds: punitive/custodial and treatment-oriented. All prisons are custodial (and therefore punitive, as custody implies the loss of rights and the denial of certain comforts), but some are more oriented toward treating and rehabilitating offenders than others. Punitive/custodial prisons and treatment-oriented prisons differ in several ways (Cressey, 1965).

One important difference between the two types of prisons is in their pattern of authority. In punitive/custodial prisons, authority is based only on rank, so that persons of lower status (for example, guards) have to obey the orders of persons of higher status (for example, the warden) because they might be fired if they do not. This, of course, is a traditional social-exchange relationship. In the ideal treatment-oriented prison, in contrast, authority is based on possession of technical knowledge, so that the advice of "experts," such as psychiatrists and psychologists, is followed because it is believed to be correct rather than because the experts are of higher rank. A second difference is that in punitive/custodial prisons, because goals are specific and measurable (for example, a warden's goal of minimizing the number of riots and escapes), there is great emphasis on rules. In contrast, when the goal is more difficult to measure (for example, "rehabilitation"), there is less emphasis on rules. A third difference between the two types of prisons is the amount of decision making the guards are allowed and the form of communication between inmates and guards. In the punitive/custodial prison, where obedience to higher rank is important, a minimum amount of discretion is allowed guards. Their decision making is supposed to consist only in reporting rule violations to a central authority. Moreover, in the punitive/custodial prison, communications are formal and are restricted as much as possible to commands. In the treatment-oriented prison, communication among employees is very important, and staff members are encouraged to make decisions on their own. A final difference between the two prison types is the pattern of incentives and punishments. In the punitive/custodial prison, coercion is the usual means of bringing compliance. In the treatment-oriented prison, positive incentives, such as better living quarters or furloughs, are used to reinforce appropriate behavior.

Although both punitive/custodial prisons and treatment-oriented prisons exist in the United States and although most prisons have elements of both types, most lack the physical and human resources necessary for an effective treatment orientation and therefore are primarily of the punitive/custodial type. For this reason, our discussion of the actors in the prison will focus on the agents in punitive/custodial prisons. This discussion will center on the most important agent in such an institution, the prison guard.

THE PRISON GUARD

Although the prison administration is responsible for dealing with groups outside the prison and with setting general institutional policy, it is the prison guards who must deal on a day-to-day basis with the inmates. In most prisons, custodial officers have more impact on inmates during their stay in prison than any other group of prison employees (Glaser, 1964), probably because there are more guards than other types of prison personnel and they come into closer contact with the offenders than either the administration or the treatment staff (National Advisory Commission on Criminal Justice Standards and Goals, 1973).

Several negative aspects are associated with the position of prison guard, including dangerous and depressing working conditions and low prestige (Sykes, 1958). In spite of these factors, prison guards tend to like their work. For example, of a sample of 929 Illinois prison guards, 92% considered their jobs "almost always satisfying" or "usually satisfying" (Jacobs, 1978). In the same study, 58% described their work as "quite interesting" and only 8% described it as boring. Even though many (57%) had become guards because they "just needed a job," most of them expected to remain prison guards for at least five years.

One reason prison guards find their jobs satisfying may be that the position provides them with better salaries and other benefits than they could get elsewhere. Most prisons are located in rural areas, and being a guard may be the best job in the area a high school graduate can get. For example, guards in a prison in Clinton County, in rural upstate New York, had earnings that were a few thousand dollars above the average for residents of the county (Sheehan, 1978).

Selection of prison guards is not a particularly rigorous process. In most cases the screening mechanism consists of an employment application (38 states), a personal interview (40 states), or both. Sixteen states use a written examination in addition to one or both of these two methods. Only a few states require a background check or a trial period of service (Goldstein, 1975). In many prisons, as was true of the Attica prison before the riot, the only firm requirements are meeting minimum height, weight, vision, and hearing standards (Hawkins, 1976). A high school diploma is required in about 40 states (May, 1976). Prison guards usually receive only minimal training, consisting of only a few weeks of instruction. Before the riot at Attica, about one-third of the guards at that institution had received no formal training at all, and the rest had received only two weeks of formal training (New York State Special Commission on Attica, 1972).

The stereotype of a prison guard is a person who is cruel. However, research seems to show that it is not the personality of correctional officers but the situation that creates violence and causes mistreatment (Sykes, 1958). Zimbardo and his colleagues (Haney, Banks, & Zimbardo, 1973) set out to test the influence of the environment on the behavior of guards and inmates by simulating prison conditions.

Zimbardo and his students set up a simulated prison in the basement of the psychology building at Stanford University. Paid subjects, recruited through a newspaper advertisement, were randomly assigned to be either guards or inmates in the prison. The guards were given only minimal instructions; they were told simply to conduct themselves as they thought prison guards would behave, but they were not allowed to beat the prisoners. Although the subjects who were simulating prisoners initially tended to treat the experiment as a joke, those who simulated guards took their jobs all too seriously. Within two days the guards began treating the prisoners cruelly—forcing them into crowded cells, waking them up several times during the night for "counts" to make sure all the inmates were still in the prison, refusing to let inmates use the bathroom and giving them a bucket instead. Even Zimbardo and his students, who acted as the prison administration, became wrapped up in the mentality of the prison. When they heard a rumor that some of the prisoners' friends were going to stage a break to release the prisoners, Zimbardo, his students, and the guards moved the prisoners to a different location. Later, they discovered there was no planned prison break.

Within six days of the start of the experiment, the simulation had to be ended. The guards had become cruel; the prisoners had become passive and submissive to the guards' authority; the prison administrators had begun to believe they were actually running a prison; and one of the prisoners had apparently suffered a nervous breakdown.

Zimbardo and his associates concluded that because subjects had been randomly assigned to be either guards or prisoners, the results could not be attributed to personality differences between guards and prisoners. Rather, strong situational factors seemed to account for the way the guards, the prisoners, and even the administration acted, such as the anonymity of both guards and prisoners due to the wearing of uniforms and the emphasis on power.

Although Zimbardo's study has been criticized on methodological grounds (Banuazizi & Movahedi, 1975), its major findings have been supported by information from real prisons. When all this information is taken together, a fairly persuasive argument can be made that the prison situation plays a major role in determining guards' behavior. The influence of the situation on guards' actions is evidenced both in the attributions guards make about inmates and in the social-exchange relationships guards have with the inmates and with other prison workers.

ATTRIBUTIONAL CONSIDERATIONS

In the punitive/custodial type of prison, guards are told not to communicate with the inmates on a personal basis. Instead, the communication structure is very formal and is limited to what is necessary to keep the prison running. In other words, the same formal structure of authority by which the administration deals with the guards is used by the guards in their dealings with prisoners. Sometimes the organization of the prison is such that it is nearly impossible for guards to establish rapport with inmates. For example, the New York State Special Commission on Attica (1972) found that guards' duty shifts were arranged so that they were likely to deal with different inmates each day. When guards are relatively unacquainted with individual prisoners, their attributions are often guided by stereotypic beliefs about prisoners and certain ethnic groups gained from past experience with, and what they have heard and read about, such prisoners and ethnic-group members. That is, the mere fact of labeling someone as an inmate or as a member of an ethnic minority predisposes guards to make negative attributions about inmates. The attributions that guards make about inmates are influenced not only by stereotypes but by knowledge of their *own* behavior toward inmates as well as by direct observation of inmates' behaviors (see Figure 8–2).

Fact of Being an Inmate

The most important piece of information that a guard has about an inmate is that the inmate is a prisoner in the institution, since guards consider the mere fact of entrance into prison as prima facie evidence that the prisoner is a lawbreaker (Goffman, 1961). Knowing that a person is an inmate conveys a great deal of information to the guard.

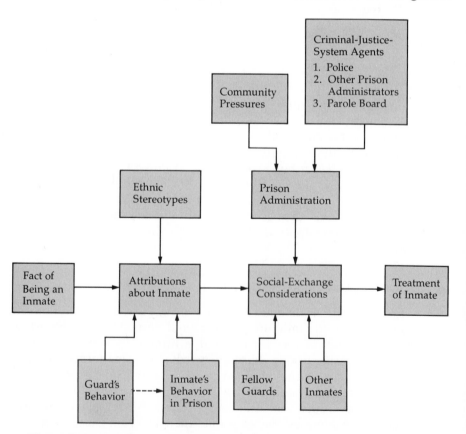

Figure 8–2. Attribution/exchange model of the guard's treatment of an inmate

Foremost, it tells the guard that there is something special about the inmate. Fewer than 40% of all persons convicted of felonies are sentenced to prison (Silberman, 1978). The figure is much smaller when the comparison is with all persons arrested for committing crimes. Consequently, a guard knows that a person who is sentenced to prison is not the usual person who is arrested for a crime. Guards know that several persons before them—the police, the prosecutor, perhaps a jury, the judge—were convinced that the inmate was guilty of the crime, especially if the inmate pleaded guilty. Thus, for the guard, the locus of causality for the crime has been determined by others to be internal to the inmate, and the guard need have no doubts.

In addition, because most first offenders who commit relatively minor crimes are placed on probation, the fact that a person is imprisoned tells the guard that he is probably not a first offender, or his crime was probably relatively serious, or both. If the inmate is a repeat offender, the guard is likely to attribute a stable criminal disposition to him. Thus, the guard will probably believe that if the inmate committed crimes in the past, he will probably commit more crimes when released from prison. If the inmate's crime was serious, the guard is likely to attribute a strong internal criminal disposition to the inmate, because there are strong inhibiting causes (such as being sentenced to prison) against such nonnormative acts. Therefore, simply on the basis of inmates' being in prison, the guard is likely to attribute a stable disposition of criminality to them. That is, the guard is likely to see prisoners as being internally responsible for their crimes and as being likely to commit more crimes in the future. In the words of the New York State Special Commission on Attica (1972, p. 120): "The inmate who refused to regard himself only as a criminal simply could not relate in any meaningful, constructive manner with a prison staff that could not regard him as anything else." The attribution of a stable criminal disposition will be even stronger if the prison is a maximum-security institution, because guards know that usually only the most dangerous criminals are sentenced to maximum-security prisons.

There are some inmates, however, to whom guards are unlikely to attribute strong internal dispositions of criminality. For example, an inmate convicted of deserting his wife, gambling, or embezzlement is unlikely to be considered a "desperate criminal" (Sykes, 1958). Nevertheless, such inmates are probably the exception, and even they are somewhat suspect, because many people who commit these crimes are not sentenced to prison.

Ethnic Identity

Another source of attributions about inmates is ethnic identity. Often when people are minimally acquainted with another person, they attribute characteristics to the other on the basis of the other's ethnic identity. Such ethnic stereotypes are another important source of guards' attributions about prisoners (Sommer, 1976). In many prisons, particularly in rural areas, there are large differences in the ethnic composition of the inmate and guard populations. Such prisons have a guard population that is mostly white and an inmate population consisting mostly of minority-group members. For example, at Attica Prison in 1971 (the year of the riot), 70% of the inmates were either black or Puerto Rican, while the staff was 100% white (Sommer, 1976). In the Illinois state prison system, 85% of the guards are white, while most inmates are black or Latino (Jacobs, 1978). One study found that guards tended to view black prisoners in stereotypical terms. That is, guards perceived black inmates "as being innately lazy, ignorant, crude, and hypersexual" (Carroll, 1974, p. 125). Studies suggest that people are likely to notice and recall information consistent with their stereotypes and to ignore information inconsistent with these stereotypes (for example, Snyder & Uranowitz, 1978). Assuming that guards have negative stereotypes about certain ethnic groups, we would expect them to interpret these inmates' behaviors in such a way as to perpetuate their negative inferences.

Somewhat different results were obtained by one investigator, who asked Illinois prison guards why there are so many minority-group members in prison (Jacobs, 1978). The response most often given (45%) was that minority-group members are poor and lack jobs, which suggests an external attribution for their winding up in prison. The next most frequent responses were that minority-group members have a subculture of violence and are brought up breaking laws (30%) and that they choose to commit more crime (22%). These data are surprising in light of other studies that describe guards as racist. For example, the McKay Commission, which investigated the Attica riot, found several guards who were prejudiced against inmates from minority groups, in spite of the guards' denial of racist attitudes. One reason for the results in the Illinois study may be that more than 25% of the Illinois correctional officers were under 30 at the time of the study and were probably less racist than the older guards. A second reason might be that the Illinois guards did not want to appear prejudiced and therefore gave the researcher socially desirable answers. Unfortunately, we do not know the extent to which the guards' answers reflected their true beliefs or their desire to win the approval of the investigator by saying the "right" things.

Some of the attributions that a guard makes about inmates are *defensive attributions*—that is, attributions that serve an ego-defensive function. One such function is to maintain the guard's belief that he or she is superior to the inmates. By viewing inmates as inferior, childish, and having criminal dispositions, which are internal, stable traits, guards can make themselves feel superior to the inmates, even if inmates are better educated, wealthier, or from a higher social class than the guards (Cressey, 1965). Such attributions make it easier for guards to perform their duties in the punitive/custodial prison. A guard who makes these attributions about inmates will deal with them as inferiors, not equals. He is unlikely to do them favors and is likely to be a strict enforcer of rules (Cressey, 1965).

Another effect of guards' attributing a criminal disposition to inmates is that it serves to justify their treatment of inmates (Goffman, 1961). Even in the experimental simulation by Zimbardo and associates, the "guards" reacted to the "inmates" as if they were criminals. Although the participants in the study were randomly assigned to be either inmates or guards, the guards behaved as though the mere fact that the prisoners were prisoners justified cruel treatment. In addition, because "inmates are believed to have been sentenced to prison because they could not or would not respect the rights of others in free society" (Sutherland & Cressey, 1974, pp. 511–512), dominating the inmates' lives is often seen as being for the inmates' "own good." Such domination is viewed as a form of education designed to correct faulty relationships with society.

Attributing a criminal disposition to inmates is actually a quite functional strategy for prison guards. "To be effective, personnel who are hired to guard must view inmates as dangerous, scheming, conniving men who are in need of close surveillance and domination" (Sutherland & Cressey, 1974, p. 511). By seeing inmates in this way, guards are likely to be sensitized at all times to potential violations and to show their authority through rule enforcement and the infliction of punishment.

In addition to attributions based on the fact that the inmate is in prison and that the inmate belongs to a certain ethnic group, guards make attributions about inmates from direct observation of their *own* behavior toward inmates and from inmates' behavior. We turn now to a discussion of these two sources of attributions.

Guards' Observation of Their Own Behavior

A great deal of work has shown that people learn about their attitudes in the same way that an impartial observer would—that is, by observing their behavior (for example, Bem, 1972). If the behavior in question is surveillance of some group of people, an impartial observer is likely to come to the conclusion that the people must, for some reason, be watched. In much the same way, the person doing the surveillance will come to the same conclusion. Thus, the person watching the group will begin to believe that the group *needs* to be watched, because otherwise the person would not be asked to perform the surveillance (Strickland, 1958). It is easy for prison guards to examine their own participation in the elaborate security arrangements found at most prisons and thereby convince themselves that unless they keep the prisoners under continuous surveillance, the prisoners will break the rules and even try to escape (Haney & Zimbardo, 1977). Guards probably reason that if prisoners have to be carefully guarded, it must be because they cannot be trusted. Although some prisoners undoubtedly would try to disobey the rules regardless of the guards' behavior, other prisoners might be led to rule breaking simply because of the way they are treated by the guards.

What this amounts to is a self-fulfilling prophecy. If guards perceive inmates as having criminal dispositions, they will treat the inmates as criminals. The inmates, in turn, will act like criminals, because they have no incentive to act any other way. Once the inmates act like criminals, the guards' attribution of criminality has been fulfilled and reinforced, and the process is likely to be repeated when new inmates arrive.

Thus, guards' treatment of inmates is likely to affect not only the guards' attributions about the inmates' behaviors but also the inmates' behaviors themselves. The behavior of inmates is perhaps the most important source of guards' attributions about inmates.

Guards' Observation of Inmates' Behavior

Inmates' behavior in prison is influenced both by the way the guards treat them and by the objective deprivations of the prison. In order to deal with the harsh physical and psychological environment of the prison, prisoners construct their own norms, known as the "inmate code." As we will see in the following section, the presence of such norms makes it harder for guards to attribute dispositions to inmates. Thus, if an inmate conforms to the code by showing hostility to a guard, the guard cannot be sure whether to attribute the behavior to the inmate code or the inmate's personal hostility toward the guard. The guard's attributional dilemma is an example of Kelley's (1972a) discounting principle: there are two facilitating causes for the inmate's behavior—one external (norms) and the other internal (personal disposition). Because the inmate code is so important in affecting the attributions that guards make about inmates, we will describe this code in some detail.

According to this code, the inmate should not (1) interfere with other inmates' interests ("Don't rat on a con"), (2) start fights with other inmates, (3) exploit other inmates through force or fraud, (4) appear weak, or (5) show respect to the guards or the values they favor (Sykes & Messinger, 1960). The inmate code is enforced through a system of rewards and punishments. The rewards include status and respect; the punishments include derisive laughter, ridicule, corporal punishments, and sometimes execution (Sutherland & Cressey, 1974).

In recent years the notion that a single inmate code applies to all prisoners has been called into question (Jacobs, 1979). In contrast to early studies on the prisoner subculture, which suggested that prison life is governed by one set of inmate norms (for example, Clemmer, 1940), more recent observations have focused on the effects of race relations on the norms governing inmates' behavior. This recent research suggests that each ethnic group has its own social organization and enforces its own norms.

According to this more recent view, race is one of the dominant factors affecting relationships among inmates. In California prisons, for instance, blacks, whites, and Chicanos maintain ethnic separation and are openly hostile to one another (Irwin, 1970). Today, in prisons across the country, black inmates tend to dominate prison life. Jacobs (1979) suggests that this dominance results from their superior numbers in prison and the fact that they, in contrast to whites, are used to facing the larger society in terms of their racial identity. Another cause is the actions of the Black Muslims in the late 1950s and early 1960s. According to Jacobs, the Muslims caused profound changes in three ways: (1) by challenging prison racism, which was evidenced in poorer job assignments and more severe discipline for blacks; (2) by forcing the prison administration to recognize them as a group rather than as individuals; and (3) by initiating suits in federal courts that resulted in a broadening of inmates' rights.

In reading the following discussion of the inmate code, you should recognize that although inmate solidarity exists to some extent, there are conflicts among ethnic groups. The inmate code is probably applied more strongly within a race than across races, and there is probably a slightly different inmate code for each ethnic group.

One result of the convict code is that each inmate has few friends in the prison, a result that is reinforced by two other factors. First, the number of people with whom any one prisoner has contact is purposely kept small by the authorities, mainly because the more prisoners who associate with one another, the more likely it is that activities counter to the administration's goal of peace in the prison will be contemplated. Second, the companionship of thieves, rapists, murderers, and predatory homosexuals cannot be considered encouraging to productive friendships (Sykes, 1958).

Another result of the inmate code is a convict status hierarchy based on the crime for which convicts were imprisoned and on their behavior in the prison. At the top of the social structure, using the first criterion, are those felons who committed crimes against persons in which violence was threatened or present (Bramwell, 1967), although in some prisons this distinction is not considered very important (Cohen & Taylor, 1972). However, in all prisons, sex offenders are at the bottom of the social ladder and are generally ostracized. Other types of inmates near the bottom are the mentally disturbed or retarded and the physically weak.

With regard to the second criterion for placement on the inmate social structure, their behavior in prison, inmates evaluate fellow inmates' ability to cope with prison life. This ability to cope is judged by several behaviors. One of the most important is the inmate's ability to take punishment without "breaking" (McCleery, 1961). A second factor is the inmate's knowledge of prison life, which enables him to live without being controlled by other inmates. A third factor is the inmate's job in the prison. Some inmates have assignments that give them access to information that can be used against other inmates. From these positions these inmates can act as middlemen between the staff and the other inmates. The top echelon of prisoners has been divided into three basic types: (1) the "politician," who acts as a middleman between the staff and inmates, (2) the "merchant," who obtains contraband, such as drugs and alcohol, for other inmates, and (3) the "right guy," who refuses to weaken even when severe punishment is meted out (Cloward, 1960).

Those high in the inmate hierarchy are usually assigned to positions of leadership by the prisoner community. As a group, prison leaders tend to have served more time in prison, have longer sentences left to be served, are more likely to have been charged with crimes of violence, and more frequently return to prison for committing new crimes than nonleaders. Generally, prison leaders have more major infractions, including previous escapes, attempted escapes, and fighting, than other inmates. On such factors as age, occupation, education, marital status, and intelligence, leaders do not generally differ from the rest of the prison population (Schrag, 1964).

A third result of the inmate code is that all prisoners live in a world governed explicitly by exchange relationships. An example of this exchange system will show how pervasive is the inmate code. Consider the giving of material goods. In almost every case, when an inmate accepts material aid from another prisoner, he must be submissive to the donor. Often, new inmates, unaware of the exchange norms that operate in a prison, will accept a gift of cigarettes and will later discover that by accepting the gift, they have incurred a debt that must be repaid in the form of sexual favors. If the receiver of the gift does not want to be bound to the giver, he must return it, sometimes even to the point that he must fight the donor to take it back (McCorkle & Korn, 1964).

In addition to affecting how prisoners perceive one another, the inmate code affects how prisoners perceive the staff. Generally, guards and prisoners come from the same socioeconomic class and have a number of common attitudes. In one study several psychological tests were given to both prison inmates and correctional-officer candidates in the Rhode Island prison system. The tests showed that the two groups had equal "violence potential," the officers being slightly more likely to engage in assaultive behavior.

In spite of these similarities, prisoners generally consider themselves superior to the guards for a number of reasons. First, many criminals, especially if they committed notorious crimes, have a strong sense of status because they have gained fame through exposure of their exploits in the media (Cohen & Taylor, 1972). Whenever the media make a celebrity out of a criminal, whether the criminal is Al Capone or Charles Manson, he is likely to consider himself more of a celebrity than most guards can ever hope to be. Second, because guards are recruited from rural communities, where most prisons are located, and most felons come from urban areas, prisoners often feel that they are more sophisticated than their guards (Cohen & Taylor, 1972). In Illinois, for instance, 35% of the prison guards grew up on farms and 36% came from small towns (Jacobs, 1978). Third, because the guards have to spend almost as many waking hours in the prison as the prisoners, many convicts feel that their guards are in no better position than they are. Finally, prisoners feel that their guards are working in the prison only because they cannot do any other kind of work (Cohen & Taylor, 1972).

In summary, the inmate code establishes a number of norms to which virtually all inmates verbally state their allegiance, because almost all inmates, regardless of their own behavior in relation to the code, want other inmates to follow the code (Sykes & Messinger, 1960). Consequently, the fact that an inmate offers vocal support for the code does not inform the guard of the inmate's true attitude toward the code. However, the inmate's behavior vis-à-vis the inmate code can be informative of the inmate's true disposition.

Inmates support the inmate code for one of three reasons (Sykes & Messinger, 1960). First, some prisoners strongly believe that inmate cohesion is an important goal because of their identification with the criminal world. Second, other inmates who may not place personal value on inmate cohesion still want their fellow prisoners to follow the code because otherwise they would probably be victims of their fellow captives. Third, a fairly small group strongly supports, but actively violates, the inmate code. These inmates take advantage of their fellow prisoners, and because they do not want their numbers to increase, they strongly support the notion that other inmates should be in favor of inmate cohesion.

To the extent that an inmate's behavior conforms to the inmate code, it is difficult for guards to determine the true motive underlying the inmate's behavior. For example, an inmate may show hostility toward a guard because he really feels hostile or because the inmate norm dictates that he act in a hostile way. In contrast, because inmate behavior that is nonnormative is very costly to enact, it will convey more information about the inmate's true dispositions than normative behavior would. Thus, a guard who observes an inmate violate the inmate code by starting lots of fights with inmates will be highly certain that the inmate is "mean" and "dangerous."

SOCIAL-EXCHANGE CONSIDERATIONS

Although prison guards' behavior toward a particular inmate is based to a large degree on the attributions they make about the inmate, their behavior is also influenced by a number of social-exchange considerations. Prison guards have social-exchange relationships with the prison administration, with fellow guards, and with other inmates as well as with the particular inmate (see Figure 8–2). Often the relationship that offers the most reward is clear, and there is no question what behavior the guard will perform. At other times, however, rewards offered by competing relationships are of similar value, so that the guard's decisions involve a more careful weighing of the costs and benefits for each of the relationships. These costs and benefits will be examined in this section.

Social Exchange with the Prison Administration

One of the most important social-exchange relationships prison guards have is with the prison administration. Their salary and the possibility of promotion are dependent on pleasing their immediate supervisors and the warden and his assistants. Before we examine the guard's relationship with the prison administration, we must first look at the pressures on the prison administration so that we can understand why the administration expects certain behaviors from guards.

At the top of the prison hierarchy are the warden and, generally, one or two assistant wardens. It is their duty to translate the formal policy laid down by the head of the prison system and the legislature into the directives that ensure continued functioning of the prison. Many wardens started as guards and rose through the ranks to their position. Thus, many are likely to have a strong commitment to the quasi-militaristic system of rank, command, and unquestioning response to orders.

Because most prisons are of the punitive/custodial type, correctional administrators generally see the function of their prisons to be incapacitation (custody) and punishment. In one survey, 50 administrators of adult prison systems were asked what the primary goal of their institution should be. The largest group, 48%, said public protection; 6% said punishment; 24% said rehabilitation; and 16% mentioned other goals (Serrill, 1975).

Maintaining the prison

Even though prison administrators generally see their function as keeping criminals away from society, with some efforts toward rehabilitation, their decisions regarding the institution are often made not on the basis of incapacitation or rehabilitation considerations but on the basis of how best to maintain the prison system (Burnham, 1975). These decisions are made even before a particular inmate comes to the prison. For example, the assignment of an inmate to a particular prison will depend as much on whether the prison has space to take him as on the inmate's own needs for inclusion in the prison by reason of its programs and its proximity to his family, friends, and lawyer (Burnham, 1975).

Even after a person is assigned to a particular prison, what programs he is allowed to enter will depend on whether these programs have space for him. And the inmate's job assignment, whether maintaining the prison grounds or helping in the warden's office, will depend primarily on the institutional needs to keep the prison running smoothly rather than on the individual inmate's needs for rehabilitation (Allen & Simonsen, 1975; see *Pugh* v. *Locke*, 1976).

When a prisoner first arrives at a prison, some kind of classification process is usually set in motion. The ideal classification process occurs in three stages (Irwin, 1974). The first stage, diagnosis, consists of gathering information about the inmate through interviews, psychological testing, and examination of his records. In the second stage, initial classification, a classification committee reviews the information and decides on an appropriate program of treatment and type of training for the inmate. In the final stage, the classification committee regularly reviews the case, evaluates the inmate's progress, and decides on changes, if needed, in his treatment and training. Although classification should ideally operate in this fashion, in actuality other considerations usually determine how an inmate will be treated while in prison. These other considerations include *custody* (the likelihood that the inmate will try to escape) and *convenience* (which programs have openings when the classification decision is made) (Sutherland & Cressey, 1974).

Prison administrators have to make decisions in light of how the probable outcomes of the decisions will affect their primary consideration of keeping the prison running efficiently. Thus, their decision making necessarily involves weighing the costs and benefits of a decision that might interfere with prison maintenance. One such decision concerns the amount of time inmates spend in "treatment." The more time they spend in educational, vocational, or therapeutic activities, the less time they can spend on activities that maintain the prison, such as working in the kitchen.

Preserving order

A major part of the administration's job in keeping the prison running smoothly and efficiently is defusing potential disturbances. A prison riot is the extreme case of blocking the smooth functioning of the prison. But even such things as petitions signed by the inmates and suits filed against the prison can interfere with the effective running of the system. To prevent such disturbances, the administration must attend to the major sources of inmate dissatisfaction. In a few prisons, the mechanism by which the administration deals with inmates' complaints is a formal inmate advisory committee composed of inmates selected by the administration to represent the other prisoners. In other prisons, a less formal approach is adopted; the administration simply meets informally with known prison leaders to discuss ways to deal with prisoners' grievances.

The prison administration may also maintain order by asking powerful inmates to use force against troublesome inmates. For example, as

revealed on CBS News' *60 Minutes* (January 11, 1981), prison administrators at a maximum-security institution in Florida were accused of
ordering a special "goon squad" of prisoners to beat up problem inmates. In exchange for performing this service for the administration,
the inmates in this goon squad were allowed to pick the boys of their
choice and to have four or five "wives" apiece. And, naturally, there was
no retaliation for their beatings.

Exchange with correctional staff

The administration's relationships with the correctional staff are also
aimed primarily at maintaining the prison. As mentioned earlier, in
punitive/custodial prisons authority is based on rank, there is great
emphasis on rules, decision making by guards is supposed to be limited,
communications are formal and restricted, and punishments are the
usual means of enforcing the rules. This system makes the social exchanges between the prison administration and the correctional staff
very explicit. In return for following the rules, the guards earn their
time toward retirement and have a chance for promotion and pay increases. In most prisons, even decisions by the treatment staff are often
aimed primarily at the continued functioning of the prison rather than
toward some rehabilitative goal. For example, a prison physician may
be asked to make decisions on the basis of punitive/custodial rather
than medical considerations (Cressey, 1965). A common practice is for
physicians to aid the administration by authorizing the transfer of a
"problem" inmate to another prison for medical reasons. Removal of
this person benefits the administration, which, in turn, makes administrative officials more likely to reward the physician with needed resources, such as space and work facilities.

Administration's need to accommodate community interest groups

In addition to the exchanges the prison administration has with inmates and with the correctional and treatment staff, the warden must
also engage in social exchanges with various community interest
groups. Community pressure on prison administrators comes from individuals and groups having conflicting purposes. Often there are those
who feel that conditions in prisons are not harsh enough, while others
take the opposite view, asserting that conditions in prisons are too
harsh. The first group feels that merely restricting prisoners' freedom is
not enough, that prisoners should also experience physical discomfort,
and that anything less than real punishment is "coddling criminals."
Police officers, prosecuting attorneys, other prison wardens, and many
politicians are usually in this first group. The second group, believing
that prisons are dehumanizing, is concerned with minimizing the dis-
comforts that prisoners are forced to endure. Members of the latter
group have helped prisoners file suits against state prison systems on
the grounds that the prison conditions constituted cruel and unusual

punishment. In this second group are such organizations as the American Civil Liberties Union, the American Friends Service Committee, and the National Association for the Advancement of Colored People.

Because the demands of the interest groups are often stated in very broad terms, wardens can often satisfy many of these groups at the same time. For example, by installing a very secure perimeter around the prison (a fence or a wall), the administrator can satisfy individuals and groups who are concerned with preventing escapes. Within that secure perimeter, however, the warden can establish a number of therapeutic, educational, vocational, and religious programs and can therefore satisfy those groups that call for rehabilitation inside prisons (Cressey, 1965). This system of compromise exists not only at the level of the individual prison but also at the level of the state correctional system. Thus, the head of the system could satisfy one interest group by making one prison very secure and another group by making another prison less restrictive with more rehabilitation programs (Cressey, 1965).

In addition to these ideology-based citizen pressure groups, there are a number of other groups that have a more economic interest in how prisons are run. Because prisons are large consumers of goods, including food, clothing, medicines, and toiletries, the suppliers of these goods have a strong interest in ensuring that the prison population does not decrease too much and that inmates do not try to produce the needed goods themselves. Where prison industry exists, local industry will oppose the new competition (Cressey, 1965; Cressey & Ohlin, 1966). Pressure on prison administrators comes even before the prison is built. Some local communities may oppose the building of prisons because of the increased crime and lower property values they fear the prison will bring. In contrast, other communities may favor construction of a prison in their district because it provides a large influx of money into the community in the form of salaries and purchased goods. Thus, powerful state legislators, who often come from relatively rural areas, may seek to locate state institutions, both prisons and mental institutions, in their districts ("The Mental Health Mess," 1981; Silberman, 1978). And when administrators contemplate the closing of a prison, citizen groups in the surrounding community are often very adamant in their opposition.

Administration's need to accommodate fellow agents of the criminal justice system

The prison administration also has social-exchange relationships with several criminal-justice-system agents: the police, other prison administrators, and the parole board. Police departments in the vicinity of the prison are very concerned with the security of the prison against escapes, and when prisons have work-release and study-release programs, police departments are particularly concerned with making sure that inmates return to the institution when they are supposed to. When prisoners escape, not only do local police departments have to spend time helping to catch the escapees, but they also face the likelihood that an escapee without any money will have to commit a crime in order to survive.

Prison administrators are also subject to pressure from other prison administrators in the same jurisdiction and in other states. For example, during the riot at Attica, the superintendent of corrections for New York State was besieged by telegrams and letters from corrections officials in New York and across the country who wanted the riot quelled and the danger to corrections officers' lives ended (Wicker, 1975). Even the governor of the state took into account the possibility that, as a result of the negotiations with the inmates at Attica, inmates at prisons in New York and elsewhere would riot and demand that the governors negotiate with them as well (Wicker, 1975).

The final group with which the prison administration must deal is the parole board. The board's policy influences the prison administration by directly affecting the number of prisoners in the institution. The greater the number of paroles granted, the more room there is for new inmates, and the less chance there is that the prison will become overcrowded. The less crowded the prison is, the better will be the prisoners' living conditions, which, in turn, can affect the likelihood that officials will have to deal with prison riots and other forms of inmate disturbances. In addition, reduced crowding is likely to increase inmates' chances of gaining access to work, educational, and rehabilitative programs within the prison, thus further decreasing prisoner dissatisfaction. Decreased inmate dissatisfaction makes it easier for the warden to run the prison. If few paroles are granted, there are less space for new inmates, more overcrowding, and fewer work, educational, and rehabilitation opportunities, all of which result in prisoner dissatisfaction and a higher likelihood of overt disturbances. Another effect of the board's policy is less direct. If the board is too conservative in granting paroles, inmates may become totally indifferent to the disciplinary sanctions of the prison guards, because conformity with prison officials' expectations will not lead to early parole. Lacking this incentive, many prisoners will be less motivated to comply with prison rules, thereby making it more difficult for administration officials to enforce compliance—the burden of which falls on the guards.

In summary, the prison administration is under pressure from the community and other agencies in the criminal justice system to keep the prison operating efficiently within legal standards and administrative guidelines. What the prison administration desires most, therefore, is a prison that operates with very few problems. The guards' task is to ensure that disciplinary problems are kept to a minimum. If guards succeed at their task, they are likely to have their salaries increased and perhaps even be promoted. The problem is that "keeping the peace" on a cellblock can be very difficult.

Many guards think it is especially difficult now to maintain order in prisons because they are handcuffed by federal judges and "reform" wardens who question the need for, and utility of, totalitarian control (Silberman, 1978). Prison guards who dislike the changes imposed by these wardens have united in unions to challenge prison policy and have threatened, as in one Georgia prison, to "lock down" the institution (that is, confine inmates to their cells) unless policy is changed or a warden fired (Mooney, 1980).

Guards' Social Exchanges with Inmates

To achieve the goal of a quiet cellblock, the guard must engage in social exchanges with the prison inmates. To understand the social-exchange relationship between guards and inmates, we must first understand the situational forces involved. We will discuss why guards form social-exchange relationships with inmates and then why inmates desire social-exchange relationships with guards.

Guards receive rewards from the prison administration for minimizing behavior that disrupts the operation of the institution, such as riots, fights, escapes, and possession of contraband material. Guards who have the fewest occurrences of these behaviors on their cellblock can expect to be rewarded in terms of salary and promotions. To achieve this goal of minimizing rule infractions, guards can rely exclusively on the use of formally approved punishment or rewards. However, for reasons to be discussed below, to minimize disruptive behavior, guards cannot effectively use either legitimate punishments or legitimate rewards. Instead, guards must enter into social exchanges with inmates in order to control their behavior.

Use of punishment to control inmates

The use of punishment to secure obedience to prison rules is largely ineffective. Most forms of physical violence have been eliminated as legitimate means of social control because of efforts at penal reform and court cases brought under the Constitution and federal statute (Cloward, 1960). Even without these reforms, however, the use of force has not been shown to be an efficient means of controlling inmates' behavior (Sykes, 1958). Although physical force can be effective for a problem involving a few inmates, only a large amount of force can be effective when many inmates are involved. In addition, the use of violence by guards may invite retaliation by inmates, who, though less well armed than the guards, greatly outnumber them. Moreover, guards know that at some point they may be held hostage by inmates, and if they have used physical violence against inmates in the past, they will probably be treated severely if taken hostage (Sykes, 1958). For example, in the Attica prison riot, several guards who were injured by inmates were those who had treated inmates harshly in the past (Wicker, 1975).

No doubt some guards do use violence against some prison inmates. However, the number of inmates involved is probably very small, because there are simply not enough guards to regularly control a prison if physical violence is used against most inmates. For example, in the mid-1970s at the maximum-security prison at Stateville, Illinois, the average ratio of guards to prisoners across shifts was 1 to 17 (Silberman, 1978).

The results from the Stanford prison experiment (Haney et al., 1973), which showed that physical aggression by guards increased over time despite a decrease in prisoner resistance, are probably not generalizable to real prisons. The simulated prison had few inmates and a relatively high ratio of guards to inmates. Furthermore, the physical aggression in the simulated prison did not include beating and torture. Therefore, one must be careful in generalizing from the physical aggression shown by the guards in the Stanford simulation study to aggression in the form of beatings in real prisons.

A punishment often used in prisons is segregating inmates who violate prison rules. This segregation occurs in one of two forms. The first, transferring the problem inmate to a more secure institution, which is known as "bus therapy" (Silberman, 1978), is beneficial to the first prison but harmful to the second, since the inmate still must be dealt with. Thus, the problem is not solved by the transfer, because the inmate "cannot be expelled from the system as a whole" (Cloward, 1960, p. 23). Moreover, although bus therapy may be effective in inducing compliant behavior from inmates at minimum- and medium-security institutions, these inmates are least likely to be recalcitrant, since they were put in these institutions precisely because they were not troublemakers. Most inmates who are severe problems are already at maximum-security institutions, and being transferred to another maximum-security institution is not much of a threat.

The second form of segregation involves placing the inmate in a special status within the prison, usually solitary confinement. Although one might expect such confinement to be a potent form of punishment, its effectiveness may be limited in that the difference between the usual status of some prisoners and the conditions of solitary confinement is not great. Moreover, the pain of solitary confinement is tempered to some degree by the increased prestige the punished inmate has in the eyes of fellow inmates (Sykes, 1958). Finally, the use of solitary confinement is restricted by the limited facilities of most prisons and by the decisions of several courts.

Silberman (1978) has argued that in recent years punishment of young black inmates has become particularly ineffective. In most large prisons today, blacks are in the majority and are, according to Silberman, less willing to obey guards' orders than white inmates were 20 years ago. Silberman suggests also that black violence against whites in prison is more an expression of outrage at past injustices than a means of achieving some end. Given this assumption, it is not surprising that punishment of black inmates would be ineffective.

Use of formal incentives to control inmates

Just as punishments are ineffective in controlling inmates' behavior, so too are the formal incentives offered to inmates for observing the prison's rules. One form of incentive is "good time"—a portion of the inmate's sentence automatically subtracted for good behavior. Like other so-called privileges such as mail, visitors, and recreation, the privilege of gaining good time is given to all inmates when they enter the prison, so that inmates have little to gain by complying with the rules of the prison (Sykes, 1958). A second incentive available to inmates who follow prison rules is early release from prison by parole. As with good time, however, inmates who comply with the rules are not rewarded with parole. Instead, when inmates violate the rules, they are likely to be punished by not receiving parole. Thus, both good time and parole serve as negative incentives (that is, withdrawal of a reward that inmates already possess) rather than positive incentives (that is, the granting of rewards that inmates do not have). Neither one necessarily serves as a powerful influence on many inmates' behavior, because inmates may come to view early release as a "right" to which they are entitled regardless of their behavior in prison. In addition, inmates may believe that the immediate rewards obtained from violating the prison rules are more valuable than early release, which may be years away. Finally, inmates may feel that the two incentives, good time and parole, will not be withdrawn even if their rule violations are discovered. In especially overcrowded prisons, inmates may be correct.

For the reasons just discussed, the formal mechanisms of controlling inmates are inadequate to control the deviant behavior of many inmates. But because prison guards are responsible for the management of inmates and receive their rewards on the basis of how well the inmates are controlled, it is clear that guards must have some means by which they can achieve their goal of control in the prison. The system of social exchanges between guards and inmates allows guards to gain some control of the inmates' behavior.

Guards' perspective of social exchange with inmates

In addition to the inadequacy of punishments and incentives, two factors lead guards to enter into social-exchange relationships with prisoners. First, because the guard must deal directly and continuously with prisoners, he or she cannot maintain the social distance required by the punitive/custodial prison (Sykes, 1958). Second, it is often necessary that inmates take over some of the guard's duties both because prisons are understaffed and because generally there are more prisoners than there is work for them to do. Generally, the duties the prisoners assume are minor tasks, such as delivering mail or housekeeping duties. An extreme example of this transfer of duties existed in Arkansas prisons before a federal court ruling declared the situation unconstitutional. When the inmates worked in the fields, a few inmates actually guarded the others with shotguns (*Holt* v. *Sarver*, 1970).

The forces that lead guards to enter into social-exchange relationships with prisoners are very powerful, and the usual result is that a system of accommodation develops. A common form of this accommodation is for guards to enforce prison rules selectively. Thus, guards are willing to tolerate violations of less important rules in exchange for adherence to the important rules of the institution (Sykes, 1958). A second form of such accommodation is for guards to allow some inmates fulfillment of their needs through illegitimate means in exchange for these inmates' maintaining social control over other prisoners (Cloward, 1960). Guards may allow these inmates to obtain information, material goods, or status, thus creating an inmate elite that serves an important role in keeping the prison quiet. As a result of its privileged status, the inmate elite has a vested interest in maintaining the status quo. Inmate disturbances, such as escapes or riots, are a source of embarrassment to the guards and may lead them to seek social exchanges with inmates who can better maintain control of the prisoner population. If the guard fails to fulfill his or her part of the exchange, the inmate can organize other prisoners to embarrass the guard, which may cause the administration to wonder whether the guard can effectively perform his or her duties (Cloward, 1960).

Prison guards have compelling reasons to enter into social-exchange relationships with prison inmates. To understand why some inmates form social-exchange relationships with guards, we need to know more about the objective conditions of imprisonment, the resulting psychological state of inmates, and the alternatives available to them.

Inmates' perspective on social exchange with guards

Although there is evidence that individual inmates may react to imprisonment in idiosyncratic ways, generally it appears that punitive/custodial institutions affect prisoners negatively (Bukstel & Kilmann, 1980). The objective deprivations that a prisoner endures are many. Indeed, when a convicted felon enters a prison for the first time, he is struck by the tremendous differences between the enclosed world of the prison and the "free world" outside. These differences are evident in virtually every aspect of the prison but particularly in the physical facility and the limitations it imposes on inmates: crowding, lack of personal space, deprivations that prisoners must endure. Within a few days after the inmate has entered the prison, he has been shocked by his new environment and forced to change his behavior to meet the demands of the prison.

Clemmer (1971) termed this adaptation to the new environment "prisonization," the process by which a new inmate is integrated into the life of the prison. The first step in this process is a change in the person's status, which changes the way he sees himself and the way others see him. No one action causes this change. Rather, it is a series of actions: for example, in many states the prisoner is identified by a number instead of a name, he is made to wear the same clothes as the rest of the inmates, and he is given a very short haircut identical to that given other inmates. As a result of these actions, inmates are stripped of their personal identity. It should be noted, however, that some states are relaxing these restrictions.

One aspect of the prison experience that greatly affects how the prisoner responds to imprisonment is the physical facility itself. Environmental psychologists have argued that the design of an institutional building generally reflects how the outside world views those who are institutionalized (Ittelson, Proshansky, Rivlin, & Winkel, 1974). A fortress-like maximum-security prison that has bars thicker than the ones used to cage gorillas signals that punishment is the primary goal of the institution.

Another source of distress for inmates is the degree of crowding. In one study, Paulus, Cox, McCain, and Chandler (1975) found that inmates housed under highly crowded conditions (dormitories accommodating from 26 to 44 inmates) were generally less tolerant of overcrowding than inmates who were housed under less crowded conditions (single-occupant cells). In addition, Paulus et al. found that the longer inmates were confined in a crowded environment, the less tolerance they had for high levels of crowding. Finally, in a subsequent series of studies at six federal prisons, McCain, Cox, and Paulus (1980) found that prisoners in higher-density housing generally had a higher rate of illness complaints (as measured by voluntary visits to a medical facility) than those in lower-density housing, and this effect appeared to be independent of the length of the inmates' stay in the particular type of housing.

Crowding and the lack of privacy seem to affect everyone, but these effects may be aggravated in the prison setting by characteristics of the prisoners. Kinzel (1970) found that violent prisoners are more sensitive to physical closeness, particularly when approached from the rear, than nonviolent prisoners. Thus, for some prisoners, being crowded and having their personal space invaded may have particularly harmful consequences. Because crowding seems to affect both individual inmates and the quality of institutional services, crowding is considered a contributing cause to some prison riots (Clements, 1979).

Other important deprivations that prisoners have to endure include separation from family and friends, anxiety over physical and emotional integrity, and the absence of heterosexual relationships (Sykes, 1958). In evaluating these deprivations, a prisoner judges his condition on the basis of the outcomes he received before his imprisonment, the present outcomes received by prisoners around him, and the outcomes of others with whom he regularly interacts—the guards.

Inmates' evaluation of the outcomes. In addition to the objective deprivations a prisoner endures, he also suffers because the outcomes he experiences are below those he expects or feels he deserves (his comparison level). As mentioned in Chapter 1, a person's comparison level is determined by the level of the person's previous outcomes, what the person observes similar others receiving, and the outcomes received by the person with whom he or she is interacting. A prisoner's comparison level is determined by what he received in the past (in the outside world), by what he observes other prisoners are receiving, and by the outcomes the guards and other prison staff members he interacts with are receiving. If a prisoner compares his outcomes with those he experienced when he was free or those he observes the prison staff receive, he is likely to see himself as relatively deprived. Even if he compares himself with other inmates, he may still feel deprived because his job may be of low status or he may have fewer privileges than other inmates.

In addition to the frustration resulting from being objectively deprived and from receiving outcomes below his comparison level, a prisoner often feels frustrated because his environment exercises a great deal of control over his life. Related to the distress over not being able to control his life is the distress caused by not knowing how long this lack of control will last. In most jurisdictions offenders are sentenced to an indefinite term of imprisonment. Thus, when a person is sentenced to prison, he is not sure exactly how long he will remain there. That determination is made by the parole board (see Chapter 9).

How inmates cope with the prison environment. A prisoner who is objectively deprived, who is below his comparison level, and who feels little control over his fate can attempt to change his situation either *psychologically* or *behaviorally*. The psychological alternative will be discussed first. Thibaut and Kelley (1959) suggest that when a person must remain in a nonvoluntary relationship and his outcomes are below his comparison level, he can lower his comparison level and thus lessen his discontent. His comparison level can be lowered in one of two ways: "(1) devaluating the outcomes believed to exist in the unavailable alternative relationships or (2) decreasing the salience of the good outcomes in these relationships" (p. 174). Alternative relationships can be devalued by minimizing the good aspects (for example, "Freedom on the outside really isn't that important to me") or by maximizing the negative aspects (for example, "If I were free, I'd have to worry about finding a job and a place to live"). A related way that a prisoner can devaluate the outcomes that exist in the outside world is to overvaluate his present outcomes (for example, "Here in prison, at least I have a roof over my head, three warm meals a day, and plenty of time to read and think").

When people decrease the salience of the good outcomes in alternative but unattainable relationships, they are constructing the situation in their mind so that they do not notice the good outcomes they cannot have. Prisoners draw a distinction between "doing hard time" and "doing easy time." When a prisoner constantly thinks about his life on the streets, his friends, and all that he is missing by being in prison, inmates say he is "doing hard time." Using Thibaut and Kelley's terminology, the prisoner can be said to be maintaining his comparison level where it was, because the good outcomes in his alternative relationships (the outside world) are still salient to him. The salience of these outcomes makes him feel deprived. In contrast, a prisoner who "does easy time" makes these unattainable relationships less prominent in his life. For example, Farber (1944) reported,

> Prisoner 24, who had cut off all personal contact with the outside, says, "I don't do hard time. It's much easier if you get the outside off your mind and just forget about your family, your folks and your wife." For some cases at least, cutting off personal relations with the outside seems to be an effective means of avoiding frustration [p. 176].

Farber also reported that those prisoners who had the least contact with their families and friends were less frustrated than those who had brief, intermittent contact. For inmates who had some contact with friends and family, the salient comparison level was still the outside world.

Instead of, or in addition to, these psychological redefinitions of their situation, inmates may use behavioral alternatives to improve their condition. One behavioral alternative available to inmates is to acquire goods and services lawfully through such channels as the prison store and gifts from outside. There are two problems with legal channels. First, inmates' consumption demands are often greater than the money they receive from work in the prison and outside sources (Gleason, 1978). Second, many of the things prisoners want, such as drugs or alcohol, cannot be obtained legally. Consequently, inmates use a different behavioral alternative, exchanges with fellow prisoners or with guards or with both groups.

The reason inmates will enter exchange relationships is to obtain physical and psychological rewards that they do not want to do without. According to Sheehan (1978, pp. 91–92),

> Most of the men at Green Haven [a prison in New York] are in prison precisely because they were not willing to go without on the street. They are no more willing to go without in prison, so they hustle to obtain what they cannot afford to buy. Some men sell special services. Inmates who want to be sure of getting their clothes back from the laundry "buy" a laundryman for a carton of cigarettes a month. . . . Hustling usually involves breaking a prison rule. Some men gamble. Some sell sexual favors. . . . A great deal of the

hustling involves appropriating state property for one's personal use, in which case it is usually called swagging.[1]

Because inmates are usually unable to deal with the hardships of imprisonment by purely psychological means, they must rely on social exchanges with other inmates to satisfy many of their needs. Many such social exchanges involve violation of prison rules and therefore usually require the cooperation of the prison guards. Without such cooperation, inmates run the continuous risk of losing their benefits through confiscation and of losing their position in the prison that enables them to obtain the benefits. Clearly, then, inmates are dependent on the guards to reduce the harshness of prison life.

Mutuality of exchange between guards and inmates

Because guards need the cooperation of certain inmates in order to control the prison population, it is in the interest of both parties, prisoners and guards, to engage in social exchanges. Both parties profit from the exchange. The prisoners help maintain control over other inmates through the use of threats or by providing information to the guards, and in exchange, the guards allow these inmates to acquire illegitimate benefits and to use them in illicit exchanges with other inmates. As discussed earlier, each party has power over the other to ensure that mutual obligations are met. In other words, "Each is captive and captor of the other" (Cloward, 1960, p. 42). As an illustration of the exchanges between guards and inmates, consider the following interview with an inmate of an Eastern penitentiary:

> Interviewer: I notice that you finally got that job as chief clerk in the company. You've been working on that for some time, haven't you?
> Prisoner: Yeah, I got it, and it sure took some doing. But it's worth it. You can make that kind of a job pay off.
> Interviewer: How do you mean "pay off"?
> Prisoner: Well, you get a lot of information about things on that job. You see papers, you hear guards talk, you overhear telephone conversations. Sometimes, if something big is cooking, the sergeant passes the word to me. And then I decide who to pass it on to. Like I said, you just know things that other guys don't know, and that means you got an edge on them.
> Interviewer: You mean by "edge" that you can sort of have things your way with the other inmates?
> Prisoner: Yeah, sort of like that. You don't have to take no crap off anybody. If a guy gets wise, you can fix him good.
> Interviewer: How would you go about "fixing" him?
> Prisoner: It's easy enough. Suppose I hear there's going to be a shakedown. So I pass the word, but not to this guy. He don't know it's coming, so he gets caught hands down with a bunch of crap in his locker. Maybe he gets restricted, or a couple of days in the "hole."

[1]From A PRISON AND A PRISONER by Susan Sheehan. Copyright © 1978 by Susan Sheehan. Reprinted by permission of Houghton Mifflin Company. The material in this book originally appeared in *The New Yorker*.

Interviewer: How did you manage to get this job?

Prisoner: Angles, angles.

Interviewer: Give me an example.

Prisoner: Well, it's mostly a matter of handling the company sergeant. I been working on him for a long time, and he finally paid off. It's a matter of knowing what a guy wants.

Interviewer: And what did the sergeant want that you could supply him with?

Prisoner: Information. Like I said, everybody wants information.

Interviewer: In the sergeant's case, you mean information about other prisoners.

Prisoner: Yeah, something like that. Just a word now and then about a little something that's going on that he don't know about. That's about all it takes.

Interviewer: How do the other prisoners feel about that?

Prisoner: What does it matter? What they don't know won't hurt them.

Interviewer: And what about you? Does it hurt you?

Prisoner: Listen, buddy, this ain't no dude ranch. Doing time is no picnic. It's every man for himself. You got to work the angles to survive. If you don't put the finger on a man, he'll put the finger on you. I don't rat out on just any old guy . . . only the ones that got it coming [Cloward, 1960, pp. 38–39].[2]

Although a guard generally benefits from a social-exchange relationship with an inmate, there are two additional relationships that limit the scope of the guard/inmate exchange. The guard must take into account his relationship with fellow guards as well as with other inmates.

Social Exchange with Fellow Guards

Even though a guard must cooperate with inmates, his first loyalty must be to his fellow guards because, should a dangerous situation occur, he must be able to count on their support. In many ways, guards show the same solidarity and brotherhood as police officers, particularly if a fellow guard is harmed (see Chapter 3). For example, the guards at Attica felt justified in using deadly force when they retook the prison, because of rumors that the rioting inmates had murdered several guards who had been taken hostage (Stotland, 1976). One means by which guards demonstrate their readiness to help their fellow guards is to display constantly, to prisoners and guards alike, an attitude of fearlessness and toughness. Another way for a guard to show readiness to aid fellow guards is not to give the appearance of being too friendly with inmates. If he does, he may be perceived by fellow guards as being "wired up" by the inmates and therefore not to be counted on in an emergency. Informal social sanctions are likely to be applied to guards

[2]From "Social Control in the Prison," by R. A. Cloward. In R. A. Cloward, O. R. Cressey, G. H. Grosser, R. McCleery, L. E. Ohlin, G. M. Sykes, and S. L. Messinger (Eds.), *Theoretical Studies in Social Organization of the Prison.* Copyright © 1960 by the Social Science Research Council, New York. This and all other quotations from this source are reprinted by permission.

who show too close a relationship with inmates. The general perception is that a guard who shows fear or friendliness toward inmates cannot be relied on in a dangerous situation (Haney & Zimbardo, 1977).

This loyalty to fellow guards does not eliminate the guard/inmate social-exchange relationship; it only modifies it. Certainly a guard would do nothing that endangered the life of a fellow guard. The guard will be likely to maintain his exchange relationship with an inmate if it is not likely to cause harm to a fellow guard, if it serves to maintain order and security in the prison, and if it does not harm the guard's relationship with other inmates.

Social Exchange between Guards and Other Inmates

The social-exchange relationship between the guard and a particular inmate is affected by the guard's relationship with other inmates as well as with fellow guards. The guard must be aware that to preserve the value of the resources he or she possesses—access to information, access to material rewards—he or she must invest in certain prisoners but not in others. To the extent that a guard allows many inmates to have access to these resources, their value, following traditional market principles, is reduced. Thus, the guard will enter social-exchange relationships with inmates who can best provide what he or she wants: control over other inmates. If other inmates are not under the control of the inmate with whom the guard has a social-exchange relationship, the guard will want to enter an exchange relationship with someone who does have this control.

Guards must also be concerned with their public image among the prisoners. Generally, guards want to appear "tough," because they know that their effectiveness depends to a large extent on their reputation for controlling inmates. Inmates may try to exploit a guard who appears friendly or "soft," and therefore he or she will have difficulty dealing with them. Hence, guards are told to be "firm and fair but not friendly" with inmates (Haney & Zimbardo, 1977).

Even though guards must have an image of being tough, it is important that they not treat an inmate unfairly, because other inmates may come to the aid of the unfairly treated inmate. The inmate's friends could make the guard's job difficult by creating a situation, such as a littered, noisy cellblock, that makes the guard appear incapable of meeting his or her responsibilities. Inequitable treatment of an inmate is likely to arouse strong reactions from other inmates for two reasons. First, to the extent that inmate solidarity exists, whether solely because the harmed person is a fellow inmate or on some other basis, such as race, harm to one inmate is harm to all inmates. Second, unfair treatment of one inmate by a guard establishes by implication the precedent that the guard can treat other inmates unfairly. To ensure that they will not be subject to arbitrary treatment, the inmates will "punish" the guard for his or her unfair behavior, by making the guard's job difficult.

Thus far, we have examined prisons from the standpoint of the principal actor in the prison, the prison guard. We have seen that the guard's treatment of an inmate depends on his or her attributions about the inmate and on several social-exchange relationships. In the next section we will examine the interaction of people in prison in terms of the decision-making stages discussed earlier in this book. These stages—reporting, arrest, trial, and sentencing—occur in the prison because the prison is a minisociety and, therefore, a mini–criminal justice system.

THE PRISON AS A MINI–CRIMINAL JUSTICE SYSTEM

Criminals commit crimes not only on the streets but also inside prisons. The inmates who are victims of these crimes must decide whether to report them. Guards must decide whether to file misconduct charges against the offenders. If charges are filed, a hearing is held to determine guilt or innocence and to set punishment if guilt is established. These stages are direct analogues of the stages in the criminal justice system. We will briefly discuss the parallels between the two systems.

Reporting Crimes

A striking example of social exchange as it operates in prisons concerns the reporting of crimes, usually assaults, to the prison authorities. As discussed in Chapter 2, the decision to report is based on a weighing of benefits and costs that are likely to result from reporting. The victim of a prison assault may see little to be gained from reporting the incident to authorities. Victims may believe that guards are reluctant to act on such complaints because the complaints are evidence of the guards' failure to perform their duty (Davis, 1971). An example of what happens when assaults are reported to prison authorities can be found in a study of the Philadelphia prison system. In one year, of the estimated 2000 assaults that occurred, just 96 were reported to prison authorities. "Of this 96, only 64 were mentioned in the prison records. Of these 64, only 40 resulted in internal discipline against the aggressors; and only 26 incidents were reported to the police for prosecution" (Davis, 1971, p. 32).

Not only does the victim have little to gain by reporting, but there may be considerable costs as well. A victim who reports a crime to authorities may run the risk of being a double victim, in that the original perpetrator or his friends may punish the victim for having "ratted" to the authorities. Fear of a second, possibly worse, victimization for reporting the incident may be especially prominent among victims of sexual assault. A number of studies indicate that most sexual aggressors are black whereas most victims are white (for example, Irwin, 1970; Lockwood, 1980; Scacco, 1975), and therefore sexual assaults may be, in part, an attempt to assert authority over a member of a group that traditionally has had more power than blacks (Silberman, 1978). If, as has been argued, homosexual rape in prison is a crime of violence and power (Moss, Hosford, & Anderson, 1979; Silberman, 1978; Toch, 1977; compare Brownmiller, 1975, on heterosexual rape), then it seems likely that aggressors would be likely to reassert their power against a victim who reported them to the prison guards.

If a threat of retaliation exists, the victim may have to be placed in isolation for his protection. Being placed in protective solitary confinement carries certain costs: prisoners in such cells cannot leave their cells to exercise or to take showers, their food is usually cold, and they cannot participate in educational, vocational, or therapeutic programs. Moreover, a stigma as a perceived informer or homosexual attaches to a prisoner who has been in protective custody, and this stigma will follow the inmate even if he is transferred to another prison (Toch, 1977). Finally, asking to be placed in protective confinement is an admission of weakness in a society that values fearlessness. This admission is not likely to be forgotten. For these reasons, it is believed, inmates are extremely reluctant to report their victimizations to the prison authorities.

Because the rewards from reporting incidents are small and the costs are fairly great, it is not surprising that most victims of assaults in prison attribute their injuries to bumping into a door, or if they admit that another inmate caused the injuries they say they do not know who assaulted them. Among prisoners the norm is not to invoke legitimate authority if a crime has occurred ("Never rat on a con"), and therefore most victims do not report crimes to guards.

Guards' Discretion

When an inmate is caught violating a prison rule, the guard must write up a report of the incident. Although guards in punitive/custodial prisons are not supposed to have any discretion in the issuing of incident reports, in fact they do. "Officially, guards are enjoined to report rather than to conceal or to overlook deviant behavior of inmates; but the novice soon learns the informal rule that you 'con them, chastise them, coerce them, *but never charge them*'" (Cloward, 1960, p. 36). As previously stated, guards will sometimes overlook an inmate's violation of minor rules in exchange for the inmate's following major rules. For example, guards may be willing to allow inmates to have some alcohol or marijuana but will strictly enforce rules against violence (Coleman, 1980). An additional consideration is the guard's estimation of the probability that a major violation might result while he or she is dealing with a minor violation. Sometimes guards will overlook a minor violation for fear that a major violation might occur while they are off the cellblock dealing with the minor infraction (Nacci, Teitelbaum, & Prather, 1977).

Another reason that guards may be reluctant to write up an incident report is that such a report may call into question whether they could have acted sooner and thus prevented the incident in the first place. Further, if guards reported every offense that occurred on their cellblocks, the entire prison would become bogged down in a morass of adjudication and disposition hearings (Cloward, 1960; Sykes, 1958). These processes would disrupt the efficient operation of the prison and, hence, incur the anger of the prison administration. Therefore, the guard is likely to report only major offenses. If a guard writes a number of misconduct reports during his or her shift, while guards on other shifts do not write many misconduct reports, the prison administration is likely to view the guard as unable to maintain order (Silberman, 1978). The guard may then be sent to a position that allows less contact with inmates and may find that his or her opportunities for promotion are limited. If inmates wanted to have a certain guard transferred, they could deliberately cause trouble while he or she was on duty. Eventually, the guard would be transferred, and the inmates would have, in effect, "fired" him or her (Sutherland & Cressey, 1974).

Not only can guards use their discretion to avoid writing misconduct reports, but they can also use it to be supervigilant of some inmates. Guards take special interest in a "troublemaker" who has been transferred from another prison for discipline problems. They are likely to be particularly vigilant of this inmate's actions, much as the police are when an ex-con returns from prison to the community, because they will believe that his disciplinary problems stem from a stable "troublemaker" disposition. This vigilance was certainly in evidence at Attica before the riot in 1971. Inmates who had been involved in disturbances at other New York prisons and had been transferred to Attica were watched especially closely by the guards (Wicker, 1975).

Disciplinary Hearing

After an infraction of the prison rules is reported, the convict may be put in an isolated cell or may be denied some privileges pending a hearing on the charges of misconduct. At the hearing, which is usually conducted by a committee consisting of a senior correctional officer and treatment personnel, the guard making the complaint gives his or her account of the offense. The inmate can then state his version of the incident and may be allowed to provide witnesses.

A decision by the United States Supreme Court has defined an inmate's rights at a disciplinary hearing (*Wolff* v. *McDonnell*, 1974). The court held that although a disciplinary hearing is not part of a criminal prosecution, an inmate who might lose good-time credits (a reduction of sentence given by the prison system in return for the inmate's good behavior) is entitled to the following rights: (1) notice of the charges against him, (2) the opportunity to present evidence and call witnesses at a hearing, unless doing so would be dangerous, and (3) a statement expressing the disciplinary committee's reasons for its decision and the evidence it relied on to reach that decision. The court decided that inmates had no right to confront and cross-examine witnesses at disciplinary hearings, because such a right might be useless, given the reluctance of inmates to speak, and might be dangerous to both inmates and staff because of the possibility of reprisal. Moreover, because the court wanted to maintain the "rehabilitative function" of disciplinary hearings, which would be destroyed in an adversary situation, it decided that inmates had no blanket right to counsel at such hearings.

There is probably a bias for an inmate to be found guilty of the misconduct with which he was charged. First, many other persons have found the offender to have a criminal disposition, and the commission of an offense in prison is consistent with that disposition. Second, the members of the hearing board are probably more tied by social-exchange relationships to the guard than to the inmate. Thus, if the evidence comes down to a "swearing contest" between the guard and the inmate, the guard will almost certainly be believed.

Should the inmate be found guilty, he is then "sentenced" to some form of punishment. This punishment generally is a loss of some or all privileges—for example, movies, athletic events, visiting, and correspondence (Sutherland & Cressey, 1974). Often, too, good time is revoked. A serious infraction of prison rules can result in the forfeiture of some or all of this good time. A serious offender may also be sent to solitary confinement. If the inmate is seen as a troublemaker and as likely to commit additional misconducts on release from solitary confinement, he may be transferred to another prison.

Generally, hearing boards are likely to impose some form of punishment in order to deter both the offender and others from committing similar offenses. The board may reason that the misconduct itself is further evidence that the inmate's criminal disposition has not changed, and the board may feel that his disposition will not change unless he is punished. Social-exchange considerations also dictate that the inmate receive some punishment for his offense (Sutherland & Cressey, 1974). If the inmate is not punished, the nonpunishment may be seen as a reprimand to the guard who reported the offense, and the incident may lower the morale of other guards. Further, the failure to impose some form of punishment may be a signal to other inmates that such behavior is condoned. Indeed, there is evidence that if inmates perceive that *all* disciplinary violations will be punished, there will be fewer infractions (Edinger & Auerbach, 1978). Thus, even though the hearing board may have preferred that the offense not be reported, once it is reported, the board is under strong pressure to back up the guard who issued the report.

SUMMARY

The prison administration is charged with the responsibility of running the prison and preserving order. This task is not easy, because prisons are often overcrowded and lack sufficient facilities. Moreover, prison administrators are often under pressure from the community and from other agents in the criminal justice system.

The actor with the primary responsibility for dealing with prison inmates is the prison guard. The guard's behavior toward inmates is based on attribution and social-exchange considerations. The guard's attributions about inmates are based on the fact that the inmates are in prison, ethnic stereotypes, the guard's own behavior toward the inmates, and the inmates' behavior in prison. The guard's relationship with the prison administration is premised on the notion that the guard will be rewarded if he or she maintains order in the area for which he or she is responsible. Because formal punishments and incentives are not fully effective in controlling inmates, guards must enter into informal social-exchange relationships with some prisoners in order to gain their cooperation. These inmates also gain from being in a social-exchange relationship with guards. The guard/inmate relationship is limited by the social-exchange relationships the guard has with fellow guards and with other prisoners.

The prison is a mini–criminal justice system that encompasses re-porting, arrest, trial, and punishment. The same considerations that affect decision making in the criminal justice system outside the prison walls also affect decision making within the prison.

The prison is not the end of the criminal justice process, although it is sometimes portrayed as such. Most inmates are released from prison, and it is to this last stage of the criminal justice system that we turn next.

CHAPTER NINE

Parole and Return to Society

Virtually everyone who is sent to prison eventually returns to society, for only about 3% of inmates die in prison (Fox, 1975). Most of the inmates who leave prison are released through some form of conditional release, generally parole (U. S. Department of Justice, 1979). This chapter will briefly describe the history of parole and will then focus on the attributional and exchange considerations that parole boards use in deciding to release offenders. Finally, we will discuss how members of society react to these released offenders and how parole boards decide whether to revoke parole.

A BRIEF HISTORY OF PAROLE

Parole is the "release of an offender from a penal or correctional institution, after he has served a portion of his sentence, under the continued custody of the state and under conditions that permit his reincarceration in the event of misbehavior" (*Attorney General's Survey of Release Procedures*, 1939, Vol. IV, p. 4). In the United States today 72% of inmates are released from prison through parole, although the range is from under 20% in four states to more than 90% in eight states (National Advisory Commission on Criminal Justice Standards and Goals, 1973). Because parole is so important in the lives of most inmates and because in many cases it constitutes the sentencing decision, the parole decision has recently become the subject of much research.

Although parole is said to have its origins in the release of military prisoners who promised not to fight again (Dressler, 1965), most scholars consider it an outgrowth of the English and Irish systems of penology. For several decades before the American War of Independence,

England had transported its prisoners to the colonies. After the war, it turned to other colonies, primarily Australia and the surrounding islands. In 1840 Captain Alexander Maconochie became governor of one of these penal colonies, Norfolk Island, east of Australia, and immediately implemented a mark and grading system that he had proposed in 1837. By receiving marks for good conduct and labor, a convict could move through four levels of incarceration—"strict imprisonment at first, then work on government chain gangs, followed by a period of partial freedom, but with restrictions on the prisoner's movement, and finally a ticket-of-leave that enabled him to be transferred to Australia for the remainder of his time before attaining full liberty" (Tappan, 1960, p. 712). Because Maconochie was considered too lenient in his handling of the Norfolk Island convicts (the most serious of the English criminals), he was replaced in 1844 after serving four years as governor.

His system, however, had a great influence on the "progressive stage system," introduced in England in 1857 by Sir Joshua Jebb, and on the "Irish system," introduced in Ireland in 1854 by Sir Walter Crofton. Under Crofton's plan prisoners about to be released lived in small groups apart from the other inmates. During this period, employment and police supervision after discharge were arranged. Once released, the "ticket-of-leave man" was required to report monthly to the local police in his community and to conform to a set of rules, on pain of revocation (Tappan, 1960).

The opening of the Elmira Reformatory in New York State in 1876 is generally considered the beginning of parole in the United States (National Advisory Commission on Criminal Justice Standards and Goals, 1973). Young felons were sentenced to Elmira for an indeterminate length of time, dependent on the number of "marks" earned by good behavior. During the six-month parole term that followed release, the parolee had to report regularly to a volunteer guardian, or sponsor.

During the last quarter of the 19th century and the beginning of the 20th, the concepts of reformatories for young offenders, of indeterminate sentences, and of parole were put into practice throughout the United States. Soon this sentencing system was extended to prisoners of all ages. By 1922, 45 states had parole laws, and by 1945 they existed in all states (National Advisory Commission on Criminal Justice Standards and Goals, 1973).

In the United States today parole eligibility depends on requirements set by statutes and on the sentence imposed by the court (Goldfarb & Singer, 1973). In most jurisdictions and for most crimes, a felon is eligible for parole after he has served one-third of his sentence. For more severe crimes an inmate must serve about two-thirds of his sentence (Krantz, 1976). Differences among states' statutes make it difficult to generalize about length of incarceration, percentage of prisoners released by parole, or even the composition of the parole board. For example, parole-granting agencies range from parole boards of three or more full-time members in 17 states and the federal system to boards with part-time or honorary members in 11 states to ex officio boards in 7 states to the governor with an advisory board in 6 states to some other kind of agency in the remaining 9 states (Tappan, 1960).

PAROLE DECISION MAKING

As a general statement, the parole decision-making process can be said to occur in four stages. In the first stage, the prison staff makes a report on the inmate, including a discussion of his participation in vocational, educational, and therapeutic activities, institutional misconducts, attitude toward parole, and attitude toward the crime. In some jurisdictions this report is prepared by the inmate's counselor, who makes a recommendation for or against parole, and then is passed on to his treatment team, usually consisting of the counselor, a supervising caseworker, and other counselors who know the inmate. This group also recommends a decision to parole or not to parole.

In the second stage of the parole process, the inmate's case is passed from correctional personnel to a member of the parole staff, often called a case analyst. The parole case analyst considers the inmate's behavior and activities while in prison, as did the prison correctional staff, but also examines the inmate's parole plan for his release from prison. This parole plan comprises the inmate's intended living arrangements and employment if he is granted parole.

From the case analyst, the parole case goes to the parole-board member or members who conduct the parole hearing. This hearing represents the third stage of the decision-making process. In some states the parole hearing is conducted by a hearing examiner appointed by the parole board. The parole hearing serves a number of functions (Dawson, 1969, p. 253). First, it is the primary focus for gathering information and making the parole decision. All the reports from the prison staff and from persons in the parole system are geared toward this stage of the parole process. Second, the hearing is a time when the parole board can verify information in the inmate's case file and the inmate can present his version of any facts in the file that he thinks are incorrect. Third, the inmate can present new information, and the parole board can request information not included in the file. Finally, the hearing gives the parole board a better understanding of the person it is considering for parole. Ideally, the members would be thoroughly familiar with the inmate's case file before the hearing began. In practice, however, board members often do little more than quickly read a summary of the case file just before the hearing begins. "Under these circumstances excessive weight may be given to the impressionistic observations of the board members, to the formal criminal record of the offender, or to the inferences contained in the parole summary" (Tappan, 1960, p. 727). At the end of the hearing, the hearing examiner makes a recommendation to the parole board.

In the fourth and final stage, the parole decision is made. Most jurisdictions require only a majority for parole decisions (Tappan, 1960, p. 727). Parole boards, like sentencing judges, can achieve one or more goals in their parole decisions. Although boards differ in their stated goals, most try to achieve some combination of the following: (1) punishing offenders on the basis of crime seriousness, (2) incapacitating offenders who are likely to commit a dangerous crime in the future, (3) rehabilitating offenders, and (4) reinforcing institutional discipline (Stanley, 1976). Another goal that it has been suggested parole boards can achieve is the reduction of disparity in sentencing by releasing similarly situated offenders after they have served equal amounts of time in prison (National Advisory Commission on Criminal Justice Standards and Goals, 1973). However, one study indicated that the variation in time actually served in prison was only slightly less than the variation in sentence lengths, indicating that the parole board was not reducing disparity (Gottfredson, 1979).

When the decision is made—just after the hearing or some weeks later—depends on the jurisdiction. As will be discussed later, in most cases the parole board agrees with the recommendation of the hearing examiner, possibly because the board members are usually political appointees and often do not have a professional background in correctional casework (Krantz, 1976). The parole release decision is often made with only a minimal amount of time spent on each case. For instance, in New York in the early 1970s, the parole board spent, on the average, about six minutes per case, including a review of the file and deliberation before reaching the decision (New York State Special Commission on Attica, 1972).

The 1939 *Attorney General's Survey of Release Procedures* volume on parole characterized the then-current parole practice as "purely discretionary . . . aside from general principles relating to public safety." Thus, parole decisions were said to "rest on the intuition of the paroling authority, largely unguided by the laws that establish this broad grant of power or even by specific board standards" (p. 13). In the years since that report, most jurisdictions have not changed their procedures, although the federal government has limited discretion somewhat by establishing parole guidelines. Aside from the federal government and a few states that are experimenting with a guidelines table, parole decisions are still made largely by "intuition." Indeed, it has been found that parole experts were no better than students at predicting which inmates would commit a new crime while on parole (Hakeem, 1961). And a study in New York comparing recidivism rates of inmates who were granted parole and those who had to serve their entire sentences found no difference between the two groups (Citizens' Inquiry on Parole and Criminal

Justice, 1974). It would appear that the parole board was a poor judge of who was rehabilitatable and who was not (Wilson, 1975).

Just like other agents in the criminal justice system, parole decision makers are concerned with the causes of a criminal's past behavior. This information is important to parole-board members because their major concern is with the probability of recidivism—that is, with whether the criminal behavior is likely to continue. Therefore, they want to know whether the criminal's actions were the result of a "criminal disposition" and whether that disposition still exists. Consequently, in their search for the causes of the criminal behavior, parole decision makers make causal attributions, which serve as organizing frameworks for understanding the criminal's past and predicting his future behavior. Using what is called a "protocol method," by which board members were asked to "think aloud" as they examined parole case files, it was found that these decision makers frequently made causal attributions for the criminal's behavior (Carroll & Payne, 1977b).

Like judges, members of parole boards have a limited amount of time with which to deal with any individual parole case. The members therefore have to use some kind of shortcut in order to make parole decisions. In some states, base expectancy scales, which summarize how successful on parole certain types of offenders have been in the past, are used to help with the parole decision. Some of the factors that have proved useful are past criminal record, type of offense, age of the offender, and drug and alcohol use. Generally, the following have been found to be good predictors of parole failure: a long criminal record, an offense against property rather than against a person, youth, and drug and alcohol problems (Goldfarb & Singer, 1973).

Since 1974, the United States Board of Parole (now called the United States Parole Commission) has used a system that gives guidelines to the appropriate parole recommendation. The guidelines are based on two dimensions, severity of offense and probability of successful parole. Severity of offense is divided into six categories, and the commission has specified a number of examples for each category (for instance, immigration-law violations are placed in the low-severity category, embezzlement of less than $20,000 and theft of a motor vehicle in the moderate-severity category, and robbery and extortion in the very-high-severity category). The probability of successful parole is measured by an 11-point salient-factor score, which is based on nine factors such as number of prior convictions, number of prior incarcerations, and age at first commitment. The fewer the prior convictions and incarcerations and the older the age at first commitment, the higher is the salient-factor score and the greater is the expected probability of a successful parole.

Together, the two dimensions, severity of offense and probability of successful parole, form a table so that the decision maker merely has to find the appropriate rating of severity and match that with the probability of success (see Table 9–1). The cells in the table show the range of time to be served before parole is normally granted. The actual parole recommendation within a particular range is based on factors about the person under consideration. Recommendations outside the range in the table must be accompanied by extra justification based on particular aggravating or mitigating factors in the individual case. Recently, a few states have experimented with guidelines similar to those used by the federal parole system (Cosgrove, 1976).

Proponents of parole decision guidelines believe that these guidelines establish justice and promote the protection of society. For example, the Georgia Board of Pardons and Paroles (1979) argues that justice is established because the guidelines weigh the inmate's crime severity and criminal record, guide the board to the same decision in similar cases, and centralize decision making in a statewide decision-making authority. Society is protected, the board argues, because the guidelines keep career criminals in prison longer and preserve the deterrent value of imprisonment, since more severe crimes result in longer prison terms. In addition, the board argues that the guidelines are better for the inmates because decisions under the guidelines (1) are easily understood, (2) result in relatively prompt decisions, which result in less inmate anxiety about the uncertainty of the release date, and (3) mean that inmates do not have to enroll in vocational and educational programs to "con" the board into believing that they are "model inmates."

Even though several jurisdictions are using statistical guidelines, research has shown that not every person can make effective use of this

TABLE 9–1. Guidelines used by the United States Board of Parole for adult cases: Customary total time served before release (in months)

Offense categories	Salient-factor score (probability of favorable parole outcome)			
	9–11 (very good)	6–8 (good)	4–5 (fair)	0–3 (poor)
Low severity	6–10	8–12	10–14	12–16
Low/moderate severity	8–12	12–16	16–20	20–25
Moderate severity	12–16	16–20	20–24	24–30
High severity	16–20	20–26	26–32	32–38
Very high severity	26–36	36–45	45–55	55–65
Highest severity	Ranges greater than those above are not given because of the small number of cases.			

Adapted by permission of the publisher from GUIDELINES FOR PAROLE AND SENTENCING, by Don M. Gottfredson, Leslie T. Wilkins, and Peter B. Hoffman (Lexington, Mass.: Lexington Books, D. C. Heath and Company, Copyright © 1978, D. C. Heath and Company).

kind of statistical information. For example, college students, when given both base-rate information (the frequency of some characteristic in the population) and case-specific information (a description of one particular case), tend to rely on the case-specific information even when it contradicts the base-rate information (Kahneman & Tversky, 1973; Nisbett, Borgida, Crandall, & Reed, 1976). In a series of experiments using parole cases, Carroll (1980) found that base-rate information was sometimes used, particularly when it was stated in verbal rather than numerical terms. Carroll also found that parole experts used base rates regarding parole outcomes more than students and that both groups were more likely to rely on information about parole failure than parole success. That is, they seemed to "look for bad comments."

Although there is some evidence that parole boards make use of statistical prediction tables, it is unlikely that statistical tables will be the sole basis for parole decisions. There are several reasons: (1) the belief that decisions should be individualized for each criminal; (2) the fact that statistical predictions will be wrong some of the time (even though the proportion of erroneous predictions is actually less than with clinical decisions); and (3) the assumption that statistical tables will omit some important case factors (Kastenmeier & Eglit, 1973). There are two additional reasons that parole boards may be reluctant to use base expectancy tables (Carroll, 1980). First, parole decision makers may be reluctant to state all the considerations that enter into their decisions (for example, concern over public opinion). Second, the use of statistical prediction tables makes parole decision makers less necessary and reduces their status.

Rather than using statistical prediction tables to make a parole decision, parole boards in most states make the decision after being exposed to a great deal of information about the inmate and to judgments about the inmate by agents of the criminal justice system. How all this information is assimilated and used by the parole decision maker is a social-psychological question. To deal with this question, we will examine the parole decision in two stages: first, in terms of the attributions the parole-board member makes about the inmate and, second, in terms of the social-exchange considerations that affect the decision. The two stages and the relevant information at each stage are presented in Figure 9–1.

ATTRIBUTIONAL CONSIDERATIONS

If the jurisdiction does not use base expectancy tables, parole-board members, like judges, will rely on their past experience with several types of offenders to make their decisions. Attribution theorists call the results of this past experience in making judgments about others "causal schemata." More specifically, a causal schema is "a general conception the person has about how certain kinds of causes interact to

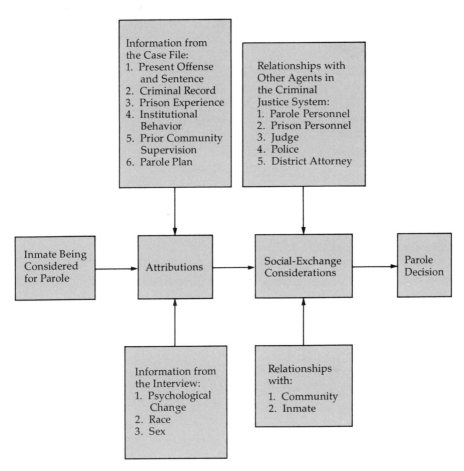

Figure 9–1. Attribution/exchange model of the parole decision

produce a specific kind of effect" (Kelley, 1972b, p. 151). On the basis of their past experience with similar offenders, parole-board members will attribute a disposition to an inmate. Using the protocol technique mentioned earlier, in which parole-board members verbalize their thoughts about real parole cases, researchers have shown that parole-board members do employ causal schemata (Carroll & Payne, 1977b). Reliance on causal schemata derived from past experience simplifies the decision process by limiting the number of causal factors that have to be considered, thereby permitting more decisions to be made in a given period of time. Another consequence of the use of causal schemata is that individual differences among those being judged are often glossed over. As the President's Commission on Law Enforcement and Administration of Justice (1967a, p. 181) noted, "The information on offenders often is fitted into a highly stereotyped format. The repetitious character of parole hearings, coupled with the sameness of reporting style and jargon, make it very difficult for board members to understand the individual aspects of a given case and to assess them wisely."

In summary, it appears that parole decision makers, like judges and other actors in the criminal justice system, make causal attributions. As discussed in Chapter 7, research has shown that sentencing decisions can be explained in terms of the two dimensions of the Weiner attribution model, internal/external and stable/unstable. In jurisdictions where the parole/no-parole decision is, in effect, a resentencing decision (such as the federal parole system), both dimensions are important. In other jurisdictions, however, the parole decision is concerned more with the likelihood of future crime (stable/unstable dimension) than with punishing the past offense (internal/external dimension). These attributions of stability and internality are formed on the basis of information contained in the parole client's case file and information obtained from the parole board's interview with the client.

Information from the Case File

Most of the information parole-board members use to make attributions comes from the parole client's case file. This file, which is usually prepared by a member of the parole staff, includes information about the client's present offense, criminal history, and prior involvement with correctional agencies, as well as institutional reports on the client's behavior while in prison and a summary of the client's plans if released from prison. Because information from the case file is the main source of the parole-board members' attributions, the most important items in it will be discussed first.

Present offense and sentence

One of the central facts contained in the case file is the crime for which the inmate was convicted. In most cases, the parole board considers the crime to be the result of internal rather than external factors. This "internal bias" is to be expected, because parole-board members are undoubtedly aware that other agents of the system who have made prior decisions about the locus of causality (for example, prosecutor, judge) have judged the crime as resulting primarily from internal causes. Thus, in only a few cases will the board consider situational factors to be the predominant influence (Dawson, 1969). Moreover, this internal bias is consistent with what is called the "fundamental attributional error" (Ross, 1977), which is "the tendency for attributers to underestimate the impact of situational factors and to overestimate the role of dispositional factors in controlling behavior" (p. 183). As was true with the sentencing decision, the more serious the crime, the more likely are parole-board members to attribute an internal criminal disposition to the inmate, which, in turn, makes it likely that the inmate will spend more time in prison.

Related to the present offense as an indicator of the inmate's criminal disposition is the judge's sentencing decision, which is also in the inmate's file. If a sentence seems unusually short or long, the board is likely to believe that the judge had some additional information about the offender that did not appear in the presentence report (Dawson, 1969). The parole board must conjecture about what this information was and about the judge's motives. It seems likely that board members interpret an unusually long sentence as evidence that the judge believed the offender has a criminal disposition and an unusually short sentence as evidence of the absence of a criminal disposition.

Criminal record

A second piece of information in the inmate's case file is his or her criminal record. A criminal record is the factor most often mentioned by parole boards as a reason for denial of parole (Dawson, 1969), presumably because the longer the criminal record, the more likely the person is to commit another crime. In some states, parole eligibility is denied or postponed for inmates who have prior convictions. Even in states where parole is possible for offenders with fairly long criminal records, parole is likely to be denied at the first hearing (Dawson, 1969). Thus, an extensive criminal record operates at the parole stage of the criminal justice system much as it did at the sentencing stage. As one would expect, the greater the number of prior convictions, the greater is the likelihood of attributing a more stable criminal disposition. A study involving actual decisions made by the Pennsylvania Parole Board found that when board members made stable criminal attributions about an inmate, they also tended to consider the inmate to have a high risk of committing a subsequent offense (Carroll, 1978a).

In addition to the crimes for which the inmate was convicted, the parole board is likely to be concerned with prior offenses for which the inmate was *not* convicted. This information is usually obtained directly from the presentence report, which is included in the inmate's parole file (Dawson, 1969). These same prior offenses for which there were no convictions were also considered at the sentencing stage (see Chapter 7). Thus, the probation officer's presentence report has an impact not only at the sentencing stage but even years later at the parole stage. And, as was true at the sentencing stage, these arrests without convictions are used as evidence of an internal disposition of criminality (Dawson, 1969).

Prison experience

A third factor contained in the inmate's case file is his or her prison experience, including both prior incarcerations and the inmate's present incarceration. Generally, if the inmate's present confinement is his or her first incarceration in a prison, even if the inmate had other convictions that resulted in probation, the parole board is more likely to be lenient than if the person had been in prison before. This is so because the parole board feels that the shock value of an inmate's first experience in prison is likely to have a stronger impact on criminal tendencies (Dawson, 1969). In attributional terms, the parole board's action can be seen as attributing greater evil intent to an inmate who has previously been in prison than to an inmate who is in prison for the first time. That is, if an inmate commits a crime in spite of the inhibiting cause of knowing how bad prisons are, then he or she must really have a criminal disposition.

A related factor is the type of prison in which the inmate is presently incarcerated. Board members' perceptions of different institutions seem to affect the parole decision concerning inmates of similar backgrounds who committed similar crimes but who are incarcerated in different institutions. As we saw in the preceding chapter, inmates in maximum-security institutions suffer more deprivations, particularly with regard to freedom, and thus are punished more than inmates in less secure institutions. This more severe punishment could have one of two effects on the parole board's decision. One could argue that a prisoner who has suffered more because of the institution he or she is in should serve less time than a prisoner in a less severe institution to make the punishment of the two inmates equitable. Alternatively, one could argue that an inmate in a maximum-security prison who has been in the company of people with stable and internal criminal dispositions has learned more about crime and therefore deserves a longer sentence to deter him or her from committing a crime when paroled.

A study that investigated the effects of the type of institution on a parole board's decision found that inmates imprisoned in a maximum-security institution served longer sentences than inmates in a less secure institution (Scott & Snider, 1973). Inmates in a maximum security institution served, on the average, eight months more than the minimum sentence imposed by the judge, while inmates imprisoned in a nonmaximum-security institution in the same state served, on the average, three months less than their minimum sentence. When the crimes for which the offenders were imprisoned were scaled on a crime-seriousness index, the inmates in the maximum-security institution were found, as one would expect, to have committed more severe crimes. However, when the average scaled seriousness score for each institution was divided into the average term of imprisonment at that institution, the researchers found that inmates in the maximum-security institution received more punishment per unit of crime seriousness than inmates in the less secure institution. In effect, the type of institution the inmate was in was a better predictor of the amount of time spent in prison than were the inmate's intelligence, prior criminal involvement, race, and education.

The researchers interpreted the importance of the institution in the parole board's decision as due to the board's reliance on stereo-types about the typical offender from a particular prison. These stereotypes were seen as affecting the board's perceptions and judg-ments regarding a particular inmate from that prison. This interpreta-tion fits nicely within our attribution framework. An internal criminal disposition is more likely to be attributed to an inmate of a maximum-security prison than to an inmate of another type of penal institution.

Institutional behavior

A fourth type of information contained in the inmate's case file con-cerns the inmate's behavior while in prison. Generally, the parole board is looking to see whether the inmate's behavior inside the institution provides evidence of a changed disposition. First, the board will look at the inmate's involvement in institutional programs (Dawson, 1969). Generally, these programs, if they exist at the prison, are of three types: vocational, educational, and therapeutic. If an inmate can prove to the board that he has learned a skill or gained an education or received some therapeutic counseling, then he has a much better chance of showing that his past criminal behavior will no longer be necessary when he is released on parole. Because not all prisons have well-developed vocational, educational, or therapeutic programs or enough staff to admit every inmate who wants to enter one of these programs, an inmate's lack of involvement in these programs may not provide the parole board with useful information about the stability of the inmate's criminal disposition.

Another institutional behavior that parole boards examine very closely is the inmate's adjustment to the daily life of the prison (Daw-son, 1969). Institutional adjustment includes satisfactory performance of assigned work and, more important, few violations of the prison rules, especially during the six months prior to the parole hearing. Gen-erally, it appears that the more disciplinary infractions inmates com-mit, the less likely they are to be paroled (Carroll & Coates, 1980). This result is probably due to parole-board members' judgments that disrup-tive inmates cannot adjust to their status and respect authority (Daw-son, 1969) and that such inmates are more likely to commit crimes in the future because they show continuing evidence of a stable criminal disposition (Carroll, Wiener, Coates, & Alibrio, 1981; Holland, Holt, & Brewer, 1978). Although poor institutional adjustment, particularly in-cident reports for assaultive behavior, is often sufficient reason to deny parole, good institutional adjustment is probably not sufficient reason to grant parole (Dawson, 1969). One explanation is that most inmates show fairly good institutional adjustment, probably because there are so many strong inhibitory causes for bad behavior, such as punishment by the prison staff, denial of parole, and a longer stay in prison. Moreover, a prisoner may have a good institutional record not because he committed few violations but, as we saw in the preceding chapter, because guards did not cite him for infractions of institutional rules. It should also be noted that good institutional behavior has not been found to be highly predictive of success on parole (Stanley, 1976).

Prior community supervision

A fifth piece of information in the inmate's file is his or her past behavior while under supervision in the community. Inmates with criminal records are likely to have had experience on probation or parole or both. This prior experience is considered a particularly important indication of the inmate's probable success on parole (Dawson, 1969). Inmate's who did not commit a new crime while under supervision in the past are more likely to be granted parole, whereas inmates who committed crimes on probation or parole are considered poor parole risks (Cosgrove, 1976).

Parole plan

A final factor from the inmate's case file that is used in the parole board's attribution decision is the inmate's parole plan, which can be a useful indicator of the stability of the inmate's criminal disposition (Dawson, 1969). Generally, this plan consists of the inmate's intended residence and place of employment in the community to which he or she will be paroled, and usually it must be approved by the parole officer who will deal with the inmate when he or she is released to the community. A workable parole plan is usually considered very favorably by the parole board because it shows that the inmate is seriously considering "going straight." Moreover, it provides evidence that any situational factors that may have led to the inmate's previous crime will no longer be present.

Information from Interview with Inmate

In addition to the information in the inmate's case file, parole board members use information from the interview they conduct with the inmate.

One of the most important items of information parole-board members can gain from the interview with the inmate is whether the inmate has changed psychologically during his or her stay in prison. Board members want to know whether inmates' attitudes toward their crimes and themselves have changed. Usually, this means that the inmate has gained "insight" into his or her problems that led to committing crimes (Dawson, 1969). In attributional terms, important evidence of a change in the inmate's stable criminal disposition is the realization that his or her problem is internal to himself or herself. Parole boards feel that inmates have made progress when they accept responsibility for their criminal behavior rather than blaming others or the environment.

Although a parole board would like to find that all prisoners had changed their dispositions from criminal to noncriminal, board members are usually very cautious in interpreting inmates' acceptance of responsibility as evidence of a change in disposition, because the inmates may be trying to "con" them (Dawson, 1969). If the board uses verbalization of attitudinal change as one of several criteria for parole, then it is likely that many inmates will try to convince the board that they have recognized their problems. However, because of the facilitating causes for inmates to make this sort of statement, parole boards are likely to discount much of the inmates' statements. Therefore, an inmate usually has to be very persuasive at the parole hearing in order to convince board members that he or she really has undergone a true psychological change.

Because board members want to respond positively only to a true change in disposition, it is important for them to judge whether the inmate is telling the truth. In a study of the parole interview process in Pennsylvania, Ruback (in press) examined content and nonverbal factors that were related to the interviewers' perception of male parole clients' honesty. Almost two-thirds of the clients were judged to be lying about their original offense, any misconducts in prison, their parole plan, or their "desire to go straight," although only if they were perceived to be lying about their original offense or prison misconducts was their overall perceived honesty adversely affected. Ruback found a relatively strong positive relation between quantity of discussion and perceived honesty, such that clients were judged more honest the more information they volunteered about themselves. Quantity of discussion may be perceived as reflecting a strong motivation to be released, whereas reticence may be perceived as an attempt to hide something. Consistent with research on nonverbal behavior, parole clients were judged to be more honest the more gestures they made and the more they smiled. Moreover, clients' perceived honesty during the interview affected interviewers' parole recommendations; the more honest clients were perceived to be, the more strongly they were recommended for parole, a result that was supported by a multiple regression analysis of over 800 parole decisions in Pennsylvania (Carroll et al., 1981). It should be noted, however, that not all parole boards place great weight on the interview with the inmate. For example, a study in California indicated that the parole interview did not seem to affect interviewers' judgments and therefore either was of no use at all or served only to justify a decision that had already been made (Garber & Maslach, 1977).

Inmate's Race and Sex

The prisoner's race and sex are two observable characteristics that might seem intuitively to be important factors in the attribution of a criminal disposition. On the surface, race does appear to have an effect on the parole decision. For instance, in Illinois 77% of the white inmates, 75% of the inmates with Spanish surnames, and 67% of the black inmates were paroled during the years 1970–1972 (Heinz, Heinz, Senderowitz, & Vance, 1976). However, when such other factors as criminal record and prison disciplinary record were statistically controlled, race was not a significant factor in the parole decision.

The prisoner's sex is another factor that one might think would be important in the parole decision-making process. It is difficult to test the importance of the sex of the inmate in the parole decision because relatively few women are in prison and therefore eligible for parole. Nevertheless, analysis of the type of considerations that parole boards use in their decisions shows that the considerations are not, in the main, noticeably different (Heinz et al., 1976). Although women do seem to have a higher parole release rate than men, women also tend to commit less severe crimes than men. Therefore, it cannot be concluded that sex is the reason for the difference in parole release rates between the sexes.

Importance of Stability Attributions

Using the information in the inmate's file and knowledge gained from the parole interview, parole-board members make attributions of both stability and internality. Research suggests, however, that the attributions of stability may have more impact on the parole decision. In a study of the kinds of attributions board members make and the effect these attributions have on actual parole decisions, Carroll (1978a) asked the five members of the Pennsylvania Board of Probation and Parole to give their opinions on the underlying cause of the offense and on the reason for the inmate's criminal history. These opinions, or attributions, were then coded for stability and internality. The stability dimension was significantly related to parole decisions. The data suggested that stable causes produced greater perceived risk of subsequent crime, and it was this greater perceived risk that made board members less willing to parole the inmate. This finding is reinforced by the fact that board members considered special deterrence, risk of future crime, and likelihood of rehabilitation to be the most important factors in their parole decisions. Internality was found to have no significant effect on parole decisions, apparently because this dimension is related to evaluating the seriousness of the crime and assigning punishment for it and the Pennsylvania board leaves this decision to the judge through the sentence. It should be pointed out that the emphasis on the stability dimension may be unique to Pennsylvania. That is, other boards may well consider internal factors in their parole decisions.

SOCIAL-EXCHANGE CONSIDERATIONS

Although the attributions the parole board makes about the inmate are an important factor in its parole decision, there are other factors that affect the final decision. These factors pertain to social-exchange relationships in which the parole board is involved. Parole boards engage in social-exchange relationships with three groups of people: (1) other agents in the criminal justice system, (2) the community, and

(3) the inmate and his or her family (see Figure 9–1). Many of these exchange relationships are explicitly mandated by the legislature. Although jurisdictions differ, parole boards are often directed to aid in the maintenance of order in prisons, protect the public, punish crime, and treat the offender. These sometimes conflicting goals often mean that parole boards must choose the most important exchange relationship from among many. In the exchange with the inmate and his or her family, perceived fairness plays a particularly important role in the parole board's decision-making process.

Social Exchange with Other Agents in the Criminal Justice System

In earlier chapters we found that the judge's bail-setting decision is heavily influenced by the recommendation of the prosecuting attorney and that the sentencing decision is based largely on the recommendation of the probation officer. Similarly, at the parole stage, the decision of the board members is based on the judgments of workers with less authority. For instance, in Illinois a correctional sociologist goes over the inmate's file, has a brief interview with the inmate, and then writes a brief summary of the inmate's criminal record and behavior in prison, concluding with a prognosis, on a five-point scale, of the likelihood that the inmate will violate parole. Using a statistical technique called multiple regression analysis, Heinz et al. (1976) found that the best predictor of the parole board's decision in Illinois was the correctional sociologist's prognosis. In a similar study in Pennsylvania, the parole board's decisions were virtually identical to those of the hearing examiner and were highly correlated with those of the parole case analyst (Carroll & Coates, 1980). Like the judge's reliance on the probation officer's sentencing recommendation, the parole board's reliance on the judgments of others is a clear example of social exchange: in exchange for the information and recommendations contained in the reports of the case analyst and hearing examiner, the parole board pays these persons' salaries and promotes those who it believes are doing a good job.

The parole decision affects virtually every agent in the criminal justice system. The most immediate effect of a parole decision is on the prison where the inmate is incarcerated. As discussed in Chapter 8, the parole decision affects the prison in two ways. First, it affects the size of the institutional population. For example, by reducing the extent to which parole is granted, the United States Parole Commission has contributed to an increase in the federal prison population (Armbrust & Deloney, 1977). Second, the parole decision reinforces the type of behavior that the board explicitly values—for example, involvement in institutional programs, no institutional misconduct. Sometimes the board even lectures the inmate about the kind of behaviors and attitudes it wants to see (Dawson, 1969). Thus, parole can be an incentive for good behavior, and parole boards perform a valuable service to the prison staff by rewarding behavior that helps maintain order in the prison, even though its effectiveness as an incentive is limited by the factors described in Chapter 8. Although the new federal parole guidelines have explicitly excluded behavior in prison as a factor in the parole decision, some states (such as North Carolina) have, in their guidelines, kept institutional behavior as a factor because of their desire to maintain prison discipline (Cosgrove, 1976).

Another group of criminal justice agents who are in a social-exchange relationship with the parole board is the judges who sentenced the offenders. Here, the relationship is fairly straightforward: "The sentencing decision is sometimes influenced by the trial judge's expectations of the probable parole decision and the parole decision is influenced by the sentence selected" (Dawson, 1969, p. 258). Aside from the reciprocal effects of these two decisions, there is also a sometimes more-than-tacit agreement between the two parties with regard to the equalization of penalties. As discussed in Chapter 7, disparity in sentencing is a major problem. At the parole stage of the system, this disparity can be reduced or eliminated because the board can keep similar offenders (those who committed the same offense) in prison for the same length of time, although the research discussed earlier found little evidence of reduction in disparity (Gottfredson, 1979).

The police and district attorney of the community where the offender was convicted are sometimes consulted about the parole decision (Dawson, 1969). Most of the time, the police disapprove of parole, probably because they interpret the inmate's release on parole as increasing the likelihood of crime in their community. Prosecuting attorneys are less likely to express disapproval, although they too sometimes oppose the offender's release to the community. Because both the police and district attorneys routinely oppose offenders' release, the board, in most cases, discounts the opposition of these two groups.

In addition to opposing the release of particular inmates, district attorneys may also oppose the general release policy of the parole board. For example, in Georgia the parole board has been automatically releasing many inmates who were sent to prison after their probation was revoked, if their time already served on probation was greater than the minimum portion of the sentence needed to be served before parole could be considered. The policy was based on a ruling that time spent on probation was the same as time spent in prison and was intended to help alleviate the severe overcrowding in Georgia prisons. The Fulton County District Attorney (Atlanta) expressed his strong disagreement with this policy when he first learned of it (King, 1981).

Social Exchange with the Community

The parole board, in its parole decisions, considers both general public acceptance of parole and actual or expected public attitudes toward that individual parole decision. The more likely a particular parole decision is to damage favorable public attitudes toward parole, the less risk of a future criminal offense the parole board will accept. Other community concerns are also present in the parole decision: "Criteria having little to do with the question of risk may be used by parole officials in dealing with certain cases, particularly those involving crimes seen as 'heinous.' The concern is more for meeting general social norms and responding according to public expectations" (National Advisory Commission on Criminal Justice Standards and Goals, 1973, p. 395). For example, the Illinois Parole and Pardon Board took only ten minutes to deny parole to Richard Speck, who was serving a 400-to-1200-year prison sentence for the murder of eight nurses in Chicago in 1966 ("Illinois Denies Parole Bid," 1976).

Often, parole boards are reluctant to release assaultive offenders because of the fear of adverse community reaction if the offender violates parole by again committing a violent crime (Dawson, 1969). Parole boards show this reluctance even though some assaultive offenders, particularly murderers, are not likely to commit another violent crime. Because it takes only one violent crime by a parolee to create adverse community sentiment, the board is much less likely to grant parole to an assaultive offender than to a nonassaultive offender, even if the two have the same probability of committing a crime while on parole. Thus, the board would probably be more willing to risk a forger committing another forgery while on parole (a relatively probable occurrence) than a murderer committing another murder while on parole (a relatively improbable occurrence).

Another type of community sentiment is present after prison riots. Often, there is pressure on the parole board to become more "liberal"—that is, to increase the risk of violation acceptable for parole. In this way, pressure within the institutions is also reduced (National Advisory Commission on Criminal Justice Standards and Goals, 1973).

The social exchanges that the parole board makes with the case analysts and hearing examiners who work for it, with other agencies in the criminal justice system, and with the community can have a major impact on the board's final parole decisions. Maintaining good social-exchange relationships with all these groups is sometimes very difficult, because different groups might want different decisions. For example, the case analyst and hearing examiner might recommend that an inmate be paroled, while the police and the local community might recommend against parole. The board's final decision must take into account these considerations, as well as factors about the inmate.

Social Exchange with Offenders and Their Families

In addition to its social-exchange relationships with other agents of the criminal justice system and with the community, the parole board also is concerned with equitable treatment of the offender and his or her family. As mentioned previously, one way in which the board seeks fairness is to equalize penalties for similar offenders who have received different sentences. A second way the board tries to be fair to offenders is to release them, even if they are poor risks, because they have served enough time in prison for the offenses they committed (National Advisory Commission on Criminal Justice Standards and Goals, 1973). When this rationale is used, the board is considering the prison sentence in terms of retribution. By serving his or her time in prison, the inmate is now "even" with society, and additional time would be unfair to him or her. A final concern with fairness is to the offender's family. As long as inmates are in prison, they cannot support their families. This consideration is particularly important for nonsupport offenders. For example, the Wisconsin parole board is likely to parole such offenders when they become eligible for parole because they are unlikely to commit a serious criminal violation, further incarceration is unlikely to promote their rehabilitation, and if paroled they may provide economic as well as emotional support to their families (Dawson, 1969).

After an inmate is paroled, his or her contact with the criminal justice system does not end. First, the parolee must maintain regular contact with the parole agent who monitors his or her behavior. Second, the police, who are aware of the parolee's release from prison, are likely to be particularly observant of his or her actions. In addition, citizens who know of parolees' imprisonment are likely to react to them differently than if they were noncriminals. We turn now to a discussion of the parolee's return to society.

RETURN TO SOCIETY

Parole is the means by which about 75% of prison inmates in this country are returned to society. These persons, who are usually the best risks, are supervised by parole officers until their parole terms expire. What is ironic is that the 25% or so of prison inmates who are *not* released on parole, because they are poor risks, are not subject to the supervision of a parole officer when they are released after serving their *full* terms. Thus, the people who need supervising the most (those inmates who serve their entire sentences) are the ones who receive the least supervision and the least help when they return to society.

At this point, it is necessary that a brief comparison of probation and parole be made. Probation, as discussed in Chapter 7, is the supervision of a convicted felon who is allowed to remain in society without a term of imprisonment, subject to some restrictions laid down by the judge and regular reporting of his or her activities to a probation officer. Parole supervision is very similar to probation supervision. Indeed, in some states the same department and the same officers handle probation and parole cases. The major difference between the two occurs if the person violates the terms of the release. In the case of probation, it is the judge who holds a hearing and, if the evidence warrants it, revokes probation and imposes a prison sentence. In contrast, in the case of parole, a member or members of the parole board hear the evidence regarding the alleged parole violation. If the facts warrant it, the person is returned to prison to serve time on the sentence for which he or she had been paroled. Because probation and parole are similar in so many respects, the reader may assume that what we have to say about parole in the remainder of this chapter holds for probation as well.

In this section, we will discuss the inmate's return to society. Specifically, we will look at (1) the conditions and requirements of parole, (2) how society in general and the police in particular deal with the returned inmate, and (3) the factors affecting the decision to revoke parole.

Conditions and Requirements of Parole

The parole officer who will supervise the returned offender already has some knowledge of the offender through his or her field investigation into and approval of the inmate's parole plan, which includes an approved residence and place of employment. However, this knowledge is only superficial, and not until the parole officer has met with the ex-convict a number of times does the officer really know what the offender is like.

In most states the parole officer has a number of duties in addition to making preparole investigations. One of his or her major duties is to serve as a counselor for the ex-prisoner. Because the offender has been in prison for (generally) at least a year and sometimes much longer, he or she has to make new adjustments to society. By providing guidance in decisions, the parole officer serves a valuable function. The parole officer also helps offenders in their dealings with public agencies— for example, in obtaining food stamps or regaining custody of a child who was placed in foster care while the offender was in prison. A third duty of the parole officer, the one with which we usually associate the officer, is making sure that the client obeys the rules and conditions of parole.

Parole conditions for each parolee consist of two kinds: (1) general prohibitions that apply to all offenders, such as prohibitions against leaving the state or getting married without permission, and (2) specific conditions that apply to the parolee in particular, such as participating in a program for alcoholics or maintaining employment. Many of these conditions have been characterized as being moralistic and impractical and impinging on the human rights of the parolee (Arluke, 1969).

Society's Reactions to the Parolee

People who have served time in prison are often called "ex-cons," a name that brings forth a number of associations, almost all negative. To live in the outside world without again becoming involved in crime, the former prisoner must overcome the negative perceptions of the persons with whom he or she comes into contact, foremost of whom are the police and the inmate's employer.

As mentioned in Chapter 3, the police often consider persons with arrest and conviction records prime suspects when crimes occur. This scrutiny is much more evident when the persons are former prison inmates. In many states the local police are usually notified about parolees in their area. This notification may come as early as the pre-parole investigation, when the parolee's living plan is investigated prior to his or her appearance before the parole board. In other states, the notification is made by the parole officer when the parolee comes to the community. Because many of the police believe that former prisoners are likely to commit crimes again, some police departments maintain a separate file and identification system for parolees (Dawson, 1969).

The employer is another member of society whose judgments about the returned offender affect the offender's adjustment to society. Many employers are reluctant to hire ex-offenders because they fear that the former felon will commit another crime. In addition, employers feel that the ex-convict will not have a steady habit of coming to work. Finally, many ex-convicts leave prison unskilled and unschooled. The work conditions of prisons are often not very conducive to learning how to perform a job well. Because prisoners receive little if any pay for their work in prison, they often perform only the minimum amount of work required to keep them from having a report filed against them. In the outside world, most employers are not content with having employees do only the least amount of work that they can get away with.

Perhaps the most important person that parolees have to deal with is the parole officer. Recent evidence shows that many parolees have to contend with negative attributions made about them by their parole officers. One such study found that

> the parolee was in general defined both by the parole agency and by relevant persons in the community as a person to be distrusted. He was often cast in the role of a problematic person, and admitted to normal social positions, such as employee or student, only hesitantly or as a special favor. He often felt "treated like a child." Most parolees lacked those evidences of accreditation on which all of us depend when presenting ourselves in a new community, such as acceptable identification, references, clothing appropriate for various occasions, a telephone where he could be reached, explanations about the recent past [Studt, 1967, p. 8].

Moreover, it has been argued that because parole officers receive rewards and punishments on the basis of how much or how little trouble their clients cause the parole agency, these officers are strongly motivated to keep their clients under control (McCleary, 1978). One method is to offer parolees rewards for good behavior. For example,

McCleary found that some parole officers promised an early release from parole supervision if clients did not cause any trouble for two years. What the parole officers failed to mention to the clients was that the standard practice in the jurisdiction was to discharge parolees after two years of supervision. Thus, the "reward" was of less value than might at first appear. Another method of controlling parolees was to classify them so that quick action could be taken if they proved uncontrollable. Thus, a "noncriminal" label, which included alcoholics and addicts, enabled the parole officer to transfer the parolee quickly to a treatment program (and off his or her caseload) if the parolee started causing trouble for the officer. Labeling a client as a "dangerous person" enabled the parole officer to revoke the client's parole easily if the client caused trouble. However, using this label was costly in that the parole officer had to place the dangerous person under an intensive supervision schedule. McCleary concluded that because parole officers must control their caseloads if they are to be rewarded, the officers are likely to type clients as noncriminals or dangerous persons so as to solve their own problems rather than to meet their clients' needs.

Revocation of Parole

Nationwide, two-thirds of parolees are successes—that is, they are not returned to prison before their parole expires (Morris & Hawkins, 1970). However, the one-third who are not successes amount to several thousand people a year who are returned to prison. Revocation of parole may follow one of two types of violation: (1) a parolee may violate one of the conditions of his or her parole (for example, by leaving the community for a week without telling the parole officer), or (2) a parolee may commit a new crime. The first type of violation is usually called a technical parole violation, and the second type is usually called a criminal parole violation. However, the fact that a parolee has violated parole does not necessarily mean that the parole will automatically be revoked. As is true at other stages of the criminal justice system, the attributions made about the offender and a number of social-exchange considerations between agents of the criminal justice system significantly affect the decision to revoke or not to revoke parole. Because it is the parole officer who initiates the revocation, the officer is the person on whom we will focus.

A parole officer can learn about a violation of parole in three ways: through personal observation, from police reports, or from reports from other persons (Dawson, 1969). Although parole officers are supposed to meet regularly with their clients, many times these meetings are short and little information is gained. Thus, personal observation is restricted because the officer often must deal with 60 or 70 cases and can devote less than half of his or her time to interviews. The rest of the officer's time is spent on administrative work (Miles, 1965).

Attributional considerations

Assuming that a parolee has violated a condition of the parole, many of the factors a parole officer considers in deciding whether to initiate revocation are the same ones that prosecutors consider when they decide whether to prosecute an offender for violating the law (see Chapter 4). These factors include the parolee's prior criminal record, his or her intent regarding the present offense, and the likelihood of obtaining a conviction (that is, a revocation). However, in contrast to the prosecutor, the parole officer has additional information on which to make a judgment. This information comes from personal contact with the parolee and is used by the parole officer to make attributions about the parolee (see Figure 9–2).

The parole officer's relationship with the parolee is a major determinant of the attribution decision. If the parolee has been open and cooperative with the parole officer, the officer is more likely to see the violation as a one-time aberration (unstable cause) than if the parolee has been secretive and uncooperative. Thus, through his or her personal knowledge about the parolee, the officer develops some idea about the existence or absence of a stable criminal disposition. If the parolee's pattern of good behavior is broken on a single occasion, the parole officer is likely to make an attribution to some unique situational feature rather than to an enduring disposition of criminality. In contrast, if a parolee's behavior is consistently bad over time and across situations, the parole officer is likely to make an attribution to an enduring disposition of criminality rather than to a feature of the environment.

A second factor that influences the attributions a parole officer makes

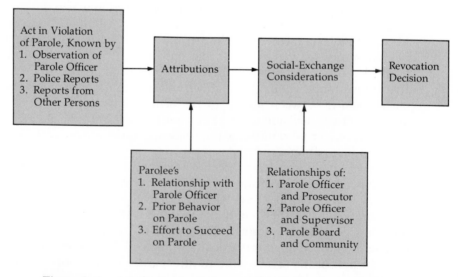

Figure 9–2.   Attribution/exchange model of the parole revocation decision

about the offender is the parolee's behavior on parole before the violation. Prior violations for which no revocation proceedings were begun are important because (1) they indicate a stable criminal behavior pattern and (2) they show the parole officer that the parolee will take advantage of him or her. Taking advantage of the parole officer is likely to lead to the attribution of dishonesty.

In addition to prior parole violations, the parole officer will consider the parolee's effort to succeed at a noncriminal life in society. A parole officer will look for stable effort from the parolee and may overlook a minor violation if the parolee had shown consistent effort to have a successful parole. Suppose, for example, that a parolee had maintained a job for three months and had regularly reported to his parole officer. In all ways he was a model parolee. Should he leave the state to visit a relative without first telling his parole officer, it is very unlikely that the parole officer will initiate parole revocation proceedings.

Social-exchange considerations

Although the attributions the parole officer makes about the parolee are an important factor in the revocation decision, the final judgment is determined by several social-exchange considerations. One of the most important of these is the type of violation involved, for different factors come into play with each type of violation. For technical parole violations, the main consideration is the seriousness of the violation. As discussed earlier, most of the parole rules are extremely moralistic and would be difficult for anyone to follow, much less someone who has been convicted of a crime and has lived for a year or more with criminals. Hence, a parole officer is not likely to initiate revocation proceedings just because a parolee has committed a minor technical parole violation.

In contrast, when the violation consisted in committing a new crime, it is clear that the violation is serious enough for revocation proceedings to be started. The Supreme Court in recent years has required certain safeguards that protect parolees from the indiscriminate use of revocation proceedings. In two important decisions (*Morrissey* v. *Brewer*, 1972; *Gagnon* v. *Scarpelli*, 1973), the court mandated (1) that a preliminary hearing be held to determine, first, whether there exists sufficient evidence against the parolee to justify a revocation hearing and, second, whether the parolee should be incarcerated pending the hearing and (2) that a revocation hearing be held to determine whether the alleged violation of parole warrants revocation.

Sometimes the prosecuting attorney will drop the charges against the parolee for the new crime because after the revocation hearing the parolee will be returned to prison anyway and a conviction for the new crime is not worth the trouble. In other cases, the new charges are brought against the parolee and a conviction is gained. Then, usually after the parolee has been returned to prison, parole revocation proceedings are begun. It is clear from this description of the parole revocation proceedings that the parole officer and the prosecutor can work closely together to determine whether revocation proceedings will be initiated or whether the second crime will be prosecuted or both.

Another consideration is the relationship between the parole officer and his or her supervisor. The number of revocations instituted against parole violators, particularly technical parole violators, results partly from administrative fiat, because virtually every parolee is likely to violate at least one condition of his or her parole during the parole period. Administrative orders concerning revocations are directed both at the type of violations for which revocation is appropriate and at the number of revocations that should be instituted. For example, in California, money was allocated to reduce parole officers' caseloads from 70 to 35. It was expected that there would be fewer violations because of the more intensive supervision that would follow. Actually, the number of technical parole violations increased. Supervisors then met with their staffs and told them that the number of revocations for technical parole violations had to be reduced and that promotions of both supervisors and officers were contingent on a low revocation rate for technical parole violations. Not surprisingly, a year later the rate of technical parole violations was reduced (Takagi, 1967).

This example vividly illustrates not only the direct exchanges that exist in the parole bureaucracy—following orders in exchange for promotion—but also the effect of caseload size on revocation rate. More revocations are likely to be initiated when the average caseload is small, because the parole officer has more time to supervise the parolees under his or her charge and therefore is more likely to detect violations. In addition, when the caseload is small, the officer has more time to fill out the forms necessary for parole revocation. When the caseload is large, overlooking a parole violation is easier and means less work for the parole officer.

The recommendations of the parole officer to revoke parole are generally followed. For example, of 1700 revocation proceedings initiated by parole officers in California, supervisors disagreed with officers in only 13 cases (Takagi, 1967). The high percentage of agreement among the parole officer and his or her supervisor and the supervisor's superiors is similar to other situations we have encountered in the criminal justice system, such as the high agreement found between the probation officer and the judge.

Agreement between supervisors and parole officers facilitates the smooth working of the system. Superiors who decide not to follow the recommendations of their subordinates create excessive costs for the subordinates, which could result in greater costs for the superiors. For example, supervisors who go against parole officers' recommendations might find that the officers slow down in their work production. Or officers might follow the rules literally, a situation that would probably result in a great deal of paperwork. In either case, parole officers' actions would be costly to supervisors, who would have to explain to *their* supervisors why their offices were not functioning smoothly. These possible costs might make supervisors think twice before disagreeing with subordinates.

If a parolee's parole has been revoked, because of either a technical parole violation or a criminal parole violation, the parole board must decide how much time the parolee must serve in prison before he or she is again eligible for parole. This time to be served is often called "back time." A study of parole revocation and back-time setting for criminal parole violators in Pennsylvania (Carroll & Ruback, 1981) found that the parole board was more likely to revoke parole if the sentence on the original offense was shorter and if the new offense involved a weapon. More back time was likely to be set if the original offense was a homicide. Interestingly, the researchers found that parole-board members and hearing examiners seemed to use different decision criteria and set different amounts of back time in their initial recommendations. Hearing examiners tended to consider parole performance, while board members appeared to focus on the seriousness of the prior criminal record. Thus, board members seemed to treat the back-time-setting decision as a resentencing decision, punishing offenders for their criminal disposition rather than predicting their probable success on parole.

Two social exchanges are evidenced in the parole board's treatment of revocation and back-time setting as a resentencing decision. The first exchange is between the board and the parolee. There is an implicit contract in inmates' being paroled (in some states there is an explicit written contract) that they will be released to society on the condition that they follow the rules of parole. Violation of those rules results in a breach of the contract, and parolees must be put in the position they were in before they were paroled. The second social exchange is between the parole board and the community. Every parole revocation decision is, in effect, an admission by the board that it made a mistake in releasing the inmate. The board's mistake harmed society in general, and the board must redress that harm by punishing the offender. By revoking parole and imposing back time, the board reduces some of the community's negative reaction to the board's failure to keep the violator behind bars. Moreover, revocation and back-time ensure that the violator will not commit another violation during the period of the back time.

In some states a parolee can be discharged from parole early if his or her behavior has been satisfactory. In one study, when parole agents recommended that the parolee be continued on parole, the parole board agreed with the initial recommendation in 506 of 510 cases (Kingsnorth, 1969). In contrast, when the recommendation was for discharge from parole, the parole board agreed with the initial recommendation in only 372 of 902 cases, although the board did seem to follow the advice of one of the intervening decision makers (the hearing examiner) to a very high degree. Continuation on parole is a conservative action that eliminates the possibility of community outrage should a discharged parolee commit a crime during what would have been his or her parole period. In this decision to discharge, the board weighs the value to the parolee (in terms of freedom) and to the parole bureaucracy (in terms of more available resources) against the risk of the parolee's committing a new crime and the adverse community reaction that would result. From this research, it appears that the board opts for the less risky decision of continuation on parole.

THE FUTURE OF PAROLE

Although a number of states have adopted parole decision guidelines, partly in response to criticism of the parole process, there have been calls for the abolition of parole (for example, von Hirsch & Hanrahan, 1979). Basically, von Hirsch and Hanrahan argue that imprisonment should depend on "the degree of blameworthiness of the offender's criminal conduct" (p. 103). They therefore suggest that the date of release from prison can and should be decided at or shortly after the sentencing decision, subject only to adjustments for prison overcrowding and, to some extent, for disciplinary infractions the offender may commit. Von Hirsch and Hanrahan also argue that parole supervision should be eliminated completely, although they favor a system of voluntary social services for released prisoners. Finally, they would abolish parole revocation for new criminal conduct because they believe revocation procedures provide insufficient safeguards against imprisoning the innocent.

SUMMARY

Because parole boards, like sentencing judges, are under severe time and caseload pressures, they must often rely on their past experience and the judgments of other experts in the criminal justice system. The parole decision itself is based on both attributional and social-exchange considerations. Attributions are based on information contained in the inmate's case file (present offense and sentence, criminal record, prison experience, institutional behavior, prior community supervision, and parole plan) and information obtained from the interview (primarily perceived psychological change). The parole board's decisions are also affected by the board's social exchanges with other agents in the criminal justice system (parole personnel, prison administrators, judges, the police, and district attorneys), with the community, and with the inmate.

Once inmates are released from prison on parole, they are placed under the supervision of a parole officer, who helps them adjust to society and makes sure that they abide by the rules imposed on them as a condition of their parole. If parolees violate the conditions of their parole, their parole may be revoked, and they may be returned to prison. The revocation decision is based on both attributional considerations (the parolee's relationship with the parole officer, prior behavior on parole, and effort to succeed on parole) and social-exchange considerations (the parole officer's relationships with supervisors and with the prosecutor and the parole board's relationship with the community).

CHAPTER TEN

Summary and Conclusions

The criminal justice system is an enormously complex bureaucracy that handles hundreds of thousands of people every year. In the previous chapters we described the criminal justice system as it operates in urban areas in the United States today. We discussed the system as it is, not how it is supposed to work or how people with vested interests might say it does work.

We focused on decisions made by agents in the criminal justice system. As discussed earlier, the most important characteristic of these decisions is that they involve discretion. Decision makers in the criminal justice system exercise discretion because of ambiguities in the laws, the belief that persons should be treated as individuals, the limited resources of the criminal justice system, and the need to accommodate the interests of those inside and outside the system.

It should also be noted that these decisions are often subject to time pressures, which are of two types. Some decisions have to be made quickly, and usually under stress, because of the nature of the decision itself. The decisions of victims, bystanders, and the police officers are often of this type. A second type of time pressure affecting decision makers in the criminal justice system results from a large backlog of cases. These caseload pressures force decision makers to act quickly even though they might prefer to make their decisions more thoughtfully. The decisions of prosecutors, judges, and parole boards are often subject to this type of time pressure. Both types of time pressure force decision makers to rely on their past experience and on the judgments of others.

THE ATTRIBUTION/EXCHANGE MODEL OF THE CRIMINAL JUSTICE SYSTEM

Attribution theory and social-exchange theory are two broad theoretical frameworks that encompass much of human behavior. Our specific concern in this book was to use these theories to understand the decisions of agents of the criminal justice system. Although these agents have different responsibilities and duties, there are common considerations that affect both the attributions and the social exchanges of these decision makers. Table 10–1 presents an outline of these common factors considered by the various decision makers in the criminal justice system. The following discussion of the table will summarize the important points described in earlier chapters and will bring together the similarities of the various types of decisions.

Attributional Considerations

Three factors seem to have an important impact on the attributions made by decision makers in the criminal justice system: the seriousness of the offense, the offender's prior record, and the judgments of other agents in the criminal justice system. These factors will be discussed in order of importance in affecting the final attribution, from most to least important.

Seriousness of the offense

Not surprisingly, the most important factor affecting the attributions of the decision makers listed in Table 10–1 is the seriousness of the offense of the person suspected, accused, or convicted of committing the offense (to whom we will refer subsequently as the offender). The crime itself is what decision makers use as a key to understanding the offender's disposition. The more serious the crime, the more "criminal" the offender will be judged by every decision maker in the system. As we saw earlier, this criminal disposition is then translated into punishment, such that the more serious the crime, the more punishment the decision maker will decide on.

TABLE 10–1. Important factors in the attribution/exchange model of the criminal justice system

Actors	Factors affecting attributions	Important social-exchange relationships
Victim and bystander	1. Seriousness of the offense	1. Suspected offender
Police		
Attorney	2. Prior criminal record	2. Peers
		3. Other agencies
Judge	3. Judgments of other decision makers	4. Victim
Juror		
Probation officer		5. Community
Prison guard		
Parole board		
Parole officer		
Public		

Prior criminal record

The offender's past behavior is also important in determining agents' attributions. This past behavior is evidenced by a prior criminal record. Agents' knowledge of an offender's prior criminal record serves two functions. First, it provides evidence of a stable criminal disposition. One encounter with the criminal justice system could have resulted from any of several causes. A subsequent encounter with the criminal justice system shows consistency across time, thus weakening any notion that the first encounter was either an error by the criminal justice system or a one-time action by the offender. Second, the evidence of a criminal record and the resulting stable criminal attribution probably reduce the degree of certainty that decision makers in the criminal justice system require of themselves before processing the offender on to the next stage of the system. For example, police officers are more likely to stop a person who has been arrested before than someone who has not, even though both might be performing the same behavior, because the person's prior criminal record has raised the possibility that he or she has a criminal disposition. The subsequent suspicious behavior serves to confirm that attribution.

Other agents' judgments

One other factor affects attributional judgments—the judgment of other agents in the criminal justice system. As persons are processed through the criminal justice system, certain information follows them. Reports about an offender contain not only information about the offender's crime and past record but also the judgments of other agents in the criminal justice system. For example, parole-board members examining a parole client's file will usually find information from police records regarding the offense, the probation officer's presentence report, correctional officers' judgments about the offender's behavior in prison, and the parole staff's recommendations regarding parole.

Other agents' judgments serve a function similar to that of a prior criminal record. The judgments of agents who have considered the offender at an earlier stage of the criminal justice system serve to increase the confidence that agents at later stages of the system have in their own attributions. Thus, parole boards probably feel confident that they are facing true criminals, because decision makers at every stage of the system—police officers, prosecuting attorneys, juries, judges—had previously decided that the offender had a criminal disposition. This confidence is increased because they also know that because of plea bargaining, the offender was almost certainly arrested for and charged with more crimes and more serious crimes.

Social-Exchange Considerations

Just as there are common factors affecting the attributions of the actors, there are also common exchange relationships that most decision makers in the criminal justice system have. Social-exchange theory assumes that people seek to maximize their outcomes. Although the sources of the rewards differ for each actor, there are five important social-exchange relationships that affect most of the actors in the criminal justice system: (1) with the offender, (2) with peers, (3) with other agencies, (4) with the victim, and (5) with the community.

Social exchange with the offender

At all stages of the criminal justice system, from the initial reporting of a crime to the release of an offender, decision makers in the system have a social-exchange relationship with the offender. For some of these decision makers, the exchange relationship is direct. For example, victims or bystanders who know the offender may let this relationship affect their decision to report the crime to the police. At the very least, they will consider the relationship before reaching a decision. Similarly, police officers, prison guards, and parole officers who know the offender will weigh the costs and benefits that will result from arresting the offender or reporting the offender's act. Equity considerations usually play a prominent role in decisions made by agents of the system. That is, the decision maker desires to treat the offender fairly, as compared with the treatment of similarly situated offenders.

Social exchange with peers

One of the most important social-exchange relationships a decision maker has is with his or her peers. Victims and bystanders rely on covictims, cobystanders, and friends for support and advice regarding their decision to report a crime to the police and thus become involved with the criminal justice system. Social exchange with peers is particularly important for police officers and prison guards, because both groups must rely to a great extent on their fellow officers for help and protection and, therefore, would not want to disrupt these important social-exchange relationships in any way. And, as we saw in Chapter 6, during deliberation jurors are often under great pressure to conform with the majority.

Social exchange with other agents of the system

The criminal justice system is a series of interrelated and interdependent agencies that, in spite of sometimes conflicting interests, must find ways of working together. If an offender is to be convicted and sentenced to prison, police officers must obtain evidence that will not be excluded at trial, the prosecuting attorney must charge the offender with the appropriate offenses, and the judge must sentence the offender to prison. If these agencies do not work together, the system will not operate efficiently, and all its agents may suffer as a consequence.

As discussed in earlier chapters, agencies sometimes have conflicting interests, which they must attempt to resolve. For example, the police might be interested in stopping a particular type of crime—say, drug crimes. To do this, they would probably decide to increase the number of arrests for crimes involving the sale or possession of drugs. Because it is easier to arrest people than to indict and convict them, the likely result of a large increase in the number of drug arrests would be a large backlog of cases for the prosecutor's office to deal with. To reduce the large volume, the prosecutor might be more likely to drop weak cases and plea-bargain others. If this did indeed occur, the police might well believe that their efforts to reduce drug crimes by increasing the number of arrests were wasted. One solution to this problem might be for the police to concentrate on the quality rather than the quantity of their arrests. Thus, to reduce drug crimes they might focus on building strong cases against major drug dealers. Then, once an arrest was made, the prosecutor would be more likely to obtain a conviction.

An example of a second type of disagreement is the frequent lack of cooperation between two police agencies investigating a case. For instance, city and county police agencies may each want the glory of capturing a criminal and therefore may be reluctant to share their information with each other. Such a problem existed in Atlanta in connection with the multicounty investigation of the missing and murdered black children and youths (Willis, 1981).

Social exchange with the victim

Decision makers from the police to the parole board have a social-exchange relationship with the victim (if there is one), whether or not they acknowledge this relationship. At times, the victim is the forgotten person in the criminal justice system. It is true that various decision makers often consider the victim's desires before making a decision. For example, the police and prosecuting attorney take the victim's wishes into account in the arrest and charging decisions, and for many offenses, if the victim prefers not to press charges against the offender, the police and prosecuting attorney will honor this wish. A judge who sentences a convicted criminal may take the victim's statement into account if, for example, the offender made restitution to the victim. Similarly, parole boards may consider a statement by the victim or the victim's family when deciding whether an inmate should be paroled. But in many cases, victims are forgotten by the criminal justice system. Victims may appear repeatedly in court only to learn that the defendant has had the case postponed. Moreover, victims often are not compensated for their losses and suffering. Recently, though, more concern has been expressed for the victim, as evidenced by the institution of compensation programs for victims in many states.

Social exchange with the community

Police officers and administrators, district attorneys, judges, prison administrators, and parole-board members are all cognizant of their direct or indirect relationships with the community, because the community ultimately has the political power to make their lives uncomfortable or even to remove them from their positions. For example, city police administrators are usually appointed by elected officials, such as the mayor. If the community is dissatisfied with police service, the mayor may appoint new police administrators, or if the mayor is defeated in an election, the new mayor will often appoint new police department heads. Most state trial-court judges and many chief district attorneys are elected to office. For these officials the community can exert a direct influence on the prosecution of cases and the sentencing of offenders by not reelecting them. Prison administrators and parole-board members usually owe their allegiance to the governor or to one of the governor's appointees. If the community at large is upset with the operation of the prison system or the parole system, pressure will be exerted on the governor and on prison administrators or parole-board members to institute change. Whether their relationships with the community are direct or indirect, most criminal justice agents know that public dissatisfaction with the operation of the criminal justice system can mean trouble for their agencies and themselves.

Although we believe that the attribution/exchange theoretical framework is the most useful perspective for viewing how the criminal justice system operates in practice, we want to make clear that there are other theories and frameworks that could be used to consider the entire system. Some of these theories may even do a better job at explaining a particular issue than the framework we have chosen. For instance, the material on persuasion and attitude change (for example, Hovland, Janis, & Kelley, 1953) might be particularly applicable to understanding persuasion techniques in the courtroom. Although these other theories could be used to explain the behaviors of actors in the criminal justice system, we believe that none of them provides as extensive and coherent a framework as the attribution/exchange framework we have used here.

We have described the criminal justice system as it is today. It may be different ten years from now because, like any part of society, it is subject to a number of pressures. In the next sections we will examine these pressures. First, we will consider societal factors affecting the criminal justice system. We will then examine the role that social science, particularly social psychology, has played and might play in affecting the criminal justice system.

PRESSURES ON THE CRIMINAL JUSTICE SYSTEM

The societal factors affecting the criminal justice system differ in their stability over time. One group of factors, which we will call *constant pressures*, are relatively permanent pressures on the criminal justice system. A second group of factors, which we will call *cyclical pressures*, change in a recurring pattern. A final group of factors, which we will call *recent pressures*, have only recently begun to exert influence on the criminal justice system.

Constant Pressures

There are three constant pressures on the criminal justice system. The first, and most important, source of pressure is the existence of crime. The second major source of pressure is public dissatisfaction with the operation of the criminal justice system. The final major source of pressure is other agencies in the criminal justice system and other agents within the same agency.

Existence of crime

The most consistent pressure on the criminal justice system is the existence of crime. There will always be crime because, contrary to the popular adage, crime often does pay, or at least criminals think it pays better than other available alternatives. Crime pays because, unless the criminal justice system is enormously expanded and individuals are constantly watched, there is absolutely no way that all criminals can be caught and punished. If criminals know that there is a chance that they will not be punished, many are likely to take that risk. Moreover, criminals may be more likely to focus on the money they will obtain if their crime is successful than on the penalty they will pay if caught (Carroll, 1978b; see also Zimring & Hawkins, 1973). If we assume that people will always want more money, we can probably also safely assume that people will commit crimes to obtain that money. The major implication of the perpetual existence of crime is that the criminal justice system will never go out of business and, indeed, will probably be hard pressed to deal with all those who are suspected of committing crimes.

Public dissatisfaction

In addition to the constancy of crime, there is also the constancy of public dissatisfaction. For the foreseeable future, some portion of the public will probably be dissatisfied with the operation of the criminal justice system. This dissatisfaction will exist for several reasons. First, because the resources of the criminal justice system are limited, some criminals will be able to escape capture, trial, and/or prison. That is, the agents of the criminal justice system must be selective in their enforcement of the law, and their decision will almost certainly displease some segment of society. If the displeased portion of the public happens to have political clout, one can expect with some confidence that the next administration will "clean up the streets" by being "tough on crime." A second type of dissatisfaction will arise from groups of citizens who feel that they are inordinately and unfairly singled out by law enforcement agencies. These groups, which include racial, sexual, and political minorities, are often heard to raise cries of "police harassment."

Because citizens are likely to be dissatisfied with the operation of the criminal justice system generally and with certain agencies specifically, criminal justice agents are likely to value their relationships with other agents more than their relationships with their "enemies" outside it. This attitude is likely to foster a strong in-group solidarity with other agents and to increase the value of social-exchange relationships with these agents.

In-group solidarity

As we have suggested at several points in the book, agents of the criminal justice system often believe that they are subjected to unjustified criticism by members of the community, mainly because average citizens are not aware of how difficult decision making in the criminal justice system is. As a result, many agents may see themselves as an oppressed group, and, as such, they have closer ties to one another than to people outside the criminal justice system. They are particularly likely to have strong ties to people who have the same role that they do.

Because of the importance agents in the criminal justice system place on their relationships with other agents in the system, they are likely to show an in-group solidarity, which is evidenced in many ways—for example, in the presence of police officers from around the country at the funeral of a fellow police officer killed in the line of duty. Agents are also likely to defend the actions of agents in other jurisdictions doing the same task. For example, during the prison riot in Attica in 1971, Commissioner Oswald received letters of support from prison wardens around the country (see Chapter 8).

Cyclical Pressures

Cyclical pressures are those that change in a recurring pattern. Three important cyclical pressures affect the criminal justice system. The first, economic pressure, affects not only the criminal justice system but all society. The second and third are pressures that society places specifically on the criminal justice system. These pressures concern which laws are enforced and what purpose law enforcement serves.

Economic pressures

As discussed above, crime is always likely to exist, because there will always be people who want something they do not have and who will resort to crime to obtain it. In addition, not having property or wealth can exacerbate existing problems, such as marital discord, thus leading to such problems as domestic violence. The effect of the economy on crime is particularly severe when the nation enters a recession. More people are without work and therefore without the money to obtain all that they would like to have. Thus, property crimes such as larceny are more likely to occur when the economy is bad. In addition, when times are bad for a person or family, tension and frustration are likely to be increased, which may lead to more crimes of violence as well.

The nature of crime

Related to recurring economic cycles is the emphasis that society places on a particular type of crime. The type of crime that society would like to see suppressed, as well as the definition of what constitutes a crime, changes in a recurring fashion. Which laws are enforced by agents in the criminal justice system depends to a large extent on society's changing definition of what crime is. For example, DeFleur (1975), in her investigation of drug arrests in Chicago in the 1950s and 1960s, found that the kind of arrests made by the police depended on the public's attitudes toward a particular type of drug. Thus, in the 1950s most drug arrests were of sellers and possessors of heroin because of the public's concern with heroin addiction. By the late 1960s most drug arrests were of white middle-class teenagers for marijuana possession and sale. As marijuana becomes more accepted by society, enforcement is likely to focus again on heroin and other "hard drugs." Another example of society's changing attitude toward a particular type of crime is draft resistance. During the Vietnam War, hundreds of protesters were arrested for resisting the draft. By the end of the war, many of these convicted draft resisters were being paroled early because the crime was no longer thought serious.

Punishment versus treatment

As we have discussed earlier in reference to sentencing (see Chapter 7), there are several reasons that people who are convicted of breaking the law are sentenced to prison or given probation: individual deterrence, general deterrence, incapacitation, retribution, moral outrage, and rehabilitation. Probably the two most important and most conflicting reasons are retribution and rehabilitation, or, more simply, punishment and treatment. Both have been considered legitimate reasons for imprisonment, and prison sentences today generally include both as justifications. Although punishment has usually been the more important of the two, the relative importance of treatment has changed over the last 150 years.

Immediately after the American Revolution, punishment was the sole purpose of criminal sentences. The only issue was whether the punishment would be physical pain or psychological pain resulting from being humiliated in front of one's neighbors. Beginning with the early-19th-century notion of repentance in a penitentiary, a prison sentence was viewed as a means of treating the offender. That is, during confinement prisoners would have the time to think about their past wrongdoing and atone for it, thus "treating" themselves. The reformatories of the latter 19th century continued this notion of treatment. Youths were sent to these reformatories for an indeterminate period, which ended when they showed through their good behavior that they had "reformed." By the beginning of the 20th century, the dominant goal of sentencing was probably treatment rather than punishment.

At present, sentencing includes both treatment and punishment as goals. The notion that criminal justice should be individualized for each offender follows directly from the treatment notions of the 19th century. Although many people have argued—particularly during the 1960s, when there was optimism about the possibilities of rehabilitation—that offenders should be treated rather than punished (for example, Menninger, 1968), in recent years many others have argued that treatment is ineffective and ought not to be considered in sentencing and parole decisions (for example, Wilson, 1975). Today, many decision makers give only lip service to the individualization of treatment (Erickson & Gibbs, 1979).

There is likely to be a continued conflict between the proponents of treatment and the proponents of punishment. Although punishment has been and probably will be the more important rationale over the long run, there have been and probably will be times when treatment is viewed as the primary purpose of sentencing. Which of the two is dominant at any particular time depends on which phase of the cycle we are in.

Recent Pressures

Many developments during the past several years have influenced the criminal justice system. These developments have been of three types: legal changes, administrative changes, and societal changes.

Legal changes

The most significant legal pressure on the criminal justice system has come from the Supreme Court of the United States. Most of the Supreme Court's decisions that significantly expanded the right of the defendant, which have been discussed previously, were made while Earl Warren was chief justice. These decisions include *Mapp* v. *Ohio* (which applied the exclusionary rule to the states) and *Miranda* v. *Arizona* (which required that suspects be told their rights before a confession could be used as evidence against them). In recent years the Supreme Court has been less active in granting new rights to the accused. As Table 10-2 shows, however, there has been no shortage of cases brought in federal courts alleging violation of the United States Constitution or federal statute.

TABLE 10–2. Frequency of general procedure issues raised in Federal Courts of Appeals and the Supreme Court of the United States, July 1976 through June 1977

Issue raised	Courts of Appeals[a]	Supreme Court	Total cases brought
Search and seizure	409	18	427
Electronic surveillance	53	2	55
Arrest	36	0	36
Identification	44	1	45
Confessions	109	1	110
Exclusionary rule	56	6	62
Prosecutorial discretion	31	2	33
Indictments	107	2	109
Grand jury	59	0	59
Preliminary hearing	9	1	10
Joinder and severance	77	1	78
Bail	15	0	15
Discovery	117	0	117
Continuance	32	0	32
Speedy trial	66	2	68
Defendant's competency	14	0	14
Guilty pleas	87	1	88
Double jeopardy	77	10	87
Right to counsel	129	2	131
Jury problems	115	2	117
Conduct of the trial judge	189	4	193
Conduct of the prosecutor	102	0	102
Sentencing	199	3	202
Parole	53	1	54
Probation	23	1	24
Prisoners' rights	97	4	101
TOTAL	2305	64	2369

[a]Including the ten circuits and the D. C. Circuit Court of Appeals
Based on *Georgetown Law Journal,* Project criminal procedure, 1978, *67,* 317–698, pp. 672–673. Copyright © 1980 by the *Georgetown Law Journal.* Used with permission of the publisher.

Administrative changes

One of the recent pressures from both political conservatives and liberals has been to structure decision making in the criminal justice system. Such guidelines please both political conservatives, who view the guidelines as a way to eliminate judges who are "soft" on criminals, and political liberals, who view the guidelines as a way to eliminate arbitrary decision making and discrimination.

A second administrative change has occurred because agencies in the criminal justice system have become more cost-conscious. In their efforts to economize, these agencies have turned to programs that are cheaper than traditional modes of dealing with offenders. For example, pretrial diversion is more economical for the state than processing the offender through trial and prison. That pretrial diversion is also less damaging to the offender is a side cost or benefit, depending on one's viewpoint. A second example of cost cutting in the criminal justice system is the recent trend toward deinstitutionalization. Because maintaining offenders in a halfway house or counseling them while they are on parole is much less costly than housing them in prison, many states have begun to release offenders earlier than formerly. Early release is also due, in part, to the overcrowding in many prisons.

The major result of the increasing effort to reduce the cost of processing offenders through the criminal justice system will probably be that agents will be granted more discretion. That is, the number of people who commit crimes will probably remain constant or increase, while the criminal justice system will probably have the same or fewer resources (such as money and personnel) to deal with them. An inevitable result is that criminal justice agents will have more discretion when deciding whether an offender should enter or remain in the criminal justice system.

Societal changes

Three societal changes have had and will have important repercussions on the operation of criminal justice agencies in the United States. The first of these is the greater number of women entering the labor force. As more women enter the working world, they will have more opportunities to commit crime. In addition, with the rise in sentiment for treating women the same as men, differences in treatment of the sexes are likely to be eliminated. Data from the Federal Bureau of Investigation's *Uniform Crime Reports* (Webster, 1980) indicate that from 1970 to 1979 the number of women arrested for committing crimes increased by 62%, although almost all of this increase resulted from the increased participation of women in property crimes rather than crimes against persons.

A second societal change is the increasing concern for innocent people. There are more and more newspaper editorials, magazine articles, books, movies, and television programs on the high cost that victims, bystanders, and witnesses pay when they become involved with the criminal justice system. This increasing exposure is likely to result in tangible benefits for such people. For example, many states have instituted compensation programs for victims. In addition, the federal government has sponsored several programs to help witnesses (see Cain & Kravitz, 1978).

A final societal change concerns the greater interest and sophistication of the public in the operation of the criminal justice system. Citizens have organized neighborhood watch groups, which look out for suspicious behavior in their neighborhoods and report suspected crimes to the police. Other citizens have organized court watch groups, which observe judges. Finally, this increased interest and sophistication of the public is evidenced by citizens' reading more about the criminal justice system and students' taking courses related to it.

We have briefly discussed several types of pressures on the criminal justice system. An important question is what impact these pressures will have on the system. In the next section we will consider this question.

Impact of the Pressures on the Criminal Justice System

Although the various types of pressures will have an impact on the criminal justice system, it is likely that this impact will be relatively small. An example of the minimal adjustment of agents of the criminal justice system to changes imposed from the outside is the police response to the *Miranda* decision (1966), which required that all persons arrested for a crime be warned of their constitutional rights to remain silent, to hire an attorney, and to have an attorney appointed if they cannot afford one. Some authors (for example, Milner, 1971) have suggested that the police are using subtle means to limit the effectiveness of the *Miranda* rules. For example, many officers allow the suspect only a few seconds to determine whether an attorney is needed. Thus, although the agents are complying with the letter of the law by reading suspects their rights, they are not meeting the spirit of the law—that is, ensuring that suspects can fully exercise their rights.

A second example of the minimal adjustment the criminal justice system makes to outside pressures is the adjustment to pressures for fixed sentences for each type of crime. Although the intent of fixed sentencing standards is to reduce and structure judges' discretion, some have argued that the discretion will not be eliminated or structured but only moved from the judge to the prosecuting attorney (for example, Alschuler, 1978). Indeed, there is some evidence that when sentencing standards have been imposed, prosecuting attorneys have avoided the impact of the mandatory sentences by charging defendants with less serious crimes than they might have. However, other experts have suggested that as long as the sentencing standards are reasonable, neither too lenient nor too severe, prosecuting and defense attorneys are less likely to bypass the standards through plea bargaining (Rossett, 1972).

These minimal adjustments to outside pressures are consistent with the argument made by many persons that regardless of the type of pressure, the criminal justice system, like any complex organization, is concerned primarily with maintaining itself and thus with minimizing the impact of outside pressures (for example, Chambliss & Seidman, 1971).

TRENDS AFFECTING PSYCHOLOGY AND THE CRIMINAL JUSTICE SYSTEM

Two important factors suggest that in the immediate future there will be more psychological research on the criminal justice system. These are changes in education and in government funding.

Trends in Education

As just mentioned, society generally has become more interested in understanding the criminal justice system, prompting the formation of neighborhood watch groups and court watch groups. Another result of this increased interest is an increased number of college courses relating psychology and the criminal justice system.

Recently, a survey of academic psychology departments in the United States revealed that 85 departments had at least one graduate course in which half or more of the content was related to the law (Grisso, Sales & Bayless, 1979). Most of these courses have been taught since 1973. At the graduate level there are also several other cross-disciplinary opportunities. For example, the Russell Sage Foundation sponsors a law and psychology program at Stanford University and has granted several fellowships to psychologists interested in studying law and psychology. At several universities, such as Northwestern, Minnesota, Harvard, and Chicago, students may design their own joint-degree programs in law and psychology. There are presently two programs in the country that grant both J.D. degrees in law and Ph.D. degrees in psychology: the University of Nebraska at Lincoln and the University of Maryland School of Law–Johns Hopkins Graduate School. More such programs will probably be created in the future.

At the undergraduate level, it is even more likely that departments will show increasing interest in the interrelationship of psychology and law. The fact that you are taking this course is evidence of this increased interest.

Trends in Research Funding

There is a trend toward increased funding of psychological research related to the criminal justice system. Most of the support for this research comes from federal government funding agencies. Although several federal agencies are interested in this research, most of the funding is channeled through three agencies: the Center for the Studies of Crime and Delinquency of the National Institute of Mental Health, the Law and Social Policy Section of the National Science Foundation, and the National Institute of Justice. These agencies provide funds to universities and research organizations to investigate topics related to the criminal justice system. Sometimes a researcher in a university or other organization will have an idea for a research project and will write a grant proposal asking one of these agencies to provide money for the project. If the agency believes that the project is worthwhile, it will provide funds for the investigator's and employees' salaries, supplies, equipment, and administrative costs. Sometimes an agency has an idea for a research question that it would like someone to investigate. In such a circumstance, the agency distributes a request for proposals that details the research question and the amount of money offered. Interested researchers are aksed to submit proposals on the procedures they would use to investigate the question.

Funding from federal agencies is important for research in colleges and universities because it provides money for faculty salaries and administrative costs. Because of increased costs, universities must look to sources of funding in addition to students' fees, state government appropriations, and donations from alumni. A major source of this additional funding is the federal government, through research grants. Thus, federal funding allows researchers to investigate problems which they are interested in but which, without the funding, they would not be able to study.

Federal funding is also important to research organizations that survive mainly on contracts and grants from the federal government and sometimes from state governments. These research organizations include organizations whose primary interests are in justice-related issues, such as the National Center for State Courts, as well as organizations for which justice-related research is only a small part of their work, such as the Rand Corporation.

Because federal funding is so important, the interests of the funding agencies can determine the kind of research that will be conducted. As these agencies are becoming more concerned with criminal-justice-related issues, particularly with questions that have practical value to the criminal justice system, it is likely that in the future there will be more research by psychologists on questions related to the criminal justice system.

SOCIAL PSYCHOLOGY AND THE CRIMINAL JUSTICE SYSTEM

In discussing the relation between social psychology and the criminal justice system, we will consider two issues. First, we will examine the impact that social psychology has had on the criminal justice system in the past. Second, we will conjecture about its role in the future, particularly the kinds of research that will probably be conducted.

Impact of Social Psychology

Before we can accurately assess the impact social psychology has had on the criminal justice system, we need to be aware of the limitations on the kinds of research that social psychologists can conduct and the obstacles to the application of their findings to the criminal justice system. In Chapter 1 and in subsequent chapters we explicitly discussed some of these limitations. Nevertheless, the limitations should be briefly mentioned again.

First, we need to be aware that some decisions by agents in the criminal justice system cannot be studied at all. For example, many decisions are made in private and without record. A prison guard's decision not to write a misconduct report about a disruptive inmate is such a decision.

Second, because social psychologists are often unable to study actual decisions, they have had to rely on simulated decisions, using college students. As discussed in Chapter 6, for example, there are problems of external validity when college students are used to simulate the decision making of actual jurors. A third limitation of social-psychological research is posed by ethical considerations. Some questions cannot be investigated because to do so would be wrong ethically, if not legally. For example, eavesdropping on actual jury deliberations would be an investigation of this type.

In addition to these research limitations, three major obstacles affect the impact of social-psychological research on the legal process (Tanke & Tanke, 1979). First, by the time a specific issue comes to the attention of social scientists, there is usually not enough time for relevant research to be conducted. For example, in the *Ballew* v. *Georgia* (1978) case, which concerned the constitutionality of five-person juries, interested parties had less than six months from the time the Supreme Court agreed to hear the case until written arguments were due. Clearly, this period is insufficient to design studies, collect and analyze data, and present results. Given this shortage of time, Tanke and Tanke (1979) conclude that "unless a substantial body of relevant research and criticism is available at the beginning of the appellate process, social science participation in the decision is practically impossible" (p. 1132).

A second obstacle to social-scientific participation in the legal process is the nature of the appellate review process. Generally, appellate courts review only the information in the trial record. Therefore, the testimony of expert witnesses and results from relevant studies can be subjected to scrutiny only through the adversary process of cross-examination. Without this opportunity for critical evaluation, appellate judges must rely on their own nonexpert interpretations of the studies. Often, these judges are not aware of the inadequacies of the research and consequently can reach erroneous conclusions (Zeisel, 1971; Zeisel & Diamond, 1974).

A third obstacle to the use of social-scientific research in the legal process is the concept of legal precedence. Once a court has reached a decision in a case, the reasoning or rule involved in it serves as a justification for decisions in later cases. Only if compelling evidence is offered will subsequent courts overrule the precedent. Some writers have suggested that social-scientific research will only rarely be judged conclusive enough to warrant overruling a legal precedent (for example, Tanke & Tanke, 1979).

Even if social psychologists could overcome all these limitations, there is no assurance that agents in the criminal justice system would use the information that social psychology could offer. We have already discussed several reasons that parole boards are reluctant to use decision-making guidelines (see Chapter 9): the commitment to individualize decisions for each criminal; the knowledge that statistical predictions will necessarily be wrong for some cases (even though the percentage of errors will be less than with clinical decisions); the presumption that statistical tables will overlook significant case factors; the probability that for reasons of public opinion, people will not want to put into writing the factors that affect their decisions; and the reduction in the need for and status of the decision makers. Moreover, agents of the criminal justice system may be reluctant to use research findings because these agents are unfamiliar with social-psychological research and with statistics. For example, Justice Powell has expressed his reluctance to rely "on numerology derived from statistical studies" (*Ballew* v. *Georgia*, 1978, p. 246).

In spite of the above-mentioned limitations of social-psychological research and the reluctance of criminal justice agents to use the research, in several instances social-psychological research has been used in the criminal justice system. As discussed in Chapter 6, the Supreme Court has relied on social-psychological evidence in its rulings on the constitutionally permissible size of juries. Relying on evidence that 6- and 12-member juries do not give discernibly different verdicts, the court in *Williams* v. *Florida* (1970) held that a jury of 6 persons was permissible in criminal trials. In *Ballew* v. *Georgia* (1978), the court reaffirmed the constitutionality of the 6-person jury but held that conviction by a 5-person jury violated the Constitution. The evidence relied on for this decision included social-psychological research on groups and mock juries (for example, Saks, 1977). It should be noted, however, that social scientists have criticized the court for misreading the data (for example, Saks & Hastie, 1978; Zeisel, 1971).

Thus, social-psychological research has been used in the past and will probably be used in the future. Given our belief that social-psychological research should affect future judgments concerning the criminal justice system, the question is what issues social psychologists should investigate in the future.

Future Research

Probably the most important criterion for future work in the criminal justice system by social psychologists is that the work be relevant and useful to decision makers in the system. How can this criterion be met?

Tanke and Tanke (1979) have outlined three strategies social scientists should use to produce and present data that will be considered in the judicial process. The same general approaches could be used for other stages of the criminal justice process. First, social scientists should identify empirical questions that will be relevant to legal decision makers. They can identify such questions by (1) examining reports of recent cases, both trial and appellate, through such reference publications as *United States Law Week* and the *Criminal Law Reporter*, (2) reading law review articles that analyze trends and project future developments in the law, and (3) conferring with special interest groups that engage in litigation and watch developments in the law, such as the National Association for the Advancement of Colored People and the American Civil Liberties Union. Second, social scientists should work closely with legal experts when planning experimental research relevant to legal issues. Without such advice, the research is not likely to be considered valid by decision makers. For example, "If the research is not designed to answer specific, legally relevant empirical questions in a setting that at least approximates the legal environment, it will not be useful to a court" (Tanke & Tanke, 1979, p. 1135). Finally, social scientists should present their information in ways that merit the acceptance of legal decision makers. These avenues include publishing in legal journals, presenting research in an appellate brief as an *amicus curiae* (friend of the court), and participating at the trial stage as an expert witness and as an adviser to the attorneys on the presentation of evidence.

Given that social psychologists will be conducting research that is relevant to the criminal justice system, are there some variables that should be studied before others? On this question, Wells (1978) has drawn a distinction between what he terms "estimator variables" and what he terms "system variables." Estimator variables are variables that "may be manipulable in research" but "cannot be controlled in actual criminal cases" (p. 1548). For example, research suggests that eyewitness testimony may be more accurate for moderately severe crimes than for very severe crimes (Johnson & Scott, 1976). With this knowledge, social psychologists could *estimate*, after the fact, the probable accuracy of a witness. But this information is of limited value because the criminal justice system cannot produce more accurate witnesses by controlling the severity of crimes. System variables are "variables that are (or potentially can be) under the direct control of the criminal justice system" (p. 1548). For example, the interval between the occurrence of a crime and the time that the witness testifies is a system variable. If research shows that eyewitness testimony is more accurate when this interval is short, the criminal justice system could use this knowledge to produce more accurate witnesses. Wells argues that if the goal of social-psychological research is to produce results that can be applied to the criminal justice system, system-variable research would be more useful than estimator-variable research.

Wells' preference for system-variable research may come about because, as bank robbers often say, "that's where the money is." That is, social psychologists interested in obtaining money in the form of grants from the federal government may have to conduct system-variable research, because the government is becoming increasingly cost-conscious. Thus, in the future, government funding agencies may be more likely to fund research that is useful or potentially useful than research that is of theoretical interest to a small group of psychologists.

Aside from focusing on system variables, future social-psychological research will almost certainly include evaluation of various programs in the criminal justice system. The federal government is becoming more concerned with the cost-effectiveness of its programs. That is, the government wants to know whether the taxpayers are getting their money's worth out of a particular program. Evaluation of the effectiveness of many types of criminal justice programs has become mandated by federal law, and more social psychologists will be needed to conduct this research. Indeed, the American Psychological Association Task Force on the Role of Psychology in the Criminal Justice System (American Psychological Association, 1978) has specifically pointed to evaluation as one area in which psychologists can provide valuable expertise. The reason that more social psychologists will probably be doing evaluation research on the criminal justice system is the same as that proposed for why they are more likely to focus on system variables: because that is where the money is likely to be.

SUMMARY

In the first part of this chapter, we discussed the elements of the attribution/exchange framework that are common to the various types of decisions made by agents in the criminal justice system. Regarding the attribution decision, three factors are important at most stages of the criminal justice system: seriousness of the offense, offender's prior criminal record, and judgments of other agents. Regarding the social-exchange decision, we looked at five individuals or groups with whom an agent is likely to have a social-exchange relationship: the offender, peers, other agencies, the victim, and the community.

In the second part of the chapter, we examined different kinds of forces that exert pressure on the criminal justice system and speculated about their future impact on the system. These forces included constant pressures on the system (the existence of crime, public dissatisfaction with the criminal justice system, and in-group solidarity), cyclical pressures (economic pressures, the nature of crime, and the purpose of sentencing), and recent pressures (legal, administrative, and societal changes).

In the final part of the chapter, we briefly summarized the past role of social psychology in affecting decisions in the criminal justice system. We concluded the chapter by discussing ways that future research can be made both relevant and useful to agents in the system.

References

Aaronson, D. E., Kittrie, N. N., & Saari, D. J. *Alternatives to conventional criminal adjudication: Guidebook for planners and practitioners.* Washington, D. C.: U. S. Government Printing Office, 1977.

Adams, J. S. Toward an understanding of inequity. *Journal of Abnormal and Social Psychology,* 1963, *67,* 422–436.

Adams, J. S. Inequity in social exchange. In L. Berkowitz (Ed.), *Advances in experimental social psychology* (Vol. 2). New York: Academic Press, 1965.

Adams, J. S., & Freedman, S. Equity theory revisited: Comments and annotated bibliography. In L. Berkowitz (Ed.), *Advances in experimental social psychology* (Vol. 9). New York: Academic Press, 1976.

Adorno, T., Frenkel-Brunswik, E., Levinson, D., & Sanford, N. *The authoritarian personality.* New York: Harper, 1950.

Agency stops court advice after Berkowitz bail urged. *Dallas Morning News,* August 21, 1977, p. 37A.

Allen, H. E., & Simonsen, C. E. *Corrections in America: An introduction.* Beverly Hills, Calif.: Glencoe, 1975.

Alschuler, A. W. The prosecutor's role in plea bargaining. *University of Chicago Law Review,* 1968, *36,* 50–112.

Alschuler, A. W. The defense attorney's role in plea bargaining. *Yale Law Journal,* 1975, *84,* 1179–1314.

Alschuler, A. W. Sentencing reform and prosecutorial power: A critique of recent proposals for "fixed" and "presumptive" sentencing. *University of Pennsylvania Law Review,* 1978, *126,* 550–577.

American Bar Association. *Standards relating to sentencing alternatives and procedures.* New York: Office of the Criminal Justice Project, 1968.

American Bar Association. *Standards relating to the prosecution function and the defense function.* Chicago: American Bar Association, 1971.

American Bar Association. *Standards for criminal justice* (2nd ed.). Vol. I. Boston: Little, Brown, 1980. (a)

American Bar Association. *Standards for criminal justice* (2nd ed.). Vol. III. Boston: Little, Brown, 1980. (b)

American Bar Association, Section of Criminal Justice. *Plea-bargaining: Nemesis or nirvana?* Washington, D. C.: American Bar Association, Section of Criminal Justice, 1977.

American Psychological Association. *Ethical principles in the conduct of research with human participants.* Washington, D. C.: American Psychological Association, 1973.

293

American Psychological Association. Report of the Task Force on the Role of Psychology in the Criminal Justice System. *American Psychologist*, 1978, *33*, 1099–1113.

Ares, C. E., Rankin, A., & Sturz, H. The Manhattan bail project: An interim report on the use of pre-trial parole. *New York University Law Review*, 1963, *38*, 71–92.

Arluke, N. R. A summary of parole rules. *Crime and Delinquency*, 1969, *15*, 267–274.

Armbrust, E. A., & Deloney, D. G. *Federal prison construction: Alternative approaches.* Washington, D. C.: U. S. Government Printing Office, 1977.

Asch, S. *Social psychology.* Englewood Cliffs, N.J.: Prentice-Hall, 1952.

Attorney General's survey of release procedures. Washington, D. C.: U. S. Government Printing Office, 1939.

Austin, W. The concept of desert and its influence on simulated decision makers' sentencing decisions. *Law and Human Behavior*, 1979, *3*, 163–187. (a)

Austin, W. Sex differences in bystander intervention in a theft. *Journal of Personality and Social Psychology*, 1979, *37*, 2110–2120. (b)

Austin, W., & Hatfield, E. Equity theory, power, and social justice. In G. Mikula (Ed.), *Justice and social interaction: Experimental and theoretical contributions from psychological research.* New York: Springer-Verlag, 1980.

Austin, W., Walster, E., & Utne, M. K. Equity and the law: Effect of a harmdoer's "suffering in the act" on liking and assigned punishment. In L. Berkowitz (Ed.), *Advances in experimental social psychology* (Vol. 9). New York: Academic Press, 1976.

Bailey, F. L., & Rothblatt, H. B. *Successful techniques for criminal trials.* San Francisco: Bancroft-Whitney, 1971.

Banuazizi, A., & Movahedi, S. Interpersonal dynamics in a simulated prison: A methodological analysis. *American Psychologist*, 1975, *30*, 152–160.

Bard, M., & Sangrey, D. *The crime victim's book.* New York: Basic Books, 1979.

Barkas, J. L. *Victims.* New York: Scribner's, 1978.

Barker, T. Peer group support for police occupational deviance. *Criminology*, 1977, *15*, 353–366. (a)

Barker, T. Social definitions of police corruption: The case of South City. *Criminal Justice Review*, 1977, *2*, 101–110. (b)

Begley, K. Rapists provoked, judge repeats. *Pittsburgh Press*, June 26, 1977, p. 1A.

Bem, D. J. Self-perception theory. In L. Berkowitz (Ed.), *Advances in experimental social psychology* (Vol. 6). New York: Academic Press, 1972.

Berg, K., & Vidmar, N. Authoritarianism and recall of evidence about criminal behavior. *Journal of Research in Personality*, 1975, *9*, 147–157.

Berkowitz, L. Social norms, feelings, and other factors affecting helping and altruism. In L. Berkowitz (Ed.), *Advances in experimental social psychology* (Vol. 6). New York: Academic Press, 1972.

Berscheid, E., & Walster, E. Physical attractiveness. In L. Berkowitz (Ed.), *Advances in experimental social psychology* (Vol. 7). New York: Academic Press, 1974.

Bickman, L. Bystander intervention in a crime: The effect of a mass media campaign. *Journal of Applied Social Psychology*, 1975, *5*, 296–302.

Bickman, L., & Green, S. Is revenge sweet? The effect of attitude toward a thief on crime reporting. *Criminal Justice and Behavior*, 1975, *2*, 101–112.

Bickman, L., & Green, S. Situational cues and crime reporting: Do signs make a difference? *Journal of Applied Social Psychology*, 1977, *7*, 1–18.

Bickman, L., & Lavrakas, P. J. *National evaluation program phase I report: Citizen crime reporting projects* (Vol. 1). U. S. Department of Justice, National Institute of Law Enforcement and Criminal Justice, Law Enforcement Assistance Administration, 1976.

Bickman, L., & Rosenbaum, D. P. Crime reporting as a function of bystander encouragement, surveillance, and credibility. *Journal of Personality and Social Psychology*, 1977, *35*, 577–586.

Black, D. Police encounters and social organization: An observation study. Unpublished doctoral dissertation, University of Michigan, 1968.

Black, D. The social organization of arrest. *Stanford Law Review*, 1971, *23*, 1087–1111.

Black, D. J., & Reiss, A. J., Jr. *Studies of crime and law enforcement in major metropolitan areas: Patterns of behavior in police and citizen transactions.* Field Surveys III, Vol. 2, President's Commission on Law Enforcement and Administration of Justice. Washington, D. C.: U. S. Government Printing Office, 1967.

Black, H. C. *Black's law dictionary* (4th ed.). St. Paul, Minn.: West, 1957.

Blau, P. M. *Exchange and power in social life.* New York: Wiley, 1964.

Blitman, N., & Green, R. Inez Garcia on trial. *Ms.*, May, 1975, pp. 49–54; 84–88.

Blumberg, A. S. The practice of law as a confidence game: Organizational cooptation of a profession. *Law and Society Review*, 1967, *1*, 15–39.

Blunk, R. A., & Sales, B. D. Persuasion during the voir dire. In B. D. Sales (Ed.), *Psychology in the legal process.* New York: Spectrum, 1977.

Boehm, V. Mr. Prejudice, Miss Sympathy, and the authoritarian personality: An application of psychological measuring techniques to the problem of jury bias. *Wisconsin Law Review*, 1968, *1968*, 734–750.

Bopp, W. J., & Schultz, D. O. *Principles of American law enforcement and criminal justice.* Springfield, Ill.: Charles C Thomas, 1972.

Bottomley, A. K. *Decisions in the penal process.* London: Robertson, 1973.

Bramwell, P. F. An investigation of the influence of group pressure upon prison inmate leaders and nonleaders. Unpublished doctoral dissertation, Brigham Young University, 1967.

Bray, R. M. The mock trial: Problems and prospects for jury research. In R. Dillehay (Chair), *Innovations in jury research: Concepts, methods, and policy implications.* Symposium presented at the meeting of the American Psychological Association, Washington, D. C., September 1976.

Bray, R. M., & Kerr, N. L. Use of the simulation method in the study of jury behavior. *Law and Human Behavior*, 1979, *3*, 107–119.

Bray, R. M., & Noble, A. M. Authoritarianism and decisions of mock juries: Evidence of jury bias and group polarization. *Journal of Personality and Social Psychology*, 1978, *36*, 1424–1430.

Brodsky, S. L. *Psychologists in the criminal justice system.* Urbana: University of Illinois Press, 1972.

Broeder, D. Voir dire examinations: An empirical study. *Southern California Law Review*, 1965, *38*, 503–528.

Bronson, E. J. On the conviction proneness and representativeness of the death qualified jury: An empirical study of Colorado veniremen. *University of Colorado Law Review*, 1970, *42*, 1–32.

Brosi, K. B. *A cross-city comparison of felony case processing.* Washington, D. C.: U. S. Government Printing Office, 1979.

Brown, E., Deffenbacher, K., & Sturgill, W. Memory for faces and the circumstances of encounter. *Journal of Applied Psychology*, 1977, *62*, 311–318.

Brownmiller, S. *Against our will: Men, women, and rape.* New York: Simon & Schuster, 1975.

Bukstel, L. H., & Kilmann, P. R. Psychological effects of imprisonment on confined individuals. *Psychological Bulletin*, 1980, *88*, 469–493.

Bullock, H. A. Significance of the racial factor in the length of prison sentences. *Journal of Criminal Law, Criminology, and Police Science*, 1961, *52*, 411–417.

Burchard, W. W. Lawyers, political scientists, sociologists—and concealed microphones. *American Sociological Review*, 1958, *23*, 686–691.

Burkhart, K. W. *Women in prison.* Garden City, N.Y.: Doubleday, 1973.

Burnham, R. W. Modern decision theory and corrections. In D. M. Gottfredson (Ed.), *Decision-making in the criminal justice system: Reviews and essays.* Washington, D. C.: U. S. Government Printing Office, 1975.

Cain, A. A., & Kravitz, M. *Victim/witness assistance: A selected bibliography.* Washington, D. C.: U. S. Government Printing Office, 1978.

Calhoun, L. G., Selby, J. W., Cann, A., & Keller, G. T. The effects of victim physical attractiveness and sex of respondent on social reactions to victims of rape. *British Journal of Social and Clinical Psychology*, 1978, *17*, 191–192.

Calhoun, L. G., Selby, J. W., & Warring, L. J. Social perception of the victim's causal role in rape. *Human Relations*, 1976, *29*, 517–526.

Campbell, D. T., & Stanley, J. C. *Experimental and quasi-experimental designs for research.* Chicago: Rand McNally, 1963.

Carroll, J. S. Causal attributions in expert parole decisions. *Journal of Personality and Social Psychology*, 1978, *36*, 1501–1511. (a)

Carroll, J. S. A psychological approach to deterrence: The evaluation of crime opportunities. *Journal of Personality and Social Psychology*, 1978, *36*, 1512–1520. (b)

Carroll, J. S. Judgments of recidivism risk: The use of base-rate information in parole decisions. In P. D. Lipsett & B. D. Sales (Eds.), *New directions in psycholegal research.* New York: Litton, 1980.

Carroll, J. S., & Coates, D. Parole decisions: Social psychological research in applied settings. In L. Bickman (Ed.), *Applied social psychology annual* (Vol. 1). Beverly Hills, Calif.: Sage, 1980.

Carroll, J. S., & Payne, J. W. The judgment of criminality: An attributional analysis of the parole decision. Paper presented at the meeting of the American Psychological Association, Chicago, August 1975.

Carroll, J. S., & Payne, J. W. The psychology of the parole decision process: A joint application of attribution theory and information processing psychology. In J. S. Carroll & J. W. Payne (Eds.), *Cognition and social behavior.* Hillsdale, N. J.: Erlbaum, 1976.

Carroll, J. S., & Payne, J. W. Crime seriousness, recidivism risk, and causal attributions in judgments of prison term by students and experts. *Journal of Applied Psychology*, 1977, *62*, 595–602. (a)

Carroll, J. S., & Payne, J. W. Judgments about crime and the criminal: A model and a method for investigating parole decisions. In B. D. Sales (Ed.), *Perspectives in law and psychology.* Vol. 1: *Criminal justice system.* New York: Plenum, 1977. (b)

Carroll, J. S., & Ruback, R. B. Sentencing by parole board: The parole revocation decision. In B. D. Sales (Ed.), *Perspectives in law and psychology.* Vol. 2: *The trial process.* New York: Plenum, 1981.

Carroll, J. S., Wiener, R. L., Coates, D., & Alibrio, J. J. A multistage model of parole decision making. Unpublished manuscript, Loyola University of Chicago, 1981.

Carroll, L. *Hacks, blacks, and cons.* Lexington, Mass.: Lexington Books, 1974.

Carter, R. M., McGee, R. A., & Nelson, E. K. *Corrections in America.* Philadelphia: Lippincott, 1975.

Carter, R. M., & Wilkins, L. T. Some factors in sentencing policy. *Journal of Criminal Law, Criminology, and Police Science*, 1967, *58*, 503–514.

Casper, J. D. *American criminal justice: The defendant's perspective.* Englewood Cliffs, N. J.: Prentice-Hall, 1972.

Cavoukian, A. Eyewitness testimony: The ineffectiveness of discrediting information. Paper presented at the meeting of the American Psychological Association, Montreal, September 1980.

Chambliss, W. J., & Seidman, R. B. *Law, order, and power.* Reading, Mass.: Addison-Wesley, 1971.

Chapman, J. R., & Gates, M. (Eds.). *Women into wives: The legal and economic impact of marriage.* Beverly Hills, Calif.: Sage, 1977.

Citizens' Inquiry on Parole and Criminal Justice. *Prison without walls: Report on New York Parole.* New York, 1974.

Clarke, S. H., Freeman, J. L., & Koch, G. G. *The effectiveness of bail systems: An analysis of failure to appear in court and rearrest while on bail.* Chapel Hill: Institute of Government, University of North Carolina at Chapel Hill, 1976.

Clements, C. Crowded prisons: A review of psychological and environmental effects. *Law and Human Behavior,* 1979, *3,* 217–225.

Clemmer, D. *The prison community.* New York: Holt, Rinehart & Winston, 1940.

Clemmer, D. Imprisonment as a source of criminality. In D. Dressler (Ed.), *Readings in criminology and penology.* New York: Columbia University Press, 1964.

Clemmer, D. The process of prisonization. In L. Radzinowicz & M. E. Wolfgang (Eds.), *The criminal in confinement.* New York: Basic Books, 1971.

Clifford, B. R. & Bull, R. *The psychology of person identification.* London: Routledge & Kegan Paul, 1978.

Cloward, R. A. Social control in the prison. In R. A. Cloward, D. R. Cressey, G. H. Grosser, R. McCleery, L. E. Ohlin, G. M. Sykes, & S. L. Messinger (Eds.), *Theoretical studies in social organization of the prison.* New York: Social Science Research Council, 1960.

Cloyd, J. W. The processing of misdemeanor drinking drivers: The bureaucratization of the arrest, prosecution, and plea bargaining situations. *Social Forces,* 1977–1978, *56,* 385–407.

Cochran, P. A. A situational approach to the study of police-Negro relations. *Sociological Quarterly,* 1971, *12,* 232–237.

Cohen, J. S. Trial tactics in criminal cases. In H. Toch (Ed.), *Legal and criminal psychology.* New York: Holt, Rinehart & Winston, 1961.

Cohen, S., & Taylor, L. *Psychological survival: The experience of long-term imprisonment.* New York: Random House, 1972.

Cole, G. E. The decision to prosecute. *Law and Society Review,* 1970, *4,* 331–343.

Cole, G. F. Criminal justice as an exchange system. *Rutgers Camden Law Journal,* 1971, *3,* 18–31.

Coleman, J. R. What I learned last summer. *Psychology Today,* November 1980, pp. 14–21.

Coombs, C. H. Thurstone's measurement of social values revisited forty years later. *Journal of Personality and Social Psychology,* 1967, *6,* 85–91.

Cosgrove, C. A. A screening model for parole decision-making. Paper presented at the meeting of the American Psychological Association, Washington, D. C., August 1976.

Cressey, D. R. Prison organizations. In J. G. March (Ed.), *Handbook of organizations.* New York: Rand McNally, 1965.

Cressey, D. R., & Ohlin, L. E. *Working with criminals: A study of social organization and change.* New York: Russell Sage Foundation, 1966.

Critchley, T. A. *A history of police in England and Wales* (2nd ed.). Montclair, N. J.: Patterson Smith, 1967.

Crump, D. Determinate sentencing: The promises and perils of sentence guidelines. *Kentucky Law Journal,* 1980, *68,* 1–100

Culhane, J. California enacts legislation to aid victims of criminal violence. *Stanford Law Review*, 1965, *18*, 266–273.

Darrow, C. Attorney for the defense. *Esquire*, May 1936, pp. 36–37; 211–213.

Daudistel, H. C. On the elimination of plea-bargaining: The El Paso experiment. In W. F. McDonald & J. A. Cramer (Eds.), *Plea-bargaining*. Lexington, Mass.: Lexington Books, 1980.

Daudistel, H. C., Sanders, W. B., & Luckenbill, D. F. *Criminal justice: Situations and decisions*. New York: Holt, Rinehart & Winston, 1979.

Davis, A. J. Sexual assaults in the Philadelphia prison system. In S. E. Wallace (Ed.), *Total institutions*. Hawthorne, N. Y.: Aldine, 1971.

Davis, J. H., Bray, R. M., & Holt, R. W. The empirical study of decision processes in juries: A critical review. In J. L. Tapp & F. J. Levine (Eds.), *Law, justice, and the individual in society: Psychological and legal issues*. New York: Holt, Rinehart & Winston, 1977.

Davis, J. H., Kerr, N. L., Atkin, R. S., Holt, R., & Meek, D. The decision processes of 6- and 12-person mock juries assigned unanimous and two-thirds majority rules. *Journal of Personality and Social Psychology*, 1975, *32*, 1–14.

Davis, J. H., Kerr, N. L., Stasser, G., Meek, D., & Holt, R. W. Victim consequences, sentence severity, and decision processes in mock jurors. *Organizational Behavior and Human Performance*, 1977, *18*, 346–365.

Dawson, R. O. *Sentencing: The decision as to type, length, and conditions of sentence*. Boston: Little, Brown, 1969.

DeFleur, L. B. Biasing influences on drug arrest records: Implications for deviance research. *American Sociological Review*, 1975, *40*, 88–103.

DeJong, W., Morris, W. N., & Hastorf, A. H. Effect of an escaped accomplice on the punishment assigned to a criminal defendant. *Journal of Personality and Social Psychology*, 1976, *33*, 192–198.

Denno, D., & Cramer, J. A. The effects of victim characteristics on judicial decision making. In W. F. McDonald (Ed.), *Criminal justice and the victim*. Beverly Hills, Calif.: Sage, 1976.

Dermer, M., & Thiel, D. L. When beauty may fail. *Journal of Personality and Social Psychology*, 1975, *31*, 1168–1176.

Dershowitz, A. M. Background paper in the report of the Twentieth Century Fund Task Force on Criminal Sentencing. New York: McGraw-Hill, 1976.

Deutsch, M. Equity, equality, and need: What determines which value will be used as the basis of distributive justice? *Journal of Social Issues*, 1975, *31(3)*, 137–149.

Diamond, S. S., & Zeisel, H. A courtroom experiment on juror selection and decision-making. *Proceedings of the Division of Personality and Social Psychology*, 1974, *1*, 276–277.

Dodge, D. C. Plea bargaining revisited. *State Court Journal*, Fall 1978, pp. 13–16; 38–40.

Donalson, A. JPs urging Tucker's return. *Pittsburgh Press*, January 16, 1977, p. 16A.

Doob, A. N., & Kirshenbaum, H. M. Some empirical evidence on the effect of S.12 of the Canada Evidence Act on an accused. *Criminal Law Quarterly*, 1972, *15*, 88–96.

Dressler, D. *Practice and theory of probation and parole*. New York: Columbia University Press, 1965.

Ebbesen, E. B., & Konečni, V. J. Decision making and information integration in the courts: The setting of bail. *Journal of Personality and Social Psychology*, 1975, *32*, 805–821.

Ebbesen, E. B., & Konečni, V. J. Fairness in sentencing: Severity of crime and judicial decision making. Paper presented at the meeting of the American Psychological Association, Washington, D. C., September 1976.

Edelhartz, H. *The nature, impact, and prosecution of white collar crime.* Washington, D. C.: U. S. Government Printing Office, 1970.

Edinger, J. D., & Auerbach, S. M. Development and validation of a multidimensional multivariate model for accounting for infractions in a correctional setting. *Journal of Personality and Social Psychology,* 1978, *36,* 1472–1489.

Efran, M. G. The effect of physical appearance on the judgment of guilt, interpersonal attraction, and severity of recommended punishment in a simulated jury task. *Journal of Research in Personality,* 1974, *8,* 45–54.

Elwork, A., Sales, B. D., & Suggs, D. The trial: A research review. In B. D. Sales (Ed.), *Perspectives in law and psychology.* Vol. 2: *The trial process.* New York: Plenum, 1981.

Emerson, R. M. Power-dependence relations. *American Sociological Review,* 1962, *27,* 31–41.

Ennis, P. H. *Criminal victimization in the United States: A report of a national survey.* Field Surveys II, President's Commission on Law Enforcement and Administration of Justice. Washington, D. C.: U. S. Government Printing Office, 1967.

Erdelyi, M. H. A new look at the new look: Perceptual defense and vigilance. *Psychological Review,* 1974, *81,* 1–25.

Erickson, B., Lind, E. A., Johnson, B. C., & O'Barr, W. M. Speech style and impression formation in a court setting: The effects of "powerful" and "powerless" speech. *Journal of Experimental Social Psychology,* 1978, *14,* 266–279.

Erickson, M. L., & Gibbs, J. P. On the perceived severity of legal penalties. *Journal of Criminal Law and Criminology,* 1979, *70,* 102–116.

Farber, M. L. Suffering and time perspective of the prisoner. *University of Iowa Studies in Child Welfare,* 1944, *20*(409), 153–227.

Feldman, R. S., & Rosen, F. P. Diffusion of responsibility in crime, punishment, and other adversity. *Law and Human Behavior,* 1978, *2,* 313–322.

Feldman-Summers, S., & Lindner, K. Perceptions of victims and defendants in criminal assault cases. *Criminal Justice and Behavior,* 1976, *3,* 135–149.

Felkenes, G. T. *The criminal justice system.* Englewood Cliffs, N.J.: Prentice-Hall, 1973.

Festinger, L. A theory of social comparison processes. *Human Relations,* 1954, *7,* 117–140.

Festinger, L., Schachter, S., & Back, K. *Social pressures in informal groups.* New York: Harper, 1950.

Fischer, C. T. Unpublished research interviews with victims of crime. Duquesne University, 1977.

Fishman, J. J. The social and occupational mobility of prosecutors: New York City. In W.F. McDonald (Ed.), *The prosecutor.* Beverly Hills, Calif.: Sage, 1979.

Flanagan, T. J., Hindelang, M. J., & Gottfredson, M. R. (Eds.). *Sourcebook of criminal justice statistics—1979.* Washington, D. C.: U. S. Government Printing Office, 1980.

Fontaine, G., & Emily, C. Causal attribution and judicial discretion: A look at the verbal behavior of municipal court judges. *Law and Human Behavior,* 1978, *2,* 323–337.

Forst, B., & Brosi, K. B. A theoretical and empirical analysis of the prosecutor. *Journal of Legal Studies,* 1977, *6,* 177–191.

Fosdick, R. B. *American police systems.* Montclair, N. J.: Patterson Smith, 1972.

Fox, V. *Introduction to criminology.* Englewood Cliffs, N. J.: Prentice-Hall, 1975.

Frankel, M. E. Lawlessness in sentencing. *University of Cincinnati Law Review,* 1972, *41,* 1–54.

Frase, R. S. The decision to file federal criminal charges: A quantitative study of prosecutorial discretion. *University of Chicago Law Review*, 1980, *47*, 246–330.

Gallup, G. H. *The Gallup Poll: Public opinion 1972–1977.* Wilmington, Del.: Scholarly Resources, Inc., 1978.

Garber, R. M., & Maslach, C. The parole hearing: Decision or justification? *Law and Human Behavior*, 1977, *1*, 261–281.

Garcia, L. I., & Griffitt, W. Impact of testimonial evidence as a function of witness characteristics. *Bulletin of the Psychonomic Society*, 1978, *11*, 37–40.

Gaylin, W. *Partial justice: A study of bias in sentencing.* New York: Knopf, 1974.

Gelfand, D. M., Hartman, D. P., Walder, P., & Page, B. Who reports shoplifters? A field-experimental study. *Journal of Personality and Social Psychology*, 1973, *25*, 276–285.

Georgetown Law Journal, Project criminal procedure, 1978, *67*, 317–698.

Georgia Board of Pardons and Paroles. Parole decision guidelines make a better parole system, 1979.

Gerbasi, K. C., Zuckerman, M., & Reis, H. T. Justice needs a new blindfold: A review of mock jury research. *Psychological Bulletin*, 1977, *84*, 323–345.

Gigler, R. Burglar alarms trip police-security firms feud. *Pittsburgh Press*, December 12, 1976, p. 1F.

Glaser, D. *The effectiveness of a prison and parole system.* New York: Bobbs-Merrill, 1964.

Gleason, S. E. Hustling: The "inside" economy of a prison. *Federal Probation*, 1978, *42*, 32–40.

Goffman, E. *Asylums: Essays on the social situation of mental patients and other inmates.* Garden City, N. Y.: Anchor Books, 1961.

Goldberg, F. Toward expansion of *Witherspoon:* Capital scruples, jury bias, and the use of psychological data to raise presumptions in the law. *Harvard Civil Rights—Civil Liberties Law Review*, 1970, *5*, 53–69.

Goldfarb, R. L. *Ransom.* New York: Harper & Row, 1965.

Goldfarb, R. L., & Singer, L. R. *After conviction.* New York: Simon & Schuster, 1973.

Goldkamp, J. S., & Gottfredson, M. R. Bail decision making and pretrial detention: Surfacing judicial policy. *Law and Human Behavior*, 1979, *3*, 227–249.

Goldman, N. The differential selection of juvenile offenders for court appearance. Unpublished doctoral dissertation, University of Chicago, 1951.

Goldstein, B. *Screening for emotional and psychological fitness in correctional officer hiring.* Washington, D. C.: American Bar Association, 1975.

Goldstein, J. Police discretion not to invoke the criminal process: Low-visibility decisions in the administration of justice. *Yale Law Journal*, 1960, *69*, 543–594.

Gottfredson, D. M., Wilkins, L. T., & Hoffman, P. B. *Guidelines for parole and sentencing.* Lexington, Mass.: Lexington Books, 1978

Gottfredson, M. R. Parole board decision making: A study of disparity reduction and the impact of institutional behavior. *Journal of Criminal Law and Criminology*, 1979, *70*, 77–88.

Gouldner, A. W. The norm of reciprocity: A preliminary statement. *American Sociological Review*, 1960, *25*, 161–178.

Green, E. Sentencing practices of criminal court judges. *American Journal of Correction*, July-August 1960, pp. 32–35.

Green, E. *Judicial attitudes in sentencing.* London: Macmillan, 1961.

Greenberg, M. S. A preliminary statement on a theory of indebtedness. In M. S. Greenberg (Chair), *Justice in social exchange.* Symposium presented at the meeting of the Western Psychological Association, San Diego, March 1968.

Greenberg, M. S. A theory of indebtedness. In K. J. Gergen, M. S. Greenberg, &

R. H. Willis (Eds.), *Social exchange: Advances in theory and research*. New York: Plenum, 1980.

Greenberg, M. S., Ruback, R. B., & Wilson, C. E. Theft victims' decision to call the police: The supportive role of the bystander. Manuscript submitted for publication, 1981.

Greenberg, M. S., Ruback, R. B., Wilson, C. E., & Mills, M. K. Theft victims' decision to call the police: An experimental approach. In G. Cooke (Ed.), *The role of the forensic psychologist*. Springfield, Ill.: Charles C Thomas, 1980.

Greenberg, M. S., Wilson, C. E., Carretta, T., & DeMay, A. Historical trends in perceived seriousness of crimes: Thurstone-Coombs revisited. *Replications in Social Psychology*, 1979, *1*, 36–38.

Greenberg, M. S., Wilson, C. E., & Mills, M. K. Victim decision-making: An experimental approach. In V. J. Konečni & E. B. Ebbesen (Eds.), *The criminal justice system: A social-psychological analysis*. San Francisco: W. H. Freeman, 1982.

Greenberg, M. S., Wilson, C. E., Ruback, R. B., & Mills, M. K. Social and emotional determinants of victim crime reporting. *Social Psychology Quarterly*, 1979, *42*, 364–372.

Greenwood, P. W., Chaiken, J. M., Petersilia, J., & Prusoff, L. *The criminal investigation process*. Vol. 3: *Observations and analysis*. Santa Monica, Calif.: Rand, 1975.

Gregory, W. L., Mowen, J. C., & Linder, D. E. Social psychology and plea bargaining: Applications, methodology, and theory. *Journal of Personality and Social Psychology*, 1978, *36*, 1521–1530.

Griffitt, W., & Jackson, T. Simulated jury decisions: Influence of jury-defendant attitude similarity-dissimilarity. *Social Behavior and Personality*, 1973, *1*, 1–7.

Grisso, T., Sales, B. D., & Bayless, S. Law-related graduate courses in psychology departments: A national survey. Paper presented at the meeting of the American Psychology-Law Society, Baltimore, October 1979.

Hagan, J. Extra-legal attributes and criminal sentencing: An assessment of a sociological viewpoint. *Law and Society Review*, 1974, *8*, 357–383.

Hagan, J. Law, order, and sentencing: A study of attitude in action. *Sociometry*, 1975, *38*, 374–384.

Hager, P. Debt repaid to society—literally. *Pittsburgh Press*, September 4, 1977, p. 13A.

Hakeem, M. Prediction of parole outcomes from summaries of case histories. *Journal of Criminology, Criminal Law, and Police Science*, 1961, *52*, 145–150.

Hall, D. J. Role of the victim in the prosecution and disposition of a criminal case. *Vanderbilt Law Review*, 1975, *28*, 931–985.

Haney, C., Banks, C., & Zimbardo, P. Interpersonal dynamics in a simulated prison. *International Journal of Criminology and Penology*, 1973, *1*, 69–97.

Haney, C., & Zimbardo, P. The socialization into criminality: On becoming a prisoner and a guard. In J. L. Tapp & F. J. Levine (Eds.), *Law, justice, and the individual in society: Psychological and legal issues*. New York: Holt, Rinehart & Winston, 1977.

Hans, V., & Doob, A. N. Section 12 of the Canada Evidence Act and the deliberations of simulated jurors. *Criminal Law Quarterly*, 1976, *18*, 235–253.

Harding, A. *A social history of English law*. London: Penguin, 1966.

Harries, K. D., & Lura, R. P. The geography of justice: Sentencing variations in U. S. judicial districts. *Judicature*, 1974, *57*, 392–401.

Harvey, J. H., & Weary, G. *Perspectives on attributional processes*. Dubuque, Iowa: William C. Brown, 1981.

Hatvany, N., & Strack, F. The impact of a discredited key witness. *Journal of Applied Social Psychology*, 1980, *10*, 490–509.

Hawkins, G. *The prison.* Chicago: University of Chicago Press, 1976.

He didn't sit still for subway holdup. *New York Times,* June 4, 1978, p. 6, sec. 4.

Hegland, K. F. *Trial and practice skills in a nutshell.* St. Paul, Minn.: West, 1978.

Heider, F. Social perception and phenomenal causality. *Psychological Review,* 1944, *51*, 358–374.

Heider, F. *The psychology of interpersonal relations.* New York: Wiley, 1958.

Heinz, A. M., Heinz, J. P., Senderowitz, S. J., & Vance, M. A. Sentencing by parole board: An evaluation. *Journal of Criminal Law and Criminology,* 1976, *67*, 1–31.

Heinz, A. M., & Kerstetter, W. A. Victim participation in plea-bargaining: A field experiment. In W. F. McDonald & J. A. Cramer (Eds.), *Plea-bargaining.* Lexington, Mass.: Lexington Books, 1980.

Hemsley, G. D., & Doob, A. N. The effect of looking behavior on perceptions of a communicator's credibility. *Journal of Applied Social Psychology,* 1978, *8*, 136–144.

Hendrick, C., & Shaffer, D. R. Effect of pleading the Fifth Amendment on perceptions of guilt and morality. *Bulletin of the Psychonomic Society,* 1975, *6*, 449–452.

Heumann, M. *Plea bargaining.* Chicago: University of Chicago Press, 1978.

Hindelang, M. J. *Criminal victimization in eight American cities.* Cambridge, Mass.: Ballinger, 1976.

Hindelang, M. J., & Davis, B. J. Forcible rape in the United States: A statistical profile. In D. Chappell, R. Geis, & G. Geis (Eds.), *Forcible rape: The crime, the victim, and the offender.* New York: Columbia University Press, 1977.

Hindelang, M. J., & Gottfredson, M. The victim's decision not to invoke the criminal justice process. In W. F. McDonald (Ed.), *Criminal justice and the victim.* Beverly Hills, Calif.: Sage, 1976.

Hogarth, J. *Sentencing as a human process.* Toronto: University of Toronto Press, 1971.

Holland, T. R., Holt, N., & Brewer, D. L. Social roles and information utilization in parole decision-making. *Journal of Social Psychology,* 1978, *106*, 111–120.

Homans, G. C. *Social behavior: Its elementary forms* (2nd ed.). New York: Harcourt Brace & World, 1961.

Homans, G. C. *Social behavior: Its elementary forms* (2nd ed.). New York: Harcourt Brace Jovanovich, 1974.

Hopkins, J. R. Sexual behavior in adolescence. *Journal of Social Issues,* 1977, *33*(2), 67–85.

Horowitz, I. A. Juror selection: A comparison of two methods in several criminal cases. *Journal of Applied Social Psychology,* 1980, *10*, 86–99.

Hovland, C. I., Janis, I. L., & Kelley, H. H. *Communication and persuasion.* New Haven, Conn.: Yale University Press, 1953.

How safe is immunity? *Time,* August 11, 1980, p. 58.

Huston, T. H., Ruggiero, M., Conner, R., & Geis, G. Bystander intervention into crime: A study based on naturally-occurring episodes. *Social Psychology Quarterly,* 1981, *44*, 14–23.

Illinois denies parole bid. *Pittsburgh Press,* September 16, 1976, p. 5A.

Irwin, J. *The felon.* Englewood Cliffs, N. J.: Prentice-Hall, 1970.

Irwin, J. Adaptation to being corrected: Corrections from the convict's perspective. In D. Gleason (Ed.), *Handbook of criminology,* Chicago: Rand McNally, 1974.

Ittelson, W. H., Proshansky, H. M., Rivlin, L.G., & Winkel, G. H. *An introduction to environmental psychology.* New York: Holt, Rinehart & Winston, 1974.

Izzett, R., & Leginski, W. Group discussion and the influence of defendant characteristics in a simulated jury setting. *Journal of Social Psychology,* 1974, *93*, 271–279.

Jacobs, J. B. What prison guards think: A profile of the Illinois force. *Crime and Delinquency,* 1978, *24,* 185–196.

Jacobs, J. B. Race relations and the prisoner subculture. In N. Morris & M. Tonry (Eds.), *Crime and justice: An annual review of research* (Vol. 1). Chicago: University of Chicago Press, 1979.

Jacoby, J. E. The charging policies of prosecutors. In W. F. McDonald (Ed.), *The prosecutor.* Beverly Hills, Calif.: Sage, 1979.

Janoff-Bulman, R. Characterological versus behavioral self-blame: Inquiries into depression and rape. *Journal of Personality and Social Psychology,* 1979, *37,* 1798–1809.

Johnson, C., & Scott, B. Eyewitness testimony and suspect identification as a function of arousal, sex of witness, and scheduling of interrogation. Paper presented at the meeting of the American Psychological Association, Washington, D. C., September 1976.

Jones, C., & Aronson, E. Attribution of fault to a rape victim as a function of respectability of the victim. *Journal of Personality and Social Psychology,* 1973, *26,* 415–419.

Jones, E. E., & Davis, K. E. From acts to dispositions: The attribution process in person perception. In L. Berkowitz (Ed.), *Advances in experimental social psychology* (Vol. 2). New York: Academic Press, 1965.

Jones, E. E., & McGillis, D. Correspondent inferences and the attribution cube: A comparative reappraisal. In J. H. Harvey, W. J. Ickes, & R. F. Kidd (Eds.), *New directions in attribution research* (Vol. 1). Hillsdale, N. J.: Erlbaum, 1976.

Jones, E. E., & Nisbett, R. E. The actor and observer: Divergent perceptions of the causes of behavior. In E. E. Jones, D. E. Kanouse, H. H. Kelley, R. E. Nisbett, S. Valins, & B. Weiner (Eds.), *Attribution: Perceiving the causes of behavior.* Morristown, N. J.: General Learning Press, 1972.

Judson, C. J., Pandell, J. J., Owens, J. B., McIntosh, J. L., & Matschullat, D. L. A study of the California penalty jury in first degree murder cases. *Stanford Law Review,* 1969, *21,* 1302–1497.

Juhnke, R., Vought, C., Pyszczynski, T. A., Dane, F. C., Losure, B. D., & Wrightsman, L. S. Effects of presentation mode upon mock jurors' reactions to a trial. *Personality and Social Psychology Bulletin,* 1979, *5,* 36–39.

Jurors refuse to indict wife in husband's death. *Atlanta Journal and Constitution,* November 22, 1980, p. 11A.

Jurow, G. New data on the effect of a "death qualified" jury on the guilt determination process. *Harvard Law Review,* 1971, *84,* 567–611.

Jury acquits man of arson charge after nine hours of deliberation. *Recorder and Times* (Brockville, Ontario), October 18, 1980, p. 3.

Kahneman, D., & Tversky, A. On the psychology of prediction. *Psychological Review.* 1973, *80,* 237–251.

Kalven, H., Jr., & Zeisel, H. *The American jury.* Boston: Little, Brown, 1966.

Kaplan, J. The prosecutorial discretion—A comment. *Northwestern University Law Review,* 1965, *60,* 174–193.

Kaplan, K. J., & Simon, R. J. Latitude and severity of sentencing options, race of the victim, and decisions of simulated jurors: Some issues arising from the Algiers Motel trial. *Law and Society Review,* 1972, *7,* 87–98.

Kaplan, M. F., & Kemmerick, G. D. Juror judgment as information integration: Combining evidential and nonevidential information. *Journal of Personality and Social Psychology,* 1974, *30,* 493–499.

Kaplan, M. F., & Miller, L. E. Reducing the effects of juror bias. *Journal of Personality and Social Psychology,* 1978, *36,* 1443–1455.

Kassin, S. M., & Wrightsman, L. S. On the requirements of proof: The timing of judicial instruction and mock juror verdicts. *Journal of Personality and Social Psychology,* 1979, *37,* 1877–1887.

Kastenmeier, R. W., & Eglit, H. C. Parole release decisionmaking: Rehabilitation, expertise, and the demise of mythology, *American University Law Review,* 1973, *22,* 477–525.

Kelley, H. H. Attribution theory in social psychology. In D. Levine (Ed.), *Nebraska Symposium on Motivation* (Vol. 15). Lincoln: University of Nebraska Press, 1967.

Kelley, H. H. Attribution in social interaction. In E. E. Jones, D. E. Kanouse, H. H. Kelley, R. E. Nisbett, S. Valins, & B. Weiner (Eds.), *Attribution: Perceiving the causes of behavior.* Morristown, N.J.: General Learning Press, 1972. (a)

Kelley, H. H. Causal schemata and the attribution process. In E. E. Jones, D. E. Kanouse, H. H. Kelley, R. E. Nisbett, S. Valins, & B. Weiner (Eds.), *Attribution: Perceiving the causes of behavior.* Morristown, N.J.: General Learning Press, 1972. (b)

Kerr, N. L. Beautiful and blameless: Effects of victim attractiveness and responsibility on mock jurors' verdicts. *Personality and Social Psychology Bulletin,* 1978, *4,* 470–482. (a)

Kerr, N. L. Severity of prescribed penalty and mock jurors' verdicts. *Journal of Personality and Social Psychology,* 1978, *36,* 1431–1442. (b)

Kerr, N. L., Atkin, R. S., Stasser, G., Meek, D., Holt, R. W., & Davis, J. H. Guilt beyond a reasonable doubt: Effects of concept definition and assigned decision rule on the judgments of mock jurors. *Journal of Personality and Social Psychology,* 1976, *34,* 282–294.

Kerr, N. L., Nerenz, D., & Herrick, D. Role playing and the study of jury behavior. *Sociological Methods and Research,* 1979, *7,* 337–355.

Kerstetter, W. A., & Heinz, A. M. Pretrial settlement conference: An evaluation. Washington, D. C.: Department of Justice, 1979.

Keyes, R. Dressed to run . . . from the law. *Pittsburgh Press,* November 30, 1980, Family Magazine, p. 2.

Kidd, R. F. Crime reporting: Toward a social psychological model. *Criminology,* 1979, *17,* 380–394.

King, B. Prisoners get early freedom: DOR policy upsets Fulton DA. *Atlanta Constitution,* April, 10, 1981, p. 1A.

Kingsnorth, R. Decision-making in a parole bureaucracy. *Journal of Research in Crime and Delinquency,* 1969, *6,* 210–218.

Kinzel, A. F. Body-buffer zone in violent prisoners. *American Journal of Psychiatry,* 1970, *127,* 59–64.

Kirby, M. P. Recent research findings in pretrial release. Unpublished paper, Pretrial Services Resource Center, Washington, D. C., September 1977.

Klotter, J. C. *Legal guide for police.* Cincinnati: Anderson, 1977.

Knudten, R. D., Meade, A., Knudten, M., & Doerner, W. The victim in the administration of justice: Problems and perceptions. In W. F. McDonald (Ed.), *Criminal justice and the victim.* Beverly Hills, Calif.: Sage, 1976.

Knudten, R. D., Meade, A. C., Knudten, M.S., & Doerner, W. G. *Victims and witnesses: Their experiences with crime and the criminal justice system* (Executive summary). Washington, D. C.: U. S. Government Printing Office, 1977.

Konečni, V. J., & Ebbesen, E. B. External validity of research in legal psychology. *Law and Human Behavior,* 1979, *3,* 39–70.

Koza, P., & Doob, A. N. The relationship of pre-trial custody to the outcome of the trial. *Criminal Law Quarterly,* 1975, *17,* 391–400.

Krantz, S. *Corrections and prisoners' rights in a nutshell.* St. Paul, Minn.: West, 1976.

LaFave, W. R. *Arrest: The decision to take a suspect into custody.* Boston: Little, Brown, 1965.

La Fave, W. R. The prosecutor's discretion in the United States. *American Journal of Comparative Law*, 1970, *18*, 532–548.

La Fave, W. R. *Search and seizure: A treatise on the Fourth Amendment* (Vol. 1). St. Paul, Minn.: West, 1978.

LaFave, W. R., & Scott, A. W., Jr. *Handbook on criminal law.* St. Paul, Minn.: West, 1972.

Landy, D., & Aronson, E. The influence of the character of the criminal and his victim on the decisions of simulated jurors. *Journal of Experimental Social Psychology*, 1969, *5*, 141–152.

L'Armand, K., & Pepitone, A. On attribution of responsibility and punishment for rape. Paper presented at the meeting of the American Psychological Association, San Francisco, August 1977.

Latané, B., & Darley, J. M. *The unresponsive bystander: Why doesn't he help?* New York: Appleton-Century-Crofts, 1970.

Law Enforcement Assistance Administration. *Crimes and victims: A report on the Dayton-San Jose pilot survey of victimization.* Washington, D. C.: U. S. Government Printing Office, 1974.

Law Enforcement Assistance Administration. *Criminal victimization in the United States—1973.* Washington, D. C.: U. S. Government Printing Office, 1976. (a)

Law Enforcement Assistance Administration. *Criminal victimization in the United States—1976.* Washington, D. C.: U. S. Government Printing Office, 1976. (b)

Law Enforcement Assistance Administration. *Criminal victimization in the United States: A comparison of 1974 and 1975 findings.* Washington, D. C.: U. S. Government Printing Office, 1977. (a)

Law Enforcement Assistance Administration. *Forcible rape: A national survey of the response by police* (Vol. 1). Washington, D. C.: U. S. Government Printing Office, 1977. (b)

Law Enforcement Assistance Administration. *Forcible rape: A national survey of the response by prosecutors* (Vol. 1). Washington, D. C.: U. S. Government Printing Office, 1977. (c)

Law Enforcement Assistance Administration. *Trends in expenditure and employment data for the criminal justice system 1971–1977.* Washington, D. C.: U. S. Government Printing Office, 1980.

Leippe, M. R., Wells, G. L., & Ostrom, T. M. Crime seriousness as a determinant of accuracy in eyewitness identification. *Journal of Applied Psychology*, 1978, *63*, 345–351.

Lemert, E. M., & Rosberg, J. The administration of justice to minority groups in Los Angeles County. *University of California Publications in Culture and Society*, 1948, *2*, 1–27.

Lempert, R. O. Uncovering nondiscernible differences: Empirical research and the jury-size cases. *Michigan Law Review*, 1975, *73*, 644–708.

Lerner, M. J. The justice motive in social behavior: Introduction. *Journal of Social Issues*, 1975, *31*(3), 1–19.

Lerner, M. J., & Miller, D. T. Just world research and the attribution process: Looking back and ahead. *Psychological Bulletin*, 1978, *85*, 1030–1051.

Lerner, M. J., Miller, D. T., & Holmes, J. G. Deserving and the emergence of forms of justice. In L. Berkowitz (Ed.), *Advances in experimental social psychology* (Vol. 9). New York: Academic Press, 1976.

Letkemann, P. *Crime as work.* Englewood Cliffs, N. J.: Prentice-Hall, 1973.

Leventhal, G. S. Fairness in social relationships. In J. W. Thibaut, J. T. Spence, & R. C. Carson (Eds.), *Contemporary topics in social psychology.* Morristown, N. J.: General Learning Press, 1976.

Levine, J. P. The potential for crime overreporting in criminal victimization surveys. *Criminology,* 1976, *14,* 307–330.

Lockwood, D. *Prison sexual violence.* New York: Elsevier North-Holland, 1980.

Loftus, E. F. Reconstructing memory: The incredible eyewitness. *Psychology Today,* December 1974, pp. 116–119.

Loftus, E. F. Leading questions and the eyewitness report. *Cognitive Psychology,* 1975, *7,* 560–572.

Loftus, E. F. *Eyewitness testimony.* Cambridge, Mass.: Harvard University Press, 1979.

Loftus, E. F., & Palmer, J. C. Reconstruction of automobile destruction: An example of the interaction between language and memory. *Journal of Verbal Learning and Verbal Behavior,* 1974, *13,* 585–589.

Lundman, R. J. Routine police arrest practices: A commonweal perspective. *Social Problems,* 1974, *22,* 128–141.

Many queries, few replies in bail case. *New York Times,* April 22, 1979, p. 1, sec. 4.

Maryniak, P. DA staffers leave for greener pastures. *Pittsburgh Press,* June 18, 1979, p. 4A.

May, E. Prison guards in America. *Corrections,* 1976, *2*(6), 3–5; 12; 36–40.

McCain, G., Cox, V. C., & Paulus, P. B. The effect of prison crowding on inmate behavior. Final report on LEAA grant 78-NI-AX-0019. University of Texas at Arlington, 1980.

McCleary, R. On becoming a client. *Journal of Social Issues,* 1978, *34*(4), 57–75.

McCleery, R. H. The governmental process and informal social control. In D. R. Cressey (Ed.), *The prison: Studies in institutional organization and change.* New York: Holt, Rinehart & Winston, 1961.

McConahay, J. B., Mullin, C. J., & Frederick, J. The uses of social science in trials with political and racial overtones: The trial of Joan Little. *Law and Contemporary Problems,* 1977, *41,* 205–229.

McCorkle, L. W., & Korn, R. Resocialization within walls. In D. Dressler (Ed.), *Readings in criminology and penology.* New York: Columbia University Press, 1964.

McDonald W. F. The prosecutor's domain. In W. F. McDonald (Ed.), *The prosecutor.* Beverly Hills, Calif.: Sage, 1979.

McDonald, W. F., Cramer, J. A., & Rossman, H. H. Prosecutorial bluffing and the case against plea-bargaining. In W. F. McDonald & J. A. Cramer (Eds.), *Plea-bargaining.* Lexington, Mass.: Heath, 1980.

McFatter, R. M. Sentencing strategies and justice: Effects of punishment philosophy on sentencing decisions. *Journal of Personality and Social Psychology,* 1978, *36,* 1490–1500.

Medea, A., & Thompson, K. *Against rape.* New York: Farrar, Straus & Giroux, 1974.

Menninger, K. *The crime of punishment.* New York: Viking Press, 1968.

The mental health mess. *Atlanta Journal and Constitution,* January 11, 1981, p. 2D.

Merola, M. Modern prosecutorial techniques. *Criminal Law Bulletin,* 1980, *16,* 232–272.

Middle-class leaders in Harlem ask for crackdown on crime. *New York Times,* December 24, 1968, pp. 25, 46, sec. L.

Miles. A. P. The utility of case records in probation and parole. *Journal of Criminal Law, Criminology, and Police Science,* 1965, *56,* 285–293.

Miller, F. W. *Prosecution: The decision to charge a suspect with a crime.* Boston: Little, Brown, 1970.

Miller, W. Ideology and criminal justice policy: Some current issues. *Journal of Criminal Law and Criminology*, 1973, *64*, 141–162.

Milner, N. A. *The court and local law enforcement: The impact of Miranda*. Beverly Hills, Calif.: Sage, 1971.

Mitchell, H. E., & Byrne, D. The defendant's dilemma: Effects of jurors' attitudes and authoritarianism. *Journal of Personality and Social Psychology*, 1973, *25*, 123–129.

Monahan, J. (Ed.). *Who is the client?* Washington, D. C.: American Psychological Association, 1980.

Mooney, B. Inmate: New warden, guards in power duel. *Atlanta Constitution*, November 18, 1980, p. 2C.

Moriarty, T. Crime, commitment, and the responsive bystander: Two field experiments. *Journal of Personality and Social Psychology*, 1975, *31*, 370–376.

Morris, N. *The future of imprisonment*. Chicago: University of Chicago Press, 1974.

Morris, N., & Hawkins, G. Rehabilitation: Rhetoric and reality. *Federal Probation*, 1970, *34*(12), 9–17.

Moss, C. S., Hosford, R. E., & Anderson, W. R. Sexual assault in prison. *Psychological Reports*, 1979, *44*, 823–828.

Moulds, E. F. Chivalry and paternalism: Disparities of treatment in the criminal justice system. In S. K. Datesman & F. R. Scarpatti (Eds.), *Women, crime, and justice*. New York: Oxford University Press, 1980.

Moylan, C. E., Jr. Hearsay and probable cause: An *Aguilar* and *Spinelli* primer. *Mercer Law Review*, 1974, *25*, 741–786.

Munsterberg, H. *On the witness stand*. New York: S. S. McClure, 1908.

Myers, D. G., & Kaplan, M. F. Group-induced polarization in simulated juries. *Personality and Social Psychology Bulletin*, 1976, *2*, 63–66.

Myers, D. G., & Lamm, H. The group polarization phenomenon. *Psychological Bulletin*, 1976, *83*, 602–627.

Myers, M. A. Social contexts and attributions of criminal responsibility. *Social Psychology Quarterly*, 1980, *43*, 405–419.

Myers, M. A., & Hagan, J. Private and public trouble: Prosecutors and the allocation of court resources. *Social Problems*, 1979, *26*, 439–451.

Nacci, P. L., Teitelbaum, H. E., & Prather, J. Population density and inmate misconduct rates in the federal prison system. *Federal Probation*, 1977, *41*(2), 26–31.

Nagel, I. H. The behavior of formal law: A study of bail decisions. Unpublished manuscript, Indiana University School of Law, 1981.

Nagel, I. H., Cardascia, J., & Ross, C. E. Sex differences in the processing of criminal defendants. In D. K. Weisberg (Ed.), *Women and the law: The social historical perspective*. Cambridge, Mass.: Schenkman, 1980.

Nagel, S. *The legal process from a behavioral perspective*. Homewood, Ill.: Dorsey Press, 1969.

Nagel, S. S. Judicial backgrounds and criminal cases. *Journal of Criminal Law, Criminology, and Police Science*, 1962, *53*, 333–339.

Nagel, S. S., & Neef, M. Plea bargaining, decision theory, and equilibrium models: Part I. *Indiana Law Journal*, 1976, *51*, 987–1024. (a)

Nagel, S. S., & Neef, M. Plea bargaining, decision theory, and equilibrium models: Part II. *Indiana Law Journal*, 1976, *52*, 1–61. (b)

National Advisory Commission on Criminal Justice Standards and Goals. *Corrections*. Washington, D. C.: U. S. Government Printing Office, 1973.

National Advisory Commission on Criminal Justice Standards and Goals. *A call for citizen action: Crime prevention and the citizen*. Washington, D. C.: U. S. Government Printing Office, 1974.

National District Attorneys Association. *The prosecutor's screening function: Case evaluation and control.* Washington, D. C.: National Center for Prosecution Management, 1973.

National Probation and Parole Association. *Guides for sentencing.* New York: Carnegie Press, 1957.

Nedrud, D. R. The career prosecutor. *Journal of Criminal Law, Criminology, and Police Science,* 1960, *51,* 343–355.

Nemeth, C. Interactions between jurors as a function of majority vs. unanimity decision rules. *Journal of Applied Social Psychology,* 1977, 7, 38–56.

Newman, D. J. Pleading guilty for considerations: A study of bargain justice. *Journal of Criminal Law, Criminology, and Police Science,* 1956, 47, 780–790.

Newman, D. J. *Conviction: The determination of guilt or innocence without trial.* Boston: Little, Brown, 1966.

Newman, D. J. Role and process in the criminal court. In D. Glaser (Ed.), *Handbook of criminology.* Chicago: Rand McNally, 1974.

New York State Special Commission on Attica. *Attica: The official report of the New York State Special Commission on Attica.* New York: Bantam Books, 1972.

Niederhoffer, A. *Behind the shield: The police in urban society.* Garden City, N. Y.: Doubleday, 1967.

Nimmer, R. T. The system impact of criminal justice reforms. In J. L. Tapp & F. J. Levine (Eds.), *Law, justice, and the individual in society: Psychological and legal issues.* New York: Holt, Rinehart & Winston, 1977.

Nisbett, R. E., Borgida, E., Crandall, R., & Reed, H. Popular induction: Information is not necessarily informative. In J. S. Carroll & J. W. Payne (Eds.), *Cognition and social behavior.* Hillsdale, N. J.: Erlbaum, 1976.

No prosecution in suicide. *Boston Globe,* August 12, 1980, p. 4.

Oaks, D. H. Studying the exclusionary rule in search and seizure. *University of Chicago Law Review,* 1970, *37,* 665–753.

O'Mara, J. J. Standard jury charges: Findings of a pilot project. *Pennsylvania Bar Association Quarterly,* 1972, *43,* 166–175.

Ostrow, M. Letter in response to Rosenhan's article "On being sane in insane places." *Science,* 1973, *180,* 356–365.

Packer, H. L. Two models of the criminal process. *University of Pennsylvania Law Review,* 1964, *113,* 1–68.

Packer, H. L. *The limits of the criminal sanction.* Stanford, Calif.: Stanford University Press, 1968.

Parkinson, M. G. Language behavior and courtroom success. Paper presented at the meeting of the British Psychological Society, University of Bristol, England, July 1979.

Partridge, A., & Eldridge, W. B. *The second circuit sentencing study: A report to the judges of the second circuit.* Washington, D.C.: Federal Judicial Center, 1974.

Paulus, P. B., Cox, V. C., McCain, G., & Chandler, J. Some effects of crowding in a prison environment. *Journal of Applied Social Psychology,* 1975, *5,* 86–91.

Penrod, S. Evaluating social scientific methods of jury selection. Paper presented at the meeting of the Midwestern Psychological Association, St. Louis, May 1980.

Penrod, S., Loftus, E. F., & Winkler, J. The reliability of eyewitness testimony: A psychological perspective. In R. M. Bray & N. Kerr (Eds.), *Psychology of the courtroom.* New York: Academic Press, in press.

Pepinsky, H. E. Police decision-making. In D. M. Gottfredson (Ed.), *Decision-making in the criminal justice system: Reviews and essays.* Washington, D. C.: U. S. Government Printing Office, 1975.

Pepitone, A., & DiNubile, M. Contrast effects in judgments of crime severity and the punishment of criminal violators. *Journal of Personality and Social Psychology*, 1976, *33*, 448–459.

Phares, E. J., & Wilson, K. G. Responsibility attribution: Role of outcome severity, situational ambiguity, and internal-external control. *Journal of Personality*, 1972, *40*, 392–406.

Phillips, S. *No heroes, no villains: The story of a murder trial*. New York: Vintage Books, 1978.

Piliavin, I., & Briar, S. Police encounters with juveniles. *American Journal of Sociology*, 1964, *70*, 206–214.

President's Commission on Law Enforcement and Administration of Justice. *The challenge of crime in a free society*. Washington, D. C.: U. S. Government Printing Office, 1967. (a)

President's Commission on Law Enforcement and Administration of Justice. *Task force report: The police*. Washington, D. C.: U. S. Government Printing Office, 1967. (b)

Probation report urged freedom for Berkowitz. *Dallas Morning News*, August 19, 1977, p. 12A.

Quinney, R. *The social reality of crime*. Boston: Little, Brown, 1970.

Rankin, A. The effect of pretrial detention. *New York University Law Review*, 1964, *39*, 641–664.

Reid, S. T. *Crime and criminology*. Hinsdale, Ill.: Dryden Press, 1976.

Reiss, A. J., Jr. *Studies in crime and law enforcement in major metropolitan areas*. Field Surveys III, President's Commission on Law Enforcement and Administration of Justice. Washington, D. C.: U. S. Government Printing Office, 1967.

Reiss, A. J., Jr. *The police and the public*. New Haven, Conn.: Yale University Press, 1971.

Reiss, A. J., Jr. Public prosecutors and criminal prosecution in the United States of America. *Juridical Review*, April 1975, *20*, 1–21.

Rhodes, W. M. Plea bargaining: Who gains? Who loses? (Executive summary). Unpublished manuscript, Institute for Law and Social Research, Washington, D. C., 1978.

Rosenhan, D. L. On being sane in insane places. *Science*, 1973, *179*, 250–258.

Ross, L. The intuitive psychologist and his shortcomings: Distortions in the attribution process. In L. Berkowitz (Ed.), *Advances in experimental social psychology* (Vol. 10). New York: Academic Press, 1977.

Rossett, A. I. The negotiated guilty plea. *The Annals: Combatting Crime*, 1967, *374*, 70–81.

Rossett, A. I. Trial and discretion in Dutch criminal justice. *UCLA Law Review*, 1972, *19*, 353–390.

Rothblatt, H. B. Bargaining strategy. *Trial*, 1973, *9*(3), 20–21.

Rothman, D. J. *The discovery of the asylum: Social order and disorder in the new republic*. Boston: Little, Brown, 1971.

Rotter, J. B. Generalized expectancies for internal versus external control of reinforcement. *Psychological Monographs*, 1966, *80*(1, Whole No. 609).

Ruback, R. B. Perceived honesty in the parole interview. *Personality and Social Psychology Bulletin*, in press.

Rubinstein, J. *City police*. New York: Farrar, Straus & Giroux, 1973.

Rubinstein, M. L., & White, T. J. Alaska's ban on plea-bargaining. In W. F. McDonald & J. A. Cramer (Eds.), *Plea-bargaining*. Lexington, Mass.: Lexington Books, 1980.

Saks, M. J. "Scientific" jury selection: Social scientists can't rig juries. *Psychology Today*, August 1976, pp. 48–50; 55–57.

Saks, M. J. *Jury verdicts*. Lexington, Mass.: Heath, 1977.

Saks, M. J., & Hastie, R. *Social psychology in court*. New York: Van Nostrand Reinhold, 1978.

Scacco, A. M. *Rape in prison*. Springfield, Ill.: Charles C Thomas, 1975.

Scaring off witnesses: Testifying can be time consuming, costly—and risky. *Time*, September 11, 1978, p. 41.

Schrag, C. Leadership among prison inmates. In D. Dressler (Ed.), *Readings in criminology and penology*. New York: Columbia University Press, 1964.

Schulhofer, S. J. Due process of sentencing. *University of Pennsylvania Law Review*, 1980, *128*, 733–828.

Schulman, J. A systematic approach to successful jury selection. *Guild Notes*, 1973, *2*, 13–20.

Schulman, J., Shaver, P., Colman, R., Emrich, B., & Christie, R. Recipe for a jury. *Psychology Today*, May 1973, pp. 37–44; 78–84.

Schwartz, S. H. Normative influences on altruism. In L. Berkowitz (Ed.), *Advances in experimental social psychology* (Vol. 10). New York: Academic Press, 1977.

Schwartz, S. H., & Gottlieb, A. Bystander reactions to a violent theft: Crime in Jerusalem. *Journal of Personality and Social Psychology*, 1976, *34*, 1188–1199.

Schwarz, L., Jennings, K., Petrillo, J., & Kidd, R. F. Role of commitments in the decision to stop a theft. *Journal of Social Psychology*, 1980, *110*, 183–192.

Scott, J. E., & Snider, P. J. Effects of different perceptions of penal institutions on the severity of punishment. In I. Drapkin & E. Viano (Eds.), *Victimology: A new focus* (Vol. 5). Lexington, Mass.: Lexington Books, 1973.

Seedman, A. A., & Hellman, P. *Chief*. New York: Avon, 1975.

Selby, J. W., Calhoun, L. G., & Brock, T. A. Sex differences in social perception of rape victims. *Personality and Social Psychology Bulletin*, 1977, *3*, 412–415.

Sellin, T. *Culture conflict and crime*. New York: Social Science Research Council, 1938.

Serrill, M. S. Is rehabilitation dead? *Corrections*, 1975, *1*(5), 3–7; 10–12; 21–32.

Shaffer, D. R., Rogel, M., & Hendrick, C. Intervention in the library: The effect of increased responsibility on bystander willingness to prevent a theft. *Journal of Applied Social Psychology*, 1975, *5*, 303–319.

Shaffer, D. R., & Sadowski, C. Effects of withheld evidence on juridic decisions II: Locus of withhold-strategy. *Personality and Social Psychology Bulletin*, 1979, *5*, 40–43.

Sheehan, S. *A prison and a prisoner*. Boston: Houghton Mifflin, 1978.

Shin, H. J. Do lesser pleas pay: Accommodations in the sentencing and parole processes. *Journal of Criminal Justice*, 1973, *1*, 27–42.

Shotland, R. L., & Stebbins, C. A. Bystander response to rape: Can a victim attract help? *Journal of Applied Social Psychology*, 1980, *10*, 510–527.

Shotland, R. L., & Straw, M. K. Bystander response to an assault: When a man attacks a woman. *Journal of Personality and Social Psychology*, 1976, *34*, 990–999.

Siegel, L. J., Sullivan, D. C., & Greene, J. R. Decision games applied to police decision making—An exploratory study of information usage. *Journal of Criminal Justice*, 1974, *2*, 131–146.

Sigall, H., & Ostrove N. Beautiful but dangerous: Effects of offender attractiveness and nature of the crime on juridic judgment. *Journal of Personality and Social Psychology*, 1975, *31*, 410–414.

Silberman, C. E. *Criminal violence, criminal justice*. New York: Random House, 1978.

Simon, R. J. (Ed.). *The jury and the defense of insanity*. Boston: Little, Brown, 1967.

Skogan, W. G. Crime and crime rates. In W. G. Skogan (Ed.), *Sample surveys of the victims of crime.* Cambridge, Mass.: Ballinger, 1976.

Skolnick, J. H. *Justice without trial: Law enforcement in democratic society* (2nd ed.). New York: Wiley, 1975.

Smith, E. D., & Hed, A. Effects of offenders' age and attractiveness on sentencing by mock juries. *Psychological Reports,* 1979, *44,* 691–694.

Smith, M. Percy Foreman: Top trial lawyer. *Life,* April 1, 1966, pp. 92–101.

Snyder, M., & Uranowitz, S. W. Reconstructing the past: Some cognitive consequences of person perception. *Journal of Personality and Social Psychology,* 1978, *36,* 941–950.

Sommer, R. *The end of imprisonment.* New York: Oxford University Press, 1976.

Southern California Law Review. Comment: Prosecutorial discretion in the initiation of criminal complaints. *Southern California Law Review,* 1969, *42,* 519–545.

Spitzer, R. L. On pseudoscience in science, logic in remission, and psychiatric diagnosis: A critique of Rosenhan's "On being sane in insane places." *Journal of Abnormal Psychology,* 1975, *84,* 442–452.

Stanko, E. A. Would you believe this woman? Prosecutorial screening for "credible" witnesses and a problem of justice. Paper presented at the meeting of the American Sociological Association, New York City, August 1980.

Stanley, D. T. *Prisoners among us: The problem of parole.* Washington, D.C.: Brookings Institution, 1976,

Steffensmeier, D. J., & Terry, R. M. Deviance and respectability: An observational study of reactions to shoplifting. *Social Forces,* 1973, *51,* 417–426.

Stevens, C. W. Many are praising Massachusetts law controlling guns. *Wall Street Journal,* June 20, 1980, p. 10.

Stewart, J. E., II. Defendant's attractiveness as a factor in the outcome of criminal trials: An observational study. *Journal of Applied Social Psychology,* 1980, *10,* 348–361.

Stoddard, E. R. The informal "code" of police deviancy: A group approach to "blue-coat crime." *Journal of Criminal Law, Criminology, and Police Science,* 1968, *59,* 201–213.

Stone, J. *Human law and human justice.* Stanford, Calif.: Stanford University Press, 1965.

Stotland, E. Self-esteem and violence by guards and state troopers at Attica. *Criminal Justice and Behavior,* 1976, *3,* 85–96.

Stotland, E., & Berberich, J. The psychology of the police. In H. Toch (Ed.), *Psychology of crime and criminal justice.* New York: Holt, Rinehart & Winston, 1979.

Strickland, L. H. Surveillance and trust. *Journal of Personality,* 1958, *26,* 200–215.

Strodtbeck, F. L., & Hook, L. H. The social dimensions of a twelve man jury table. *Sociometry,* 1961, *24,* 397–415.

Strodtbeck, F. L., James, R. M., & Hawkins, C. Social status in jury deliberations. In E. E. Maccoby, T. M. Newcomb, & E. L. Hartley (Eds.), *Readings in social psychology* (3rd ed.). New York: Holt, Rinehart & Winston, 1958.

Studt, E. The reentry of the offender into the community. Washington, D.C.: U. S. Government Printing Office, 1967.

Sudnow, D. Normal crimes: Sociological features of the penal code in a public defender office. *Social Problems,* 1965, *12,* 255–276.

Sue, S., Smith, R. E., & Caldwell, C. Effects of inadmissible evidence on the decision of simulated jurors: A moral dilemma. *Journal of Applied Social Psychology,* 1973, *3,* 344–353.

Suggs, D., & Sales, B. D. Using communication cues to evaluate prospective jurors during the voir dire. *Arizona Law Review,* 1979, *20,* 629–642.

Suggs, D., & Sales, B. D. Juror self-disclosure in the voir dire: A social science analysis. *Indiana Law Journal*, 1981, *56*, 245–271.

Suls, J. M., & Miller, R. L. (Eds.). *Social comparison processes: Theoretical and empirical perspectives*. Washington, D. C.: Hemisphere, 1977.

Sutherland, E. H. White collar criminality. *American Sociological Review*, 1940 *5*, 1–12.

Sutherland, E. H., & Cressey, D. R. *Principles of criminology* (7th ed.). Philadelphia: Lippincott, 1966.

Sutherland, E. H., & Cressey, D. R. *Criminology* (9th ed.). Philadelphia: Lippincott, 1974.

Sykes, G. M. *The society of captives: A study of a maximum security prison*. Princeton, N. J.: Princeton University Press, 1958.

Sykes, G. M., & Messinger, S. L. The inmate social system. In R. A. Cloward, D. R. Cressey, G. H. Grosser, R. M. McCleery, L. E. Ohlin, G. M. Sykes, & S. L. Messinger (Eds.), *Theoretical studies in social organization of the prison*. New York: Social Science Research Council, 1960.

Takagi, P. T. Evaluation systems and adaptations in a formal organization: A case study of a parole agency. Unpublished doctoral dissertation, Stanford University, 1967.

Tanke, E. D., & Tanke, T. J. Getting off a slippery slope: Social science in the judicial process. *American Psychologist*, 1979, *34*, 1130–1138.

Tapp, J. L. Psychology and the law: An overture. *Annual Review of Psychology*, 1976, *27*, 359–404.

Tapp, J. L. Psychological and policy perspectives on the law: Reflections on a decade. *Journal of Social Issues*, 1980, *36*(2), 165–192.

Tappan, P. W. *Crime, justice, and correction*. New York: McGraw-Hill, 1960.

Taylor, S. E., & Fiske, S. T. Salience, attention, and attribution: Top of the head phenomena. In L. Berkowitz (Ed.), *Advances in experimental social psychology* (Vol. 11). New York: Academic Press, 1978.

Thibaut, J. W., & Kelley, H. H. *The social psychology of groups*. New York: Wiley, 1959.

Thurstone, L. L. The method of paired comparisons for social values. *Journal of Abnormal and Social Psychology*, 1927, *21*, 384–400.

Tiffany, L. P., McIntyre, D. M., Jr., & Rotenberg, D. L. *Detection of crime: Stopping and questioning, search and seizure, encouragement and entrapment*. Boston: Little, Brown, 1967.

Tivnan, E. Jury by trial. *New York Times Magazine*, November 16, 1975, p. 30.

Toch, H. *Living in prison*. New York: Free Press, 1977.

Twentieth Century Fund Task Force on Criminal Sentencing. *Fair and certain punishment*. New York: McGraw-Hill, 1976.

Ugwuegbu, D. C. E. Racial and evidential factors in juror attribution of legal responsibility. *Journal of Experimental Social Psychology*, 1979, *15*, 133–146.

U.S. Department of Justice. *Parole in the United States: 1978*. Washington, D.C.: U. S. Government Printing Office, 1979.

U. S. Department of Justice. *Summary report: Expenditure and employment data for the criminal justice system—1978*. Washington, D. C.: U. S. Government Printing Office, 1980.

U. S. Department of Justice, Federal Bureau of Prisons. *National prisoner statistics: State prisoners, admissions, and releases*. Washington, D. C.: U. S. Government Printing Office, 1970.

Valenti, A., & Downing, L. Differential effects of jury size on verdicts following deliberation as a function of the apparent guilt of a defendant. *Journal of Personality and Social Psychology*, 1975, *32*, 655–663.

Van Caenegem, R. C. *The birth of the English common law.* London: Cambridge University Press, 1973.

Van Kirk, M. *Response time analysis* (Executive summary). Washington, D. C.: U. S. Government Printing Office, 1978.

Vera Institute of Justice. *Programs in criminal justice reform: Ten-year report 1961–1971.* New York: Vera Institute of Justice, 1972.

Vidmar, N. Effects of decision alternatives on the verdicts and social perceptions of simulated jurors. *Journal of Personality and Social Psychology,* 1972, *22,* 211–218.

Vidmar, N. The other issues in jury simulation research. *Law and Human Behavior,* 1979, *3,* 95–106.

Villasenor, V. *Jury: The people vs. Juan Corona.* Boston: Little, Brown, 1977.

von Hirsch, A., & Hanrahan, K. J. *The question of parole: Retention, reform, or abolition.* Cambridge, Mass.: Ballinger, 1979.

Wald, P. Pretrial detention and ultimate freedom: A statistical survey, foreword. *New York University Law Review,* 1964, *39,* 631–640.

Walker, M. Threat to spill biggest names in the game. *Manchester Guardian Weekly,* December 3, 1978, p. 5.

Waller, I., & Okihiro, N. *Burglary—The victim and the public.* Toronto: University of Toronto Press, 1978.

Walster, E., Berscheid, E., & Walster, G. W. New directions in equity research. *Journal of Personality and Social Psychology,* 1973, *25,* 151–176.

Walster, E., Berscheid, E., & Walster, G. W. New directions in equity research. In L. Berkowitz (Ed.), *Advances in experimental social psychology* (Vol. 9). New York: Academic Press, 1976.

Walster, E., Walster, G. W., & Berscheid, E. *Equity: Theory and research.* Boston: Allyn & Bacon, 1978.

Webster, W. *Uniform crime reports for the United States, 1979.* Washington, D. C.: U. S. Government Printing Office, 1980.

Weinberg, H. I., & Baron, R. S. The discredible eyewitness. Paper presented at the meeting of the Midwestern Psychological Association, St. Louis, May 1980.

Weiner, B. *Theories of motivation: From mechanism to cognition.* Chicago: Markham, 1972.

Weiner, B. "On being sane in insane places": A process (attributional) analysis and critique. *Journal of Abnormal Psychology,* 1975, *84,* 433–441.

Weiner, B., Frieze, I., Kukla, A., Reed, R., Rest, S., & Rosenbaum, R. M. Perceiving the causes of success and failure. In E. E. Jones, D. E. Kanouse, H. H. Kelley, R. E. Nisbett, S. Valins, & B. Weiner (Eds.), *Attribution: Perceiving the causes of behavior.* Morristown, N.J.: General Learning Press, 1972.

Weiten, W. The attraction-leniency effect in jury research: An examination of external validity. *Journal of Applied Social Psychology,* 1980, *10,* 340–347.

Weiten, W., & Diamond, S. S. A critical review of the jury simulation paradigm. *Law and Human Behavior,* 1979, *3,* 71–94.

Wells, G. L. Applied eyewitness-testimony research: System variables and estimator variables. *Journal of Personality and Social Psychology,* 1978, *36,* 1546–1557.

Wells, G. L., Lindsay, C. L., & Ferguson, T. J. Accuracy, confidence, and juror perceptions in eyewitness identification. *Journal of Applied Psychology,* 1979, *64,* 440–448.

Westcott, D. R., Greenberg, M. S., & Ruback, R. B. Social influence and theft victims' decision to call the police. Paper presented at the meeting of the American Psychological Association, Montreal, September 1980.

Westley, W. A. *Violence and the police: A sociological study of law, custom, and morality.* Cambridge, Mass.: MIT Press, 1970.

What to wear in court. *Newsweek,* December 16, 1974, p. 52.

Whobrey, L., Sales, B. D., & Elwork, A. Applying social psychological research to witness credibility law. In L. Bickman (Ed.), *Applied social psychology annual* (Vol. 2). Beverly Hills, Calif.: Sage, in press.

Wicker, T. *A time to die.* New York: Quadrangle Books, 1975.

Wilder, D. A. Homogeneity of jurors: The majority's influence depends upon their perceived independence. *Law and Human Behavior,* 1978, *2,* 363–376.

Wiley, M. G., & Hudik, T. L. Police-citizen encounters: A field test of exchange theory. *Social Problems,* 1974, *22,* 119–127.

Wilkins, L. T. Perspectives on court decision-making, In D. M. Gottfredson (Ed.), *Decision making in the criminal justice system: Reviews and essays.* Washington, D. C.: U. S. Government Printing Office, 1975.

Willis, K. Handling of kids' evidence angers some lawmen. *Atlanta Journal and Constitution,* February 28, 1981, p. 1A.

Wilson, D. W., & Donnerstein, E. Guilty or not guilty? A look at the "simulated" jury paradigm. *Journal of Applied Social Psychology,* 1977, *7,* 175–190.

Wilson, J. Q. *Thinking about crime.* New York: Basic Books, 1975.

Wilson, J. Q. *Varieties of police behavior* (2nd ed.). Cambridge, Mass.: Harvard University Press, 1978.

Winick, C. The psychology of the courtroom. In H. Toch (Ed.), *Psychology of crime and criminal justice.* New York: Holt, Rinehart & Winston, 1979.

Wolfgang, M. E. *Patterns in criminal homicide.* Philadelphia: University of Pennsylvania Press, 1958.

Wolfgang, M. E., & Riedel, M. Race, judicial discretion, and the death penalty. *Annals of the American Academy of Political Science,* 1973, *407,* 119–133.

Woman jailed for giving gun to boyfriend in court. *Pittsburgh Press,* June 17, 1978, p. 7A.

Worgan, D. S., & Paulsen, M. G. The position of a prosecutor in a criminal case: A conversation with a prosecuting attorney. *Practical Lawyer,* 1961, *7*(7), 44–58.

Wortman, C. B. Causal attributions and personal control. In J. H. Harvey, W. H. Ickes, & R. F. Kidd (Eds.), *New directions in attribution research* (Vol 1). Hillsdale, N. J.: Erlbaum, 1976.

Wright, D. B. Duties of a prosecutor. *Connecticut Bar Journal,* 1959, *33,* 293–296.

Yale Law Journal. Comment: The influence of the defendant's plea on judicial determination of sentence. *Yale Law Journal,* 1956, *66,* 204–222.

Yarmey, A. D. *The psychology of eyewitness testimony.* New York: Free Press, 1979.

Zeisel, H. ". . . And then there were none": The diminution of the federal jury. *University of Chicago Law Review,* 1971, *38,* 710–724.

Zeisel, H., & Diamond, S. S. Convincing empirical evidence on the six-member jury. *University of Chicago Law Review,* 1974, *41,* 281–295.

Zeisel, H., & Diamond, S. S. The jury selection in the Mitchell-Stans conspiracy trial. *American Bar Foundation Research Journal,* 1976, *1,* 151–174.

Zeisel, H., & Diamond, S. S. The effect of peremptory challenges on jury and verdict: An experiment in a federal district court. *Stanford Law Review,* 1978, *30,* 491–531.

Zerman, M. B. *Call the final witness.* New York: Harper & Row, 1977.

Zimring, F., & Hawkins, G. *Deterrence: The legal threat in crime control.* Chicago: University of Chicago Press, 1973.

Name Index

Subject Index